CHRISTIAN

SERIES EDITORS

Timothy Gorringe   Serene Jones   Graham Ward

CHRISTIAN THEOLOGY IN CONTEXT

Any inspection of recent theological monographs makes plain that it is still thought possible to understand a text independently of its context. Work in the sociology of knowledge and in cultural studies has, however, increasingly made obvious that such divorce is impossible. On the one hand, as Marx put it, 'life determines consciousness'. All texts have to be understood in their life situation, related to questions of power, class, and modes of production. No texts exist in intellectual innocence. On the other hand, texts are also forms of cultural power, expressing and modifying the dominant ideologies through which we understand the world. This dialectical understanding of texts demands an interdisciplinary approach if they are to be properly understood: theology needs to be read alongside economics, politics, and social studies, as well as philosophy, with which it has traditionally been linked. The cultural situatedness of any text demands, both in its own time and in the time of its rereading, a radically interdisciplinary analysis.

The aim of this series is to provide such an analysis, culturally situating texts by Christian theologians and theological movements. Only by doing this, we believe, will people of the fourth, sixteenth, or nineteenth centuries be able to speak to those of the twenty-first. Only by doing this will we be able to understand how theologies are themselves cultural products—projects deeply resonant with their particular cultural contexts and yet nevertheless exceeding those contexts by being received into our own today. In doing this, the series should advance both our understanding of those theologies and our understanding of theology as a discipline. We also hope that it will contribute to the fast developing interdisciplinary debates of the present.

Irenaeus of Lyons

Identifying Christianity

John Behr

OXFORD
UNIVERSITY PRESS

OXFORD
UNIVERSITY PRESS

Great Clarendon Street, Oxford, OX2 6DP,
United Kingdom

Oxford University Press is a department of the University of Oxford.
It furthers the University's objective of excellence in research, scholarship,
and education by publishing worldwide. Oxford is a registered trade mark of
Oxford University Press in the UK and in certain other countries

© John Behr 2013

The moral rights of the author have been asserted

First published 2013
First published in paperback 2015

Impression: 1

All rights reserved. No part of this publication may be reproduced, stored in
a retrieval system, or transmitted, in any form or by any means, without the
prior permission in writing of Oxford University Press, or as expressly permitted
by law, by licence or under terms agreed with the appropriate reprographics
rights organization. Enquiries concerning reproduction outside the scope of the
above should be sent to the Rights Department, Oxford University Press, at the
address above

You must not circulate this work in any other form
and you must impose this same condition on any acquirer

Published in the United States of America by Oxford University Press
198 Madison Avenue, New York, NY 10016, United States of America

British Library Cataloguing in Publication Data
Data available

ISBN 978–0–19–921462–4 (Hbk.)
ISBN 978–0–19–921463–1 (Pbk.)

Links to third party websites are provided by Oxford in good faith and
for information only. Oxford disclaims any responsibility for the materials
contained in any third party website referenced in this work.

For my students

Preface

It is an honour to be asked by the editors, Timothy Gorringe, Serene Jones, and Graham Ward, to write this volume on Irenaeus of Lyons for their series Christian Theology in Context. Irenaeus presents an unusual challenge for such a task, as, on the one hand, he is the first prolific author of the Christian tradition, and yet, on the other hand, the information that we have to contextualize what remains of his work is rather slim. We know some tantalizing details, teased out in Chapter 1, about his early life in Asia Minor; yet we know neither how he arrived in Lyons nor any details of his life there. As for Christianity in the city and surrounding region, we have only the sparsest details outside the scarce allusions that Irenaeus himself makes; these have also been discussed in Chapter 1. We do, of course, know something of the more general history of the city and area, about trade with, and immigration from, the East, about Gaul under Roman rule, and some reports of the pagan religions that had been practised there, but this provides us with very little to help us understand Irenaeus' theological context in Gaul. All this is in stark contrast to the abundant material that we have from a few decades later for contextualizing Origen within the rich intellectual and religious history of Alexandria, the detailed account by Eusebius of his life, travels, and eventual move to Caesarea, and his own voluminous work with its plentiful contextualizing comments.

While there are only a few points in Irenaeus' major work, *Against the Heresies*, that allow parts of its five books to be dated, the nature of the work is such that its real context is the history and diversity of Christianity in Rome over the course of the second century: it is to this that Irenaeus responds, and so I have presented this, in Chapter 1, as the background to Irenaeus' life and work. Irenaeus' response, however, and his elaboration of 'Orthodoxy' and 'Heresy', have their own history of interpretation, which has undergone significant modifications over the last couple of centuries and especially in recent decades. As such, this is another 'context' for situating and interpreting Irenaeus, which I have addressed outside the main body of this work, in the Introduction and Conclusion. Thus the contextualizing of Irenaeus undertaken in this contribution to the series is multi-faceted: Irenaeus' own historical context and our own context as we read Irenaeus in his, allowing him, in turn, to address us.

The following two books regretfully appeared in print too late to be taken into account in this work: Paul Foster and Sara Parvis (eds) *Irenaeus: Life, Scripture, Legacy* (Minneapolis: Fortress Press, 2012); Anthony Briggman, *Irenaeus of Lyons and the Theology of the Holy Spirit* (OECS; Oxford: Oxford University Press, 2012).

Contents

Abbreviations	x
Introduction	1
1. Irenaeus of Lyons: Ambassador for Peace, Reconciliation, and Toleration	13
Vienne and Lyons	16
The Christian Communities in Rome	21
Irenaeus and Florinus, Eleutherus and Victor	47
Irenaeus and Polycarp	57
The Chronology of Irenaeus' Life and Writings	66
2. Against the Heresies	73
Structure	74
Refutation and Overthrowal (*haer. 1–2*)	103
3. The Glory of God (*haer. 3–5*)	121
The Concise Word	124
The Arc of the Economy	144
The Work of God	162
The Symphony of Salvation	185
Living Human Beings, the Martyrs	198
Conclusion	205
Bibliography	211
Index	233

Abbreviations

Abbreviations for Greek Classical and Patristic texts are those found in the following: H. G. Liddell and R. Scott, *A Greek–English Lexicon*, rev. H. S. Jones with R. McKenzie, 9th edn with revised supplement (Oxford: Clarendon Press, 1996); G. W. Lampe, *A Patristic Greek Lexicon* (Oxford: Clarendon Press, 1961).

For Latin writers, I have followed *The SBL Handbook of Style for Ancient Near Eastern, Biblical, and Early Christian Studies*, ed. Patrick H. Alexander, John F. Kutsko, James D. Ernest, Shirley A. Decker-Lucke, and David L. Petersen (Peabody, MA: Hendrickson, 1999).

The two most frequently used abbreviations, *haer.* (Irenaeus of Lyons, *Adversus Haereses*) and *h.e.* (Eusebius of Caesarea, *Historia Ecclesiastica*), are usually given without the author's name.

I have followed the translations listed in the Bibliography, modifying them occasionally to bring out particular aspects. When also giving the original text of Irenaeus, within square brackets, I have indicated by a preceding 'R.' that a Greek word or phrase is the retroversion conjectured by Rousseau in his edition.

AB	*Analecta Bollandiana*
ACW	Ancient Christian Writers
ANF	Ante-Nicene Fathers
ANRW	*Aufstieg und Niedergang der römischen Welt: Geschichte und Kultur Roms in Spiegel der neueren Forschung*
ATR	*Anglican Theological Review*
CCSL	Corpus Christianorum: Series Latina
CQ	*Classical Quarterly*
CSCO	Corpus scriptorum christianorum orientalium
DACL	*Dictionnaire d'Archéologie Chrétienne et de Liturgie*, ed. F. Cabrol and H. Leclercq (Paris, 1907–53)
DCB	*Dictionary of Christian Biography*, ed. W. Smith and H. Wace, 4 vols (London, 1877–87).
DSp.	*Dictionnaire de spiritualité*, ed. M. Viller et al. (1937–)
ETL	*Ephemerides théologiques et religieuses*
FC	Fathers of the Church
GCS	Die griechische christliche Schriftsteller der ersten [drei] Jarhunderte

GNO	Gregorii Nysseni Opera
Greg.	*Gregorianum*
HJ	*Heythrop Journal*
HTR	*Harvard Theological Review*
JECS	*Journal of Early Christian Studies*
JEH	*Journal of Ecclesiastical History*
JR	*Journal of Religion*
JTI	*Journal of Theological Interpretation*
JTS	*Journal of Theological Studies*
LCL	Loeb Classical Library
LSJ	H. G. Liddell and R. Scott, *A Greek–English Lexicon*, rev. H. S. Jones with R. McKenzie, 9th edn with revised supplement (Oxford: Clarendon Press, 1996)
LV	*Lumière et vie*
MT	*Modern Theology*
NHS	Nag Hammadi Studies
NPNF	Nicene and Post Nicene Fathers
NRT	*Nouvelle reveu théologique*
NTS	*New Testament Studies*
OCA	Orientalia Christiana Analecta
OCP	*Orientalia christiana periodica*
OECS	Oxford Early Christian Studies
OECT	Oxford Early Christian Texts
PG	Patrologia Graeca
PO	Patrologia Orientalis
PTS	Patristiche Texte und Studien
RB	*Revue Biblique*
REG	*Revue des études grecques*
RSPT	*Revue des sciences philosophiques et théologiques*
RSR	*Revue de science religieuse*
SC	Sources chrétiennes
SJT	*Scottish Journal of Theology*
SM	*Studia Moralia*
StPatr	*Studia Patristica*

ST	*Studia Theologica*
SVF	*Stoicorum Veterum Fragmenta*, ed. J. von Armin (Leipzig: Teubner, 1903–24)
SVTQ	*St Vladimir's Theological Quarterly*
TU	Texte und Untersuchungen
TS	*Theological Studies*
TSK	*Theologische Studien und Kritiken*
WUNT	Wissenschaftliche Untersuchungen zum Neuen Testament
VC	*Vigiliae Christianae*
ZAC	*Zeitschrift für antikes Christentum*
ZKT	*Zeitschrift für katholische Theologie*
ZNTW	*Zeitschrift für die neutestamentliche Wissenschaft und die Kunde des Urchristentums*

Introduction

There is an uncanny parallel, and strange reversal, between the times of Irenaeus of Lyons, at the end of the second century, and our own, and perhaps even a return. The discoveries over the past century of long-lost texts written by those whom he opposed have been loudly publicized and have stimulated much scholarly endeavour. These texts, it is claimed, give us access to early alternative and equally legitimate approaches to Christianity, ones that were marginalized, excluded, and condemned by patriarchal bishops, among whom Irenaeus stands first in line. As a result, the controversies in which he was engaged are again very much alive today. But the tides have now turned. Presuming we already know, and have always known, what Irenaeus had to say in his positive exposition of the Christian faith, attention is more often given to the manner in which he dealt with his opponents, his strategies of denunciation, his 'construction of orthodoxy', and his exercise of a newly emerging episcopal office controlling its flock and persecuting others. The rediscovery of these proscribed texts thus appears as a rich resource for alternative approaches to Christianity, free from the constraints of the self-proclaimed 'orthodox' position. This is not surprising, for, as Bart Ehrman points out, 'virtually all forms of modern Christianity, whether they acknowledge it or not, go back to *one* form of Christianity that emerged as victorious from the conflicts of the second and third centuries'.[1] That this is so is in no small measure due to the work of Irenaeus, and so, with our new historical perspective, his claims are subject to new critical enquiry. Standing at the very foundation of all the diverse forms of Christianity we see today, Irenaeus must be read with all due diligence and seriousness, whether one regards his work negatively or positively. This is, moreover, not simply an exercise of history but a necessary task of the work of understanding Christian identity today. Becoming a controversial figure, which previously he had never been, Irenaeus has also never been more contemporary and important.

---

[1] Bart D. Erhman, *Lost Christianities: The Battles for Scripture and the Faiths We Never Knew* (Oxford: Oxford University Press, 2003), 4.

For all its contemporary relevance, understanding Irenaeus is nonetheless a historical task. Over the last decades, much great work has been done on the history of Christianity, especially in Rome and its gradually evolving structures, which enables us to understand Irenaeus' activity with much greater historical accuracy. Excellent work has also been done, with much sophistication, attempting to bring to light the theologies and world-views of the newly rediscovered texts, giving voices to the supposedly marginalized and excluded. Yet, ironically, this '"gospel" of diversity'[2] has little place for Irenaeus, who is instead usually vilified and his own literary and ecclesial activity cast in terms drawn from later centuries. Rather than understanding Irenaeus' exposition of Christian theology on its own terms, with all the diversity that it embraced in its own time and for which thereafter it served as the bedrock, modern scholars often depict Irenaeus as the first representative of an increasingly intolerant patriarchal episcopacy, as seen in later centuries, but held to be emerging already during the second century, exercising its power and authority by excluding and condemning others, those, that is, who today are held in high esteem as free-thinking seekers of higher spiritual illumination and tolerant of diversity. And yet this image is simply not historically accurate.

As we will see in Chapter 1, those whom Irenaeus describes as 'heretics' are precisely those who, of their own accord rather than through episcopal condemnation, left the 'Great Church', to use the expression of the second-century pagan doctor Galen, to found their own church, such as Marcion, or who gradually drifted away, as did the disciples of Valentinus, denigrating as merely 'psychic' those who, unlike themselves, were not truly 'spiritual'. It was, as we will see, the 'heretics' who were intolerant, and the Catholic Church that preached toleration and was open to diversity; the 'Great Church' was catholic not because it was a universal monolithic institution, but because it embraced diversity. This is, it has to be said, a rather 'unorthodox' claim in today's scholarly climate. To be clear, I do not mean to suggest that Christian leaders such as Irenaeus accepted any and every teaching claiming to be Christian—clearly not! Nor do I mean to imply that during the course of the second century the 'Great Church' already had a fixed and clear self-understanding of its own faith and its parameters. But, when Marcion came before the presbyters in Rome with his particular understanding of a radical distinction between

---

[2] The phrase is that of Andreas J. Köstenberger and Michael J. Kruger, *The Heresy of Orthodoxy: How Contemporary Culture's Fascination with Diversity has Reshaped our Understanding of Early Christianity* (Wheaton, IL: Crossway, 2010), 16.

the God of the Old Testament and the God of Christ, he was not well received. And this was an occasion to become clearer about the faith that was shared between the different representatives of the 'Great Church'. Yet it nevertheless was Marcion who separated from that common body, with its diversity, to establish a church that agreed with himself. The 'Great Church' at that time, as we will see, did not have an organ by which an excommunication could be imposed, if this was even thought of as a possibility. And, in turn, when Irenaeus did intervene in the life of the Christian community in Rome, it was not with a demand that 'heretical' books be burnt or that false teachers be excommunicated, but to make clear who had separated themselves and to urge toleration and acceptance of diversity among those who remained together, such as with regard to the celebration of Pascha, for, as he put it, 'our diversity in practice confirms our unity in faith'.[3]

Apart from the question of historical accuracy in reconstructing the situation of Christianity in Rome in the second century, the issue of historical perspective is more complex than might be supposed and is both the reason for the renewed controversy about matters already worked over in the second century and for why much modern scholarship finds Irenaeus' own account of the Christian faith, despite its presumed familiarity, strangely unfamiliar, even alien territory. Ehrman rightly points out that the source for our modern controversies lies with the debates about the historical reliability of Scripture that emerged during the Enlightenment, together with a developing secular discourse of science and renewed reflection on the nature of truth.[4] Of particular importance here was the attempt, beginning with Herman Reimarus (1694–1768), whose literary 'Fragments' were published posthumously by Gotthold Lessing (1729–81), to rediscover, behind the claims of the apostles, the real Jesus.[5] He was followed by many other notable scholars, such as Ferdinand Christian Baur (1792–1860), with his strong contrast between the proclamation of the kingdom of God by Jesus and the proclamation of the crucified and exalted Christ by Paul, and Albert Schweitzer (1875–1965), who pointed out that images of Jesus produced by previous historical quests in fact reflected the times and circumstances of the authors rather than the apocalyptic Judaism within which Schweizter would

---

[3] Irenaeus, 'Letter to Victor', in Eusebius, *h.e.* 5.24.13.
[4] Ehrman, *Lost Christianities*, 168 ff.
[5] See esp. Herman Reimarus, 'The Intention of Jesus and his Disciples', in *Reimarus: Fragments*, ed. Charles H. Talbert, trans. Ralph S. Fraser (Eugene, OR: Wipf and Stock, 2009).

himself insist that Jesus must be understood. Subsequent phases of the quest for the historical Jesus during the course of the second half of the twentieth century were given a boost by the discovery of previously hidden caches of material and culminated, most notoriously, in the work of the 'Jesus Seminar'.

It was also Lessing, ever the controversialist, who more than anyone else recast what was understood by the phrase 'the canon of truth' or the 'rule of faith' ('canon' and 'rule' being the same word, derived from Greek and Latin respectively).[6] For Lessing, the 'regula fidei' was 'not drawn from the writings of the New Testament', 'was in existence before a single book of the New Testament existed', 'is even older than the *Church*', and therefore it was 'this *regula fidei*, and *not the Scriptures* [that] is the rock on which the Church of Christ was built'.[7] The 'canon' or 'regula' is here understood in terms of particular teachings—on God, Christ, and his work—and is detached from Scripture, by which Lessing seems only to have understood the writings of the New Testament, for the 'Old Testament', now read merely historically, plays no other role for him. Subsequent elaboration of this original teaching is, correspondingly, understood either positively, as Newman's 'development of doctrine', or negatively, as Harnack's 'Hellenization of Christianity' or 'acute Hellenization' in the case of 'Gnosticism'.

Karen King rightly points out that there are certain assumptions at play in much of this scholarship.[8] First there is 'the association of truth and chronology'—that is, the assumption that what is earlier is necessarily truer. This is combined with, second, 'the notion that truth is pure; mixing is contamination', and, third, 'the assumption that truth ("orthodoxy") is characterized by unity, uniformity, and unanimity; falsehood ("heresy") by division, multiformity, and diversity'. King would see these assumptions as deriving from an uncritical appropriation of the anti-heretical strategies of early Christian writers, and so she describes the purpose of her book as being 'to consider the ways in which early Christian polemicists' discourse of orthodoxy and heresy has been intertwined with twentieth-century scholarship on Gnosticism in order to show where and how that involvement has distorted our analysis of ancient texts'. 'At stake', she continues, 'is not only

---

[6] See esp. Gotthold Lessing, 'Necessary Answer to a Very Unnecessary Question of Herr Hauptpastor Goeze of Hamburg', in *Lessing: Philosophical and Theological Writings*, ed. H. B. Nisbet, Cambridge Texts in the History of Philosophy (Cambridge: Cambridge University Press, 2005), 172–7.
[7] Lessing, 'Necessary Answer', §§2–5, emphasis in original.
[8] Karen King, *What is Gnosticism?* (Cambridge, MA: Belknap Press of Harvard University Press, 2003), 228–9.

the capacity to write a more accurate history of ancient Christianity in all its multiformity, but also our capacity to engage critically the ancient politics of religious difference rather than unwittingly reproduce its strategies and results'.[9] And this is not merely a historical exercise, though it is that as well, for, as King notes, with respect to the problem of describing 'Gnosticism', the difficulty 'has been and continues to be primarily an aspect of the ongoing project of defining and maintaining a normative Christianity'.[10]

Such assumptions are certainly at work in much modern scholarship, with its quest to uncover the original historical Jesus and his unadulterated message or the original doctrinal core of Christianity. In both cases, a pure original essence is sought, which can then be used as a criterion to demonstrate the distortions or falsifications of what happens later. But it is again striking that, if parallels are to be found in the second century, they again lie with protest figures such as Marcion, whom Harnack famously compared to Luther standing before the Roman Church. He it was who claimed to have preserved, or critically determined, the original message of the apostle Paul before it was distorted by false apostles, who upheld a single Gospel account expurgated of all error rather than a diversity of witnesses, and who established his own church of like-minded believers. It might well be the case that the assumptions of modern scholarship derive from the narratives of orthodoxy and heresy elaborated in the fourth century, together with the exercise of power and authority that comes to be deployed thereafter, but this does not help us understand the dynamics of the second century. It is necessary to be sensitive to the different discourses on orthodoxy and heresy elaborated by different figures in different epochs, and a first step towards this would be to turn King's project around, as it were, and to disentangle the early discourse on orthodoxy and heresy from the assumptions operative within twentieth-century scholarship and their roots in the historicizing perspective of recent centuries, so that we can hear how second-century figures, such as Irenaeus, construed the debate on their own terms.

A death blow to any search for a single origin of the Christian faith was dealt by Walter Bauer in his claim that Christianity was a diverse phenomenon from the beginning, that 'varieties of Christianity' arose around the Mediterranean, and that in some places what would later be called 'heretical' was initially normative.[11] In and through the struggles between

---

[9] King, *Gnosticism?*, 19.   [10] King, *Gnosticism?*, 18.
[11] Walter Bauer, *Rechtgläubigkeit und Ketzerei im ältesten Christentum* (Tübingen: Mohr, 1934); trans. of 2nd edn. (1964, ed. G. Strecker) by R. Kraft et al., *Orthodoxy and Heresy in Earliest Christianity* (Philadelphia: Fortress Press, 1971).

these various group, one form eventually came to dominate as 'orthodox', enabling us to speak of their predecessors as 'proto-orthodox', while others lost and became 'lost Christianities', to use the title of Ehrman's book, until the rediscovery of their own texts. Although some of Bauer's reconstructions are inaccurate and have been dropped, the idea that Christianity was originally a diverse phenomenon has now been generally accepted. While Bauer still utilized fairly static notions of orthodoxy and heresy, others developed the 'varieties' model in a more historically dynamic fashion into a 'trajectories' model of early Christianity, tracing the movement of different trends over time.[12] And yet, in a sense, the 'varieties' and 'trajectories' models still operate on the basis of some of the assumptions outlined by King: they construe these different groups as defined and fixed entities, in varying degrees independent, and supposes that we can view them as different horses in a rerun of a race, keeping our eye all the time on the one we know to be the eventual winner and so defining the race itself in the terms given by the winner.[13] Determining the reason why one group eventually came to dominate is no longer sought, as in early modern times, on the basis of a pure originating source, but rather, in equally modern terms, through the interaction of historical and socio-political forces.

One very concrete benefit of this work has been to recognize that the study of early Christianity needs to be attuned to the different geographical settings of the figures and texts studied, recognizing the differences between them, and, more recently, the differences even within particular local regions, especially large urban centres such as Rome.[14] Another distinct advantage is that it shifts historical study away from a quest for a single origin, in a (modern) reconstruction of either the real Jesus or a single apostolic deposit, to focus instead on responses to Christ, in their unsurprising diversity. Apart from Christ's writing in the sand (John 8:6), which no one is said to have read anyway and has long since been smoothed over, we have only reports, accounts, and interpretations of

---

[12] Cf. James M. Robinson and Helmut Koester, *Trajectories through Early Christianity* (Philadelphia: Fortress Press, 1971).

[13] See the discussion in David Brakke, *The Gnostics: Myth, Ritual, and Diversity in Early Christianity* (Cambridge, MA: Harvard University Press, 2010), 5–18. Brakke adapts the analogy of a horse race from Philip Rousseau, *Pachomius: The Making of a Community in Fourth Century Egypt*, The Transformations of the Classical Heritage (Berkeley and Los Angeles: University of California Press, 1985), 19.

[14] See in particular Peter Lampe, *From Paul to Valentinus: Christians at Rome in the First Two Centuries*, trans. M. Steinhauser (Minneapolis: Fortress Press, 2003).

Christ's life and actions, death and resurrection, the earliest of which, the letters of Paul, are already a response to conflicting interpretations. The history of Christianity can be written only as a history of these different interpretations, and an account of the identity of the Church, in theological as well as sociological terms, must reflect its historical reality as a community of interpretation.[15]

The voices in this dialogue are necessarily personal and particular. But it is also of the nature of dialogue that each voice will contribute to the shaping of other voices. In this way, more recent historical and critical work, including King and others such as Rebecca Lyman, Judith Lieu, and David Brakke, has not been concerned simply to point out the original diversity of voices, each expressing distinct claims with one eventual winner, but rather to understand the concrete rhetorical and social practices involved in these conversations and the various identities being fashioned through them.[16] It is not merely that the typologies of the varieties of early Christianity used by twentieth-century scholarship to reify distinct theological systems or social groups are not adequate maps of historical reality, needing simply to be refined. It is rather that such an approach does not do justice to the complexity of the means by which concrete early Christian figures developed understandings of themselves as Christian and their relations to others doing the same but differently. Focusing on the analysis of identity formation, King argues, requires being

> oriented toward the critical analysis of practices, such as producing texts; constructing shared history through memory, selective appropriation, negotiation, and invention of tradition; developing ritual performances such as baptism and meals; writing and selectively privileging certain theological forms (e.g. creeds) and canons; forming bodies and gender; making places and marking time; assigning nomenclature and establishing categories, defining 'others' and so on.[17]

A key feature of this approach is that it recognizes the hybrid nature of any identity thus established.

---

[15] For Paul's letters as being part of the history of interpretation and reinterpretation, fashioning the basis of a Christian hermeneutics, see Margaret M. Mitchell, *Paul, The Corinthians and the Birth of Christian Hermeneutics* (Cambridge: Cambridge University Press, 2010).

[16] Cf. Rebecca Lyman, 'Hellenism and Heresy', *JECS* 11/2 (2003), 209–22; Judith M. Lieu, *Christian Identity in the Jewish and Graeco-Roman World* (Oxford: Oxford University Press, 2004); Karen King, 'Which Early Christianity?', in Susan Ashbrook Harvey and David G. Hunters (eds), *The Oxford Handbook of Early Christian Studies* (Oxford: Oxford University Press, 2008), 66–84.

[17] King, 'Which Early Christianity?', 73.

'Hybridity', as David Brakke points out, is somewhat akin to the older notion of 'syncretism'. But, whereas that term expressed a negative view towards what it saw as the mixing of extraneous elements to a pure original essence, 'hybridity' emphasizes the inescapably fluid nature of human existence and interaction, the way in which different voices mutually influence one another and the rhetorical dimension in which this happens and boundaries are drawn. Rather than seeing 'the Gnostics' or other 'heretical' groups as syncretistic representatives of early Christianity, drawing in elements that do not belong to an original essence, attention is focused instead on the way in which all figures in early Christianity, as indeed any historical figure in any age, draw creatively upon the diverse cultural elements available to them. As Brakke puts it: 'The boundedness, continuity, and natural evolution of incipient beliefs and doctrines that we have attributed to early Christian groups were not in fact there in social life, but were invoked rhetorically in the multilateral process of identity formation and boundary setting in which all early Christians were engaged.'[18] Within this dynamic, and fluid, situation, one can see claims to 'orthodoxy' and 'heresy' as being rhetorical constructs attempting to set boundaries and establish identity. Our goal, as Brakke puts it, 'should be to see neither how a single Christianity expressed itself in diverse ways, nor how one group of Christians emerged as the winner in a struggle, but how multiple Christian identities and communities were continually created and transformed'.[19]

Rather than dissolving all early Christianity into 'a soup of hybridity', to use Brakke's delicious image,[20] it is nevertheless still possible to make distinctions among forms of Christianity and to identify concrete historical social groupings that did occur on the ground. Although interpretative categories or scholarly constructs, such as 'apocalyptic Judaism', are not social categories, corresponding to historical groups with which particular figures would identify, social categories, on the other hand, while always also being interpretative ones, involving the kind of practices mentioned above, do and did, Brakke rightly insists, actually exist.[21] The modern category 'Gnosticism', which was never used by Irenaeus but introduced in 1669 by Henry More, has proved to be untenable and seeking to define its 'essence' impossible.[22] Yet there was neverless, Brakke convincingly

---

[18] Brakke, *The Gnostics*, 12.   [19] Brakke, *The Gnostics*, 15.
[20] Brakke, *The Gnostics*, 15.   [21] Brakke, *The Gnostics*, 16–18.
[22] On Henry More's coinage of the term 'Gnosticism', see Bentley Layton, 'Prolegomena to the Study of Ancient Gnosticism', in L. Michael White and O. Larry Yarbrough (eds), *The Social World of the First Christians: Essays in Honor of Wayne A. Meeks* (Minneapolis: Fortress, 1995), 334–50, at 348–9. As Brakke notes (*The Gnostics*, 4): 'When modern scholars depict

argues, a specific group who did identify themselves as the 'Gnostics' whose existence can be discerned on the basis of Irenaeus' report, their own texts, and the various ritual and social practices described therein.

Likewise, in second-century Rome, a microcosm of Christianity throughout the Empire, there clearly were communities of Christians who were perceived, even by non-Christians, as belonging together, as the 'Great Church', and who identified themselves, together, in various ways and through various practices, as orthodox in distinction to the heretics—those, that is, who had separated from them. Intriguingly, given the new directions we have seen in contemporary scholarship, it was this 'Great Church' that was precisely the place, as noted above and as we will see further in Chapter 1, in which diversity was recognized as an integral element of its catholicity. Certainly some, such as Marcion, departed from this broad body, rather than being cast out, after his attempts at reformation along his own lines were not received, and others, such as Valentinus and his disciples, gradually drifted away, considering themselves possessors of higher knowledge. And certainly such splits and tensions helped the 'Great Church' clarify its own identity as a communal body of interpretation and ecclesial practice. But, rather than imagining this, as much twentieth-century scholarship has done by taking its cue from fourth-century narratives interpreted through the assumptions of the historicism of recent centuries, in terms of static and bounded reified identities needing to be preserved or retrieved, it would be better to adapt one of the key themes of Irenaeus' theology, that of a symphony, comprised of different voices throughout time, each lending themselves to the melody being played, with different timbres and tonalities, inflections and themes, and each in turn being shaped by the symphony. Speaking theologically, moreover, this symphony is not, therefore, constructed by any individual voice or all the voices together but is governed by its own rhythm and rules, so that, to use Irenaeus' words, it is God who 'harmonizes the human race to the symphony of salvation' (*haer.* 4.14.2).

In an intriguing manner, then, it seems that, after its quest for a historically pure original essence of Christianity, modern scholarship is seeking to recover a concern for catholicity in the manner of none other than Irenaeus. Through a careful historical analysis, in a modern spirit, of his writings, we

---

many different ancient groups as belonging to the same category—Gnosticism—they replicate Irenaeus' notion of false gnosis but neglect his careful delineation of its diversity.' See also Michael Allen Williams, *Rethinking 'Gnosticism': An Argument for Dismantling a Dubious Category* (Princeton: Princeton University Press, 1996); King, *Gnosticism?*

will find that Irenaeus' concerns are emphatically not those of recent centuries. He does not attempt to retrieve the 'real historical Jesus', understood as the life and teaching of Jesus prior to his Passion, but rather to understand this same Jesus on the basis of his Passion through the interpretation of the Scriptures—that is, what we now call the 'Old Testament' or the 'Hebrew Scriptures'—following the apostles in an ongoing reflection and dialogue. This Scripture is not read merely historically but as a thesaurus, a treasury of words and images that fit together as a mosaic depicting Christ, and so his concern is for the coherence of this interpretation with Scripture, rather than the historicity of the accounts of the evangelists or the 'real history' behind those accounts.[23] This does not mean that he dismisses history, but that he recognized, as we noted above, that in all this we are always already dealing with interpretations, and, in a sense, his own theology is therefore more historically grounded than those quests for the 'historical Jesus' in that it does not presume to get behind the Passion or bracket the Cross, as if it had never happened, but accepts it as the defining moment.

In a similar manner, when, at the beginning of the third book of *Against the Heresies*, Irenaeus lists the succession of teachers in Rome, all of whom, he claims, have consistently taught the same, this is not cast in terms of maintaining, statically, an original deposit of teachings separate from the Scriptures, as those following in Lessing's wake would do, but that in their preaching, bound up as this is with the interpretation of Scripture, these figures were all part of the same symphony, with all the diachronic and synchronic diversity that this entails. This symphony is continuously unfolding and, moreover, it is public, in contrast to those who, from time to time, prefer to play their own tunes in private. Such discordant voices certainly continue, nevertheless, to influence voices sharing in the symphony. But, as ones who have separated themselves from the symphony of the one body of Christ, their similar but separate tunes can be described as 'demonically inspired' mimicry after the model of Simon Magus, and can be correlated in various ways, in the case of Irenaeus, at least, with a fair

---

[23] His concern is so much with the scriptural nature of the apostolic preaching, rather than its historicity, that he does not really raise the question of the historical accuracy or reliability of the Gospels, or when he does, obliquely, he comes to rather surprising conclusions, such as his claim that at the time of his public teaching Jesus was over 40 years old (*haer.* 2.22.5–6); it is the coherence of Scripture, and the rhetorical coherence resulting from understanding Christ through the Scriptures, that is of primary importance for Irenaeus. Facing the question of conflicting details in different Gospels a generation later, Origen made the notorious claim, but one that highlights the point being made here, that 'spiritual truth is often preserved in material falsehood, so to speak' (*Jo.* 10.20)

degree of respect for their own diversity. And, having argued briefly, in five chapters, for this continuous symphony, Irenaeus' real concern is shown in the remaining three books: 'since the tradition from the apostles does thus exist in the Church, let us revert to the scriptural demonstration given by the apostles who did also write the Gospel' (*haer.* 3.5.1). The title Irenaeus gives to this work, *Refutation and Overthrowal of Knowledge falsely so-called*, as we will see, describes the task of the first two books and this seems to have been the initial scope of Irenaeus' project. If the remaining three books are a 'refutation', they are so in that they present a 'demonstration' of the mosaic or symphony itself, so that one should not be misled by the title to categorize Irenaeus, as is often done, simply as an anti-heretical writer.

There is certainly a single 'hypothesis' grounding the approach of Irenaeus. As Hellenistic philosophy well knew, building upon Aristotle and Epicurus, 'first principles' cannot be demonstrated, whether by a historical quest or empirical evidence, for this would be but to substitute another 'first principle': 'first principles' are always and in every case accepted on faith. Yet Irenaeus' 'hypothesis' does in fact cohere with the two occasions in which the apostle Paul uses the technical formula of reception and delivery or traditioning: 'I received what I also delivered to you', that the eucharistic offering received from the Lord himself was to be enacted, 'proclaim[ing] the Lord's death until he comes' (1 Cor. 11:23–6), and that 'Christ died for our sins in accordance with the Scriptures, that he was buried, that he was raised on the third day in accordance with the Scriptures' (1 Cor. 15:3–4). It is not simply the death and resurrection of Christ that are 'of first importance', but their interpretation 'in accordance with the Scriptures' in the context of a community that celebrates the Eucharist together proclaiming Christ's death. This 'hypothesis' also functions as a criterion or a 'canon of truth', by which Irenaeus does not mean, unlike Lessing, a set of doctrines detached from the Scriptures and their interpretation, but rather an expression, which can vary depending on context, of the coherence of Scripture as a mosaic of Christ. The purpose of the 'canon' was not to demarcate a set of teachings that must be accepted and to curtail reason or further thought, but instead to make further reflection possible. As Eric Osborn put it: 'the rule did not limit reason to make room for faith, but used faith to make room for reason. Without a credible first principle, reason was lost in an infinite regress.'[24]

---

[24] Cf. Eric Osborn, 'Reason and the Rule of Faith in the Second Century', in Rowan Williams (ed.), *The Making of Orthodoxy: Essays in Honour of Henry Chadwick* (Cambridge: Cambridge University Press, 1989), 40–61, at 57.

In many ways, then, Irenaeus is indeed a very contemporary figure and has perhaps never been as important as today for understanding Christian identity in a truly catholic—that is, all-encompassing—manner, and for contemporary critical thought as it seeks to understand more fully the dynamics of identity formation in an inclusive manner, at least of those who would be part of the same project, and also as it re-examines its own assumptions, negotiating the complex relations between history and interpretation, faith and reason, and ancient texts as historical documents and as Scripture. My own work on Irenaeus began over two decades ago, in my doctoral research at the University of Oxford under the supervision of Metropolitan Kallistos (Ware), to whom I continue to owe a great deal. It has also continued over those decades, translating Irenaeus' *Demonstration of the Apostolic Preaching*, and exploring the way in which particular theologians, each in his or her own context, contributed to the 'symphony' of theology on the way to Nicaea and beyond, rather than as the elaboration of a theological system on the basis of an unchanging deposit or as a development of that deposit. My own understanding of Irenaeus has grown most, however, from teaching generations of students at St Vladimir's Orthodox Theological Seminary in New York, most recently in a seminar class dedicated to Irenaeus, and it is to them that I gratefully dedicate this book.

1

Irenaeus of Lyons: Ambassador for Peace, Reconciliation, and Toleration

'No early Christian writer has deserved better of the whole Church than Irenaeus.'[1] This assessment by H. B Swete from a century ago is unfortunately borne out both by the historical treatment of his writings and information about his life and also by much modern scholarship. Judged by standards of later writers, Irenaeus was not a particularly prolific author. Yet only two of his writings have survived, and even then not in the original language. The first is the work for which he is primarily known, the five books entitled *The Refutation and Overthrowal of Knowledge falsely so-called* (haer. 4.Pref.1; cf. h.e. 5.7.1) or, in its shorter, more popular title, *Against the Heresies* (h.e. 3.23.3). The Greek text of this work was consulted by Photius in Baghdad in the ninth century, but was probably lost in the sacking of the city in 1258.[2] Apart from one paragraph towards the end, it survives only in a Latin version probably made in the third or early fourth century. In 1904, a manuscript was discovered in Erevan that contained an Armenian version of books four and five of *Against the Heresies* and the complete text of the second work, *The Demonstration of the Apostolic Preaching*, probably made in the last quarter of the sixth century. According to Eusebius, Irenaeus also wrote a treatise *Concerning Knowledge*, written against the Hellenes (h.e. 5.26), and 'a little book of various discourses in which he mentions the Epistle to the Hebrews and the so-called Wisdom of Solomon, quoting certain passages from them' (h.e. 5.26). Eusebius also mentions that Irenaeus wrote a letter to Florinus, entitled *On the Sole Sovereignty* or *That God is not the Author of Evil* (h.e. 5.20.1, 4–8), and one to Victor (h.e. 5.24.11–17), and quotes extracts from both these works. He notes in passing that Irenaeus also wrote a work concerning Florinus called *On the Ogdoad*,

---

[1] H. B. Swete, foreword in F. R. M. Hitchcock, *Irenaeus of Lyons: A Study of his Teaching* (Cambridge: Cambridge University Press, 1914).

[2] Cf. B. Hemmerdinger, 'Les "Notices et extraits" des bibliothèques grecques de Bagdad par Photius', *REG* 69 (1956), 101–3.

which he claims was written when Florinus was turning to Valentinian teaching, and a letter to Blastus called *On Schism* (*h.e.* 5.20.1). We have an extract preserved in Syriac from a letter to Victor about Florinus, and it is likely that the *Letter of the Churches of Vienne and Lyons to the Churches of Asia and Phrygia*, lengthy extracts from which were quoted by Eusebius, is from Irenaeus himself (*h.e.* 5.1–3).[3] Apart from the information provided by these works, which we will examine carefully in this chapter, we have no further information about his life or activities. Although he is commemorated, on 28 June, as a martyr, the evidence for his martyrdom is late.[4]

Subsequent generations seem to have remembered Irenaeus primarily for his anti-heretical writings, his theological orientation thereafter being taken as assumed. This is shown by the fact that, although he is cited by, among others, Basil of Caesarea and Maximus the Confessor, and some lengthy extracts from his works are preserved in the *Sacra Parallela* attributed to John of Damascus, it is primarily the first book of *Against the Heresies*, in which Irenaeus describes the various teachings of his opponents, that has been preserved in Greek by being incorporated into later anti-heretical writings, such as those of Hippolytus and Epiphanius. It is ironic that Irenaeus' work, which, in von Balthasar's words, marks the 'birth of Christian theology' and which was produced in a conscious struggle with living opponents, would later be used systematically only by those cataloguers of heresies for whom these teachings were largely no longer a living force.[5]

With regard to modern scholarship, Swete could not have foreseen the massive assault that would be launched two decades later as the methodology of 'Quellenforschung' (source criticism) was pushed to its limits. The most arresting monument of this is the work of Friedrich Loofs. His work is like an autopsy: building on the suggestions of Harnack[6] and

---

[3] On Irenaeus' authorship, see P. Nautin, *Lettres et écrivains chrétiens des IIe et IIIe siècles* (Paris: Cerf, 1961), 54–61, 93–5.

[4] The first to refer to Irenaeus as a martyr is Jerome (*c*.342–420), who describes him as 'Bishop of Lyons and martyr' (*Comm. Isa.* 17); although it is possible, as H. Dodwell suggested, that this is a later scribal error, for Jerome never refers to him as a martyr elsewhere; see H. Dodwell, *Dissertationes in Irenaeum* (Oxford, 1689), 259–64. The first full report of his martyrdom is by Gregory of Tours (*c*.540–94), *Historia Francorum* 1.27.

[5] Hans Urs von Balthasar, *The Glory of the Lord: A Theological Aesthetics*, ii. *Studies in Theological Style: Clerical Styles*, trans. A. Louth, F. McDonagh, and B. McNeil (Edinburgh: T&T Clark, 1984), 31–2. Cf. F. M. M. Sagnard, *La Gnose valentinienne et le témoignage de saint Irénée* (Paris: Vrin, 1947), 82.

[6] A. von Harnack, 'Der Presbyter-Prediger des Irenäus (IV, 27, 1–32, 1), Bruchstücke und Nachklänger der ältesten exegetisch-polemischen Homilien', in *Philotesia: Paul Kleinert zum LXX Geburtstag* (Berlin: Trowitzsch, 1907), 1–37.

Bousset,[7] Loofs dissected *Against the Heresies* into its various supposed sources, even if these 'sources' are no longer extant, and, by discounting any traces of their influence, delimited what he claimed was 'Irenaeus himself'. Not surprisingly he concluded: 'As a theological writer, Irenaeus was much less important than previously supposed... Even slighter a figure was Irenaeus as a theologian.'[8] The imposing character of Loofs's work was such that it effectively halted work on Irenaeus for the following decades. Only over the course of the second half of the twentieth century was there a renewed appreciation for his theology and his theological method.[9]

Yet, with the rediscovery of many of the writings of his opponents at Nag Hammadi and the renewed fascination with 'Gnosticism', Irenaeus has again come to be regarded with disdain. He is 'the lonely Irenaeus' and 'the ugly Irenaeus', as Charles Hill ironically entitles two chapters in his book on 'the great Gospel conspiracy'.[10] The image of Irenaeus in much modern scholarship is of a bishop concerned for his own authority and intolerant towards others, using unjustifiable (by modern standards) rhetoric in demonizing his opponents with the general label of 'Gnosticism', showing how they all derive from a single figure, Simon Magus, in a genealogy that stands opposed to the true succession of legitimate bishops traced back to the apostles, all in the aid of establishing a monolithic and patriarchal universal Church. This 'ugly' character is, it is often claimed, also 'lonely', for his community, with its own claims to 'orthodoxy' and 'catholicity', is only one among many and diverse others, each with its own legitimate claim to represent Christianity. Such has been the prevalence of this image of the heresiologist in much modern literature that, although it has been pointed out that Irenaeus does not designate all his

---

[7] W. Bousset, *Jüdisch-christlicher Schulbetried in Alexandria und Rom: Literarische Untersuchungen zu Philo und Clemens von Alexandria, Justin und Irenäus* (Göttingen, 1915), 272–82.

[8] F. Loofs, *Theophilus von Antiochien Adversus Marcionem und die anderen theologischen Quellen bei Irenaeus*, TU 46.2 (Leipzig: Hinrichs, 1930), 432. Such an assessment was accepted as standard by most handbooks in the middle of the twentieth century. For instance, Johannes Quasten, in his widely used *Patrology*, states: 'The whole work suffers from a lack of clear arrangement and unity of thought. Prolixity and frequent repetition make its perusal wearisome... Evidently he did not have the ability to shape his materials into a homogenous whole' (*Patrology*, i (Utrecht: Spectrum, 1950), 289).

[9] Especially important were Gustaf Wingren, *Man and the Incarnation: A Study in the Biblical Theology of Irenaeus*, trans. R. Mackenzie (London: Oliver and Boyd, 1959 [1947]), and Philippe Bacq, *De l'ancienne à la nouvelle alliance selon S. Irénée: Unité du livre IV de l'Adversus Haereses* (Paris: Éditions Lethielleux, Presses Universitaires de Namur, 1978).

[10] Charles E. Hill, *Who Chose the Gospels? Probing the Great Gospel Conspiracy* (Oxford: Oxford University Press, 2010).

opponents as 'Gnostic' but uses that term very carefully and specifically, it still colours many assessments of him.[11] Similarly, although certain groups did adopt the term 'Gnostic' to designate themselves, and, it should be added, used derogatory terms (notably 'psychic' and 'fleshly' rather than 'spiritual') to designate others, it is Irenaeus' own rhetoric that is held to be inexcusable.[12] As we examine, in this chapter, the activity of Irenaeus, set within what we know of Christianity in Rome, not only its diversity but also the instances of various groups who split off from the broad fellowship of the various communities and so prompted in turn a greater awareness of what holds this fellowship together, we will be able to appreciate, with greater sensitivity and accuracy, Irenaeus as an advocate of toleration and diversity in contrast to those who lacked this irenic quality.

VIENNE AND LYONS

We pray, father Eleutherus, that you may rejoice in God in all things and always. We have requested our brother and comrade Irenaeus to carry this letter to you, and we ask you to hold him in esteem, as zealous for the covenant of Christ. For if we thought that office could confer righteousness upon any one, we should commend him among the first as a presbyter of the Church, which is his position. (*h.e.* 5.4.2)

With this commendation, Irenaeus enters the historical scene, in a manner befitting his name and presaging his future activity, engaged on an embassy of peace. His mission was connected with disturbances occasioned by the rise of a new prophetic movement in Asia and Phrygia, led by Montanus and often known by his name as 'Montanism', reverberations of which seem to have spread to Rome, disrupting the Christian communities there. Just having undergone, in 177 CE,[13] the most bloody pogrom of Christians yet seen, the confessors of Vienne and Lyons wrote to Eleutherus, a leader of one of the Christian communities in Rome, and sent another letter to their

---

[11] See, e.g., the conclusion of David Brakke (*The Gnostics*, 28): 'We can try to get beyond Irenaeus' vision of false *gnosis*—ironically enough, with his own unwitting help.'

[12] Cf. Brakke, *The Gnostics*, 35: 'Their sincere use of this positive epithet for themselves inspired Irenaeus' ironic and sarcastic use of it for other Christians whose teachings he found equally ludicrous and pretentious.'

[13] Eusebius is not consistent regarding the date of this persecution: his *Chronicon* would place the persecutions during the seventh year of Marcus Aurelius' reign (166–7), while his later *Ecclesiastical History* places the events a decade later, in his seventeenth year (177), the date that is generally accepted. Cf. Robert M. Grant, 'Eusebius and the Martyrs of Gaul', in *Les Martyrs de Lyon (177)*, Colloques Internationaux du Centre National de la Recherche Scientifique, no. 575 (Paris: CNRS, 1978), 129–36.

brethren in Asia and Phrygia, so acting, in Eusebius' words, as 'ambassadors for the sake of the peace of the churches' (*h.e.* 5.3.4).

Irenaeus had come to Gaul from the East, as had many immigrants for several centuries. The region had been inhabited by the Celts, or Gauls as the Romans called them, who originated from the so-called Hallstatt culture (named after a site near Salzburg, Austria), migrating to Provence around 750 BCE and beginning what is known as the La Tène culture (named after a site near Lake Neuchâtel, Switzerland). Around the same time, the Mediterranean coasts of Gaul were settled by Ionian Greeks from Phocaea (50 miles north-west of ancient Smyrna), in search of metals and other raw materials.[14] Marseilles (Massalia) was founded around 600 BCE at the mouth of the Rhône, and other colonies along the Riviera soon after, to facilitate trade. There is evidence of coins being minted there, and of trade with the Gauls, in whose graves have been found Greek, Etruscan, and Massalian items, including luxurious pieces in gold, silver, and amber. In the following centuries, the Gauls spread out across Europe, even sacking Rome in 386 BCE, before they were driven out from the city, to travel as far east as Asia, where some settled (the 'Galatians'). The Romans gradually settled the area after the defeat of Hannibal in 202 BCE, who had been joined by the Gauls. By 121 BCE, the Romans had moved into the lower regions of the Rhône, establishing the first Roman colony at Narbonne (Narbo Martius) in 118 BCE, and their influence extended, thereafter, from the Atlantic to the Rhine and as far north as modern Holland. The most important phase of this colonization was, of course, the campaigns against Gaul and Britain led by Julius Caesar between 58 and 50 BCE. He opens his *Commentaries on the Gallic Wars* by noting that Gaul was divided into three regions: that inhabited by the Belgae, north and west of the Marne and Seine rivers; that of the Aquitani, dwelling between the Garonne river and the Pyrenees; and the largest region in which the Gauls themselves lived. In his accounts, we can see something of the culture of the Gauls, together with indications that aspects of Greek and Roman culture had taken hold; for instance, their religious leaders, the Druids (who along with the 'Knights' were distinguished from the commoners), were reported to have practised human sacrifices and even to have known the Greek alphabet.[15]

---

[14] For this period of Gaul, see A. Trevor Hodge, *Ancient Greek France* (Philadelphia: University of Pennsylvania Press, 1999).

[15] Caesar, *Bell. gall.* 6.13–14.

It is in the aftermath of these wars that the towns of Vienne (Vienna) and Lyons (Lugdunum) were established as colonies for the veterans.[16] But, after Caesar's assassination in 44 BCE, the Allobroges drove the Roman veterans out of Vienne, which had been capital of the Allobroges, and these veterans in turn settled in the nearby town of Lyons, thus initiating a long-standing rivalry between the two towns. In the following year, Mark Antony was sent to install another colony of veterans in Vienne, and Lucius Munatius Plancus, a general during the wars, was sent to be the governor of Lyons, establishing it as a proper colony. Lyons lies on the hill of Fourvière (the *Forum vetus*, or old forum), at the confluence of the Rhône and Saône rivers, and at the intersection of major trade roads. Despite the fact that Vienne was the older town, Lyons soon outstripped its rival in importance, becoming the capital of the Three Gauls, with an annual celebration of the Three Gauls, and the third division of Gaul was named after it as Lugdunensis.[17] It was the birthplace of the future emperors Claudius (10 BCE–54 CE) and Caracalla (188–217 CE), and is mentioned by a number of Roman writers, from Livy (59 BCE–17 CE) to Ammianus Marcellinus (330–400 CE). The archaeological remains from Lyons demonstrate the assimilation of Gallic and Roman religion and the arrival of cults from the East. For instance, in the Musée de la Civilisation Gallo-Romaine in Lyons there is an altar base that has separate reliefs of the Mother Goddesses (prominent among the Celtic deities and always depicted as a triad), Mercury (a popular god in Gaul, with inscriptions to him on three first-century altars), Sucellus (a Gallic male fertility god), and Fortuna, and another altar, dating to 160 CE, from a shrine to Cybele, the Great Mother of the Phrygian gods. Befitting its importance, Lyons had two Roman theatres, which can still be seen today on the Fourvière. The larger of the two was built by Augustus around 17–15 BCE, and later expanded by Hadrian (117–38 CE) to seat 10,000 spectators, while the smaller Odéon nearby seated only 2,500. To the north, across the Saône, lay the city's circus and amphitheatre, built in 19 CE.

It is in connection with the amphitheatre that we first hear of Christians in Lyons suffering in the arena in 177 CE. The Christian communities there and in Vienne were only a few decades old, for their letter to the

---

[16] For descriptions and images of these towns and their archaeological remains, see 'Sites and Museums in Roman Gaul I', *Athena Review: Journal of Archaeology, History, and Exploration*, 1/4 (1998),<www.athenapub.com> (accessed 10 September 2012).

[17] For the festival of the Three Gauls, see D. Fishwick, 'The Federal Cult of the Three Gauls', in *Les Martyrs de Lyon (177)*, 33–45.

Christians in Asia and Phrygia seems to indicate that the founders of the two churches in Gaul were among the martyrs.[18] The community in Lyons was led by Pothinus, who was imprisoned during the persecution and subsequently martyred. He was already over 90 years old (*h.e.* 5.1.29), and so presumably was one of the original founding fathers. The fact that the letter mentions Vienne before Lyons, together with its particular style and theological tenor, makes it probable that the letter was written by Irenaeus as the leader of the community in Vienne, and that he assumed a general oversight of Lyons while Pothinus was imprisoned and became leader of the larger community after Pothinus' martyrdom.[19] Many of the Christians in these towns, as Irenaeus himself, were immigrants from the East. The letter mentions Attalus, a Roman citizen, who was a native of Pergamum (*h.e.* 5.1.17), Alexander, a physician from Phrygia who had spent many years in various parts of Gaul (*h.e.* 5.1.49), and Alcibiades, who seems to have been connected with the Montanist movement (*h.e.* 5.3.2–4). The same may be true of Vettius Epagathus, who, though young and 'noble', acted as the advocate for the Christians, 'having the Advocate in himself, the Spirit, more abundantly than Zacharias' (*h.e.* 5.1.9–10).[20] These Christian communities were also diverse: Sanctus, the deacon of Vienne, replied to his interrogators in Latin (*h.e.* 5.1.20); Blandina was a slave girl, whose nameless mistress was also martyred (*h.e.* 5.1.17), and who also encouraged a 15-year-old boy called Ponticus (*h.e.* 5.1.53); along with Attalus, several others appear to have been Roman citizens (*h.e.* 5.1.47); Maturus was a 'recent convert' (*h.e.* 5.1.17), as perhaps was also Biblis, who initially denied her faith before 'recovering herself' and being martyred (*h.e.* 5.1.25–6). Finally the letter records that a number of the Christians had pagan servants, who were also seized and interrogated (*h.e.* 5.1.14). As only eleven were specifically mentioned, ten by name and the anonymous mistress of Blandina, despite the severity of the persecution, the communities were not too large to be counted, but big enough to

---

[18] Cf. *h.e.* 5.1.13. For Christianity in Gaul, see Élie Griffe, *La Gaule Chrétienne à l'Époque Romaine*, i, *Des origines chrétiennes à la fin du IVe siècle* (Paris: Picard, 1947); John Behr, 'Gaul', in Margaret M. Mitchell and Frances M. Young (eds), *The Cambridge History of Christianity*, i, *Origins to Constantine* (Cambridge: Cambridge University Press, 2006), 366–79; and *Les Martyrs de Lyon (177)*.

[19] Cf. Nautin, *Lettres et écrivains*, 54–61, 93–5; L. Doutreleau, 'Irénée de Lyon (saint). I. Vie. II. Œuvres', in *DSp*., fasc. L–LX, pp. 1923–38, at 1928–9.

[20] The mention here of Zacharias is an allusion to the priestly father of John the Baptist (Luke 1:6), though it is also given as the (baptismal?) name of Vettius in the martyrologies. Cf. Nautin, *Lettres et écrivains*, 50.

survive such an ordeal, and, while predominantly of Eastern background, as were their leaders, they were made up of a wide cross-section of society.[21]

Irenaeus also provides information about various others in his region who were promoting teachings that he regarded as false and would devote a great deal of time and attention to refuting. He himself had read some of the 'writings [ὑπομνήνατα]' circulating among the followers of Ptolemaeus, a disciple of Valentinus, and had become acquainted with their teachings through personal contact (haer. 1.Pref.2). He also claims to have received the testimony of women who were duped into the mystery of the 'union' but later repented (haer. 1.6.3). Irenaeus' other great struggle was with the followers of a certain Marcus, another disciple of Valentinus, who seems to have indulged in number and letter mysticism to a quite extraordinary degree and also used various apocryphal writings. Marcus had been active in Asia, where, according to Irenaeus, he seduced the wife of 'a certain deacon from among our own people in Asia' (haer. 1.13.5). It is possible that Irenaeus had encountered Marcus in Asia, but his greatest and more immediate concern in Gaul was with the followers of Marcus, who had deceived many people, especially women, though that is of course a *topos*, 'in our own regions around the Rhône' (haer. 1.13.7). Irenaeus describes at length the various elaborate rituals performed by Marcus and other followers of Valentinus. According to Irenaeus, in one Marcus 'gives thanks over the cup mixed with wine and draws out at great length the prayer of invocation', making the cup appear to be purple or red, through some kind of trickery, so that it appears that 'Grace from above has dropped her own blood into the cup', and then, handing the cups over to the women, he had them 'giving thanks over them in his presence' (haer. 1.13.2). The other ritual among them was a 'spiritual marriage', involving a 'bridal chamber' in which they 'complete the mystic teaching with invocations of those who are being initiated' (haer. 1.21.3), and anoint the heads of those being initiated with a mixture of oil and water (haer. 1.21.4). Irenaeus clearly wants his readers to believe that what goes on in these 'bridal chambers' is nothing other than ritualized

---

[21] The later martyrologies record forty-nine names of those who perished, though some of the names seem to refer to the same person. Cf. H. Quentin, 'La liste des martyrs de Lyon de l'an 177', *AB* 39 (1921), 113–38; Nautin, *Lettres et écrivains*, 49–50. The number of Christians in both communities was certainly larger, though, again, since Eusebius mentions that the letter contained a list of the names of those who survived (*h.e.* 5.5.3), the overall number could not have been too extensive.

debauchery, just as Christians themselves were accused of Thyestean feasts and Oedipal intercourse.

Several aspects of the letter of the confessors of Gaul indicate that the martyrs were aligned with the new prophets active in Phrygia and associated with Montanus—for instance, the description of Vettius Epagathas (*h.e.* 5.1.9–10) and perhaps also Alexander the Phrygian (*h.e.* 5.1.49–51). More explicitly, an extract from the letter, taken out of its original context by Eusebius, describes how Alcibiades led a very austere life, partaking of nothing but bread and water, but that it was revealed to Attalus, after his first contest in the amphitheatre, that Alcibiades was 'not doing well in refusing the creatures of God' and in fact was 'a stumbling block' to others, whereupon Alcibiades learnt his lesson and they 'partook of everything, giving thanks to God, for they were not deprived of the grace of God, but the Holy Spirit was their advocate' (*h.e.* 5.3.2–3). This emphasis on the guidance of the Spirit echoes the language of the Montanists, but is deployed to correct any excessive rigour, and significantly bases itself upon the authority of the martyrs rather than a claim to charismatic or institutional authority. It seems that this embassy of peace found a positive response from Eleutherus, though this was not the end of the problem for Rome or for Asian Christianity.[22] Nor was it the last time that Christians from Gaul addressed issues in Rome, as we will see.

THE CHRISTIAN COMMUNITIES IN ROME

The way in which the confessors of Gaul introduce Irenaeus to Eleutherus—'if we thought that office could confer righteousness upon any one, we should commend him among the first as a presbyter of the Church, which is his position'—points to the troubles in Rome being not simply reverberations from the New Prophecy in Asia, but more immediately concerning the role of the office of presbyter within the Church and between the different communities in Rome. To understand the scene into which Irenaeus stepped, we must first take a step back to consider the history of Christianity in Rome.

Recent scholarship, especially that of Peter Lampe, has shown clearly that the origins of Roman Christianity lie in 'fractionated' communities that slowly coalesced, through struggle, separation, and exclusion over the

---

[22] Cf. Christine Trevett, *Montanism: Gender, Authority, and the New Prophecy* (Cambridge: Cambridge University Press, 1996), 56–9.

course of the first two centuries.²³ Christians had made their way to Rome by the middle of the first century, as traders, immigrants, and travellers, establishing communities in an ad hoc manner. When the apostle Paul wrote his letter to the Romans, in the second half of the 50s, Christians had already been in Rome 'for a number of years' (Rom. 15:23). Paul also knows of a number of different communities: Prisca and Aquila and 'the church in their house [τὴν κατ'οἶκον αὐτῶν ἐκκλησίαν]' (Rom. 16:5), those who 'belong to the family of Aristobulus' and those who 'belong to the family of Narcissus' (Rom. 16:10, 11), together with two further groups some of whose names are mentioned (Rom. 16:14, 15).²⁴ Yet Paul sent only one letter, clearly expecting the Christians in Rome to pass his greetings on to one another. Likewise, writing at the beginning of the second century, Ignatius of Antioch specifies that he is writing 'to all the churches' in Rome, but nevertheless addressed his letter to 'the Church... in the country of the land of the Romans', clearly unsure whom he was addressing.²⁵ In reverse, Christians in Rome could write a letter collectively, as we see with the so-called *First Epistle of Clement*, and also could send aid and assistance collectively to Christians abroad, something that by the late second century was praised by Dionysius of Corinth as their 'ancestral custom' (*h.e.* 4.23.10). Despite being many and presumably diverse communities, Christians in Rome clearly sensed that they were also members constituting a single body.

Hermas

We begin to catch a tantalizing glimpse of the relations between the leaders of the communities in the second quarter of the second century with *The Shepherd of Hermas*.²⁶ The author addresses 'the leaders of the Church [τοῖς προηγουμένοις τῆς ἐκκλησίας]', and those who take 'the first

---

²³ Lampe, *Paul to Valentinus*, is a thorough review and examination of all the literary and archaeological evidence. See also George La Piana, 'The Roman Church at the End of the Second Century', *HTR* 18 (1925), 201–77, and 'Foreign Groups in Rome during the First Centuries of the Empire', *HTR* 20 (1927), 183–403; James S. Jeffers, *Conflict at Rome: Social Order and Hierarchy in Early Christianity* (Minneapolis: Fortress Press, 1991); and Markus Vinzent, 'Rome', in Mitchell and Young (eds), *The Cambridge History of Christianity*, i, *Origins to Constantine*, 397–412.

²⁴ On pre-Pauline Christianity in Rome, see Lampe, *Paul to Valentinus*, 1–16; and for Rom. 16, see Lampe, *Paul to Valentinus*, 153–83, 359–60.

²⁵ Ignatius, *Rom.*, 4.1, Pref.

²⁶ On *The Shepherd of Hermas*, see Carolyn Osiek and Helmut Koester, *Shepherd of Hermas*, Hermeneia (Minneapolois: Augsburg Fortress, 1999).

seats [τοῖς πρωτοκαθεδρίταις]', urging them to reform their ways.²⁷ There is evidently discord and tension between them, especially 'regarding privileges and reputation [περὶ πρωτείων καὶ περὶ δόξης τινός]'.²⁸ He notes how those who have an exalted attitude, wishing to have 'the first seat', avoid 'the assembly of righteous men' and 'shun them', preferring to remain 'in a corner' with the 'double-minded', giving empty speech to the empty-minded.²⁹ Yet there is also a developed sense of community and cooperation. In one vision, Hermas is given two books, and directed to

send one to Clement and one to Grapte: Clement then shall send it to the cities abroad, for this is entrusted to him [ἐκείνῳ γὰρ ἐπιτέτραπται]; and Grapte shall exhort the widows and orphans; but in this city you shall read it yourself with the elders who are in charge of the Church [μετὰ τῶν πρεσβυτέρων τῶν προϊσταμένων τῆς ἐκκλησίας].³⁰

Since there is no mention of a monarchical bishop for the city, as there would be in a later period, it seems that each leader or elder was responsible for the oversight (ἐπισκοπή) and well-being of their own community.³¹ Meeting together in assembly, they also assigned specific tasks—secretarial and charitable—for their communal work, giving concrete expression to their communal life.

Beyond this, however, we can probably see in Hermas' call to repentance and purification an attempt at church reform, as Einar Thomassen has suggested, intended to lead to greater integration.³² In one of his visions, Hermas sees the Church as a great tower being built from different stones.³³ Some stones are square and fit tightly together, as if one stone; these represent the apostles, bishops, teachers, and deacons who have lived righteously. Others have been smoothed by the sea and are also ready to take their place in the building; these are they who have suffered for the name. Yet others, however, are found on dry ground, cracked and

---

²⁷ Hermas, Vis. 2.2.6, 2.4.2–3, 3.9.7, cf. Matt. 23:6; Mark 12:29; Luke 11:43, 20:46.
²⁸ Hermas, Sim. 8.7.4–6
²⁹ Hermas, Mand. 11.12–13; cf. Acts 26:26.
³⁰ Hermas, Vis. 2.4.2–3; the Clement here is unlikely to be the author of the First Epistle of Clement.
³¹ Hermas uses 'caring' (ἐπισκέπεσθαι) in the sense of 'to care for needy, to visit them' (cf. Mand. 8.10, Vis. 3.9.2, Sim.1.8), and in Sim. 9.7.2 speaks of 'bishops' as 'ever sheltering the destitute and the widows by their ministry [οἱ δὲ ἐπίσκοποι ... τῇ διακονίᾳ ... ἐσκέπασαν]'. Likewise in Gaul, Pothinus was described as having been entrusted with 'the ministry of episcopacy in Lyons [τὴν διακονίαν τῆς ἐπισκοπῆς]' (h.e. 5.1.29).
³² Einar Thomassen, 'Orthodoxy and Heresy in Second Century Rome', HTR 97/3 (2004), 241–56, at 251–2.
³³ Hermas, Vis. 3.2.4–7.6.

misshapen in various ways, and are cast away from the tower; and these represent different kinds of sinners. Those who wish to repent may still do so, while the tower is being built, and through repentance they will find their place in the tower. Those, however, who have departed, thinking that they have found a better way, will fall into the fire, having 'apostatized from the living God' (cf. Heb. 3:12). In this way, 'the Church of God shall be purified', with the double-minded 'rejected' (ἀποβληθῆναι) from it, so that 'the Church of God shall be one body, one mind, one spirit, one faith, one love, and then the Son of God shall rejoice and be glad in them, when he has received his people in purity'.[34] Hermas is here describing a moral reformation of the Church. The divisions and dissensions he saw around him in Rome, principally in claims for privileges or honours, were unacceptable to him. The Church should be one, and the way he proposes this be achieved is through repentance. As far as we can tell, his vision was never realized, and, when the discipline of repentance was institutionalized in later centuries, it was within a very different context.[35]

Cerdo

An example of a figure who withdrew from the broader fellowship of the Church during this period is Cerdo. According to Irenaeus, Cerdo came to Rome during the time of Hyginus (c.136–40 CE), and then, 'entering the Church and making confession [of the faith], he thus remained, at one time teaching in secret, and then again confessing, but then, being denounced by some for teaching falsely, he withdrew from the gathering of the pious'.[36] It seems that, upon his arrival in Rome, Cerdo met together with his followers somewhere apart in the city, teaching them and worshipping with them, and this no doubt continued after he separated from the broader communion of Christians in the city. What is particularly striking about this description is not only that there is no indication of any kind of 'excommunication' by the broader Church or particular figures within it, if they even had any such notion or the means for its execution, but that, as with the double-minded arrogant man described by Hermas, it was Cerdo himself who separated from them,

---

[34] Hermas, *Sim.* 2.18.2–4.
[35] Cf. Thomassen, 'Orthodoxy and Heresy', 252.
[36] *Haer.* 3.4.3: εἰς τὴν ἐκκλησίαν ἐλθὼν καὶ ἐξομολογούμενος, οὕτως διετέλεσε, ποτὲ μὲν λαθροδιδασκαλῶν, ποτὲ δὲ πάλιν ἐξομολογούμενος, ποτὲ δὲ ὑπό τινων ἐλεγχόμενος ἐφ' οἷς ἐδίδασκε κακῶς καὶ ἀφιστάμενος τῆς τῶν θεοσεβῶν συνοδίας.

breaking fellowship or communion with them, so isolating himself in schism. That it is reported in such words decades later by Irenaeus, rather than in more active terms, is grounds for accepting that it describes accurately what happened in Rome in the 130s CE.

Marcion

This same dynamic is even more evident with the most notorious figure from the second century, the successor of Cerdo according to Irenaeus (*haer.* 3.4.3), and that is Marcion.[37] Marcion had also come to Rome from the East, from Sinope in Pontus, and 'flourished under Anicetus' (142–66 CE, *haer.* 3.4.3.). He was a rich shipowner by background, and when he arrived in Rome it is reported that he donated 200,000 sesterces to the Church, the price of a moderate-sized farm or house in the city, though it is unclear whether this was to a common fund or to a particular church community.[38] Marcion worked for several years composing a book that he called the *Antitheses*, pointing out the contradictions between the depiction of God in the Law and the Gospel, and so arguing that they must, therefore, be speaking of two different gods, the Creator of this world and the one who redeems us from the realm and dominion of the Creator. It was probably on the basis of the *Antitheses* that Marcion prepared his version of the *Gospel* and *Apostolikon*, an edited version of the Gospel of Luke and ten letters of Paul respectively, removing any positive references to the Old Testament.[39] Marcion and his followers

---

[37] For Marcion, the foundational work still remains Adolf von Harnack, *Marcion: Das Evangelium vom fremden Gott: Neue Studien zu Marcion*, 2nd edn (1924; repr. Darmstadt: Wissenschaftlich Buchgesellschaft, 1996); abridged translation, *Marcion: The Gospel of the Alien God*, trans. John E. Steely and Lyle D. Bierma (Durham, NC: Labyrinth Press, 1990). See now Gerhard May and Katharine Greschat (eds), *Marcion und seine kirchengeschichtlich Wirkung: Marcion and his Impact on Church History. Vorträge der Internationalen Fachkonferenz sur Marcion, gehalten vom 15–18 August 2001 in Mainz* (Berlin: de Gruyter, 2002); Harry Y. Gamble, 'Marcion and the "Canon"', in Mitchell and Young (eds), *The Cambridge History of Christianity*, i, *Origins to Constantine*, 195–213, and Sebastian Moll, *The Arch-Heretic Marcion*, WUNT 250 (Tübingen: Mohr Siebeck, 2010).

[38] Tertullian, *Praescr.*, 30. For the price comparisons, see Lampe, *Paul to Valentinus*, 245.

[39] Following the conclusions of Charles E. Hill, *From the Lost Teaching of Polycarp*, WUNT 186 (Tübingen: Mohr Siebeck, 2006), 92: 'It certainly seems to be the case that Marcion's versions of the *Gospel* and *Apostolikon* required the prior explanation of the *Antitheses* in order to be understood (Tertullian, *Marc.* 4.1.1, even called Marcion's Gospel "the Gospel according to the *Antitheses*"), so that the latter might have appeared first and independently, but not the former. It may also be significant that Irenaeus speaks of Marcion's followers as maintaining the exclusivity of Marcion's *Gospel* and edition of Paul's letters (*haer.* 3.12.12), as it could indicate that a full explanation of their import came only from these successors.' As Hill

were also accused of drawing two particular conclusions from their ditheism. First, a radical disdain for the material order, finding expression in a radical asceticism that proscribed marriage and prescribed sexual abstinence. And, second, a docetic understanding of Christ, denying his real human existence and thus the reality of his birth and death.

According to Tertullian, Marcion introduced his 'new god' in July 144 CE.[40] This is probably the point at which, as Epiphanius relates, Marcion, on his own initiative, asked to meet the 'presbyters and teachers' of the city to discuss with them the meaning of Christ's injunction not to put new wine in old wineskins.[41] What happened next is unclear. Tertullian uses vocabulary that suggests that the presbyters themselves took the final step, ejecting Marcion from the Christian community in Rome.[42] This is the scene as Harnack dramatically portrays it, with Marcion standing, as Luther, before an organized Roman Church gathered in council and standing in judgement over him, while he stands for the truth of the Gospel.[43] But, as Lampe points out, what else could they do, once put on the spot in such a manner and being asked to reject their Scriptures and turn to a new god? 'What would have happened if Marcion had been satisfied in his house community with only teaching his own followers? If he had not had the missionary impulse of a reformer of Christianity who sought to force decisions on other congregations by means of a synod?'[44] From what we have seen, and will see again for several more decades, the 'fractionated' Christian communities in Rome, though clearly having a unified sense of their own faith sufficient not to accept Marcion's teaching, had not yet coalesced into a body organized enough to take upon itself the action of collectively excluding a figure such as Marcion. Within a few years, however, writers such as Justin Martyr would begin critiquing Marcion's teaching as heretical.

Epiphanius, while describing the scene as one of excommunication, records words attributed to Marcion that do not fit with such an action,

---

further suggests, this also raises the possibility that, when Marcion published his *Antitheses*, he may not yet have determined to reject the other Gospels besides Luke, and that there is evidence that he was familiar with a fourfold Gospel collection and adapted from, or harmonized his text with, certain portions of Matthew and Mark.

[40] Tertullian, *Marc.* 1.19.
[41] Epiphanius, *Pan.* 42.2.1; the saying as given by Epiphanius is closer to Matt. 9:16–17 than Luke 5:36–37.
[42] Tertullian, *Praescr.* 30: ... *eiecti* ... *relegati* ...
[43] Harnack, *Marcion*, 27 (trans. 18): 'Who does not here think of Luther?!'
[44] Lampe, *Paul to Valentinus*, 393.

but that are instead more in keeping with what we have seen previously: Marcion himself 'caused the split [τὸ σχίσμα], forming his own sect [τὴν αἵρεσιν] and saying "I will split your church and cast a split in it forever"'.[45] The result indeed was that Marcion zealously began to establish and organize his own church community, as 'an *anti-movement*',[46] that spread out across the Mediterranean. It is unclear just how large a following he had in Rome, though one might well suppose that the followers of Cerdo were assumed into this new body. Marcion and his followers undoubtedly thought of themselves as being the one true Christian Church, and those who did not accept his teachings he derided, echoing Paul, as 'false apostles and Jewish evangelists'.[47] Marcion, like Hermas, wanted to reform the Church; but, unlike Hermas, he was convinced that what needed correcting were theological errors, rather than a general moral reform through repentance, and, again unlike Hermas, he had the determination and means to carry out his own vision. This he did, but only by establishing his church as a separate organization, a separate body not in communion with the greater body of Roman Christian communities.

Valentinus

A fascinating counterpoint to Marcion is provided by another contemporary figure in Rome. According to Irenaeus, 'Valentinus came to Rome in the time of Hyginus [c.136–140], flourished [ἤκμασε] under Pius [c.140–155], and remained until Anicetus [c.155–166]' (*haer*. 3.4.3).[48] He had come to Rome from Alexandria, and after leaving Rome continued his teaching activity in Cyprus.[49] He was widely regarded, even by his opponents, as brilliant, in both intelligence and eloquence.[50] He is reported to have composed psalms and hymns; a fragment of a 'linguistically exquisite'

---

[45] Epiphanius, *Pan*. 42.2.8. Cf. Lampe, *Paul to Valentinus*, 393, n. 24: 'This appears to be tradition since it contradicts Epiphanius' context.'

[46] Moll, *The Arch-Heretic Marcion*, 44, who concludes: 'It is this factor which demonstrates that it is incorrect to claim that Marcion's movement was just another circle of Christians within the great laboratory of Rome, thus supporting the thesis that at this time there was in fact no such thing as "orthodoxy" or "heresy".'

[47] Cf. Harnack, *Marcion*, 36–7, 196 (trans. 26–7, 123).

[48] For what we know of Valentinus' biography, see Einar Thomassen, *The Spiritual Seed: The Church of the 'Valentinians'* (Leiden: Brill, 2008), 417–22; for Valentinus and the Valentinians more generally, see Thomassen, *Spiritual Seed*, and Ismo O. Dunderberg, *Beyond Gnosticism: Myth, Lifestyle, and Society in the School of Valentinus* (New York: Columbia University Press, 2008).

[49] Epiphanius, *Pan*. 31.2.3, 7.1–2.

[50] Cf. Tertullian, *Val*. 4., Jerome, *Comm. Os*. 2.10.

metrical hymn is preserved by Hippolytus.[51] Valentinus also had a number of disciples, who went on to become important figures in their own right, in particular Ptolemaeus and Heracleon.

What is most intriguing about Valentinus himself and his sojourn in Rome is that, despite all his notoriety in subsequent heresiology, there is no indication at all of any concrete condemnation of his teaching in Rome during this period or for decades after. Tertullian reports that Valentinus aspired to become the bishop of Rome, but that, when another candidate, who had been a confessor, was chosen, he left the Church in indignation and, inflamed with 'the desire for revenge', applied himself 'to exterminate the truth', picking up a 'certain old opinion' and developing it 'with the subtlety of a serpent'.[52] Although clearly anachronistic, for we have seen nothing yet of an office of 'the bishop of Rome', Tertullian may well be taken as implying that Valentinus was seeking to gain a wider acceptance of his teaching beyond his own community, as had Marcion earlier, though with important differences. Irenaeus' words about Valentinus 'flourishing' in Rome give no sense of any disturbance regarding him.[53] Irenaeus also claims that the anti-Valentinian writers before himself had little success with their polemic, for the reason that they were not fully familiar with the teachings of Valentinus (*haer.* 4.Pref.2).[54] Moreover, Irenaeus reports that, even as late as the 180s CE, the Valentinians would discuss their attitude towards members of the Church, 'whom they do themselves term "vulgar" and "ecclesiastic"', and were then surprised that the faithful were reluctant to have fellowship with them (*haer.* 3.15.2). Finally, and most interestingly, when Irenaeus does intervene in the 190s CE, as we will see below, by urging Victor to action, he makes no reference to any earlier condemnation of Valentinus and his teaching; by this point, merely invoking the name of Valentinus is sufficient. The only exception to this pattern in Rome is Justin Martyr, to whom we will turn after further considering the case of Valentinus.

Asking why Valentinus was not condemned in Rome, Einar Thomassen considers three possibilities.[55] The first is that Valentinus was not in fact a

---

[51] Hippolytus, *Ref.* 6.37.6–8; the comment is that of Lampe, *Paul to Valentinus*, 295.
[52] Tertullian, *Val.* 4.
[53] Epiphanius, *Pan.* 31.7, implies that it was only in Cyprus that Valentinus 'gave up the faith' and 'pushed completely into the extreme of impiety'.
[54] Such writers would have included the author of the verse in *haer.* 1.15.6 (cited below), probably Polycarp, Miltiades also in Asia Minor (cf. Tertullian, *Val.* 5, *h.e.* 5.28.4), and Hegesippus (cf. *h.e.* 4.22.5).
[55] Thomassen, 'Orthodoxy and Heresy', 245–6.

'Valentinian'. This might be indicated by Tertullian, for, having described his turning to heresy after failing to become the bishop of Rome, Tertullian reports teachings that were quite different from what we know of Valentinus' own.[56] However, Justin, a contemporary of Valentinus, does clearly describe Valentinus as a heretic. A second possibility would be that his views were 'tolerated', either passively or actively. The difficulty here is that our sources are simply silent: there is no indication that he was condemned, but neither is there any indication that his teaching gained widespread acceptance. There is simply no basis for claiming, as some have, that he was widely regarded as being an admired teacher. Thomassen concludes that the quandary is best understood in terms of the 'fractionated' communities in Rome that were in the gradual process of coalescence into an organized institutional body over the course of the second century: 'There was no unitary "church" from which one could be expelled. And, by the time "the church" was finally established, the Valentinians, like Marcion and his followers, had long ago departed to create their own churches.'[57]

This conclusion needs to be nuanced somewhat. In the case of Marcion, while there may not have been a unitary church sufficiently organized as an institution to undertake an action of excommunication, if any had even thought of this as a possibility, there was undoubtedly a body of communities that had a coherent and cohesive enough sense of their faith not to accept Marcion's teaching: his very action thereafter, establishing his own church, testifies to that. In the case of Valentinus, the gradual separation of the ways, such that his name alone is sufficient to urge action against a later teacher, also testifies to the same lack of broad acceptance that increased over the intervening decades.

Thomassen raises the further intriguing suggestion that Valentinus should also be considered as a reformer, just as Hermas and Marcion before him.[58] It is clear that unity is a fundamental theme in Valentinus' teaching. The divine realm of the pleroma is characterized by unity, whereas this world, with its divisions, dissensions, and strife, is a result of a fall from that unity, albeit a fall that originated within the realm of the Aeons. The true church of the spiritual seed (that is, the Valentinians themselves) is a manifestation of a supra-cosmic reality that has descended

---

[56] A similar line is taken by Christoph Markschies, *Valentinus Gnosticus? Untersuchungen zur valentinianischen Gnosis mit einem Kommentar zu den Fragmenten Valentins*, WUNT 65 (Tübingen: Mohr Siebeck, 1992).
[57] Thomassen, 'Orthodoxy and Heresy', 255–6.
[58] Thomassen, 'Orthodoxy and Heresy', 253–55.

to this cosmic realm, the body of the Saviour, to return the spiritual seed to their original state of unity, through the mysteries of unification such as the 'bridal chamber'. While such metaphysical and soteriological themes are certainly being worked out across the broad span of a salvation history, they also reflect contemporary social and ecclesial realities. Accepting that *The Gospel of Truth* is indeed by Valentinus, one can see such an immediate application in the following passage:

> For the place where there is envy and strife is deficient, but the place where [there is] unity is perfect. Since the deficiency came into being because the Father was not known, when the Father is known, from that moment on the deficiency will no longer exist. As in the case of the ignorance of a person, when he comes to have knowledge, his ignorance vanishes of itself, as darkness vanishes when the light appears, so also the deficiency vanishes in the perfection. So from that moment on the form is not apparent, but it will vanish in the fusion of Unity, for now their works lie scattered. In time Unity will perfect the spaces. It is within Unity that each one will attain himself; within knowledge he will purify himself from multiplicity into Unity, consuming matter within himself like fire, and darkness by light, death by life. If indeed these things have happened to each one of us, then we must see to it above all that the house will be holy and silent for the Unity. [It is] as in the case of some people who moved out of dwellings having jars that in spots were not good. They would break them, and the master of the house would not suffer loss. Rather \<he\> is glad because in place of the bad jars [there are] full ones which are made perfect. For such is the judgement which has come down from above. It has passed judgement on everyone; it is a drawn sword, with two edges, cutting on either side. When the Word appeared, the one that is within the heart of those who utter it—it is not a sound alone but it became a body—a great disturbance took place among the jars because some had been emptied, others filled; that is some had been supplied others poured out, and some had been purified, still others broken up. (*Gospel of Truth*, 24.25–25.15)

As Thomassen points out, 'his description is, *mutatis mutandis*, not at all different from that in Hermas'.[59]

The 'jars', just as the 'stones' in the vision of Hermas, have an immediate ecclesiological application. Valentinus believes that, by coming to a true knowledge of the Father, the 'fractionated' communities of Rome can be brought into unity. By implication, the divisions that he sees, primarily between himself and the other Christian communities, are a result of their not knowing the Father: the deficiency, the lack of unity, exists 'because the Father was not known'.

---

[59] Thomassen, 'Orthodoxy and Heresy', 254.

Yet, whereas Marcion provoked a split by trying to force others to accept his new god, Valentinus took a different approach from those who did not know the 'Father' whom he would proclaim. Rather than rejecting the others, Valentinus did not regard them as 'heretics' to be condemned, but as potential true spiritual Christians needing education and conversion. Valentinian ecclesiology thus differentiates between an inner circle of the 'spiritual', and an outer circle of 'psychics' who remained beholden to an impoverished understanding of the Scriptures; their beliefs are not false *tout court*, but rather superficial or immature, needing further education and growth to flower into true knowledge.[60] There was no need for the 'spiritual' believers to break fellowship with the others, for it was part of their mission to bring them into a higher level of knowledge. In fact, it would have been an advantage to Florinus, in the 190s CE, to present himself as a presbyter connected with Victor, as we will see. The Valentinians thus presented themselves to the 'psychic' Christians using the same terms and expressions of faith as they did, but among themselves they would interpret these words in a different manner.[61]

We can see this endeavour at work in the letter of Ptolemaeus to Flora.[62] In this letter, Ptolemaeus cautiously leads Flora to a deeper understanding of the Mosaic Law, in particular, it seems, attempting to resolve her perplexity regarding Marcion's teaching and those who opposed him regarding the origin of the Law. Some, Ptolemaeus says, have mistakenly claimed that it was ordained by the God and Father, while others err equally by claiming that it was created by the adversary: 'but they are utterly in error, they disagree with one another, and each utterly misses the truth of the matter'.[63] Rather than simply thinking of the Law contained in the books of Moses as established by a single author, we must, through careful interpretation, he argues, come to discern how it is made up of different parts, and how each part must be interpreted

---

[60] Cf. K. Koschorke, *Die Polemik der Gnostiker gegen das kirchliche Christentum*, NHS 12 (Leiden: Brill, 1978). As Dunderberg (*Beyond Gnosticism*, 191–5) notes, this qualifies the allegations about the Valentinians teaching in 'secret'; any secrecy need only have been that of a pedagogical nature, leading learners into a fuller understanding, rather than an attempt to hide their 'real teachings'. On the distinction between 'saying' and 'meaning', see Richard A. Norris, 'Theology and Language in Irenaeus of Lyon', *ATR* 76/3 (1994), 285–95, at 286–8.

[61] Cf. *haer.* 3.17.4; 5.26.2; 4.33.7; 1. Praef.; 2.14.8; 2.28.4; 3.15.2; 3.16.6, 8; 4.32.1; 5.31.1; 5.18.1; 5.8.3.

[62] On Ptolemaeus' *Epistle to Flora*, see Thomassen, *Spiritual Seed*, 119–28; Dunderberg, *Beyond Gnosticism*, 77–94.

[63] Ptolemaeus, *Ep. Fl.* 33.3.3.

correctly. Of particular concern to Flora is Christ's claim, in Matt. 19:8, that permission for divorce was 'not from the beginning' but has its origin with Moses. We must differentiate, he argues, between the legislation coming from Moses, that coming from the elders, and that coming from God himself. And, furthermore, with regard to that coming from God, we must differentiate between that which is pure (the decalogue), that which is mixed with the inferior and injustice (the lex talionis), and that which is symbolic and allegorical (those concerned with ritual). The God who established this threefold law is neither the perfect God, nor the devil, but rather 'the demiurge and maker of the universe or world and of the things within it', different in essence from the other two, but in an intermediate state, such that he can be called by the name 'intermediateness'.[64] Ptolemaeus then concludes his letter by urging Flora not to be troubled now by the desire to learn how from the one principle of all the nature of corruption and of the intermediate have come into existence; 'if God allows, you will learn later on their principle and how they came to be, as you have been granted the apostolic tradition which we also received from our predecessors, together with the understanding that we measure all that is said by our Saviour's teaching'. All this, he consoles her, will be of great benefit to her in the future, if she bears the fruit of the seed she has received.[65] In all this, as Lampe puts it, we see an 'effort to cultivate spiritual communion with the "psychic" Christians', by avoiding condemnation of 'the faith of those who unreflectively accept the whole of the Old Testament as given from the God and Father', but rather building upon this naive acceptance of these Scriptures and leading to a deeper understanding.[66]

While reaching out cautiously to others in Rome, as part of their vision for a reform that would bring all the communities into unity (Valentinus' attempt to become 'bishop', as Tertullian would have it), Valentinus and his followers also sought their own way, in a manner that increasingly withdrew from the fractiousness of Roman Christianity, as Thomassen puts it, 'in order to be, all by themselves, the true spiritual church in a unified self-sufficiency'.[67] In the terms of *The Gospel of Truth*, quoted above: 'we must see to it above all that the house will be holy and silent for the Unity.'

---

[64] Ptolemaeus, *Ep. Fl.* 33.7.3.
[65] Ptolemaeus, *Ep. Fl.* 33.7.8–10.
[66] Lampe, *Paul to Valentinus*, 388.
[67] Thomassen, 'Orthodoxy and Heresy', 254.

We have a possible fascinating insight into the concrete world of this withdrawal in a couple of inscriptions, dating to this period, found on the Via Latina. The first, a marble inscription dating to the second century, is a verse written in Ionic hexameters:

> Co[brothers] of the bridal chambers, celebrate with torches the [ba]ths for me;
> They hunger for [ban]quets in ou[r rooms]
> [La]uding the Father, and praisin[g] the Son;
> Oh, may there be flow[ing] of the only [sp]ring
> and of the truth in that very place [or: then].[68]

The address to fellow members of 'the bridal chambers' is strongly suggestive of the Valentinian character of this verse, as is the adoption of the Ionic dialect, also found in Valentinus' own only remaining poetic fragment.[69] The plaque would seem to have hung in a private villa, inviting fellow members to enter and to celebrate baptisms and eucharistic meals, receiving flowing waters from the only true spring.

The second inscription, two epigraphs also hexameters on the marble gravestone of Flavia Sophe, date to the end of the second or first half of the third century. They were discovered on 'an undetermined location along the Via Latina, outside the city, where, in a quiet area, the rows of graves along the arterial road have been here and there broken by a suburban villa'.[70]

> Longing for the fatherly light, O sister bride, my Sophe,
> In the ablutions of Ch[rist] anointed with imperishable holy balsam
> You have hastened to gaze upon the divine countenances of the Aeons,
> upon the great angel of the great counsel, the true Son,
> You have gone [to] the bridal chamber and ascended to
> the... fatherly... an[d]...
>
> This deceased did not have a usual ending of life;
> She died away and lives and sees a truly imperishable light.
> She lives to the delight of the living, is really dead to the dead.
> O earth, why are you astonished about this type of corpse?
> Are you terrified?

These verses (the first of which offers the acrositc $\Phi\lambda\alpha\beta$, which is to be completed to $\Phi\lambda\alpha\beta\iota\alpha$, the name of the deceased being Flavia Sophe) are

---

[68] For the reconstructed text and translation, and full analysis, see Lampe, *Paul to Valentinus*, 298–306.
[69] In Hippolytus, *haer.* 6.37.6–8; cf. Lampe, *Paul to Valentinus*, 305.
[70] Lampe, *Paul to Valentinus*, 309; for text and translation, see pp. 308–9.

even more strongly redolent of Valentinian teaching: the deceased has gone to the bridal chamber to look upon the paternal light, to gaze upon the countenances of the Aeons; she has received the anointing with balsam; Christ is called 'the great Angel of Great Counsel', as in the *Excerpts from Theodotus*; and the earth, the domain of the demiurge, is thus terrified. Most of these have parallels elsewhere, but, as Lampe points out, the combination of all these motifs makes it most probable that it is indeed Valentinian in character.

It is notable that both inscriptions, the only archaeological traces of likely Valentinian provenance, were found near the Via Latina. Two further pieces from the area, dating to the third and fourth centuries, also indicate that the Valentinian tradition continued in that region, while nothing else has been found elsewhere in Rome.[71] The area to which this convergence points was one where wealthy and honourable people lived. It was in a villa in this region that Marcus Aurelius was born. It was certainly a district that would provide a suitable suburban location for those seeking retreat in a 'house holy and silent', celebrating in Ionic dialect and achieving mystical union in the 'bridal chamber'. If Flora, the recipient of Ptolemaeus' letter, is to be identified with the noble but unnamed woman mentioned by Justin in his *Second Apology*, it is a further indication of the social group from which the Valentinians drew their converts. This would also confirm Irenaeus' comments that Valentinians devote their efforts to those 'who are able to pay a high price for an acquaintence with such profound mysteries' and especially women who are 'well-bred, elegantly attired, and of great wealth' (*haer.* 1.13.3, and 1.4.3). Finally, it would explain why, in the 190s CE, Victor is unaware of the activities of Florinus. In a more subtle way than Marcion, then, Valentinus also took a separationist path, realizing that the theology he promoted was not acceptable to the larger body of Christians in Rome. The very language deployed by Valentinus, differentiating between the 'pneumatic' Christians and the 'psychic' Christians, the former with a higher knowledge of things unknown to and misunderstood by the latter, is already evidence of their own recognition of their difference from the majority of other Christians in Rome.

Justin Martyr

The third main figure in Rome during this period is Justin, who also arrived from the East, a convert from a pagan family in Flavia Neapolis in

---

[71] Lampe, *Paul to Valentinus*, 311.

Samaria.⁷² In the opening chapters of the *Dialogue*, Justin describes his search for truth, through the various philosophical schools, and how he was converted to Christianity through being directed, by an anonymous old man, to the Scriptures.⁷³ His conversion seems to have happened sometime before 135 CE. He came to Rome, having visited the city once before, sometime after this date, and remained there until his martyrdom under the municipal Roman praefect Iunius Rusticus (163–8 CE). A group of disciples gathered around Justin in Rome, several of whom are known by name, and at least three of whom—Euelpistus, Hierax, and Tatian— had also come from the East.⁷⁴ In the account of his martyrdom, Justin describes how he met his disciples 'above the baths of Myrtinus' and how he 'imparted the words of truth' to those who wished to come.⁷⁵ Justin's companions all claimed to have received 'the good confession' from their parents, rather, that is, than by being converted by him.⁷⁶

Justin claimed, under interrogation, that he 'has known no other meeting-place [ἄλλην τινὰ συνέλευσιν] but there'.⁷⁷ Since he asserts elsewhere that in judicial hearings Christians are obliged 'to tell the truth in everything', it is unlikely that he was simply attempting to protect other Christians.⁷⁸ Justin and his companions did not go on Sundays to some other location for worship. In fact, Justin himself provides a rare and precious description of how his community celebrated baptism and the Eucharist, and gathered together weekly, on Sundays, for the reading of Scripture, instruction, and exhortation by the president (ὁ προεστώς) of the community, the offering of prayer and the Eucharist, and the gathering and distribution of charity.⁷⁹ He also mentions that 'to those who are absent they [the deacons] carry away' a portion of the eucharistic gifts.⁸⁰ This need not necessarily be taken to mean that the eucharistic gifts were taken only to members of his community not present on a particular occasion, but perhaps could be taken to include members of

---

⁷² Justin, *1 apol.* 1; *dial.* 120.6.

⁷³ For a comprehensive analysis of Justin's education and its correspondence to his stylized 'intellectual autobiography', see Lampe, *Paul to Valentinus*, 260–72.

⁷⁴ *M. Just.* 3 A and B; Euelpistus came from Cappadocia and Hierax from Phrygia. That Tatian, from Syria, was a disciple of Justin is related by Irenaeus (*haer.*1.28.1).

⁷⁵ *M. Just.* 3 A and B. Cf. Harlow Gregory Snyder, ' "Above the Bath of Myrtinus": Justin Martyr's "School" in the City of Rome', *HTR* 100/3 (2007), 335–62.

⁷⁶ *M. Just.* 4 A and B.

⁷⁷ *M. Just.* 3 A and B.

⁷⁸ Justin, *2 apol.* 4.4; cf. Lampe, *Paul to Valentinus*, 376–7.

⁷⁹ Justin, *1 apol.* 61, 65–7.

⁸⁰ Justin, *1 apol.* 65.5.

other communities in Rome, as a concrete expression of communion.[81] We will see further evidence of this practice later, when considering Irenaeus' involvement in the Quartodeciman controversy.

Justin was a new sight for Roman Christians: he wore the distinct mantel of the philosopher, as later did Tertullian and Heraklas, a fellow student of Origen.[82] This was an unmistakable dress, one that was often caricatured, together with the sandals, staff, and goat-like beard that accompanied it.[83] Justin was also a fairly prolific writer. Eusebius knows of a number of treatises written by this philosopher having 'an educated intelligence trained in theology, which are full of benefit' (h.e. 4.18.1–10). There was a work addressed 'To the Hellenes', on matters of common interest to Christians and to the Greek philosophers, in particular the nature of demons, and another against the Hellenes, entitled 'Refutation '[Ἐλεγχον]'. One work addressed the sole sovereignty ($\mu o \nu a \rho \chi i a$) of God, drawing from Scripture and the writings of the Hellenes, perhaps addressing the ditheism of Marcion; and another work spoke directly against Marcion.[84] Eusebius also mentions a work entitled 'Psaltes' and one 'On the Soul'. Photius mentions two further works not known to Eusebius, one concerning nature and the other a refutation of anti-Christian arguments.[85] Justin himself mentions that he also composed a 'treatise against all the heresies that have arisen [σύνταγμα κατὰ πασῶν τῶν γεγενημένων αἱρέσεων]'.[86] None of these works, however, has come down to us. The only extant writings of Justin are his two *Apologies*, addressed to the Emperor Antoninus Pius (c.150–5 CE) and thus composed in the early 150s, and his *Dialogue with the Jew Trypho*, from the later part of that decade.

In the *Apologies* and the *Dialogue*, Justin presents a philosophically sophisticated exposition of the Christian faith as it relates to key themes of general philosophical interest, especially regarding the providence of God, fate or destiny, free will, and ethical responsibility. He does so in a self-conscious and explicit engagement with Greek philosophers, regarding their own writings, and in dialogue with a Jewish figure, whether recalling an actual debate or as a literary convention, on the use and interpretation of

---

[81] Cf. Lampe, *Paul to Valentinus*, 386.
[82] Justin, *dial*. 1.2, 9.2. Cf. h.e. 4.11.8. For Herakles, see h.e. 6.19.14, and for Tertullian, his pamphlet on the matter, *De pallio*.
[83] Apuleius, *Metam*. 11.8.2; Martial, 4.53.
[84] H.e. 4.11.8–9, and h.e. 4.18.9, where he quotes Irenaeus' mention of this work (*haer*. 4.6.2).
[85] Photius, *Bibl*. cod. 125.95.
[86] Justin, *1 apol*. 26.8, words cited in h.e. 4.11.10.

the writings of Moses and the prophets. The Scriptures, he argues against Trypho, 'are not yours but ours, for we believe them, but you, though you read them, you do not catch the spirit [τὸν νοῦν] in them'.[87] Justin approaches the writings of the Greek philosophers and poets in a similar manner. Probably drawing upon the parable of the sower casting seeds upon the ground (Matt. 13), as well as ideas found in Stoicism and Middle Platonism, Justin claims that the Son of God, as the *Logos spermatikos*, implants a seed, a *sperma*, in human beings that enables them to think and live in accordance with the Logos. Having read Moses and the prophets, the poets and philosophers have received 'seeds of the truth'.[88] In this way, then, they have a dim perception of 'the whole Word', the Son, so that some, like Plato and Socrates, were able to live and think, or at least attempt to do so, according to the Word. On this basis, Justin can then claim that Christ 'was partially known even by Socrates, for he was and is the Word who is in every person', and therefore 'whatever things were rightly said among all people, are the property of us Christians... For all the writers were able to see realities darkly through the presence in them of an implanted seed of the Word.'[89]

It was thus not simply his physical appearance that would have been striking to other Roman Christians, but even more so was the openness of his approach, in its audacity startling to both Christians and pagans alike. His discourse does not oppose a Christian theology, as true, to a false Greek philosophy or Jewish tradition in terms of discrete, compartmentalized and essentialized, static entities. Rather he proclaims a universal Logos, in which each has shared and is brought to completion and fulfilment in his proclamation of the Christian faith.[90] Justin, as Rebecca Lyman rightly argues, should not be understood in terms of an opposition between Hellenism and Christianity, putting an a priori self-defined

---

[87] Justin, *dial.* 29.2. On the form of Scripture used by Justin in his different works, and his method of utilizing them, see John Behr, *The Way to Nicaea*, Formation of Christian Theology, vol. 1 (Crestwood, NY: SVS Press, 2001), 94–100. See also Oscar Skarsaune, *The Proof from Prophecy: A Study in Justin Martyr's Proof-Text Tradition: Text-Type, Provenance, Theological Profile* (Leiden: Brill, 1987).

[88] Justin, *1 apol.* 44.9–10, 59–60. On this, see Mark J. Edwards, 'Justin's Logos and the Word of God', *JECS* 3/3 (1995), 261–80, Behr, *Way to Nicaea*, 106–9, and, earlier, R. Holte, 'Logos Spermatikos: Christianity and Ancient Philosophy according to St Justin's *Apologies*', *ST* 12 (1958), 109–68.

[89] Justin, *2 apol.* 10.8, 13.4–5.

[90] On the 'cultural take-over bid', implied by this claim, see A. J. Droge, *Homer or Moses? Early Christian Interpretation of the History of Culture* (Tübingen: Mohr, 1989), and Frances Young, *Biblical Exegesis and the Formation of Christian Culture* (Cambridge: Cambridge University Press, 1997), esp. 49–75.

Christianity into philosophical clothing as an apologetic move, but rather as an expression of transcendent universalism that was 'religiously powerful precisely because the themes address problems within Roman Hellenism'.[91] His understanding of the universality and authority of the divine revelation spoken of in prophetic texts and fulfilled in Jesus as the Incarnate Logos, completing the ancient search for truth by human philosophers, was confrontational but inclusive.

In bringing together the revealed texts of the Jewish tradition and the history of Greek philosophy, he shifted cultural categories rather than destroyed their validity. He displaced the sole cultural authority of Hellenic philosophy, yet the truth of his own 'philosophy' rested on acknowledged and shared cultural concepts of transcendence and mediation as well as biblical authority or revelation.[92]

He could thus recontextualize diverse ancient traditions by exegeting their texts anew in the light of Christ, finding truth in each, yet criticizing the religious practices of polytheism or adherence to the Mosaic Law. This, Lyman argues, 'is coherent only for a Hellenist, who accepts the underlying unity of truth and the hierarchy of cultures and literatures rather than their opposition'.[93]

It is in this perspective that we can best understand Justin's account of *hairesis* ($\alpha\mathring{\iota}\rho\epsilon\sigma\iota\varsigma$). Justin, as is commonly recognized, was the first to develop a 'heresiology', drawing upon earlier themes certainly, but putting them together in a new manner.[94] In antiquity this term was used, usually neutrally, to designate a 'school of thought', whether in the historiography of Greek philosophy or the various 'schools' within Judaism, such as 'the party' of the party of the Sadducees (Acts 5:17), the Pharisees (Acts 15:5), or the Nazarenes (Acts 24:5). Within a Christian context, however, it implied division as a 'faction'. Thus Paul warns the Corinthians, 'in the first place, when you assemble as church [$\sigma\upsilon\nu\epsilon\rho\chi o\mu\acute{\epsilon}\nu\omega\nu\ \acute{\upsilon}\mu\hat{\omega}\nu\ \grave{\epsilon}\nu\ \grave{\epsilon}\kappa\kappa\lambda\eta\sigma\acute{\iota}\alpha$], I hear that there are divisions [$\sigma\chi\acute{\iota}\sigma\mu\alpha\tau\alpha$] among you; and I partly believe it, for there must be factions [$\alpha\grave{\iota}\rho\acute{\epsilon}\sigma\epsilon\iota\varsigma$] among you in order that those who are genuine [$o\acute{\iota}\ \delta\acute{o}\kappa\iota\mu o\iota$] among you may be recognized' (1 Cor. 11:18–19). Such 'factions' are, for Paul, 'works of the flesh', along with strife, dissension,

---

[91] Lyman, 'Hellenism and Heresy', 217.
[92] Lyman, 'Hellenism and Heresy', 217.
[93] Lyman, 'Hellenism and Heresy', 217.
[94] Cf. Alain Le Boulluec, *La Notion d'hérésie dans la literature greque II*^{e}*–III*^{e} *siècles* (Paris: Études Augustiniennes, 1985), for a comprehensive analysis of the use of the term in the second and third centuries, and pp. 36–91 for the background in Greek literature and Judaism and Justin's transformation of the term.

pride, envy, and drunkenness (Gal. 5:19–20). Later writers, however, began to associate the word with false teaching. For instance, 2 Peter predicts the appearance of 'false teachers among you, who will secretly bring in destructive *haireseis*' (2 Pet. 2:1). Ignatius of Antioch also designates error, which accompanies rupture with the bishop, by the term *hairesis*. Thus the Ephesians, whose 'good order in God' is praised by their bishop, are in turn praised by Ignatius, for 'all of you live according to the truth and no *hairesis* resides among you; rather you do not even listen to anyone unless he speaks about Jesus Christ in truth'.[95] Moreover, Ignatius asserts that *hairesis* is a 'foreign plant' from which he urges the Trallians to abstain, using instead 'only Christian food'.[96] Finally, although not using the term *hairesis* itself, the author of 1 Timothy warns that some will 'depart from the faith' by attending 'to deceitful spirits and teachings of demons' (1 Tim. 4:1) and urges Timothy to 'guard the deposit [τὴν παραθήκην]' and avoid the empty chatter and contradictions of 'falsely-called knowledge [τῆς ψευδωνύμου γνώσεως]' (1 Tim. 6:20).

It is not clear how much of this later literature was known to Justin.[97] The themes that we have seen, however —*hairesis* as faction, false teaching, and demonically inspired—are brought together by Justin in a particular manner. 'Heresy' is not simply false teaching; it is not simply equated with philosophy, 'Hellenization', or a foreign element of teaching intruding into a pure deposit of faith. Greek philosophy, as we have seen, is not 'false' *tout court*, but rather imperfect, needing to be discerningly interpreted. As Lyman points out: 'The underlying problem for Justin in fact is not opposition, but rather diabolical imitation.'[98] In his *First Apology*, Justin describes how, after Christ's ascension, 'the devils put forward certain men who said that they themselves were gods': Simon Magus, whose statue Justin claims (mistakenly) to have seen in Rome, bearing the inscription 'To Simon the holy god', followed by his disciple Menander, and finally Marcion.[99] He then comments that 'all who take their opinions from these are, as we said, called "Christians",' just as many are called 'philosophers' even if they 'do not agree with the philosophers in their

---

[95] Ignatius of Antioch, *Eph.* 6.2. On distinctiveness of Ignatius, see Le Boulluec, *La Notion d'hérésie*, 22–5.
[96] Ignatius of Antioch, *Trall.* 6.1.
[97] It is possible that *dial.* 82.1 alludes to the mention of 'false prophets' and 'false teachers' in 2 Pet. 2:1, rather than Matt. 7:15, which mentions only 'false prophets', and that *dial.* 7.3 and 35.2 allude to 1 Tim. 4:1.
[98] Lyman, 'Hellenism and Heresy', 218.
[99] Justin, *1 apol.* 26.1–5.

teachings', and that he has already composed his 'treatise against all the heresies'.[100] Although they are called 'Christian', Justin asserts, they are not: they are diabolically inspired 'heresies' appearing as 'Christian'. As David Brakke puts it: 'This distinction between what people or things *are called* and what they *really are* is a key part of Justin's notion of heresy: heretics simply are not what they claim to be or what naïve others may think that they are, that is, Christians.'[101]

We should be careful, however, to note Justin's historical context in Rome at the time of the *Apologies*. While it is correct to say that Justin asserts that, despite their claims to be 'Christian', Marcion and his followers (and, before them, Simon and his disciple Menander) really are not, it would be misleading to say that the initiative for this action, and the terms of reference, is Justin's. Marcion, as we have seen, chose (the verb for which, αἱρέω, is the root of the noun *hairesis*), on his own initiative and by his own actions, to separate himself off from the broader body of Christians in Rome, so forming his own 'church', or 'faction'—that is, his own *hairesis*. Moreover, unlike the case of Hermas, where strife and divisiveness were caused by jealousy regarding 'honours' and 'reputation', in Marcion's case his choice was determined by doctrinal reasons—namely, the distinction he would make between the God of the Scriptures and creation and the God of the Saviour. Furthermore, Marcion was not content to 'live and let be', as it were, but rejected other Christian teachers as false prophets and teachers of Judaism. It is also noteworthy that, while Justin depicts Menander as a disciple of Simon, he does not claim the same for Marcion. They are certainly all demonically inspired, but this demonic inspiration does not pertain merely to the falsity of their teaching, but also to the division caused by their splitting themselves off from others under a guise that might, misleadingly, seem to some, non-Christians and those whose faith is not sufficiently discerning, to be similar if not identical. Marcion and his followers certainly did not regard their own teaching as similar to that of the 'Great Church'.

It is striking that Valentinus and his followers, on the other hand, are not mentioned by Justin in his *Apologies*, written in the early 150s CE. He does mention them in the *Dialogue*, later in the 150s, and by then the situation had become much more complicated. Justin tells Trypho that there are many who come 'in the name of Jesus' but teach impiety and in various ways blaspheme 'the Creator of all and Christ, who was foretold

---

[100] Justin, *1 apol.* 26.6–8.
[101] Brakke, *The Gnostics*, 108.

by him as coming, and the God of Abraham, Isaac, and Jacob, with whom we have no communion [ὧν οὐδενὶ κοινωνοῦμεν]'. Thse last words could, again, be taken to refer to the practice of sharing eucharistic gifts between the different communities or, in this case, a refusal to do so as a mark of separation. These, he continues, though 'they style themselves Christians', are known by the name of the originator of their individual opinions, as Marcionites, Valentinians, Basilidians, and Saturnilians, as philosophers also bear the name of the father of their teaching.[102] Moreover, he acknowledges that there is variation in belief among those whom he will admit to be truly Christian. When asked by Trypho if he really believes that Jerusalem shall be rebuilt and Christians raised to be with Christ, the patriarchs, and the prophets, Justin affirms that his faith is indeed such, but that 'many who belong to the pure and pious faith, and are true Christians, think otherwise'.[103] Yet there are others, 'some who are called Christians', who are in fact really 'godless and impious heretics [αἱρεσιῶται]' who 'blaspheme the God of Abraham, and the God of Isaac, and the God of Jacob; who say there is no resurrection of the dead, and that their souls, when they die, are taken to heaven'. These, Justin asserts, should not be supposed to be Christians, any more than the Sadducees or similar sects (αἱρέσεις) should be taken to be Jews.[104] Finally he concludes by saying that 'I and others, who are right-minded Christians on all points', are indeed convinced that there will be a resurrection of the flesh and a thousand years reign in a rebuilt Jerusalem.[105]

There are several important points to draw out from these considerations. First, Justin's Christian faith is not monolithic. He recognizes doctrinal differences among those whom he regards as 'true Christians'. Within appropriate bounds, in particular the identification of God of creation and of salvation, diversity is recognized and tolerated. Moreover, he is confident enough to recognize similarity and affinity in cases where this similarity is not a demonically inspired mimicry resulting from separation through self-chosen isolation. There is similarity and difference between Plato and Christ, Justin is ready and willing to acknowledge.[106] Marcion, on the other hand, has rejected the Christ of the Christian

---

[102] Justin, dial. 35.4–6.
[103] Justin, dial. 80.2: πολλοὺς δ' αὖ καὶ τῶν τῆς καθαρᾶς καὶ εὐσεβοῦς ὄντων χριστιανῶν γνώμης τοῦτο μὴ γνωρίζειν ἐσήμανά σοι.
[104] Justin, dial. 80.3–4.
[105] Justin, dial. 80.5: ἐγὼ δέ, καὶ εἴ τινές εἰσιν ὀρθογνώμονες κατὰ πάντα, χριστιανοί...
[106] Cf. Justin, 2 apol. 13.2: 'I confess that I both pray and strive with all my strength to be found a Christian, not because the teachings of Plato are different from those of Christ, but

communities in Rome, and so any similarity there might be is nothing but demonic mimicry rooted in division and rejection. Only within these bounds, then, is Lyman right to say: 'Justin's "orthodox" Christianity therefore encouraged distinction, discernment, and exegesis of varied cultural texts as part of the teaching and recovery of the ancient universal truth of the one Logos.'[107]

Another question to consider is how other communities in Rome looked upon Justin and his companions. It is clear that Justin feels himself closely bound to other Christians in the city, defending their faith, on behalf of all, in his *Apologies*. It is possible that his deacons took portions of the eucharistic gifts to specific other communities. But there is no other indication that he attempted to cultivate relationships with them: he remained in his place 'above the baths of Myrtinus', never knowing any other assembly place. Lampe's conclusion is that we should think of Justin's group as having existed 'very autonomously, as a free school, an organization independent from the rest of the house-church communities of the city'.[108] His contacts with other Christians were minimal; he seems to have preferred the quiet life of a withdrawn philosopher. Beyond this, it is somewhat surprising, given how large a role Justin has played in history books, to realize, as Thomassen points out, that there is no indication that, despite his erudition and literary ability, Justin 'had any significant influence with Christian circles in Rome'. Thomassen further asks why it was that other Christians did not call upon Justin in the struggle with Valentinians and other heretics? Was it, he suggests, 'because the leaders of the church, unlike Justin, did not consider them heretics at all?'[109]

Or perhaps was it because other Christian communities regarded Justin himself with some suspicion? He was, after all, a strange sight and an audacious teacher, elaborating a daringly expansive vision that utilized not only the Scriptures but also the writings of the Greek philosophers and poets. In this he was in fact similar to Valentinus. Although Justin's theology of the all-embracing Logos were certainly more in line with later theological developments than was Valentinus' mythological narratives, we should not, however, underestimate the extent to which Justin's discourse would have seemed strange and exotic to other Christians in Rome. That

---

because they are not in all respects similar, as neither are those of the others, Stoics, and poets, and historians.'
[107] Lyman, 'Hellenism and Heresy', 219.
[108] Lampe, *Paul to Valentinus*, 377.
[109] Thomassen, 'Orthodoxy and Heresy', 242.

we only have three of his many writings now extant is perhaps a measure of this. That Justin did not mention Valentinus among the heresies he lists in his *Apology* but does so a few years later in the *Dialogue* also invites further consideration. We have seen that Valentinus and his followers gradually withdrew from wider Christian circles, to approach these 'psychic' and 'immature' Christians in the hope of leading them to a deeper understanding of Christianity as they saw it, to a knowledge, that is, of their 'Father'. It is possible then that the parting of the ways with the Valentinians is first seen here between two philosophically inclined teachers.

A further dimension is perhaps indicated in Justin's *Second Apology*. In this work, Justin praises a certain Christian teacher called Ptolemaeus as 'a lover of truth', who, 'in awareness of his duty and the nobility of it through the teaching of Christ, confessed his discipleship in the divine virtue', leading to his execution.[110] There is good reason for thinking that this Ptolemaeus is none other than the Valentinian author of the *Letter to Flora* considered earlier in this chapter. Justin's Ptolemaeus is the teacher of an unnamed noble lady who has converted to Christianity. She was married to a licentious pagan husband, but her community had urged her to remain with him, in the hope that he might reform his ways. When he did not, but rather fell into greater vice, she presented papers of divorce to the emperor, which were accepted. Her husband, however, denounced her and her teacher Ptolemaeus, leading to Ptolemaeus' execution along with two other Christians. The relative infrequency of the name Ptolemaeus in Rome, together with the striking coincidence of the case as Justin describes it and one of the primary concerns and most extensively discussed topics in the *Letter to Flora*—that is, the proper way to understand the difference between Christ's words on divorce and those of Moses—make it very likely that they both refer to the same Ptolemaeus in each case.[111] If this is so, then it is not so much that other Christians in Rome did not think of Valentinus and his followers as promulgating heresy, but rather that they had suspicions regarding Justin himself and his *Apologies*, prompting him to distance himself explicitly from the Valentinians in his *Dialogue* and to present his credentials as one who has converted to Christianity solely on the basis of the Scriptures. This is, therefore, a further indication that the broader community of Christians in Rome were in fact suspicious of Valentinus, his teaching, and his activities.

---

[110] Justin, *2 apol.* 2.10, 13.
[111] As accepted by Lampe, *Paul to Valentinus*, 239–40, and, with qualification, by Dunderberg, *Beyond Gnosticism*, 90–2.

And that most of Justin's works are not preserved, and were not known beyond their titles even to Irenaeus or Eusebius, might well incline us to think that he was not successful in his endeavour to distance himself from this suspicion.

There is one further event that might well have prompted Justin to change his presentation. This is the visit to Rome of Polycarp of Smyrna in the year 154 or 155 CE. Irenaeus, writing in the 180s, recalls how Polycarp, 'a man of much greater weight, and a more steadfast witness of truth, than Valentinus, and Marcion, and the rest of the heretics', came to Rome in the time of Anicetus (c.155–66) and 'caused many to turn away from the aforesaid heretics to the Church of God, proclaiming that he had received this one and sole truth from the apostles—that, namely, which is handed down by the Church' (*haer.* 3.3.4). Polycarp's opposition to Marcion is well known and documented; his opposition to Valentinus is without any other testimony and presents problems regarding the chronology and career of Valentinus, though the verses against Marcus, who had taught in Asia and may have been a disciple of Valentinus, preserved by Irenaeus (*haer.* 1.15.6, cited below), are probably to be assigned to Polycarp.[112] There is no record at all of the impact of Polycarp's visit on Justin, but the coincidence of timing is striking and suggestive. We will consider more fully the significance of Polycarp, especially as it relates to Irenaeus, later in the next section of this chapter.

The Carpocratians

There is one final group in Rome during this period about whom we have some information, before we resume our account of Irenaeus, and that is the followers of Carpocrates. Irenaeus reports that they taught that the world was created by angels, greatly inferior to the unbegotten Father, and that Jesus was merely the human son of Joseph, just like other human beings, except that his soul remained steadfast and pure, perfectly recalling what he had witnessed in the sphere of the unbegotten God (*haer.* 1.25.1). These too share in the demonic mimicry of Christianity, 'abusing the name [of Christ] as a means of hiding their wickedness', so that, 'in one way or another, people hearing the things they speak, and imagining that we are all such as they, they may turn away their ears from the preaching of truth' and be led to 'speak evil of us all, who in fact have no

---

[112] Cf. Hill, *Lost Teaching*, 69.

communion with them, either in teaching or morals or in our daily conduct' (*haer.* 1.25.3). In Rome, this group was led by Marcellina, who came to the city in the time of Anicetus (*c.*155–66 CE). Irenaeus intriguingly states that 'they style themselves "gnostics"' (*haer.* 1.25.6), a designation that probably indicates their possession of higher knowledge, their maturity as perfect Christians, rather than any commonality with another group whom Irenaeus elsewhere designates as 'the Gnostics'.[113] Irenaeus also records, for the first time in the history of Christianity, that they 'possess images, some of them painted, and others formed from different kinds of material', and claimed that a likeness of Christ was made by Pilate. Irenaeus continues, commenting that 'they crown these images, and set them up along with the images of the philosophers of the world that is to say, with the images of Pythagoras, and Plato, and Aristotle, and the rest. They have also other modes of honouring these images, after the same manner of the Gentiles' (*haer.* 1.25.6). Nothing else is known of the relationship between this group and other Christian communities in Rome, though it is clear that they thought of themselves as being Christian along with other communities, and that they appeared as such to others, at least to outsiders. Although Irenaeus says that 'we have no fellowship with them', this comment does not necessarily bear upon the situation in Rome decades earlier.[114]

Summary

From what we have seen, Christianity in Rome was a microcosm of Christianity throughout the Empire. It was made up largely of immigrants, coming from all over the Mediterranean, with their own indigenous local Christian traditions, and further enriched by their own social and educational backgrounds, not to mention their own distinct personalities and temperaments. Christianity in Rome, as far as we can discern, was diverse to begin with, and this diversity increased only with the influx of more Christian teachers and leaders. Yet, countering these decentralizing forces, there was also a strong sense of being, together, one Christian community: one spoke of *the* Church in Rome, as well as of the churches there present. Over the century that we have examined, there was, however, no clearly organized structure for this single broader community. One catches, here and there, glimpses of ways in which they related to one

---

[113] Cf. *haer.* 1.29–31; Brakke, *The Gnostics*, 46–9.
[114] Cf. Lampe, *Paul to Valentinus*, 392.

another: the assembly of presbyters indicated by Hermas, and, for that matter, in the case of Marcion. One can also catch hints of other means by which the communities worked together, enhancing their sense of communal identity: sharing the eucharistic gifts between the communities (about which we will see more), appointing certain people with the task of corresponding with Christians elsewhere in the Empire or with the oversight of domestic and international charitable activity. We have no indication of how often the assembly of presbyters met, or of how representative they were, though the case of Marcion, presenting to the presbyters and leaders his distinctive teaching, presumes that it was largely representative. Nor do we have any clear sense of how representative the other cooperative works were. Nevertheless, it is clear that not only was there a conviction that the Christian Church is a single body as an ideal, but concrete efforts were made to manifest this ideal in the functioning of the particular communities. In this way, as Thomassen notes, though initially resembling other models of decentralized religious groups, such as the semi-autonomous Jewish synagogues, the cells of mystery religions, the schools of the philosophers, or the private clubs of the *collegium* type, the Christian Church 'was an innovation in the religious sociology of antiquity'.[115] The word 'church' designated at once both the local community and the broader body; to adapt the image Paul uses for individuals as members of the church in Corinth (cf. 1 Cor. 12:27), the Christian community, individually and collectively, is the one body of Christ.

However, while the Christian communities in Rome were working out how to relate to each other collectively, not yet having a centralized authority that could exclude certain individuals or groups, some had already split themselves off from the broader fellowship: Cerdo 'withdrew from the gathering of the pious' and Marcion went his own way, establishing his own church. Perhaps the most important aspect of the history of this period, in so far as it is available to us, is that such divisions occurred on the initiative of those who separated. It is, therefore, simply mistaken to characterize these developments in terms of an original plurality and toleration gradually being replaced with an increasingly intolerant 'Orthodoxy'. If intolerance is shown anywhere, it is on the part of Cerdo and Marcion. Likewise, although providing an occasion for greater clarification regarding the faith they hold, it would be incorrect to say that 'Orthodoxy' is later than 'heresy': it was because Marcion did not find acceptance of his particular ditheistic

---

[115] Thomassen, 'Orthodoxy and Heresy', 248–9.

teaching that he went his own way. I do not mean to suggest that there was already either a clear self-understanding of an Orthodox faith expressed in a creedal statement, or even that this existed simply in an incipient form, waiting for the right time to blossom. 'Orthodoxy' and 'heresy' are defined in reaction to each other and, in so doing, condition each other. As is commonly admitted, 'Orthodoxy' developed into a creedal religion in reaction to various forms of teaching. But Marcion too reacted, not finding his teaching accepted by the broad swathe of Christianity in Rome.

It seems likely that a similar dynamic is at work in the case of Valentinus. The adoption of a language that differentiates between true believers, the 'pneumatics' who do not simply have a higher or deeper understanding of the common faith but a knowledge that recontextualizes that faith in terms of an overarching theology or mythology, and the simple 'psychics', whose faith is not totally false but inadequate, is already evidence of their own perceived difference from the majority. They had thus already differentiated themselves from the other Christian communities, even if those communities were slow to recognize the fact. The break was not as dramatic as with Marcion, but it was already implicitly there.

One final observation to be made regarding what we have seen is that the claim that 'Orthodoxy', presumed to be monolithic and intolerant, was brought to Rome from the outside needs further nuance. It is certainly the case that the arrival of Polycarp in the city in the mid-150s was a major event, paving the way for his disciple Irenaeus also to intervene in Roman affairs in subsequent decades, as we will see in the next section. But we must not forget that the other notable figures in this story—Cerdo, Marcion, Valentinus, Justin—were also immigrants in Rome who, with the exception of Justin, who was martyred there, eventually moved on. If the apostle Paul knew of half a dozen communities in Rome in the 50s, there were certainly more before Cerdo arrived in the 130s. In a very real sense, then, figures such as Cerdo, Marcion, and Valentinus were 'alien plants', to use the language of Ignatius,[116] who found no abiding place in the city.

IRENAEUS AND FLORINUS, ELEUTHERUS AND VICTOR

When Irenaeus, as a leader of the Christians in Gaul, first steps into Rome, he does so, as we have seen, on a mission of peace, bearing a letter from

---

[116] Ignatius of Antioch, *Trall.* 6.1.

the confessors of Vienne and Lyons commending Irenaeus to Eleutherus of Rome (174/5–89). Given the nature of the other letter composed by the confessors, addressed to their brethren in Asia and Phrygia, with its allusions to the Montanist movement, and what we will see later of the actions of Eleutherus' successor Victor (189–98), it seems that Eleutherus was thinking of dissociating himself and his community from the communities in Rome made up of immigrants from Asia and Phrygia, most likely using their enthusiasm for the New Prophecy as the occasion. As nothing more is heard of this incipient clash, we should conclude that Irenaeus was indeed able to effect peace between the communities in Rome.[117] Later on Victor was prepared to be in fellowship with the Montanists, and wrote letters to their home churches in Asia and Phrygia.[118]

This unprecedented proposed action of Eleutherus demonstrates a new confidence of one of the leaders of the communities in Rome, an indication in the development of monepiscopacy that we will see increase under Victor. Another indication of this is the list of the succession of the leaders of the Church in Rome given by Irenaeus in his third book of *Against the Heresies*. The list consists of twelve names: Linus, Anacletus, Clement, Evaristus, Alexander, Sixtus, Telephorus, Hyginus, Pius, Anicetus, Soter, Eleutherus (*haer.* 3.3.3). As Lampe has demonstrated, there are sufficient indications to draw some conclusions regarding the origin of this list and its purpose.[119] First, that Irenaeus interrupts the catalogue of names given in the present tense with his own historical and literary comments given in the imperfect enables us to distinguish between the list itself and his redaction of it in the context of his own work. Second, that Eleutherus' position as twelfth is emphasized ('in twelfth place'), and that the sixth bishop is 'Sixtus', indicate that the composition of the catalogue to culminate in the twelfth is intentional: the list is designed to point out Eleutherus' possession of the fullness of apostolicity. The list does not end with Eleutherus simply because he was in office when Irenaeus was composing the third book of *Against the Heresies*. The list itself is an instrument justifying Eleutherus' claims to a greater role for his position: he is not simply one among many presbyters in Rome, but the first among them, in an emerging understanding of the office of bishop as distinct from presbyter. It is noteworthy that this list does not place Peter as the first bishop of Rome; the idea that the bishop possesses an office

---

[117] Cf. Trevett, *Montanism*, 56–9; Lampe, *Paul to Valentinus*, 394–5.
[118] Cf. Tertullian, *Prax.* 1.
[119] Lampe, *Paul to Valentinus*, 404–6.

Irenaeus of Lyons 49

continuous with that of the apostles only begins in the following century with Cyprian of Carthage. As such, the list cannot be older than Eleutherus himself. We do, however, have an interesting mention of such a list from a few decades earlier. According to Eusebius, Hegesippus composed five treatises describing his travels as far as Rome around the year 160 and his meetings with various bishops. After commenting on the epistle of Clement to the Corinthians, Hegesippus made the following recollection, preserved by Eusebius:

> And the church of the Corinthians remained in the true doctrine until Primus was bishop of Corinth, and I conversed with many of them on my voyage to Rome, and spent some days with the Corinthians during which we were refreshed by the true Word. When I was in Rome, I composed a succession until Anicetus [γενόμενος δὲ ἐν Ῥώμῃ, διαδοχὴν ἐποιησάμην μέχρις Ἀνικήτου], whose deacon was Eleutherus; Soter succeeded Anicetus, and after him came Eleutherus. In each succession and in each city things are as the Law, the Prophets, and the Lord preach. (h.e. 4.22.2–3)

The phrasing of the key part of the second sentence is extremely awkward, leading to various suggested emendations. The word 'succession' (διαδοχή) seems to mean neither a bare list or catalogue of names, nor a succession of teaching in the abstract, but rather refers to a genre of literature that would have included a list of names of teachers, interspersed with anecdotes about their lives and aspects of their teaching.[120] However it is striking that, although he says that he established this list or succession to Anicetus, the other names he gives in fact come *after* Anicetus. We should probably conclude that, when Hegesippus visited Rome, he established to his satisfaction that Anicetus stood in the continuity of that true teaching which the Law, the Prophets, and the Lord preached, and which, no doubt, he would claim goes back to the apostles themselves. Yet we have no indication from Hegesippus himself of a list tracing a succession of such leaders, nor even any indication that this occurred to him. Neither have we seen, when tracing the history of Christianity in Rome, any indication, prior to Eleutherus, that any leader in Rome thought of himself as being the leader of the whole Church there,

---

[120] The expression διαδοχὴν ἐποιησάμην is confirmed by all the MSS, and also by the Syriac version. For a historical analysis of the term διαδοχή, see Allen Brent, 'Diogenes Laertius and the Apostolic Succession', *JEH* 44/3 (1993), 367–89, and *Hippolytus and the Roman Church in the Third Century: Communities in Tension before the Emergence of a Monarch-Bishop* (Leiden: Brill, 1995), 446–50.

made up of numerous and diverse communities. Neither, finally, have we seen any attempt to record the successions of leaders within particular communities, though no doubt each community did preserve with reverence the names of their departed.

Thus it would seem that, when Hegesippus wrote his memoires, a few decades later, he recalled three specific names: Anicetus, who led the community during his visit, followed by Soter, and then Eleutherus, Anicetus' former deacon. This kernel (and perhaps very idea) of a list of succession was then expanded during the time of Eleutherus, incorporating other names from the history of Christianity in Rome, some more commonly known, such as Clement and Pius, Hermas' brother, and others who are more shadowy figures. And, given Eleutherus' attempted and novel action towards other communities, the purpose of this expanded list was to promote Eleutherus' claims to a monepiscopal oversight of all the Christian communities in Rome.

We next hear of Irenaeus corresponding with a Roman presbyter called Florinus. According to Eusebius, Irenaeus' letter was known as *On the Sole Sovereignty* or *That God is not the Author of Evil* (h.e. 5.20.1). Eusebius preserves an extract from the letter, which we give here in full:

[4] These teachings [τὰ δόγματα], O Florinus, that I may speak sparingly, do not belong to a sound mind. These teachings are inconsistent [ἀσύμφωνα] with the Church, and bring those who believe in them into the greatest impiety. These teachings not even the heretics outside the Church ever dared to proclaim. These teachings, the presbyters who were before us, those who accompanied the apostles, did not hand on to you. [5] For while I was still a boy [παῖς ἔτι ὤν], I knew you in lower Asia with Polycarp, fairing illustriously in the royal court, and endeavouring to make a good impression on him. [6] I remember the events of that time more clearly than those of recent years (for what you learn from childhood grows up with the mind, becomes united with it), so that I can describe the very place in which the blessed Polycarp sat as he used to discourse [διελέγετο], and his goings and comings, and the manner of his life, and his physical appearance, and the discourses [τὰς διαλέξεις] he delivered to the people, and how he used to recount [ἀπήγγελλεν] his association with John and with the others who had seen the Lord, as how he used to remember [ἀπεμνημόνευεν] their words, and what he heard from them concerning the Lord, and concerning his miracles and his teaching [τῆς διδασκαλίας]; having received them from eyewitnesses of the 'Word of life' [cf. 1 John 1.1], Polycarp used to relate all things in harmony with the Scriptures [ἀπήγγελλεν πάντα σύμφωνα ταῖς γραφαῖς]. [7] I listened eagerly even then to these things through the mercy of God, noting them down, not on paper, but in my heart, and ever, through the grace of God, do I genuinely ruminate on them, and I can bear witness before God that if that blessed and

apostolic presbyter had heard any such thing, he would have cried out, and shut his ears and, as was his custom, would have exclaimed, 'O good God, to what time have you preserved me that I should endure [ἀνέχωμαι] these things?' And he would have fled from the place where, sitting or standing, he had heard such words. [8] And this can be shown plainly from the letters which he sent, either to the neighbouring churches strengthening [ἐπιστηρίζων] them, or to some of the brethren, admonishing [νουθετῶν] and exhorting [προτρεπόμενος] them. (h.e. 5.20.4–8)

In this way, then, Irenaeus wrote to Florinus attempting to correct him by recalling him back to their common inheritance, the teaching of those who were 'presbyters before us and who were companions of the apostles'. The content of Irenaeus' concern with Florinus is not indicated by the content of this extract, but the title given to the letter—*On the Sole Sovereignty* or *That God is not the Author of Evils*—indicates that it related to the ditheistic teaching of Marcion.[121]

This extract is also important for the incidental details it provides of Irenaeus' relation to Polycarp. He and Florinus had both heard Polycarp in lower Asia, presumably Smyrna, at a time when Florinus was 'fairing illustriously in the royal court [ἐν τῇ βασιλικῇ αὐλῇ]', probably referring to employment by the emperor in some capacity rather than a physical building, and trying to make a good impression upon Polycarp.[122] It is striking, and important to note, that Irenaeus uses the imperfect tense to describe his memories of Polycarp: the teacher 'used to discourse' and 'used to recount' his reminiscences of John and others who had seen the Lord, and he 'used to remember' their words, and, having received this from the eyewitnesses of the 'Word of life', he 'used to relate' all things 'in harmony with the Scriptures'. The overwhelming impression is that Irenaeus himself had had a long period of acquaintance with Polycarp, making notes of his teaching 'not on paper but in my heart'. We will return to the importance of this, and how it qualifies our understanding of his statement that he 'was still a boy', when we consider the chronology of Irenaeus' life at the end of this chapter.

---

[121] This is confirmed by two passages from *Against the Heresies*: 1.27.2, Marcion 'advanced the most daring blasphemy against him who is proclaimed as God by the Law and the Prophets, *declaring him to be the author of evils*', and that Jesus came 'from *that father who is above God and that made the world*'; and 3.12.12, 'And indeed the followers of Marcion do directly blaspheme the Creator, *alleging him to be the Creator of* evils ... maintaining that there are *two beings*, gods by nature differing from each other—one being good, the other evil'. Emphasis added.

[122] Cf. Hill, *Lost Teaching*, 17–21.

There are two further themes in this extract that will also be taken up later. First, although Polycarp's words 'O good God, to what time have you preserved me that I should endure these things?' may sound rather intolerant, the word 'endure' or 'forbear' becomes a key theological term for Irenaeus' understanding of the economy of God and his 'forbearance' towards the apostasy of the human race so as to bring about its salvation and its participation in his own life.[123] The second theme is how Polycarp is described as realting all things 'in harmony with the Scriptures', for Polycarp should be understood as an important exegete of the Scriptures, and, as we will see when examining Irenaeus' own work, 'harmony' or 'symphony' is a guiding concept in his theological vision.

According to Eusebius, Florinus was then drawn to the teachings of Valentinus, and Irenaeus responded with a work called *On the Ogdoad*. He does not mention the addressee of this work, nor provide any extract from it, but mentions only 'a most beautiful note' found at the end of the treatise:

> I adjure thee who mayest copy this book, by our Lord Jesus Christ, and by his glorious advent when he comes to judge the living and the dead, to compare what thou shalt write, and correct it carefully by this manuscript, and also to write this adjuration, and place it in the copy. (*h.e.* 5.20.2)

We do, however, have an extract, preserved in Syriac, of a letter from Irenaeus to Victor concerning Florinus, who, in the introduction to the extract, is described as 'a presbyter, who was a partisan of the error of Valentinus'. The text reads as follows:

> Now, however, inasmuch as the books of these men may possibly have escaped your observation, but have come under our notice, I call your attention to them, that for the sake of your reputation you may expel these writings from among you, as bringing disgrace upon you, since their author boasts himself as being one of your company. For they constitute a stumbling-block to many, who simply and unreservedly receive, as coming from a presbyter, the blasphemy which they utter against God. Just [consider] the writer of these things, how by means of them he does not injure assistants [in divine service] only, who happen to be prepared in mind for blasphemies against God, but also damages those among us, since by his books he imbues their minds with false doctrines concerning God.[124]

---

[123] This influence is reinforced if we accept, with Charles Hill, that Polycarp was the author of the *Letter to Diognetus*, in which the idea of 'forbearance' is used, in a developed manner, to understand the 'forbearance' of God to creation in a similar manner to Irenaeus. Cf. Hill, *Lost Teaching*, 149–50; *Diogn.* esp. 9.1–2.

[124] Syriac fragment no. 28 in the edition of Harvey (ii. 457); in ANF 1 (p. 576) it is numbered as fragment no. 51.

Although the inscription to the letter, and the extract itself, have no external point of corroboration, they do coincide well with what Eusebius says about Florinus and Irenaeus' work *On the Ogdoad*. If we accept the trustworthiness of this witness, it would seem that, having formerly exhorted Florinus to return to their shared inheritance, Irenaeus wrote not to Florinus himself but to Victor, urging action. As far as we can tell from the extract, however, Irenaeus does not request Victor to 'dismiss' or 'excommunicate' Florinus. Even Eusebius, when describing earlier on what happened to Florinus, simply says that he had 'fallen away from the presbytery of the Church [πρεσβυτερίου τῆς ἐκκλησίας ἀποπεσών]' as had Blastus also, who 'suffered a similar fall' (*h.e.* 5.15). Rather than thinking of Florinus as being a 'presbyter' of the 'bishop' Victor, all indications are that they both belonged together to the 'presbytery of the Church' in Rome, an arrangement that we have seen repeated over the course of the second century—but that, as we have also seen, during the second half of that century, the disciples of Valentinus were progressively distancing themselves from the broader community. It is in this context that we should read the assertion in the above extract, that Florinus was 'boasting of being one of the company' of Victor, no doubt to urge the acceptance by others of the books that he had authored or was circulating. Victor's standing among the Christians in Rome is thereby also indirectly established. Quite what Florinus was teaching is unclear.[125] In response to this, Irenaeus urges Victor to clarify the situation, not by commanding the destruction of these books, but rather by taking a stand against them.[126] It is striking that, despite his standing and authority in Rome, Victor seems to have been unaware of what was being circulated with association to his name.

Florinus was not the only Roman presbyter to receive a written rebuke from Irenaeus about this time, for he also addressed a work, *On Schism*, to Blastus (*h.e.* 5.15, 20.1), who had broken from the Church, perhaps on the

---

[125] The universal history of the tenth-century Agapius (Mahboud) of Menbidj gives an account of Florinus' literary and teaching activity, which some have thought to be Valentinian, but is not really so; this report, however, is of dubious reliability. Cf. Agapius, *Kitab al-'Unvan*, PO 7.4, pp. 516–17; Thomassen, *Spiritual Seed*, 500–1, n. 37.

[126] Contrary to Elaine Pagels's claim (*Beyond Belief: The Secret Gospel of Thomas* (New York: Random House, 2003), 147–8) that 'when Irenaeus confronted the challenge of the many spiritual teachers, he acted decisively by demanding that believers destroy all those "innumerable secret and illegitimate writings" that his opponents were always invoking'. Irenaeus nowhere demands that anyone destroy certain books. As Raymond Starr ('The Circulation of Literary Text in the Roman World', *CQ* 37/1 (1987), 213–23, at 219) points out, even emperors in this time would have had difficulty carrying out such an action.

basis of paschal practice.[127] It was regarding the celebration of Pascha, and the conflicts that had arisen concerning the Quartodeciman practice of Asian Christians—that is, their celebration of Christ's Pascha on the fourteenth of Nisan—that Irenaeus wrote one more time to Victor, and that is the last we hear of Irenaeus. Eusebius preserves extracts from this letter of Irenaeus, and embeds it within his own retelling of the controversy, told from the perspective of a fourth-century bishop. It therefore needs to be examined with some care.

According to Eusebius, 'no small controversy' arose because the communities (αἱ παροικίαι) of Asia thought it right, 'as though by a more ancient tradition', to observe the feast of the Saviour's Passover on the fourteenth day of the moon, and so 'to finish the fast on that day, whatever day of the week it might be' (h.e. 5.23.1). Yet such was not the custom 'in the churches throughout the rest of the world, for from apostolic tradition they kept the custom which still exists that it is not right to finish the fast on any day save that of the resurrection of our Saviour' (h.e. 5.23.1). Eusebius then asserts that 'many meetings and conferences of bishops [σύνοδοι δὴ καὶ συγκροτήσεις ἐπισκόπων]' were held about this, and 'all unanimously formulated in their letters the doctrine of the Church for those in every country that the mystery of the Lord's resurrection from the dead could be celebrated on no day save Sunday, and that on that day alone we should celebrate the end of the paschal fast' (h.e. 5.23.2). He asserts that still extant are the letters of those who meet in Palestine, in Rome, in Pontus, in Gaul, in Osrhoene, and in Corinth, 'and of very many more who expressed one and the same opinion and judgement and gave the same vote' (h.e. 5.23.4). Eusebius then mentions the letter from Polycrates on behalf of the bishops in Asia, addressed to Victor and the Church of Rome, in which he asserts the apostolic precedent for their practice, with Philip and John, and the other great luminaries who have shone in Asia: Polycarp of Smyrna, Thraseas of Eumenaea, Sagaris of Laodicaea, Papirius, and Melito of Sardis (h.e. 5.24.2–5). 'All these kept the fourteenth day of the Passover according to the Gospel, never swerving, but following according to the rule of the faith [τὸν κανόνα τῆς πίστεως]' (h.e. 5.24.6). After mentioning his own background, as the eighth bishop of his family, having lived for sixty-five years in the Lord, and having studied all holy Scripture, he asserts that he is 'not afraid of threats' and that 'I could mention the bishops who are

---

[127] Cf. Ps-Tertullian, Adv. omnes. haer. 8.

Irenaeus of Lyons 55

present whom you required to be called by me [οὓς ὑμεῖς ἠξιώσατε μεταληθῆναι ὑπ' ἐμοῦ], and I did so' (h.e. 5.24.7–8).

Upon receiving this letter, 'Victor, who presided at Rome', took immediate and drastic action: in Eusebius' words, Victor

immediately tried to cut off from the common unity [ἀποτέμνειν... τῆς κοινῆς ἑνώσεως] the communities of all Asia [τῆς Ἀσίας πάσης... τὰς παροικίας], together with the adjacent churches, on the ground of heterodoxy, and he indited letters announcing that all the brethren there were absolutely excommunicated [ἀκοινωνήτους]. (h.e. 5.24.9)

This action, not surprisingly, caused an uproar! Bishops issued counter requests to Victor, urging him to consider the cause of peace, unity, and love towards his neighbours (πρὸς τὸν πλησίον, h.e. 5.24.9). Among these was Irenaeus, who exhorted Victor at length not to 'cut off whole churches of God [μὴ ἀποκόπτοι ὅλας ἐκκλησίας θεοῦ]' for following a tradition of ancient custom (h.e. 5.24.11). Eusebius then transcribes two extracts from the letter of Irenaeus. The first is as follows:

For the controversy is not only about the day, but also about the actual character of the fast; for some think that they ought to fast one day, others two, others even more, some count their day as forty hours, day and night. [13] And such variation of observance did not begin in our own time, but much earlier, in the days of our predecessors who, it would appear, disregarding strictness maintained a practice which is simple and yet allows for personal preference, establishing it for the future, and none the less all these lived in peace, and we also live in peace with one another and the disagreement [διαφωνία] in the fast confirms our agreement [ὁμόνοιαν] in the faith. (h.e. 5.24.12–13)

The second extract follows immediately, recalling earlier history, and seems perhaps to have preceded the first extract.

Among these too were the presbyters before Soter, who presided over the church of which you are now the leader, I mean Anicetus and Pius and Telesphorus and Sixtus. They did not observe it themselves, nor did they enjoin it on those who followed them, and though they did not keep it they were nonetheless at peace with those from the communities in which it was observed when they came to them, although to observe it was more objectionable to those who did not do so. [15] And no one was ever rejected [ἀπεβλήθησαν] for this reason, but the presbyters before you who did not observe it sent the Eucharist to those from other communities who did [ἀλλ' αὐτοὶ μὴ τηροῦντες οἱ πρὸ σοῦ πρεσβύτεροι τοῖς ἀπὸ τῶν παροικιῶν τηροῦσιν ἔπεμπον εὐχαριστίαν], [16] and when the blessed Polycarp was staying in Rome in the time of Anicetus, though they disagreed a little about some other things as well, they immediately made peace, having no wish for strife between them on this matter. For neither was Anicetus able to persuade Polycarp not to observe it, inasmuch as he had always done so in company with John the disciple of our Lord and the other apostles with whom he had associated; nor did Polycarp persuade Anicetus to observe it, for he said that he ought to keep the custom of those who were presbyters before him. [17] And under these circumstances they communed with each other [ἐκοινώνησαν ἑαυτοῖς], and in the Church Anicetus yielded the celebration of the Eucharist to Polycarp, obviously out of respect, and they parted from each other in peace, for the peace of the whole Church was kept both by those who observed and by those who did not [πάσης τῆς ἐκκλησίας εἰρήνην ἐχόντων, καὶ τῶν τηρούντων καὶ τῶν μὴ τηρούντων]. (h.e. 5.24.14–17)

Eusebius then simply concludes his account of this controversy by saying that 'Irenaeus, who deserved his name, making an eirenicon in this way, gave exhortations of this kind for the peace of the church and served as its ambassador, for in the letters he discussed the various views on the issue which had been raised, not only with Victor but with many other leaders of the church' (h.e. 5.14.18). We have no other mention of these letters to other leaders of the Church, to indicate whether they were directed solely to leaders of communities in Rome or further afield, to Asia and perhaps elsewhere.

Eusebius has presented us with a heavily redacted account of the controversy.[128] The first point to note is that, although Eusebius says many letters are extant, including one from Irenaeus, expressing a unanimous consensus that the paschal fast should not conclude on any day save that of Sunday, the day of the resurrection, the only two letters he cites, from Polycrates and Irenaeus (no less!), testify to the opposite practice, that the apostolic tradition they knew was to conclude the fast on the fourteenth day of the moon, whatever day of the week it might be. Eusebius' interpretation of the two letters he has in hand is clearly shaped by the step taken by the Council of Nicaea in 325 to separate the date of Pascha from the Jewish calendar and to insist that it be celebrated universally on the same day, eventually coming to settle on the Sunday following the first full moon after the vernal equinox.[129] Likewise, although Polycrates does himself refer to a request from Victor to summon bishops together to

---

[128] Cf. W. L. Petersen, 'Eusebius and the Paschal Controversy', in Harold W. Attridge and Gohei Hata (eds), *Eusebius, Christianity and Judaism* (Leiden: Brill, 1992), 311–25.

[129] For the evidence we have of what was discussed at Nicaea, see Peter L'Huillier, *The Church of the Ancient Councils: The Disciplinary Work of the First Four Ecumenical Councils* (Crestwood: SVS Press, 1996), 19–26, and, more generally, Alden A. Mosshammer, *The Easter Computus and the Origins of the Christian Era*, OECS (Oxford: Oxford University Press, 2008).

give their consideration, Eusebius clearly sees the controversy in a fourth-century perspective, with many bishops meeting in diverse places to come to a conclusion. Finally, although Eusebius reports that Victor tried to 'cut off from the common unity all the communities of Asia', it is almost certain that this refers to communities of Asian Christians in Rome, with their striking paschal celebrations, rather than, again in a fourth-century perspective, the action of a pope of Rome against Christians in Asia. This is made all but certain by the reference in Irenaeus' letter, the most concrete example we have seen so far, to the practice of exchanging eucharistic gifts. It is surely impossible to imagine that eucharistic gifts were sent from Rome to Asia! If the eucharistic gifts were exchanged, and so common unity was maintained, this must have taken place within Rome. And so, in turn, if there was a rupture in communion, with Victor wanting to take action against other communities for their liturgical practices, this was also an intra-Roman event.

In this controversy, Irenaeus, again in the name of the Christians of Gaul, intervened, reminding Victor that his own predecessors had accepted a diversity of practices, 'for our disagreement in the fast confirms our agreement in the faith'. In particular it is once again the example of Polycarp that Irenaeus calls for as a precedent. And, as a result of this embassy of peace by Irenaeus, 'the peace of the whole Church was kept both by those observed and those who did not'.[130]

IRENAEUS AND POLYCARP

Polycarp was clearly an important figure for Irenaeus: an 'apostolic presbyter', a 'disciple of the apostles', one who had seen and conversed with those who had seen the Lord. We also saw above how Polycarp's visit to Rome in the mid-150s was something of a catalyst for Christianity there, convincing many to turn away from the heresies of Marcion and

---

[130] The difference of practice at stake here might be greater than is immediately apparent. What is being 'observed' (or not) has been a matter of great scholarly controversy, for the verb has no object. Cf. A. Stewart-Sykes, *The Lamb's High Feast: Melito,* Peri Pascha *and the Quartodeciman Paschal Liturgy at Sardis* (Leiden: Brill, 1998), 205, n. 288. As Eusebius records two letters from the supporters of the Quartodeciman practice, but does not provide any comparable evidence for an alternative practice, it is possible that Victor's community had *no* annual celebration of Pascha, but only the weekly commemoration of the Lord's resurrection on Sundays; the (subsequent?) celebration of Pascha on the following Sunday would seem to be a compromise position.

Valentinus, by precisely this appeal to an apostolic connection, 'proclaiming that he had received this one and sole truth from the apostles' (*haer.* 3.3.4). As this connection is of importance to Irenaeus, and a significant part of his own background, it is worth considering it and the figure of Polycarp in more detail.

The difficulty with Irenaeus' portrait of Polycarp, as an 'apostolic presbyter' and a touchstone of Orthodoxy, is that it does not correspond to what we see in Polycarp's *Letter to the Philippians*, for here he makes no claim to having known any of the disciples of the Lord, nor does he engage in any anti-heretical polemic, and seems generally rather simple and uneducated. It is thus often assumed that, in making such claims, Irenaeus is embellishing vague childhood memories for his own purposes. But that Irenaeus should have deliberately or inadvertently promoted a false picture of Polycarp is extremely unlikely, if only for the fact that he exhorts Florinus to return to what they had both heard from Polycarp himself on the basis of their shared memories.[131] Irenaeus and Florinus, moreover, were not the only ones to have known Polycarp. Furthermore, Irenaeus' portrait of Polycarp, as seen in three separate works written over several years, is so stable that it cannot be the product of vague memories, and too detailed and multi-faceted, involving many claims, that it would be rather complex for it to be a deliberate deception.

On the other hand, there are good reasons, as Hill has recently and persuasively argued, for accepting the authenticity of Irenaeus' portrait of Polycarp. The only apostle directly named by Irenaeus as having had contact with Polycarp is John. Aside from the much-debated relationship between the apostle John and John the Elder, mentioned by Papias, and seemingly conflated by Irenaeus, the evidence for the apostle John's long life and residence in Asia Minor is strong.[132] Accepting the generally

---

[131] Cf. Hill, *Lost Teaching*, 174. As Alan R. Culpepper (*John, the Son of Zebedee: The Life of a Legend*, Studies on Personalities of the New Testament (Columbia: University of South Carolina Press, 1994), 126) points out: 'Since he appeals to Florinus' memory of their shared experience, it is most unlikely that Irenaeus would have fabricated any of this. Presumably, Florinus' memory was as clear as Irenaeus'.'

[132] Cf. Frederick W. Weidmann, *Polycarp and John: The Harris Fragments and their Challenge to the Literary Traditions* (Notre Dame, IN: University of Notre Dame Press, 1999), 130: 'many and varied accounts of John's activity provide the basis for recognizing the existence of both pre-Irenaean and para-Irenaean traditions about the ministry of the apostle John in Asia Minor and specifically Smyrna'. Hill, *Lost Teaching*, 176: 'While Tertullian was certainly dependent upon the witness of Irenaeus, other sources, such as the *Acts of John*, probably the *Epistula Apostolorum*, and certainly Hegesippus and Clement of Alexandria, presume the presence of an aged apostle John in Asia Minor and are independent of Irenaeus.' Irenaeus does apparently conflate John the Apostle and John the Elder, mentioned by Papias

agreed-upon date for Polycarp's martydom as 155/6, and his claim to be 86 years old before his martyrdom, it would indeed have been possible for Polycarp to have encountered the apostle John.[133] His *Letter to the Philippians*, which is clearly an early work, may well have been written before meeting John, or more likely in a period when a claim to acquaintence with the apostles was unremarkable. As he continued advancing in years, such a claim would quite naturally become more important. Moreover, the letter is addressed to a community established by Paul rather than John, and so such reticence is again understandable. Polycarp's personal connection with 'the apostles and others who have seen the Lord' would be further substantiated if we accept Hill's argument, mentioned earlier, that the *Letter to Diognetus* is by Polycarp, for the author of this work speaks of himself, in a unique manner but in conformity with Irenaeus' many testimonies, as 'a disciple of apostles'.[134]

The *Martyrdom of Polycarp* also gives the impression of a figure with much greater stature and ability than does the *Letter to the Philippians*. It recounts a revealing exchange between Polycarp and the pro-consul, Statius Quadratus, whom Philostratus describes as a talented orator and sophist capable of discoursing on abstract philosophical themes extemporaneously.[135] When asked to 'swear by the genius of the emperor', Polycarp replies:

'If you vainly suppose that I will swear by the genius of Caesar, as you say, and pretend that you are ignorant of who I am, listen plainly: I am a Christian. And if

---

(h.e. 5.39.3) in asserting that Papias was 'a hearer of John and a companion of Polycarp' (*haer* 5.33.4), but, as Hill (*Lost Teaching*, 173, n. 14) points out, this literary conflation was aided by Irenaeus' knowledge that Papias was a contemporary of Polycarp, whereas 'his knowledge of Polycarp was not merely textual but direct and personal'. For the question of the relationship between the apostle John and John the Elder, and its implications for discerning Papias' knowledge of the activity of the apostle in 'receiving' the first three Gospels and completing them with his own, see Charles E. Hill, 'What Papias said about John (and Luke): A "New" Papian Fragment', *JTS* ns 49 (1998), 582–629, and *The Johannine Corpus in the Early Church* (Oxford: Oxford University Press, 2004), 383–96, 407–16; Richard Bauckham, *Jesus and the Eyewitnesses: The Gospels as Eyewitness Testimony* (Grand Rapids: Eerdmans, 2006), 433–7; Charles E. Hill, 'The "Orthodox Gospel": The Reception of John in the Great Church prior to Irenaeus', in Tuomas Rasimus (ed.), *The Legacy of John* (Leiden: Brill, 2009), 233–300, and *Who Chose the Gospels?*, 207–25.

[133] Cf. *M. Polyc.* 9.3, and B. Dehandschutter, 'The Martyrium Polycarpi: A Century of Research', *ANRW* 2.27.1 (1993), 485–522, at 497–501.

[134] *Diogn.* 11.1: ἀποστόλων γενόμενος μαθητής. Cf. Hill, *Lost Teaching*, 133–6, 171–7: 'As a self-description, this appears to be unique in early Christian authors' (pp. 133–4).

[135] Philostratus, *VS* 576.

you wish to learn the doctrine of Christianity, fix a day and listen [εἰ δὲ θέλεις τὸν τοῦ Χριστιανισμοῦ μαθεῖν λόγον, δὸς ἡμέραν καὶ ἄκουσον]'.
The Pro-Consul said, 'Persuade the people [πεῖσον τὸν δῆμον]'.
And Polycarp said, 'You, I should have held worthy of discussion, for we have been taught to render honour, as is meet, if it hurt us not, to princes and authorities appointed by God. But as for those, I do not count them worthy that a defence should be given'. (M. Polyc. 10.1–2)

Standing before the pro-consul himself, Polycarp is not at all intimidated, but instead tries repeatedly to engage him: give me a time and place to speak more with you, so that you might learn the teaching of Christianity! Statius Quadratius rebuffs him, directing him to speak 'to the people', perhaps knowing, as Irenaeus recalled, that Polycarp was accustomed to deliver discourses 'to the people [πρὸς τὸ πλῆθος]' (h.e. 5.20.6), and perhaps also fearing losing face in such a discussion. Yet Polycarp tries again: I would consider it worthy to have such a discussion with you. Polycarp is clearly portrayed as an experienced apologist, with enough confidence to persuade a skilled sophist of the truth of Christianity. That Polycarp's rhetorical abilities should have developed in this way in the forty or so years since writing his *Letter to the Philippians*, during the very period when the movement known as the Second Sophistic was flourishing, is only to be expected.

It is also evident from other sources that Polycarp did indeed have a high reputation. Florinus, as we have seen, while flourishing 'in the royal court', was nevertheless trying to make a good impression on Polycarp, and there is no suggestion that this connection would have harmed his career. The letters of Ignatius, written in the early years of the second century, also mention various figures who appear in the *Martyrdom of Polycarp*, again indicating that he had good social standing. Ignatius specifically requests Polycarp to send his greetings to 'the wife of the procurator with her whole house and her children', implying that they were members of his flock.[136] 'Alce' is also mentioned by name by Ignatius, in his letter to Polycarp and his letter to the Smyrnaeans; and she is mentioned again, some five decades later, by the *Martyrdom*.[137] According to the *Martyrdom*, Alce was the sister of Nicetas and the aunt of his son, Herodes; Herodes was the 'chief of police' in the city, who seized Polycarp

---

[136] Ignatius, *Polyc.* 8.2; on the word ἐπίτροπος, as the name of an office, 'procurator', rather than a personal name, see J. B. Lightfoot, *The Apostolic Fathers* (Macmillan, 1889; repr. Peabody, MA: Hendrickson, 1989), pt 2, vol. 2, pp. 358–9.
[137] Ignatius, *Polyc.* 8.2; *Smyrn.* 13.2; *M. Polyc.* 17.2.

Irenaeus of Lyons 61

and took him to the stadium, and Nicetas was the one who approached the 'magistrate' after Polycarp's death to persuade him not to hand over the body, 'lest they desert the crucified one and begin to worship this one' (*M. Polyc.* 6.2, 8.2–3, 17.2). Their social rank and knowledge of Christianity is clearly evident, and demonstrates Polycarp's own standing and reputation in Smyrna, as an able orator and a skilled apologist.

In addition, we should also recall that, besides describing how Polycarp sat and discoursed, and delivered discourses to the people, Irenaeus also recalls that Polycarp wrote letters to both neighbouring churches, strengthening (ἐπιστηρίζων) them, and to the brethren, admonishing (νουθετῶν) and exhorting (προτρεπόμενος) them (*h.e.* 5.20.8). It is also likely that the verses against Marcus quoted by Irenaeus from 'the divinely inspired elder and preacher of the truth' were composed by Polycarp:

> Marcus, thou former of idols, inspector of portents,
> Skill'd in consulting the stars, and deep in the black arts of magic,
> Ever by tricks such as these confirming the doctrines of error,
> Furnishing signs unto those involved by thee in deception,
> Wonders of power that is utterly severed from God and apostate,
> Which Satan, thy true father, enables thee still to accomplish,
> By means of Azazel, that fallen and yet mighty angel,—
> Thus making thee the precursor of his own impious actions.
>
> (*haer.* 1.15.6)

Accepting this as Polycarp's composition further indicates both his own literary ability as well as his anti-heretical activity. In all, it would be a mistake to underestimate Polycarp's literary, rhetorical, and apologetic abilities. His talent and capacity were, moreover, known not only to his own disciples, but to others in Smyrna and its environs. Even allowing for hagiographic exaggeration, his prowess is also evidenced by the crowd, as they shout out at Polycarp's martyrdom: 'This is the teacher of Asia [ὁ τῆς Ἀσίας διδάσκαλος], the father of the Christians, the destroyer of our Gods, who teaches many neither to sacrifice nor to worship.'[138]

In his work on Polycarp, Charles Hill has further argued that we have solid reasons for identifying the anonymous presbyter whose teaching is

---

[138] *M. Polyc.* 12.2, following the reading evidenced by Eusebius and adopted by Lightfoot (*Apostolic Fathers*, pt 2, vol. 3), rather than that followed by Bart Ehrman (*The Apostolic Fathers*, LCL (Cambridge, MA: Harvard University Press, 2003)), who gives 'the teacher of impiety [ἀσεβείας]'. The balance of this threefold acclamation requires that the first title, as the second and third, be positive praise.

given by Irenaeus in *haer.* 4.27-32 with Polycarp.[139] This section of Irenaeus' work begins with these words:

4.27.1. As I have heard from a certain presbyter, who had heard it from the apostles whom he had seen, and from their disciples,[140] the punishment [declared] in Scripture was sufficient for the ancients in regard to what they did without the Spirit's guidance.

And the section closes with the following:

4.32.1. In this manner indeed the presbyter, a disciple of apostles, used to discourse[141] concerning the two testaments, proving that both are from one and the same God, for there is no other God besides him who created and formed us, nor does their word have any stability who say that this world of ours was made either by angels, or by another 'certain power', or by another God.

The description of the 'certain presbyter' clearly echoes Irenaeus' descriptions that we have seen of Polycarp as one who had heard from the apostles and their disciple, and who used to discourse in a manner that Irenaeus has inscribed in his heart. The only extended treatment of Marcion's teaching in the work is *haer.* 4.27-32, and this corresponds to the discourses to which we have seen Irenaeus appeal in his *Letter to Florinus* concerning the very same problem. It is, furthermore, only here, in *Against the Heresies*, that Irenaeus claims to be passing on the teaching he had heard from the presbyter, and that the presbyter himself attributed this to an earlier source, certain unnamed 'apostles and their disciples'. Hill further suggests a number of plausible reasons why Irenaeus did not identify this 'presbyter' by name.[142] First, it is not unusual for Irenaeus to cite ecclesial authorities without mentioning their names, even when he knows their identity. Second, this extended passage follows on from a section where Irenaeus has been emphasizing the importance of obeying 'the presbyters who are in the church' who 'possess the succession from the apostles', and who 'have received the certain gift of truth' (*haer.*

---

[139] Hill, *Lost Teaching*, 8-24.

[140] This translation follows the Armenian version, rather than the Latin, which reads 'from those who had seen the apostles and their disciples', putting a generation between the presbyter and the apostles. For the reasons for preferring the Armenian, see A. Rousseau, B. Hemmerdinger, L. Doutreleau, and C. Mercier, *Irénée de Lyon: Contre Les Hérésies, Livre IV*, SC 100, 2 vols (Paris: Cerf, 1965), vol. 1, p. 263, and Hill, *Lost Teaching*, 8-10. It is generally agreed that the Armenian presents a very literal, even wooden, translation of the Greek compared with the Latin.

[141] Again in the imperfect tense, *disputabat*, or in the SC retroversion διελέγετο.

[142] Hill, *Lost Teaching*, 23-4.

4.26.2); it is likely that he expected his readers to recall the beginning of the previous book, *haer.* 3.3–4, where he named these presbyters, the various leaders in Rome and Polycarp in Smyrna. Third, the similarities between *haer.* 4.27–32, the *Letter to Florinus*, and the *Letter to Victor* are so striking that they probably come from the same period, so that Irenaeus felt no need to identify the presbyter in *haer.* 4.27–32. And, finally, it is the presbyter's character as a faithful and truly apostolic figure that is being emphasized, rather than his personal identity.

If we accept this identification, as I am persuaded to do and will assume hereafter, then it further establishes a much greater link between Irenaeus and Polycarp than is often supposed: Irenaeus did indeed enjoy Polycarp's presence, hearing his teaching, for a sufficiently long period to be able to memorize large portions of the discourses he was in the habit of delivering. There are also several further conclusions, as Hill points out, that we can draw regarding Irenaeus' debt to Polycarp.

First, in *haer.* 4.30.1, in the context of refuting Marcion's faulting of Israelites having plundered the Egyptians and using the booty to fashion a temple for their God, Irenaeus makes an intriguing aside: 'As to those believing ones who are in the royal court [*in regali aula*], do they not derive the utensils they employ from the property which belongs to Caesar?' Given how Irenaeus elsewhere describes Florinus as flourishing 'in the royal court', this comment seems directed against Florinus himself.[143] And, if Florinus is in Irenaeus' mind while writing this passage, we should probably go further back, to *haer.* 4.26, in which Irenaeus describes the 'presbyteral' reading of Scripture that manifests their 'certain gift of truth' (*haer.* 4.26.2), and criticizes those 'who are believed to be presbyters by many, but serve their own lusts, and do not place the fear of God supreme in their hearts, but conduct themselves with contempt towards others, and are puffed up with the pride of holding the chief seat, and work evil deeds in secret, saying "no man sees us"' (*haer.* 4.26.3). This again echoes very clearly Irenaeus' words to Victor regarding the activity of Florinus, especially in the word 'many': the 'many' who accepted the writings circulated by Florinus, 'as coming from a presbyter', and the 'many' who improperly regard such figures as being 'presbyters'.[144] The situation in Rome addressed by Irenaeus in his letters to Blastus, Florinus, and Victor would thus be the concrete context for Irenaeus, beginning in *haer.* 4.26, to expound upon the need to follow the tradition of the apostolic

---

[143] Hill, *Lost Teaching*, 17.
[144] Hill, *Lost Teaching*, 22.

presbyters, and culminating with his reminiscences of such a presbyter's treatment of Marcion, the teaching that had attracted the attention of Florinus, another disciple of Polycarp.

A second point of connection to be drawn between the teaching of the anonymous presbyter and Irenaeus' own work is suggested by the conclusion of section *haer.* 4.27–32, where Irenaeus reports that the presbyter used to discourse not only about how the two testaments are from the same God, for there is no other, but that the teaching of those who say that 'this world of ours was made either by angels or by another certain power or by another God' has no stability (*haer.* 4.32.1). This threefold classification has a direct and unique echo in Polycarp's dying prayer, to 'the God of angels and powers and all creation' (*M. Polyc.* 14.1). Even if these are not the very words of Polycarp himself, the prayer is certainly composed by one familiar with him and his teaching, and, most strikingly, is not paralleled by any biblical, liturgical, or other martyrological source.[145] We have every reason then for thinking that this is Polycarp's own familiar teaching. This being the case, it is significant that this threefold identification is used by Irenaeus as a structural principle organizing the arrangement of heresies catalogued in *haer.* 1.23–7. It has often been assumed that Irenaeus is here drawing upon an earlier heresiological catalogue, but the various suggested sources are now either lost, such as Justin's *Syntagma*, or merely conjectured. With Polycarp's dying prayer and the presbyter's words in *haer.* 4.32.1, we have a tangible point of reference.[146]

Irenaeus begins with Simon, Menander, Saturnilus, Basilides, and Carpocrates, all of whom taught, in various ways, that the creation was accomplished 'by angels' (*haer.* 1.23–5); Cerinthus taught that it was by 'a certain power' (*haer.* 1.26); and that it was by 'some other God' is the teaching of Cerdo and Marcion (*haer.* 1.27). Into this mix, Irenaeus has also included certain others, the Ebionites and the Nicolaitans by association, as it were: the former for having taught about Christ (that he was the natural son of Joseph and Mary) in a similar manner to Carpocrates and Cerinthus, and the latter for having taught in the same period and area as Cerinthus (*haer.* 1.26.2–3).[147] That Polycarp knew Marcion is clear from the anecdote told by Irenaeus: 'Polycarp replied to Marcion, who met him on one occasion, and said, "Do you know me?" "I do know you, the first-born of Satan"' (*haer.* 3.3.4). It is also from Polycarp that Irenaeus knew of

---

[145] Hill, *Lost Teaching*, 27–8.
[146] Cf. Hill, *Lost Teaching*, 24–5.
[147] Hill, *Lost Teaching*, 26.

the encounter between John, the disciple of the Lord, and Cerinthus: 'going to bathe at Ephesus, and seeing Cerinthus within, [John] rushed out of the bath-house without bathing, exclaiming, "Let us fly, lest even the bath-house fall down, because Cerinthus, the enemy of the truth, is within"' (haer. 3.3.4). It is also likely that Polycarp himself had an encounter with some followers of Cerinthus' teaching. According to Ignatius, there were some in Smryna teaching that Christ only 'suffered in appearance' and that he did not truly 'bear flesh', refusing to listen to the prophets or the Gospel.[148] Such teachings are clearly echoed by Irenaeus' report of Cerinthus' teaching (haer. 1.26.1).

Finally, if we accept that haer. 4.27–32 derives from Polycarp, then it also demonstrates a level of sophistication on the part of Polycarp, both as an apologist and as an interpreter of Scripture.[149] In these five chapters, Irenaeus recounts a great deal of Polycarp's argument against Marcion. It strongly suggests that Polycarp knew Marcion's *Antitheses*, even using the same word (ἀντιτιθέντας, in Rousseau's retroversion, haer. 4.28.1) in rebutting him.[150] With Polycarp having discoursed often over many years on the problem of Marcion's teaching, Irenaeus' claim that Polycarp turned many away from the teaching of Marcion in Rome is indeed believable (haer. 3.3.4). Irenaeus' recollections of Polycarp's teaching in haer. 4.27–32 also indicate his high level of exegetical sophistication. Of particular interest for our understanding of Irenaeus' own theological formation is Polycarp's insistence that, when dealing with morally dubious actions of certain figures recounted in Scripture, but who are left without reproach, one must 'search for a type', for nothing is without purpose (haer. 4.31.1). Seeing 'types' within Scripture goes back to Paul, of course, who stated that the things that befell sinners of old 'happened to them as a type [τυπικῶς]' (1 Cor. 10:11), and thereafter becomes a universal approach to reading Scripture. But with Polycarp we have good reason to see this practice as now raised to the level of a hermeneutic principle. Also of particular interest, with a view to Irenaeus' own theology, is Polycarp's description of the exodus from Egypt as being 'a typical exodus' compared with 'our true exodus', which is the exodus of the Church from among the Gentiles, being led from this world into the inheritance bestowed by

---

[148] Ignatius of Antioch, *Smyrn.* 2, 5, 7.
[149] Hill, *Lost Teaching*, 80–8. For the text and full analysis of the quotations from the presbyter given in haer. 4.27–32, see Hill, *Lost Teaching*, 37–71.
[150] Cf. Hill, *Lost Teaching*, 42, 90. For the implications of this, both for the dissemination of the *Antitheses* and for Marcion's own knowledge of the writings of the apostles, see Hill, *Lost Teaching*, 90–4.

Christ the Son of God, and which will be accompanied, as John shows in the Apocalypse, by universal plagues, as was Egypt by a local plague (*haer.* 4.30.1). With this typological reading of Scripture, as we see it in the extracts preserved for us by Irenaeus, Polycarp reserves the word 'Scripture' for what would later be called the 'Old Testament'.[151] And, if these extracts, recalled from memory by Irenaeus several decades later, are indeed from Polycarp, he is evidently extremely adept and aware in his handling of them.

From this survey of the relationship between Polycarp and Irenaeus, which is greatly indebted to the work of Charles Hill, we must conclude that, far from being a rather rustic and unsophisticated writer of only one letter, Polycarp was a gifted orator and theologian, who has the distinction of being not only an Apostolic Father, but also an apologist, a heresiologist, and a scriptural exegete. Moreover, Irenaeus was not lying when he appealed to the memory of Polycarp, nor were his reminiscences vague and confused. We can, rather, be certain that Irenaeus did in fact receive a great deal of oral teaching from his beloved teacher, a tradition that can legitimately claim to go back at least to the apostle John.

THE CHRONOLOGY OF IRENAEUS' LIFE AND WRITINGS

With the details that we have established, we can now turn to providing some dates for Irenaeus' life and literary activities. Irenaeus, as we have seen, says he was 'still a boy [παῖς ἔτι ὤν]' when he knew Polycarp in Smyrna (*h.e.* 4.20.5), and elsewhere that he knew him 'in his early youth [ἐν τῇ πρώτῃ ἡμῶν ἡλικίᾳ]' (*haer.*3.3.4). However, from what we have seen, Irenaeus' association with Polycarp was sustained over a sufficiently long period to describe him as being accustomed to delivering

---

[151] I would be less inclined than Hill (*Lost Teaching*, 87) to see in the quotation given in *haer.* 4.32.1, cited above, which asserts that the 'two testaments' come from one and the same God, a reference to two bodies of literature, though accepting, of course, that Polycarp had various writings of the apostles and evangelists available to him. Early typology relates the Scripture (the 'Old Testament') to the event, Christ and his Passion, as type and fulfilment, rather than one text to another, as is abundantly clear, for instance, with Melito of Sardis, *On Pascha*, and, as we will see, with Irenaeus. Cf. John Hainsworth, 'The Force of the Mystery: Anamnesis and Exegesis in Melito's *Peri Pascha*', *SVTQ* 46/2 (2002), 107–46. When the typological structure comes to be thought of as relating two bodies of literature, it is reconfigured: type/shadow (in the Old Testament)—image (in the New Testament)—reality (in the kingdom to come). For example, Maximus the Confessor, *cap. theol.* 1.90: 'The Law is the shadow of the Gospel. The Gospel is the image of the blessings held in store.'

discourses to the people and to have etched in his mind not only key themes of Polycarp's teaching but also lengthy analyses and quotations. Such would not be likely for one who was a 'boy' as we now use that term. But Irenaeus himself describes the ages of life in the sequence 'infants and children [*parvulos*] and boys [*pueros*] and youths [*juvenes*] and old men', specifying that the 'first stage of early life embraces thirty years, and that this extends onwards to the fortieth year... but from the fortieth and fiftieth year a man begins to decline towards old age' (*haer.* 2.22.4–5).[152] Based on this text, Lipsius concluded that, when referring to himself as having then been a 'boy [παῖς]', Irenaeus designates the period between 18 and 30 years of age, as would also be implied by his speaking of 'early youth'.[153] Accepting the date of Polycarp's martyrdom as 155/6, and his visit to Rome as 154/5, this would give us a date for Irenaeus' birth of around 130.[154]

There is one final piece of evidence relating to Irenaeus that has yet to be mentioned. The Moscow manuscript of the *Martyrdom of Polycarp* includes a further chapter, which offers this report:

This account Gaius copied from the writings of Irenaeus, and he had also lived with Irenaeus, who was a disciple of the holy Polycarp. For this Irenaeus, at the time of the martyrdom of the bishop Polycarp was in Rome, and taught many, and many most excellent and correct writings are extant, in which he mentions Polycarp, saying that he had been his pupil, and he ably refuted every heresy, and he also handed on the ecclesiastical and universal canon [τὸν ἐκκλησιαστικὸν κανόνα καὶ καθολικόν], as he had received it from the saint. (*M. Polyc.* 22.2–4)

It is possible, then, and indeed likely, even without the report of the Moscow manuscript, given what we have seen of the migration of Christians from Asia to the West, that Irenaeus accompanied Polycarp to Rome, or that Irenaeus, perhaps with his family, had travelled to Rome sometime earlier, as had many other Christians from Asia, and renewed his acquaintance with his teacher then, hearing again his refutation of the heretics.

---

[152] Aristotle (*Rh.* 2.12–14) divides life into three stages—youth, prime of life, old age—and thought that the body reaches its 'prime' between the age of 30 and 35 years, and the mind around 49 years old.

[153] R. Lipsius, 'Irenaeus', *DCB* iii. 253–79, at 254.

[154] This is the date proposed by Lipsius. Hill, *Lost Teaching*, suggests 135, so that Irenaeus would have turned 18 in 153, when Polycarp was about 83. Robert Grant (*Irenaeus of Lyons* (London: Routledge, 1997), 2) claims that *Against the Heresies* indicates that a 'boy' could be nearly 15 years old, and so places Irenaeus' birth at about 140.

Regarding the literary activity of Irenaeus, only three of his writings can be dated with certainty: first, by its direct reference to Eleutherus as the current bishop in Rome (*haer.* 3.3.3), the third book of *Against the Heresies* must have been written sometime between 178 and 189 (and books one and two before book three); and, second, his two letters to Victor (189–98). After transcribing the extract from the *Letter to Florinus*, Eusebius continues directly, 'And at the same time in the reign of Commodus' (*h.e.* 5.21.1), thus suggesting that this letter was composed between 180 and 192, during the time of either Eleutherus or Victor. The *Letter to Florinus* clearly pre-dates the *Letter to Victor, on the Ogdoad*, regarding Florinus. It is also pretty certain that these letters, with their references to Polycarp as their common teacher, were written around the same time as *haer.* 4.27–32, with its reports of his teaching and the allusion to those in 'the royal court', but that the reference to false presbyters in *haer.* 4.26 also links this section to the *Letter to Victor, on the Ogdoad*, and probably also the *Letter to Blastus, on Schism*. By this time, Florinus was circulating some controversial works, and Irenaeus, having already written to him personally, wrote to Victor to warn him of the situation.

Regarding the work *The Demonstration of the Apostolic Tradition*, although it refers in its concluding chapters to the *Refutation and Overthrowal of Knowledge falsely so-called* (*Dem.* 99), it is likely that this is a later addition, attempting to reuse this work in the polemic against heresy.[155] Even if one accepts this passage as coming from Irenaeus himself, it is possible that it only intends to refer to the first two books of *Against the Heresies*, which, as we will see in the next chapter, alone properly correspond to the title *Refutation and Overthrowal*. It is only after the opening chapters of the third book that Irenaeus sets out to demonstrate 'the scriptural proof furnished by those apostles who did also write the Gospel' (*haer.* 3.5.1). Between the second and third books of *Against the Heresies*

---

[155] As argued by Yves-Marie Blanchard, *Aux sources du canon: Le Témoignage d'Irénée* (Paris: Cerf, 1993), 113, n. 2. This suggestion was rejected by A. Rousseau (ed. and trans.), without addressing the main argument: *Irénée de Lyon: Démonstration de la prédication apostolique*, SC 406 (Paris: Cerf, 1995), 352–3. That it is a later addition is further suggested by the unique manner of translating a Greek genitive absolute at the beginning of *Dem.* 99, as discerned by Rousseau himself, and the atypical use of the term 'seal' as an equivalent of baptism. Cf. J. Behr (trans.), *St Irenaeus of Lyons: On the Apostolic Preaching* (Crestwood, NY: SVS Press, 1997), 118, n. 29. One might also add the apparently non-chiliastic interpretation of Isa. 11 in *Dem.* 61, which suggests that it was composed before *haer.* 5. Cf. Charles Hill, *Regnum Caelorum: Patterns of Millennial Thought in the Early Church*, 2nd edn (Grand Rapids: Eerdmans, 2001), 255, n. 2. On the development of Irenaeus' eschatological thought, see the following paragraphs.

would be a natural context for sketching out the apostolic preaching from the Scriptures, such as we see in the *Demonstration*. The structure of *Against the Heresies* will be further considered in the following chapter.

As such, I would modify slightly the chronology proposed by Hill for the writings of Irenaeus:

1. *haer.* 1–2
2. *Demonstration of the Apostolic Preaching*
3. *haer.* 3
4. *Letter to Florinus, on the Sole Sovereignty*
5. *Letter to Blastus, on Schism*
6. *haer.* 4
7. *Letter to Victor, on the Ogdoad*
8. *haer.* 5
9. *Letter to Victor* and letters to other church leaders.

Items 1–3 are clearly from the time of Eleutherus (178–89) and items 6–9 from the time of Victor (189–98). Items 4 and 5 could be placed either during the time of Eleutherus or early in that of Victor.

Charles Hill raises one final intriguing suggestion concerning the relationship between the *Letter to Victor, on the Ogdoad* and *haer.* 5.[156] The subtitle of the *Letter to Victor* clearly brings to mind the primary eight Aeons in the Valentinian pleroma (*haer.* 1.1.1, 3), and, as we have seen, Florinus is described by Eusebius as turning to the teachings of Valentinus (*h.e.* 5.20.1). But the term 'Ogdoad' also has eschatological overtones in Valentinian teaching, which taught that at the end of time all the spiritual seeds, having come to perfection, will ascend into that Pleroma (*haer.* 1.7.1). Irenaeus turns to the topic of eschatology in the later chapters of book five. He claims that 'the opinions of certain people are derived from heretical discourses', which have led them to misunderstand 'the economy of God and the mystery of the resurrection of the just' (*haer.* 5.32.1). These 'discourses' are probably either the ones circulated by Florinus, and so the 'certain people' are the ones whom Florinus has been misleading, or they are the works of Valentinian teachers that have been misleading others, including Florinus.

But, after having completed book four, and forcefully asserted the need to pay attention to the presbyters, Irenaeus seems to have re-examined the books of Papias, who could certainly be looked upon as such an elder and

---

[156] Hill, *Lost Teaching*, 77–80.

who also claimed to have had contact with the apostle John, or so Irenaeus believed (*haer.* 5.33.4).[157] In his treatment of eschatology, countering the claims that Florinus was circulating, Irenaeus then utilized the elements he found in Papias regarding the thousand-year kingdom in which the just are raised to reign with Christ in a fully material and abundantly fruitful earth, as had apparently been taught by the elders of Asia, who 'had seen John, the disciple of the Lord', and heard him speak of these things himself (*haer.* 5.33.3). Such chiliastic eschatology was, however, something of a departure for Irenaeus, for, following Polycarp, he had earlier taught that those who died in righteousness, such as the martyrs, entered immediately into the kingdom.[158] Yet this change of eschatological teaching served his primary purposes tremendously well, emphasizing the teaching that runs throughout Irenaeus' writings, that the one God is indeed the Creator of everything, and so, in turn, the creation that he has established is indeed good, and that everything we see within this creation serves the one economy of God, who forbears even our apostasy, so that his ultimate purpose, the fashioning of living human beings, should be fulfilled.

Already, by the late 170s, it was not simply the diversity of Christian communities in Rome, a microcosm of Christianity throughout the Empire, that was striking, but the coherence of the broad and general consensus among them, from which Marcion himself had departed many decades earlier and from which Valentinus and his disciples were progressively isolating themselves. This unity was such that it was recognized even by those outside, such as the pagan philosopher Celsus, who spoke of this community as the 'Great Church'.[159] By the time of his death, Irenaeus had done more than anyone else to expose those who had departed from the Church for what they were and to refute their teachings, to expound the Christian faith with a comprehensiveness, coherence, and a remarkable degree of hermeneutical awareness, and to promote peace and toleration within the Church.

Before we turn to an examination of his work, one final monument of Christianity in Gaul in this period, in fact the only other piece besides the literary evidence we have already considered, forms a suitable conclusion to this chapter. This is the inscription, in Greek and dating to the early

---

[157] See Ch. 1, n. 132.
[158] For Polycarp, see Hill, *Lost Teaching*, 83–5. For Irenaeus, see *haer.* 3.16.4, 4.33.9, and the descriptions of the martyrs in the *Letter of the Churches of Vienne and Lyons*, see, e.g., *h.e.* 5.1.55. For further discussion, see Hill, *Regnum Caelorum*, 254–9.
[159] Cf. Origen, *Cels.* 5.59–61; for the date of Celsus' *True Logos*, see Henry Chadwick (trans.), *Origen: Contra Celsum* (Cambridge: Cambridge University Press, 1965), p. xxviii.

third century, found in the cemetery of Saint Pierre l'Estrier in Autun, 100 miles or so north of Lyons:

> Divine race of the heavenly Fish, with a noble heart
> draw, receiving, amongst mortals, the immortal spring
> of oracular water. Friend, warm your soul
> in the eternal waters of bounteous wisdom;
> Receive the food, sweet as honey, of the Saviour of the saints;
> Eat with zest, holding the Fish in your hands.
> That I may be filled with the Fish, I ardently desire, Master and Saviour.
> That my mother may be in blessed calm, I beseech, Light of the dead.
> Ascandios, my father, so dear to my heart,
> with my sweet mother and brothers,
> in the peace of the Fish, remember your Pectorius.[160]

All the central elements of the faith of Christians in Gaul are brought together in this beautiful inscription of Pectorius: baptism, Eucharist (received in the hands), eternal life, prayers for the departed, and request for their prayers in turn. The image of Christ as the 'Fish', emphasized by the fact that the first five lines of this inscription form an acrostic spelling out 'Fish', is based both upon the symbolism of the baptismal waters and the play made upon the Greek word for 'fish' (the letters of which, $\imath\chi\theta\upsilon\varsigma$, are taken as signifying 'Jesus Christ, God's Son, Saviour'), and once again links the Christians of Gaul to Rome, where the image is found in the art of the Catacombs, and Asia and Phrygia, where it occurs in the epitaph of Abercius Marcellus, the bishop of Hieropolis in Phrygia at the end of the second century, who on his own epitaph describes how he has travelled from Nisibis to Rome and found the same faith, serving the same nourishment, everywhere.[161] If Rome, during the second century, was the crucible in which 'orthodoxy' was forged, it was Irenaeus, on the basis of the witness of the martyrs in his community and the tradition going back through Polycarp to John, who oversaw the process.

---

[160] The text is transcribed in *DACL* vol. 1, pt 2, p. 3196, where it is followed by a plate of the inscription. The translation is based on that given in F. van der Meer and C. Mohrmann, *Atlas of the Early Christian World*, trans. M. F. Hedlund and H. H. Rowley (London: Nelson, 1958), 42, where a plate of the inscription is also given.
[161] Text in J. Stevenson, *A New Eusebius: Documents Illustrative of the History of the Church to A.D. 337* (London: SPCK, 1963), 143.

2

Against the Heresies

Irenaeus' work *The Refutation and Overthrowal of Knowledge falsely so-called* is not an easy read. It is often characterized as tedious, repetitious, and unwieldy, and its author as inept. And it is indeed a difficult read for a variety of reasons. First, as there is only one complete English translation of the work available, that given in the nineteenth-century Ante-Nicene Fathers series, English-speaking readers are confronted with some 250 pages of dense text formatted in two columns with no clear guidance to the structure of the work. Moreover, if they begin at the beginning, they must wade through 100 pages describing the variety of teachings of the disciples of Valentinus and others in book one and a lengthy examination of the inconsistencies and logical contradictions of such teachings in book two. If readers make it to book three, where Irenaeus begins an exposition of his own theology, many of the elements that he discusses are now so familiar to those who know something of Christian theology that, paradoxically, he is still a difficult figure to read because, laying all this out so fully for the first time in the history of Christian theology, he does so according to his own rationale, rather than the 'logical' order of Christian theology that we might expect to see, and so he can again appear rather inept. Much work, however, has been done over recent decades examining the theological and literary method of Irenaeus, and this has given us a greater understanding of how he thinks and how his works are structured.[1] It is with this that we will begin this chapter, so that we can gain an overview of his magnum opus, before considering his objections to his opponents later in this chapter and his own exposition in the next. The larger architecture of this work, as we will see, provides important insights into Irenaeus' theological vision.

---

[1] See esp. Bacq, *De l'ancienne à la nouvelle alliance selon S. Irénée*, and the companion volumes of notes to each book of *haer.* in the SC edition.

STRUCTURE

As alluded to above, the five books of *Against the Heresies* are readily divided into two parts, the first consisting of books one and two, and the second being the remaining three books.[2] It seems that, when beginning the work, Irenaeus intended to write only the first two books. He opens the work with a preface introducing himself and the problems he will tackle. He is writing at the request of a friend, and his purpose, he says, is to expose the teaching of those who 'are discarding the truth and introducing false words and "vain genealogies" which, as the Apostle says, "promote speculation rather than the edification of God in faith"'.[3] The reference is to First Timothy, from which he also gets the phrase 'falsely-called knowledge [γνῶσις]' (1 Tim. 6:20) that he uses in the title of the work and repeatedly applies to his opponents. Such people, he continues, 'falsify the oracles of God and prove themselves evil interpreters of what has been well said'. 'They speak the same language' but, he insists, 'they mean something different' (*haer.* 1. Pref.2). And so his task is primarily one of 'exposure', for 'error does not show itself [ἐπιδείκνυται], lest on being stripped naked it should be detected'. Having come across some of the 'writings' (ὑπομνήματα) of the disciples of Valentinus, and conversing with them, so becoming familiar with their teaching, he feels it is his duty to bring to light what he has found, providing 'a concise and clear report' of their doctrine, especially 'the disciples of Ptolemaeus, an offshoot of the school of Valentinus', and 'to offer suggestions... for refuting this doctrine by showing how utterly absurd, inconsistent, and incongruous with the truth their statements are'. This is done, he adds, 'to acquaint you and all your people with the teachings that have up till now been kept secret'. He also includes in the preface disclaimers to the effect that he is 'not accustomed to writing books nor practised in the art of rhetoric' (*haer.* 1.Pref.2), and that, as he lives among the Celts, and is now accustomed to using their 'barbarous dialect', the recipient of the work should not expect 'any display of rhetoric, which I have never learned, or any excellence of composition which I have never practised, or any beauty and persuasiveness of style, to which I make no pretensions' (*haer.* 1.Pref.3). Rather, he urges the reader to accept what he sends, and to expand 'those ideas of which I send thee, as it were, only the seminal principles'.

---

[2] For an attempt to see the whole five books of *Against the Heresies* as rhetorically structured (as *prooimium, narratio, probation, refutatio,* and *recapitulatio*), see Scott D. Moringiello, 'Irenaeus Rhetor' (Ph.D., University of Notre Dame, 2008).

[3] *haer.* 1.Pref.1, 1 Tim 1:4; for the friend's request, see 3.Pref.

In concluding book one, having exposed all the diverse teachings of his opponents and their predecessors, Irenaeus is confident that 'there will not now be need of many words to overthrow their teaching', and again, a few lines later, 'since we have brought their hidden mysteries, which they guard in silence, to the light, it will not now be necessary to use many words to destroy their teaching' (*haer.* 1.31.4). He then finishes by promising to refute them all 'in the following book', using the word 'overthrow' three times in as many sentences.

Book two opens with a summary of what was done in book one and a statement of his present intention:

> In the present book, I shall establish those points which fit in with my design, so far as time permits, and overthrow, by means of lengthened treatment under distinct heads, their whole system [*regulam*, R. ὑπόθεσιν]; for which reason, since it is an exposure and overthrowal [*detectio et euersio*] of their teaching, I have so entitled the composition of this work. (*haer.* 2.Pref.2)

The first two books thus correspond to the two key words of the title given the work by Irenaeus: ἔλεγχος and ἀνατροπή, a 'refutation' or 'exposure', or rather, for Irenaeus, a refutation by exposure, and an 'overturning'. The identity of the person for whom he wrote these works is not known. One might surmise, from Irenaeus' hope that his friend, having learnt these things, can 'make them clear to all your people', that the addressee is a leader of a Christian community. The friend clearly knew Greek, and was troubled by the teachings that Irenaeus has encountered in his own region around the Rhône valley, but, given how Irenaeus refers to the 'barbarous dialect' in use in Gaul, it is unlikely that the work was intended for readers there. As mentioned in Chapter 1, Irenaeus also describes an incident regarding 'a certain deacon from among our people in Asia' (*haer.* 1.13.5), suggesting that he is not writing for those back in Asia. It is most likely that the friend was the leader of a Christian community in Rome, probably one made up largely of immigrants from Asia (he speaks of 'our people' not 'my people'). The way that Irenaeus speaks of Marcellina and her activities in Rome (*haer.* 1.25.6) also indicates a Roman setting. Such a context would give an extra edge to Irenaeus' repeated emphasis that he is bringing to light the teachings that his opponents preach in secret, for this is exactly the situation we have seen in Rome.

By the time Irenaeus reaches the end of book two, he has become acutely aware that the task, as he had initially conceived it, is incomplete and that he needs to supplement the work already done with a positive statement of the Christian faith in one God and the advent of his Son, 'as

I shall demonstrate from the Scriptures themselves, in the books which follow' (*haer.* 2.35.2). He claims that it has been 'sufficiently proved' that 'the preaching of the apostles, the authoritative teaching of the Lord, the announcements of the prophets, the dictated utterances of the apostles, and the ministration of the law' all proclaim that there is 'but one God, the Maker of all' (*haer.* 2.35.4). Nevertheless, he finishes by saying 'that I may not be thought to avoid that series of proofs which may be derived from the dominical oracles[4]... I shall... devote accordingly a special book to the Scriptures, and shall set forth from these divine Scriptures demonstrations for all those who love the truth'.[5] The Latin translation of this statement is, according to Rousseau, 'particularly flawed', and the underlying Greek can be re-created only with every possible reservation.[6] Harvey had suggested a reconstruction preserving the sense of a 'special' or a 'particular' book as the Latin has it. Rousseau, instead, suggests taking this phrase as saying 'we shall, in the following book, expound the Scriptures'.[7] If Irenaeus did indeed at this point speak of a 'special work' devoted to the scriptural demonstration, it is extremely tempting to identify this as his work *The Demonstration of the Apostolic Preaching*. Either way, as his previous comment makes clear, he knows that he has more

---

[4] The phrase 'dominical oracles' (*scripturis dominicis*, λογίων κυριακῶν) is unusual and of interest. According to Eusebius, Papias wrote a book entitled *Interpretation of the Dominical Oracles* (λογίων κυριακῶν ἐξηγήσεως, h.e. 3.39.1), and also used the expression in reporting what the elder said about Mark: 'having become the interpreter of Peter, [Mark] wrote down accurately, though not indeed in order, whatsoever he [Peter?] remembered of the things done or said by Christ. For he neither heard the Lord nor followed him, but afterwards, as I said, he followed Peter, who adapted his teaching to the needs of his hearers, but with no intention of giving a connected account of the κυριακῶν λογίων, so that Mark committed no error while he thus wrote some things as he heard them' (h.e. 3.39.15); otherwise it is used by Irenaeus only in *haer.* 1.8.1 in the analogy with the mosaic of a king, which his opponents rearrange to make a picture of a fox or a dog. The reference in *haer.* 1.8.1 is to the writings we now speak of as the Old Testament, and so I have translated the phrase as 'dominical oracles' rather than 'the words of the Lord', which is often done, but which would have easily been expressed straightforwardly in Greek, so as not to confuse this with 'the words of the Lord', which Irenaeus treats in *haer.* 4. The implications of this for understanding what Papias was doing are significant, for it is usually assumed that he is dealing with the sayings of Christ rather than the Scriptures (e.g. J. Kürzinger, *Papias von Hierapolis und die Evangelien des Neuen Testaments* (Regensburg: F. Pustet, 1983), 69–87; Bauckham, *Jesus and the Eyewitnesses*, 12, 214), but this must wait for another occasion for further investigation.

[5] *haer.* 2.35.4: *Sed ne putemur fugere illam quae ex scripturis dominicis est probationem... proprium librum qui sequitur has Scripturas reddentes ex Scripturis diuinas probationes apponemus in medio omnibus amantibus ueritatem.*

[6] SC 293, p. 355.

[7] Harvey (vol. 1, p. 388): ἴδιον τόμον ταῖσδε ταῖς γραφαῖς ἀκολούθως ἀναδιδόντες· Rousseau (SC 293, p. 355): ἐν τῇ ἑξῆς βίβλῳ ταύτας τὰς γραφὰς ἀποδιδόντες.

work to do, and more books, in the plural, to write, to fulfil the task asked of him by his friend.

In the preface to the third book, Irenaeus refers back to the first two books, the first of which 'comprises the opinions of all these men and exhibits their customs and the character of their behaviour' and the second in which 'their perverse teachings are cast down and overthrown, and, such as they really are, laid bare and open to view' (*haer* 3.Pref.). Now, in this third book, Irenaeus says he intends to 'adduce proofs from the Scriptures', so as to be lacking in nothing regarding his charge. He concludes book three by noting that, 'over and above what has already been stated, I have deferred to the following book, to adduce the words of the Lord', to use 'the very instruction of Christ' to persuade others to cease blaspheming their Creator, the God and Father of Christ (*haer.* 3.25.7). Book four opens, accordingly, with Irenaeus saying that he will, to fulfil his promise, 'add weight, by means of the words of the Lord, to what I have already advanced' (*haer.* 4.Pref.1). This book is by far the longest, yet by the end of it Irenaeus realizes that he will have to defer 'to another book, the rest of the words of the Lord, which he taught concerning the Father, not by parables, but by expressions taken in their obvious meaning, and the exposition of the epistles of the blessed apostle' and in this way he will have given his friend 'the compete work of the exposure and refutation of knowledge falsely so-called' (*haer.* 4.41.4). This task is duly accomplished in book five, though not with the order that we might have expected. Irenaeus concludes his monumental work by recapitulating, in one sentence, the whole demonstration from the Scriptures that he has given:

> For there is one Son, who accomplished his Father's will, and there is one human race, in which the mysteries of God are wrought, 'which the angels desire to see' [1 Pet. 1:12], not being able to search out the wisdom of God, through which his handiwork, conformed and incorporated with the Son, is perfected, [the Father's will] that his Offspring, the first-begotten Word, should descend to the creature, that is, to the handiwork, and be borne by it, and, on the other hand, [that] the creature should bear the Word and ascend to him, passing beyond the angels and becoming in the image and likeness of God. (*haer.* 5.36.3)

This sentence brings together the three key points of his demonstration: that there is one God, the Father and Creator, who, in the one economy or arrangement for the effecting of his will through his one Son, Jesus Christ, has brought his own handiwork, the human race, to the point of becoming in his image and likeness, rendering them like himself, at the end thus fulfilling the express intention of God at the beginning of Scripture.

Book one

With this very general overview of the five books, we can now examine the contents and structure of each. As the books are dense and unwieldy, surveying and outlining each will hopefully be of use to readers attempting to navigate this work. Irenaeus provides a detailed account of book one in the preface to book two, which, with some slight incongruity regarding the ordering of items, is clear and comprehensive, and thus gives an insight into what Irenaeus thought it was that he had done in book one.[8] After having recounted, in the preface to book one, how he has read some 'writings [ὑπομνήματα] of those who call themselves disciples of Valentinus, and met with some of them and became acquainted with their views', Irenaeus states that his purpose is to set forth 'concisely and clearly the views of those who are now teaching error [παραδιδασκόντων], I mean the followers of Ptolemaeus, an offshoot of the school of Valentinus' (haer. 1.Pref.2).[9] What follows in the first eight chapters of book one is an account of what 'they say', a construction continued throughout this section, following the order of, first, events within the Pleroma (haer. 1.1–3), second, what happened outside the Pleroma, relating to the production of the world (haer. 1.4–5), and, third, the three kinds of substances— material, psychic, and spiritual—and corresponding to this the different types of human beings (haer. 1.6–7.1). In haer. 1.7.2, Irenaeus points out that 'there are also some who maintain' a variation on the teaching about the Saviour, that the birth, baptism, and suffering refer to a psychic Christ, the son of the Demiurge, in distinction to the Saviour.[10] That haer. 1–7 (with haer. 1.7.2 being a variation within this general teaching) are meant as a complete unit is indicated by the opening words of chapter 8: 'Such, then, is their hypothesis [ὑπόθεσις]'. What follows in haer. 1.8–9 is an examination

---

[8] Cf. David H. Tripp, 'The Original Sequence of Irenaeus' "Adversus Haereses" I: A Suggestion', *Second Century*, 8 (1991), 157–62; Thomassen, *Spiritual Seed*, 11–13; I would concur with Thomassen (*Spiritual Seed*, 14, n. 14) that Tripp's proposed rearrangement of book one is unnecessary. So also Joel Kalvesmaki, 'The Original Sequence of Irenaeus, *Against Heresies* 1: Another Suggestion', *JECS* 15/3 (2007), 407–17, who suggests, alternatively, that there might have been two different editions of *Against the Heresies*.

[9] The word ὑπομνήματα is often translated as 'commentaries', but simply means 'notes', private notebooks, or more generally documents; Clement of Alexandria, for instance, uses it for his own writings as well as others. Cf. Morton Smith, *Clement of Alexandria and a Secret Gospel of Mark* (Cambridge, MA: Harvard University Press, 1973), 28. There is no need to read into this word, as used by Irenaeus, 'derogatory connotations', as does Thomassen, *Spiritual Seed*, 14–15, n. 11

[10] See Thomassen, *Spiritual Seed*, 73–6, on the attempted simplification and evolution within Valentinian teaching that this represents.

of how, on the basis of this 'hypothesis' or 'presupposition', they use passages from the writings of Paul and the evangelists, especially John, the interpretation of whose Prologue is given in their own words (*haer.* 1.8.5). This report then concludes, in the Latin version but not the Greek, with the words: 'Such are the views of Ptolemaeus' (*haer.* 1.8.5).[11] It is followed by Irenaeus' own contrasting interpretation of the Prologue of John and his claim that those who have received 'the canon of truth' through baptism are able to restore the various scriptural passages to their proper place in the scriptural mosaic depicting Christ (*haer.* 1.9).

Irenaeus then begins a new section: 'The Church, though dispersed throughout the whole world, even to the ends of the earth, has received from the apostles and their disciples this faith', in one God, one Christ, and the Holy Spirit who made known by the prophets the economies of God worked by Christ (*haer.* 1.10.1). Though not formally called a 'canon of truth', this is the fullest such statement given by Irenaeus. He continues by emphasizing that the Church has preserved this faith throughout the world, for, while languages and expression differ, 'the import of the tradition' is the same, as those who have reflected further on these matters and have spoken more fully have not changed the 'hypothesis', by introducing another God or another Christ or another Only-begotten, but brought out further aspects of the same 'hypothesis' (*haer.* 1.10). This image of the Church maintaining consistently and universally, though not statically but dynamically, the faith received from the apostles, provides the contrasting background for the purpose of the next main section: 'Let us now look at the unstable opinions of these men, and how, since there are some two or three of them, they do not say the same things about the same subject but contradict themselves in regard to things and names' (*haer.* 1.11.1).[12] Irenaeus begins with Valentinus himself, who,

---

[11] Rousseau and Doutreleau (SC 263, p. 218) suggest that Epiphanius deleted these words as he includes this section in his report on Valentinus (*Pan.* 31) rather than Ptolemaeus (*Pan.* 33); though, as Dunderberg (*Beyond Gnosticism*, 198), points out, 'the fact that Epiphanius felt free to quote Irenaeus' Great Account as part of his account of *Valentinus* indicates that this passage was not yet ascribed to Ptolemaeus in his version of Irenaeus' work'. Further consideration of the sources for the teaching recounted in *haer.* 1.1–8.5 will be given in the following paragraphs.

[12] Irenaeus begins book two by saying: 'In the first book, which immediately precedes this, exposing the "knowledge falsely so-called", I showed you, my very dear friend, all the falsehood devised by the followers of Valentinus in various and contradictory ways. We also described the views of those who existed earlier, demonstrating that they disagreed among themselves, and still much more with truth itself' (*haer.* 2.Pref.1). On the translation of the first sentence (omitting the *esse* of the Latin translation), see SC 293, p. 200. Rousseau

Irenaeus claims, 'adapted the principles of the heresy called "Gnostic" [ἀπὸ τῆς λεγομένης Γνωστικῆς αἱρέσεως] to the particular character of his own school' (haer. 1.11.1). This is the first use of the terms 'heresy' ('heretic' has not been used to this point either) and 'Gnostic'. It is important to note that it is not applied directly to Valentinus or his followers. This is confirmed by the preface to book two, which also reserves the term 'heretic' for those who follow in the wake of Simon Magus. We will take up this point again at the end of discussing book one.

The account of Valentinus is followed by a brief mention of one Secundus (haer. 1.11.2), a fuller report on 'another renowned teacher among them' (haer. 1.11.3), yet other unnamed teachers (haer. 1.11.5), 'the followers of Ptolemaeus' (haer. 1.12.1–2), and some 'who are deemed more skilful than the persons just mentioned' (haer. 1.12.3–4). Considerably more space is given to the next figure mentioned (haer. 1.13–15), that is, Marcus, no doubt because he himself had been active 'among our own people in Asia' (haer. 1.13.5), and his disciples were now active 'in our own district of the Rhône' (haer. 1.13.7). Irenaeus first recounts various activities of Marcus, such as calling down 'Charis' upon cups of mixed wine and upon women whom he promised to make prophetesses (haer. 1.13.2–3), as well as seducing them through the use of philtres and love potions (haer. 1.13.5–7). He then begins his report of Marcus' teaching with a very unusual and striking account of his reception of revelation that integrates Marcus himself, as being 'the womb and receptacle of the Sige of Colorbasus' and the 'Only-begotten', into the unfolding of the primary Tetrad.[13] Irenaeus continues for two chapters recounting this teaching, usually in terms of what the Tetrad or Sige itself said to Marcus; because of the length and complexity of what is recounted, consisting of highly elaborate numerological and alphabetical symbolism, much in these chapters almost certainly comes from a written work. Irenaeus concludes his primary

---

and Doutreleau take this sentence to refer to the 'Grand Notice' of 1.1–9; on both points they are followed by Thomassen, Spiritual Seed, 12, n. 9, 14.

[13] haer. 1.14.1: 'This Marcus, then, who claimed that he alone had become the womb and receptacle of the Sige of Colorbasus, gave birth, as being the Only-begotten, to the seed that had been placed in him, in the following manner: the supreme Tetrad itself descended to him from the invisible and unnameable places, in a female shape because, he says, it was unable to bear the male form, and indicated to him who she was, and the origin of all things, and that which she had never before revealed to either gods or humans, she expounded to him alone, speaking thus...'. See Thomassen, Spiritual Seed, 242. On 'Sige' and Colobasus, see Niclas Förster, Marcus Magus: Kult, Lehre und Gemeindeleben einer valentinianischen Gnostikergruppe. Sammlung der Quellen und Kommentar, WUNT 114 (Tübingen: Mohr-Siebeck, 1999), 166–86.

account of Marcus' teaching with verses, probably from Polycarp (*haer.* 1.15.6, quoted in Chapter 1), written against Marcus.

After giving 'the words of the saintly elder', Irenaeus then says, in the penultimate sentence of *haer.* 1.15.6, that 'we shall endeavour to state briefly the rest of their mystagogy'. What follows, in *haer.* 1.16–21, is all given in the plural form, as 'they say' or similar constructions, in contrast to Marcus' own words reported in *haer.* 1.13–15. After a further symbolic account of the pleroma (*haer.* 1.16.1–2), and some polemical words (*haer.* 1.16.3), Irenaeus turns to their account of creation (*haer.* 1.17.1), and the way in which they interpret the text of Genesis (*haer.* 1.18.1) to accord with their teaching. This is followed by an account of the formation of the human being (*haer.* 1.18.2) and other passages from Genesis, such as the construction of the ark (*haer.* 1.18.3–4). That they take various texts of the prophets to mean that their 'Propater' was unknown before the coming of Christ, Irenaeus says, is done with the intention of persuading others that 'the Lord announced another Father other than the Creator of the universe' (*haer.* 1.19.1–2). Besides these interpretations, Irenaeus reports that they used a number of apocryphal and spurious writings (*haer.* 1.19–20). Finally he reports the rite of redemption that they use, anointing their initiates' heads with a mixture of oil and water, even up to the moment of death (*haer.* 1.21). It has often been assumed that *haer.* 1.16–21 refers to the teaching and practices of Marcus' disciples, though Förster, followed by Thomassen, has argued convincingly that, apart from *haer.* 1.16.1–2, it should not: it makes no mention of Marcus whatsoever, lacks his characteristic numerology and alphabetical symbolism, and is instead much more concerned with the interpretation of scriptural texts.[14] One might add that, as the diversity among the followers of Valentinus given in *haer.* 1.11 onwards focused on their teaching regarding the pleroma, one should perhaps see *haer.* 1.17–21 as reporting 'their' general teaching on creation, anthropology, and salvation, structuring *haer.* 1.11–21 in a similar threefold manner to *haer.* 1.1–9.

A further word needs to be said about the genealogy beginning in *haer.* 1.11 and the report of the teaching given in *haer.* 1.1–9. Strikingly, none of these accounts of the teachings of Valentinus and his followers, not even that of Ptolemaeus, corresponds with the report given in the first nine chapters of book one. Thomassen argues persuasively that the account of the various Valentinian systems in *haer.* 1.11–12 has been adapted 'from

[14] Förster, *Marcus Magus*, 7–15; Thomassen, *Spiritual Seed*, 12, n. 10.

one or more heresiological or doxographic sources', most likely Justin's *Syntagma* but perhaps others as well.[15] That only three names are mentioned here—Valentinus, Secundus, and Ptolemaeus—reflects the fact, as seen clearly with the Nag Hammadi Library, that most 'Gnostic' writings were transmitted anonymously. If Irenaeus did indeed use an earlier heresiological account, then it was probably Irenaeus himself who included the report about Marcus to this, as one whose disciples were causing him particular difficulties, before going on to give general reports about 'their' teaching on creation and salvation. It appears, as we will shortly see, that in *haer.* 1.22–31 Irenaeus does the same, giving a canon of truth followed by an earlier genealogy into which he has included other figures.

The most we can thus conclude regarding the writings used by Irenaeus in *haer.* 1.1–9, as Thomassen observes, is that they circulated among a group of Valentinians in the region around the Rhône who regarded themselves as followers of Ptolemaeus, but that the authorship of these documents and what this group thought of them is unknown.[16] The report about the followers of Ptolemaeus in *haer.* 1.12, on the other hand, comes from an earlier source, with no further evidence to locate this group or establish a connection with the Ptolemaeans of *haer.* 1.1–9. Likewise with regard to 'Valentinus' in *haer.* 1.11.1: the teaching as reported there reflects that of the 'Valentinians' as they were known to the author of the source used by Irenaeus.[17] In all, it is clear that Irenaeus' primary opponents are the followers of Ptolemaeus in his own region; Ptolemaeus is mentioned in the prologue, whereas Marcus is not. Irenaeus identifies Ptolemaeus' teaching with written sources coming from his followers, and it is these that he recounts in great detail in *haer.* 1.1–9. Besides tackling this teaching on its own terms, he also knows, from an earlier heresiological account, of the diversity of teachings among the followers of Valentinus and so adapts this account to heighten the contrast between the Valentinians and the 'Great Church'. That he does not smooth out the conflicting accounts of the followers of Ptolemaeus might simply be an oversight, or perhaps an indication that he recognized that they pertain to two different groups, or alternatively that he did not attribute the writings he acquired as being from Ptolemaeus himself, but as an example of things 'they say'. The importance of the account in *haer.* 1.1–9 is not because, as

---

[15] Thomassen, *Spiritual Seed*, 19.
[16] Thomassen, *Spiritual Seed*, 21.
[17] Thomassen, *Spiritual Seed*, 26; cf. Markschies, *Valentinus Gnosticus?*, 364–79.

Thomassen argues, Irenaeus regards it as being the Valentinian equivalent of his 'canon of truth', as their common doctrine with respect to which they are always in disagreement; the account of their variations given in *haer.* 1.11–12 is not presented with respect to their differences from the supposed 'common doctrine' given in *haer.* 1.1–9.[18] It is, rather, their bewildering diversity described in *haer.* 1.11 onwards, compared with the common canon held by the Church stated in *haer.* 1.10, that perplexes Irenaeus. The account in *haer.* 1.11 onwards reflects the fact, as Thomassen puts it, that 'there never, in fact, existed a single, canonical version of the Valentinian system'.[19] The importance of the report in *haer.* 1.1–9 is thus due to the fact that it is based upon actual documents circulating among his opponents in his own region and hence can be recounted much more fully and accurately than any other account he provides.

Having treated the disciples of Valentinus, Irenaeus devotes the remaining ten chapters of book one to elaborating a geneaology of the heretics, specifically called such. He begins, again, with a 'canon of truth' (*haer.* 1.22.1), though this time much shorter and focused on there being one God who created all things, without exception, by his Word, and then comments that, as it is a complex and multiform task to refute each heresy, although his plan is to reply to each one according to its particular character, he will first 'give an account of its source and root' (*haer.* 1.22.2). The archetypal and primary figure in this genealogy is Simon Magus (*haer.* 1.23); the figures listed subsequently are all later called 'Simonians'.[20] After Simon, Irenaeus lists Menander (*haer.* 1.23.5), Saturninus (*haer.* 1.24.1–2), Basilides (*haer.* 1.24.3–7), Carpocrates (*haer.* 1.25), including Marcellina in Rome (*haer.* 1.25.6), Cerinthus (*haer.* 1.26.1), the Ebionites (*haer.* 1.26.2) and the Nicolaitanes (*haer.* 1.26.3), Cerdo (*haer.* 1.27.1) and Marcion (*haer.*

---

[18] Cf. Thomassen, *Spiritual Seed*, 13–17. Thomassen bases his argument on: the words at the beginning of *haer.* 1.8.1, 'this then is their hypothesis', though the scope of 'their' is limited to the followers of Ptolemaeus from whom Irenaeus acquired the work; the first sentence of *haer.* 2.Pref.1, referring to 'all the falsehood' devised by the followers of Valentinus, taking this as referring to *haer.* 1.1–9; and 4.Pref.2, where Irenaeus refers to the Valentinians' 'regula' (which Rousseau renders as ὑπόθεσις), 'which I have with all care delivered to you in the first book', taking this also as referring to *haer.* 1.1–9. Although the latter two statements are more general than the first, and the third written several years later, it remains the case that Irenaeus does not use *haer.* 1.1–9 elsewhere in book one as a 'standard' or 'common doctrine' by which variations are measured.

[19] Thomassen, *Spiritual Seed*, 21.

[20] It is possible that Simon's role as heresiarch results from a conflation between Simon and Paul in certain Jewish–Christian circles, as seen in the Pseudo-Clementine writings. Cf. Simone Pétrement, *A Separate God: The Origins and Teachings of Gnosticism*, trans. C. Harrison (San Francisco: Harper, 1990), 233–46.

1.27.2–4), and Tatian (*haer.* 1.28.1). Given what we saw of Polycarp in the previous chapter, it is likely that this genealogy goes back to Polycarp, identifying the heretics by their understanding of creation as having occurred by angels (Carpocrates), by a certain power (Cerinthus) or another god (Marcion), with Irenaeus adding other figures by association (such as the Ebionites, for their similar views on Christ to those of Cerinthus) or as more recent figures in Rome (such as Marcellina and Tatian). The most striking aspect of this genealogy, however, is that Valentinus, Ptolemaeus, and Marcus are glaringly absent. It could be because, as we have seen in Chapter 1, the disciples of Valentinus had not yet broken with the 'Great Church' in Rome, as had, for instance, Cerdo and Marcion. They were distancing themselves, physically and theologically, but were still seeking to reach out to the 'psychic' Christians. Although exposing and refuting their errors, Irenaeus in turn also seeks 'to endeavour with all our might to stretch out the hand to them' (*haer.* 3.25.7). In writing the later books, Irenaeus certainly does describe the teaching of the Valentinians as 'heretical', 'a recapitulation of all the heretics' (*haer.* 4. Pref.2), but we should not forget the lengthy span of time over which the books of *Against the Heresies* were written and the complex, and shifting, situation on the ground that we have examined in the previous chapter.

The only, rather oblique, point of contact in book one between the genealogy of the heretics in *haer.* 1.22–31 and the disciples of Valentinus occurs at *haer.* 1.29.1, when Irenaeus says: 'Besides these, however, from those who were said before to be Simonians a multitude of Gnostics have sprung up and shot out of the ground like mushrooms' (*haer.* 1.29.1). The remaining chapters of book one (*haer.* 1.29–31) recount very particular and peculiar teachings, involving figures such as Barbelos and Ialdabaoth. Since their very distinctive teachings, as reported by Irenaeus, are paralleled by works such as *The Secret Revelation of John*, they can perhaps be identified as an actual group, with particular teachings and practices, who identified themselves as 'The Gnostics'.[21] It is from these, Irenaeus claims, that Valentinus had 'adapted the principles of the heresy called "Gnostic" to the particular character of his own school' (*haer.* 1.11.1) so that 'a many headed beast, like the Lernaean hydra, has been generated

---

[21] On Irenaeus' use of the term 'gnostic', see Mark J. Edwards, 'Gnostics and Valentinians in the Church Fathers' *JTS* NS 40/1 (1989), 26–47; Michael Allen Williams, *Rethinking 'Gnosticism'*, 33–7. For a stalwart attempt to identify the self-understanding and practices of 'the Gnostics', and the legitimacy of doing so, see Brakke, *The Gnostics*. And, for a sensitive exposition of *The Secret Revelation of John*, see the work by Karen L. King with that title (Cambridge, MA: Harvard University Press, 2006).

from the school of Valentinus' (*haer.* 1.30.15). Although these 'Gnostics' are said to be the ultimate source for the 'falsely so-called knowledge' propounded by Valentinus and his disciples, it is only at the end of his 'exposure' that Irenaeus reveals the 'source' of the teachings against which he is contending, his final act of uncovering, as it were, in a rhetorical denouement.

We can, thus, depict the structure of book one as follows:

Book One: Refutation/Exposure of the Valentinians
Preface
   I. The 'Ptolemaean' hypothesis (*haer.* 1.1–12)
      Pleroma (*haer.* 1.1–3)
      Creation (*haer.* 1.4–5)
      Human beings (*haer.* 1.6–7)
      Their use of Scripture (*haer.* 1.8–9)
  II. The Ecclesial Rule of Truth and the Genealogy of the Valentinians (*haer.* 1.10–21)
      The Rule of Truth (*haer.* 1.10)
      The teaching of Valentinus and his followers on the Pleroma (*haer.* 1.11–16)
      Their teaching on the creation (*haer.* 1.17–19)
      Their use of Scripture (*haer.* 1.20)
      Their redemptive practices (*haer.* 1. 21)
 III. The Ecclesial Rule of Truth and the Genealogy of the Heretics (*haer.* 1.22–28)
      The Rule of Truth (*haer.* 1.22)
      The succession of the heretics (*haer.* 1.23–28)
      The 'Gnostics' (*haer.* 1.29–31.2)
Conclusion (*haer.* 1.31.3–4)

Book two

Book two of *Against the Heresies*, as we have seen, presents an 'overthrowal' of the teachings recounted in book one. It begins with a lengthy examination of the various logical problems arising from not accepting one God, but a plurality of divine beings, and issues relating to their apparently spatial understanding of the 'pleroma'—for instance, that the world was created 'outside' of it or that the true God exists 'beyond' it. In *haer.* 2.11.1, Irenaeus provides a short statement of the true faith—the one

God who by his Word created all that is—and then indicates that there are further tasks to accomplish in response to the attacks that his opponents delight in bringing: 'first of all to put to them the following enquiries concerning their own doctrines, to exhibit their improbability, and to put an end to their audacity. After this has been done, to bring forward the discourses of the Lord' (*haer.* 2.11.2). There then begins a series of questions that Irenaeus brings to his opponents' teachings regarding the Aeons in the pleroma. The reference to 'the discourses of the Lord' that he must treat does not refer ahead to later books of the work, as might be supposed, but to a section beginning in *haer.* 2.20, where Irenaeus tackles the way in which his opponents have taken 'the parables and actions of the Lord' and applied them 'to their falsely-devised system' (*haer.* 2.20.1). In working through their interpretations, Irenaeus devotes a section (*haer.* 2.25–28), just as he had done in book one with 'the rule of truth', to what he describes as 'the very method of discovery' (*haer.* 2.27.2). In *haer.* 2.29, Irenaeus 'returns to the remaining points of their system', specifically points connected with anthropology—that is, their teaching that when their mother shall finally re-enter the pleroma and receive the Saviour as her consort, 'they themselves, as being spiritual', will have been released from the animal souls and become 'intellectual spirits' (*haer.* 2.29.1). Irenaeus brings his argument to a conclusion in *haer.* 2.30.9, claiming that 'justly therefore do we convict them of having departed far and wide from the truth', and, after summarizing some of his key points against various teachers and their errors, he concludes with an extended scriptural, and almost rhapsodical, sentence:

But there is one only God, the Creator—he who is above every principality, and power, and dominion, and virtue: he is Father, he is God, he the Founder, he the Maker, he the Creator, who made those things by himself, that is, through his Word and his Wisdom—heaven and earth, and the seas, and all things that are in them: he is just; he is good; he it is who formed the human being, who planted paradise, who made the world, who gave rise to the flood, who saved Noah; he is the God of Abraham, and the God of Isaac, and the God of Jacob, the God of the living: he it is whom the law proclaims, whom the prophets preach, whom Christ reveals, whom the apostles make known to us, and in whom the Church believes: he is the Father of our Lord Jesus Christ: through his Word, who is his Son, through him he is revealed and manifested to all to whom he is revealed; for [only] those know him to whom the Son has revealed him; but the Son, eternally co-existing with the Father, from of old, yea, from the beginning, always reveals the

Father to angels, archangels, powers, virtues, and all to whom he wills that God should be revealed. (*haer.* 2.30.9)

It would be very tempting to see this as the original conclusion to the work, before he realized that he needed to demonstrate this faith clearly. However, the text as we have it continues by recapitulating his argument: *haer.* 2.31.1 begins by asserting that 'those, then, who are of the school of Valentinus being overthrown, the whole multitude of heretics are, in fact, also subverted', and continues by summarizing the various arguments he has advanced in book two, and then by describing how Simon and Carpocrates are overthrown, with their particular teachings regarding the separation of the body and soul and the teaching of the transmigration of the soul (*haer.* 2.31.2–34.4), Basilides (*haer.* 2.35.1), and 'the remainder of those who are falsely-called Gnostics' (*haer.* 2.35.2), where he again deals with exotic names created from the Hebrew tongue (*haer.* 2.35.3), before finally concluding with a paragraph relating to his further tasks, discussed above.

We can schematize the structure of book two, then, in this way:

Book Two: Overthrowal
Preface
  I. One God (*haer.* 2.1–19)
    A. The logical necessity for this (*haer.* 2.1–10)
    B. The truth that there is one God the Creator of all by his Word (*haer.* 2.11)
    C. Questions to those who teach otherwise (*haer.* 2.11–19)
  II. Christ (*haer.* 2.20–28)
    A. The supposed analogies with his parables and actions (*haer.* 2.20–24)
    B. The proper mode of enquiry (*haer.* 2.25–28)
  III. Anthropology (*haer.* 2.29–30.8)
Conclusion (*haer.* 2.30.9)
Recapitulation and refutation of other heresies (*haer.* 2.31.1–35.3)
Notice of further work (*haer.* 2.35.4)

This threefold structure—God, Christ, and the human being—the last topic being eschatologically oriented, also patterns, as we have seen, the account of the teaching of the followers of Ptolemaeus (*haer.* 1.1–9) and the followers of Valentinus more generally (*haer.* 1.11–21), which we will see repeated, in various ways, in the books that follow.

Book three

In book three, Irenaeus turns to the task of presenting 'demonstrations from Scripture' (*haer.* 3.Pref.).[22] In the preface to book four, he describes book three as having presented 'the mind of the apostles' (*haer.* 4.Pref.3). He proceeds by recounting the words of the apostles and evangelists regarding God and Christ, interspersing words from the Scriptures with those from the apostles and evangelists: the 'demonstration from Scripture' that he has in mind is the apostolic preaching drawn from the Scriptures, as exemplified concisely in his *Demonstration of the Apostolic Preaching*. As such, this book begins with a discussion of the apostolic preaching from the Gospel, and an account of the origins of the four Gospels (perhaps drawing from some kind of report on the origins of the fourfold Gospel composed in Rome earlier in the second century[23]), and the relationship of this preaching to the tradition and the succession of teaching in the Church, manifest especially in Rome, using the episcopal list culminating in Eleutherus discussed in the previous chapter, but also in Smyrna and Ephesus in Asia. Irenaeus concludes this section by stating: 'Since, therefore, the tradition from the apostles does thus exist in the Church, and is permanent among us, let us revert to the scriptural demonstration given by those apostles who did also write the Gospel, in which they recorded the doctrine regarding God, pointing out that our Lord Jesus Christ is the truth, and that no lie is in him (*haer.* 3.5.1). The 'scriptural demonstration' is specifically that provided by the apostles in the proclamation of the Gospel, which has been preserved in the Church.

The first main part (*haer.* 3.6–15) of this scriptural demonstration focuses on the one God, the Creator of all, and deals specifically with the use of the terms 'God' and 'Lord', showing that

neither would the Lord, nor the Holy Spirit, nor the apostles, have ever named as 'God', definitely and absolutely, him who was not God, unless he were truly God; nor would they have named any one in his own person Lord, except God the

---

[22] On the particularly Johannine character of book three, see Bernhard Mutschler, *Irenäus als johanneischer Theologe: Studien zur Schriftauslegung bei Irenäus von Lyon*, Studien und Texte zu Antike und Christentum, 21 (Tübingen: Mohr Siebeck, 2004), *Das Corpus Johanneum bei Irenäus von Lyon: Studien und Kommentar zum dritten Buch von* Adversus Haereses, WUNT 189 (Tübingen: Mohr Siebeck, 2006), and 'John and his Gospel in the Mirror of Irenaeus of Lyons: Perspectives of Recent Research', in Tuomas Raismus (ed.), *The Legacy of John: Second-Century Reception of the Fourth Gospel*, Supplements to Novum Testamentum, 132 (Leiden: Brill, 2010), 319–43.

[23] Cf. Claus-Jürgen Thornton, *Der Zeuge des Zeugen: Lukas als Historiker der Paulusreisen*, WUNT 56 (Tübingen: Mohr Siebeck, 1991), 40–5.

Father ruling over all, and his Son who has received dominion from his Father over all creation, as this passage has it, 'The Lord said to my Lord...' (*haer.* 3.6.1, Ps. 110:1)

Irenaeus follows this with passages from the Prophets, Paul, and Christ (*haer.* 3.6–8).[24] He concludes this exposition by commenting that 'this therefore having been clearly demonstrated here...that neither the prophets, nor the apostles, nor the Lord Christ in his own person, did acknowledge any other "Lord" or "God", but the God and Lord supreme, the prophets and the apostles confessing the Father and the Son, but naming no other as "God", and confessing no other as "Lord", and the Lord himself handing down to his disciples, that he, the Father, is the only God and Lord, who alone is God and ruler of all' (*haer.* 3.9.1). If we are indeed their disciples, he continues, we should follow their testimonies regarding this and so he turns to the evangelists, treating passages using the word 'God' from the Gospels of Matthew, Luke, Mark, and John (*haer.* 3.9–11).[25] Irenaeus appends to this treatment of the evangelists a short discussion on 'the four-formed Gospel' (*haer.* 3.11.7–9), and then turns to 'the remaining apostles and enquires into their teaching with regard to God; then in due course we shall listen to the very words of the Lord' (*haer.* 3.11.9). The second part of this intention is not undertaken until book four, and by 'the remaining apostles' he primarily means the apostles as they appear and speak in the Acts, treating Peter, Philip, Paul (again, for it is Paul as he appears in the Acts), and Stephen (*haer.* 3.12). Finally, he concludes this first part of the work on 'the one God' by treating the arguments of those who only accept Paul or reject him altogether and the inseparability of Paul and Luke (*haer.* 3.13–15).

The second main part of book three is devoted to the unity of the one Jesus Christ (*haer.* 3.16–21.9).[26] He begins by noting that there are some who treat 'Jesus' as a 'receptacle of Christ' who descended from above

---

[24] In *haer.* 3.8.1–2 Irenaeus includes two sayings from Christ using the word 'God' (Matt. 22:21, 6:24), and one (Matt. 12:29) where a word is used relatively of the devil and us (and the Lord, via Jer. 38:11). Given what he says in *haer.* 3.9.1, cited in the following sentence, these sayings of Christ form for Irenaeus a witness independent from the Gospels that he quotes in the chapters that follow.

[25] It is unclear why Luke and Mark appear here in reversed order to the account of their appearance given earlier (*haer.* 3.1.1) and later (*haer.* 3.16).

[26] Rousseau would identify *haer.* 3.16–23 as being the second of two main parts of book three, entitling it 'The one Christ, Son of God become the Son of man, to recapitulate in himself his own creation', dividing it into the following sections: 1: The Son of God truly became man (*haer.* 3.16–18); 2: Jesus is not a 'mere man' but the Son of God incarnate in the womb of the Virgin (*haer.* 3.19–21.9); 3: The Recapitulation of Adam (*haer.* 3.21.9–23).

upon him, or say that he only suffered in appearance, or, as the Valentinians, that the 'Saviour' descended upon 'the Jesus of the economy'. Given such teachings, he intends to 'take into account the entire mind of the apostles regarding our Lord Jesus Christ' (*haer.* 3.16.1). He begins with a very brief comment on John, reminding the reader that he has already 'sufficiently proved' 'that John knew one and the same Word of God, and that he was the Only-begotten and that he became incarnate for our salvation', referring back to his treatment of the Prologue of John in book one.[27] He then examines passages from Matthew relating to the birth of Christ the Saviour, with a confirmation from Paul's letters to the Romans and Galatians that the prophets did indeed promise that the Son, the one Jesus Christ, would be of the seed of David, appointed Son of God by the resurrection from the dead.[28] This is followed by texts from Mark and Luke (though without mentioning the latter's name), showing again that 'the Gospel therefore knew of no other son of Man but him who was born of Mary, who also suffered, and no Christ who flew away from Jesus before the Passion, but him who was born it knew as Jesus Christ the Son of God and that his same suffered and rose again' (*haer.* 3.16.3–5). This affirmation of the Gospels is rounded off by a further mention of John, this time quoting from the Gospel, which was written 'that you might believe that Jesus is the Christ, the Son of God and that believing you might have eternal life in his name', and the Epistle with its warning about the Antichrist who 'denies that Jesus is the Christ'.[29]

That there is but one Lord Jesus Christ, the Saviour, as established by these scriptural testimonies, rather than the variety of figures according to their 'varying hypothesis', is then the subject of an extended theological reflection (*haer.* 3.16.6–18.7). 'There is, therefore,' Irenaeus demonstrates, 'one God the Father and One Christ Jesus, who is coming throughout the whole economy, recapitulating all things in himself... so that he might draw all things to himself at the proper time' (*haer.* 3.16.6). It was not a 'Saviour' or 'Christ' who descended upon Jesus, but the Holy Spirit who descended upon the one Jesus Christ at his baptism, so that, becoming accustomed in this way to dwell in the human race, the Spirit might then dwell in human beings, 'renewing them from their old habits into the newness of Christ' (*haer.* 3.17.1). It is the identity of Christ as the suffering one that is of primary importance for Irenaeus, and to which he brings

---

[27] *haer.* 3.16.2, cf. 1.8.5–9.3.
[28] *haer.* 3.16.2–3, citing Rom. 1:1–4, 9:5; Gal 4:4–5.
[29] *haer.* 3.16.5, citing John 20:31; 1 John 2:18–19, 21–2.

back his discussion showing how it opens a way for others to enter into the life that Christ gives. Paul, Irenaeus says, made it clear that he 'knew of no other Christ besides him alone, who both suffered, and was buried, and rose again, who also was born, and whom he speaks of as human' (*haer.* 3.18.3). And likewise: 'The Lord himself, too, makes it evident who it was that suffered', by asking 'who do men say that I am?' (*haer.* 3.18.4, Matt. 16:13). In response to Peter's confession, 'You are the Christ, the Son of the Living God' (Matt. 16:16), Christ 'made it clear that he, the Son of man, is Christ the Son of the Living God', by thereafter speaking of how he must go to Jerusalem, suffer, be crucified, and rise again. This suffering is, moreover, that which will come upon all those who follow Christ, as they take up the same Cross, not another, and is seen most particularly in those who 'follow the footprints of the Lord's Passion, having become martyrs of the Suffering One' (*haer.* 3.18.4–5). He concludes this series of reflections with the point that, if Christ was to destroy sin and death, then he needed to be made that very same thing as the one he would save: 'What he did appear, that he also was: God recapitulated in himself the ancient formation of man, that he might kill sin, deprive death of its power, and vivify the human being: and therefore his works are true' (*haer.* 3.18.7). The 'vivification' that Christ provides is the life given to those who suffer with Christ, identifying themselves with him.

The final section of part two turns to those who say that Christ 'was simply a mere man' (*haer.* 3.19.1). As he has shown 'from the Scriptures that none of the sons of Adam is, in all respects and absolutely, called "God" or named "Lord"' apart from Christ himself, it is of him that Scripture asks, 'Who shall declare his generation?', for he 'was not born either by the will of the flesh or by the will of man'.[30] It is for this reason that the Lord 'gave us a sign, in the depth below and in the height above', that the one born from the Virgin should be 'God with us'.[31] The 'sign in the depth below' is that of Jonah, whom God arranged to be swallowed up to learn obedience to his Creator, indicating how God 'allowed' the human race to be swallowed up from the beginning, so that, 'acquiring a knowledge of death' and then receiving an unhoped for, but divinely foreseen, salvation in the person of Christ, they might be willing ever more to receive the life that comes from God alone. Jonah is thus the 'sign' both of the perishing human race and of the divine Saviour, who by his death conquers death (*haer.* 3.20.1–2). The second 'sign of our salvation' is

---

[30] *haer.* 3.19.2, citing Isa. 53:8, John 1:13.
[31] *haer.* 3.19.3, cf. Isa. 7:11, 14; Matt. 1:23.

the Lord himself, 'Emmanuel from the Virgin', since it is 'the Lord himself who saved them' (*haer.* 3.20.3). After dealing with Theodotion's translation of the text of Isaiah (as 'a young woman shall conceive'), and the Ebionites who follow this reading, rather than the translation of the seventy as used by the apostles and evangelists (*haer.* 3.21.1–3), Irenaeus brings in further texts relating to the virgin birth and the 'sign' given by God in the house of David, showing 'that, according to the promise of God, from David's belly the King eternal is raised up, who recapitulates all things in himself (*haer.* 3.21.9).

Recapitulated in Christ is specifically 'the ancient formation' of the human being, and it is this subject that Irenaeus treats in the third main part of book three.[32] Christ's virgin birth parallels, for Irenaeus, the original formation of Adam, from virgin earth by the Hand of the God, but taking the earth from the Virgin, instead of taking new earth from the ground, so that there might not be another formation called into being, but rather that the very same formation should be recapitulated, giving it another head and preserving the analogy (*haer.* 3.21.10). For a similar reason, Irenaeus argues, Luke traces back the genealogy of Christ to Adam, so 'connecting the end to the beginning' and summing up all descendants of Adam (*haer.* 3.22.3). Taking this retrospective perspective further, Irenaeus sets Paul's contrast between the first Adam, who became an 'animated being' (cf. Gen. 2:7: εἰς ψυχὴν ζῶσαν), and Christ, who through his Passion became the new Adam and the 'life-giving spirit' (1 Cor. 15:45: εἰς πνεῦμα ζῳοποιοῦν), within the scope of one economy, to explain how Adam is a 'type of the one to come' (Rom. 5:14): 'the Word, the Maker of all things, prefigured in him the economy that was to come of the humanity of the Son of God, God having predestined that the first human being should be animated, namely, so that he should be saved by the spiritual'. And then concludes: 'For, since he who saves already existed, it was necessary that he who would be saved should come into existence, that the One who saves should not exist in vain' (*haer.* 3.22.3).[33] Human existence is seen as being oriented from the beginning to Christ, the one who has shown himself to be the crucified Saviour, granting life through the Spirit to all those who follow him in his Passion. Irenaeus also

---

[32] *haer.* 3.21.9–23, taking the last words of 3.21.9 (*Et antiquam plasmationem in se recapitulatus est*) with *haer.* 3.21.10, as does Rousseau, though he identifies the overarching structure differently (see Ch. 2, n. 26).

[33] On this difficult text, see the discussion in Chapter 3 and the material cited in Ch. 3, n. 32.

places in parallel Mary, the obedient virgin, and Eve, the disobedient virgin, arguing that by being obedient, Mary 'became the cause of salvation both to herself and the whole human race', the 'back-referencing from Mary to Eve' indicating that 'what had been joined together could not otherwise be put asunder than by the inversion of the process by which these bonds of union had arisen' (haer. 3.22.4). Beginning with Christ and working back to Adam (and similarly from Mary to Eve), as is done in Luke's genealogy, 'indicates that it was he who regenerated them into the gospel of life, and not they him' (haer. 3.22.4). For all these reasons, Irenaeus argues, with Christ coming to find the lost sheep, 'making a recapitulation of so comprehensive an economy', it was impossible that Adam should not be saved (haer. 3.23.1–2).

The remaining two chapters of book three return briefly to the theme with which the book began, having shown that

> the preaching of the Church is everywhere consistent, remains identical, and is witnessed by the prophets, the apostles, and all their disciples, as we have shown, by the beginning, the middle, and the end, and through the whole economy of God, and the sure fact of the salvation of the human being which is ours in faith. (haer. 3.24.1)

This preaching, preserved in the Church, as a precious deposit in an excellent vessel, is not merely static, but is constantly 'being rejuvenated' (*iuuenescens*), and causes the Church itself also to be rejuvenated, as the woman who appeared to Hermas, becoming ever younger.[34] The Church not only preaches this, but is, according to Irenaeus, the place where this is being worked out: it is the locus of the Spirit, who vivifies those in the Church as the breath did the first created man. Such reflection is continued by Irenaeus in terms of God's providence over the world (haer. 3.24.2–25.1), his goodness and justice and the folly of thinking of a God who is not both (haer. 3.25.2–7). Irenaeus concludes the book with a paragraph expressing his hope and prayer that those who have rejected this teaching may not remain in the pit they have dug for themselves, but be converted to the Church of God, and stating his intention to endeavour with all his might to stretch out his hand to them, promising to do so by turning to 'the words of the Lord' in the following book (haer. 3.25.7).

We can therefore outline the structure of book three thus:

---

[34] I owe this connection to Michael Soroka.

Book Three: The Apostolic Preaching
Preface
Scripture, Tradition, Church (*haer.* 3.1–5)
   I. One God (*haer.* 3.6–15)
      A Witness of the Prophets, the Apostle, and the Lord himself (*haer.* 3:6–8)
      B Witness of the Evangelists (*haer.* 3.9–11)
      C The other apostles (i.e. Acts) (*haer.* 3.12)
      D Supplementary comments on Paul (*haer.* 3.13–15)
  II. One Lord Jesus Christ, the Saviour (*haer.* 3.16–21.9)
      A The witness of the Evangelists (3.16.2–5)
      B The identity of Christ (*haer.* 3.16.6–18)
      C The 'signs' of Salvation (*haer.* 3.19–21.9)
 III. Recapitulation of Adam (*haer.* 3.21.10–23)
         The Church as the locus of life for the human being (*haer.* 3.24–25.6)
Conclusion (*haer.* 3.25.7)

Book three is thus structured in the same threefold pattern as book two, demonstrating that there is one God, one Christ revealed in what he has done in the one economy, and the new reality that this recapitulation has brought into effect, providing a new head for those who turn to Christ.

Book four

In the fourth book, the longest of the five, Irenaeus fulfils his promise (cf. *haer.* 3.25.7) to 'add weight by means of the words of the Lord, to what I have already advanced' (*haer.* 4.Pref.1). It is again divided into three parts, corresponding to what we have seen in books two and three. The first part thus treats of the one God, under various aspects, from the words of the Lord correlated to various passages from Scripture (*haer.* 4.1–19).[35] He begins by demonstrating that the Creator and author of the Law is the one

---

[35] Both Bacq (*De l'ancienne à la nouvelle alliance selon S. Irénée*) and Rousseau (SC 100) describe the contents of the first and second parts of book four in terms of the relationship between the Two Testaments: part one (*haer.* 4.1–19) as the unity of the Two Testaments shown from the clear words of Christ; and part two (*haer.* 4.20–35) as the Old Testament as a prophecy of the New. Irenaeus, however, does not (yet) work or speak in a framework structured by two bodies of literature, an Old and a New Testament; instead he intersperses words from the Law and the Prophets together with words from the apostles, evangelists, and Christ, under, as described here, the headings of the one God, the one Christ and his economy, and the one human race.

God, the Father of Christ, the God of Jerusalem and the temple, even if these have been destroyed, as will also happen to the fashion of the whole world in which human beings grow to maturity and bear the fruit of liberty (*haer.* 4.1–5.1). A second section is devoted to showing how the Father of our Lord is the very same as the God of the patriarchs, so that there is again one and the same God (*haer.* 4.5.2–8.1). That Christ himself observed the Law, Irenaeus argues in a third section, is shown by his healing of a woman on the Sabbath and plucking and eating ears of corn on the Sabbath (*haer.* 4.8.2–3). Taking his lead from Christ's words about the householder who brings forth from his treasure things old and new (Matt. 13:52), Irenaeus devotes a fourth section to showing that the Law and Gospel are not in opposition to each other, as if they were from different gods, but, as coming from one and the same God, relate to each other in terms of greater and lesser, figure and reality, the announcement of the arrival of the king and his actual arrival, differences that correspond to the continual and unending growth of the human being towards God, that which is being made and the One who makes (*haer.* 4.9–11). It is in this perspective that we can see the Gospel as the fulfilment of the Law (*haer.* 4.12–16) and the Eucharist as the completion of the figurative sacrifices (*haer.* 4.12–19.1a).[36] Irenaeus concludes this first part of book four with a few paragraphs emphasizing the transcendence of God (*haer.* 4.19.1b–3).

Irenaeus opens chapter 20 of book four by contrasting the transcendence and immanence of God: 'As regards his greatness, therefore, it is not possible to know God, for it is impossible that the Father can be measured; but as regards his love' we learn that he has 'established, and selected, and adorned, and contains all things', among which are both our world and ourselves, for we are the one of whom Scripture says 'God formed the human being, taking clay of the earth, and breathed into his face the breath of life' (Gen. 2:7), speaking to his Word and Wisdom, the Son and the Spirit, who were always present with him, by whom and in whom he has made all things (*haer.* 4.20.1). It is Christ himself to whom all things have been delivered by the Father (Matt. 11:27), who as the slain lamb is able to open the book of the Father (Rev. 3:7, 5:12), becoming 'the firstborn of the dead' (Col. 1:18), so that all might be able to behold their King and that the paternal light might rest upon the flesh of our

---

[36] Following Bacq (*De l'ancienne à la nouvelle alliance selon S. Irénée*, 147–8) in taking the first sentence of *haer.* 4.19.1 (l. 5 in the SC edition) as concluding the section, and the second sentence as beginning the conclusion to the first part.

Lord, coming from him to us, so that we too might be invested with the paternal light and attain immortality (*haer.* 4.20.2–3). He concludes this opening section by returning to the contrast of transcendence and immanence: there is one God who has created and arranged all things by his Word and Wisdom; this is the Creator who has granted this world to the human race, and 'who, as regards his greatness, is indeed unknown to all who have been made by him... but as regards his love, is always known through him by whose means he ordained all things'. And he continues by specifying who this one is and the scope of his economy:

> Now this is his Word, our Lord Jesus Christ, who in the last times was made a human being among humans, that he might join the end to the beginning, that is, the human being to God. Wherefore the prophets, receiving the prophetic gift from the same Word, announced his advent according to the flesh, by which the blending and communion of God and the human being took place according to the good pleasure of the Father, the Word of God foretelling from the beginning that God should be seen by humans, and hold converse with them upon earth, should confer with them, and should be present with his own creation, saving it, and becoming capable of being perceived by it, and freeing us from the hands of all that hate us, that is, from every spirit of wickedness; and causing us to serve him in holiness and righteousness all our days, in order that the human being, having embraced the Spirit of God, might pass into the glory of the Father. (*haer.* 4.20.4)

This opening section to part two thus provides the starting point for a Christological rereading of the Scriptures, again with specific reference to the words of the Lord, but this time demonstrating the immanence of God through Christ and the economy.

Irenaeus begins part two with a lengthy examination of the prophetic character of the Scriptures, for 'these things did the prophets set forth in a prophetical manner' (*haer.* 4.20.5), not only in word, but in their visions, John's as well as the prophets of old, and in the actions of the prophets, patriarchs, and in the prefigurative acts of Christ himself (*haer.* 4.20.5–22). In the next three chapters, Irenaeus uses Christ's words about the harvest (John 4:35–8) to describe how, through all this prefiguration, Christ was 'sown' in the Scriptures while the Church brings forward the harvest (*haer.* 4.23–25). Irenaeus then provides a summary statement, introduced and concluded with the words 'if anyone then reads Scripture' in this way, finding in them an account of Christ and themselves being transfigured so that others cannot behold the glory of their countenance (*haer.* 4.26). This is then followed by a long statement (*haer.* 4.26.2–33) regarding this ecclesial reading of Scripture, exemplified by the presbyters, and including lengthy reports of 'a certain presbyter', whom in the last chapter we saw should be identified as Polycarp, and concluding with how a 'spiritual disciple' is able on this basis to refute all heresies and expound 'the true knowledge [γνῶσις]' that is 'the teaching of the apostles and the ancient constitution of the Church throughout the world, the distinctive manifestation of the body of Christ according to the successions of the bishops' (*haer.* 4.33.8), while the Church, with the love that she bears towards God, sends forward a multitude of martyrs to the Father (*haer.* 4.33.9). Irenaeus concludes this second part by reiterating how Marcion (*haer.* 4.34) and Valentinus 'and the other Gnostics falsely so-called' (*haer.* 4.35) have misunderstood this prophetic reading of the Scriptures.

In the remaining six chapters of book four, Irenaeus draws from the words of Christ, especially his parables, to explore the situation of human beings in response to the work of Christ. He begins with the parables of the vineyard, the wedding feast, the two sons, and the publican and the Pharisee, to show how the call of the Lord through the apostles is the same as the call of the One who spoke by the prophets (*haer.* 4.36). Developing this theme of calling, Christ's saying 'how often would I have gathered your children together, but they would not' (Matt. 23:37) provides Irenaeus with an occasion to reflect on human liberty to choose or reject God, and how, even through apostasy and the experience of mortality, we grow towards perfection so as to share in the uncreated life of God, by offering that which we are able to offer—that is, faith in him and our 'mud' maintained as soft and pliable in his Hands (*haer.* 4.37–39). And then finally, in this sequence, Irenaeus uses the parables of the sheep and the goats, and the wheat and the tares, to speak of the final judgement facing all human beings (*haer.* 4.40–41.3). All these moments deal with the human response to the work of God and, as with the third part of the two preceding books, thus have an eschatological dimension. The final paragraph concludes the work briefly, and looks forward to the next book, where he will treat 'the teaching of Paul after the words of the Lord'; 'drawing up, in another book, the rest of the words of the Lord, which he taught concerning the Father not by parable but by expressions taken in their obvious meaning, and the exposition of the epistles of the blessed apostle', he will, he says, thus provide his friend 'with the complete work of the exposure and refutation of knowledge falsely so-called' (*haer.* 4.41.4).

We can thus depict the structure of book four as follows:

Book Four: 'The Words of the Lord'
Preface
  I. The one God, the transcendent Creator and Author of the Law and Gospel (*haer.* 4.1–19)
    The Father of the Lord, Creator and Author of the Law (*haer.* 4.1–5.1)
    The Father of the Lord, the God of the Patriarchs (*haer.* 4.5.2–8.1)
    That Christ observed the Law (*haer.* 4.8.2–3)
    The Law and the Gospel, Stages of Growth (*haer.* 4.9–11)
    The Gospel as Fulfilment of the Law (*haer.* 4.12–16)
    The Eucharist as the Completion of Figurative Sacrifices (*haer.* 4.17–19.1)
    Conclusion: The Transcendence of the One God (*haer.* 4.19.1–3)
  II. Christ and the economy (*haer.* 4.20–35)
    Christ, the key (*haer.* 4.20.1–4)
    The prophetic character of Scripture (*haer.* 4.20.5–8a (finishing at line 196))
    The visions of the prophets (*haer.* 4.20.8b–11)
    The prefigurative acts of the prophets, patriarchs, and Christ (*haer.* 4.20.12–22.2)
    The Word concerning Christ, sown in the Scripture, reaped in the Church (*haer.* 4.23–25)
    The reading of, and transfiguration by reading, Scripture (*haer.* 4.26.1)
    The ecclesial reading of Scripture of the presbyters and spiritual disciples (*haer.* 4.26.2–33)
    Conclusion (*haer.* 4.34–35)
  III. Calling and judgement, from the Parables of Christ (*haer.* 36–41)
    The call of God (*haer.* 4.36)
    Human liberty (*haer.* 4.37–39)
    Judgement (*haer.* 4.40–41.3)
  Conclusion (*haer.* 4.41.4)

Book five

Although Irenaeus in the concluding paragraph of book four promises to treat 'the rest of the words of the Lord...and the epistles of the blessed apostle Paul' (*haer.* 4.41.4) and says the same in the preface to book five, Irenaeus does not in fact continue where he had left off, but rather begins again with the subject of the one God, followed by the work of

Christ, and concludes with an eschatologically oriented treatment of anthropology.[37] The preface outlines what has been done in the first four books and the material to be treated in this book, and in this way, Irenaeus says, he will have fulfilled the request of his friend.

The first part of the work, as noted, treats the one God, but this time specifically in terms of his power, a power that is made manifest in weakness, that is, in the flesh, resulting in the formation of a human being (*haer.* 5.1–14).[38] Irenaeus begins with two chapters showing how empty is the teaching of the Docetists, the disciples of Valentinus, the Ebionites, and the Marcionites, 'who despise the entire economy of God, and disallow the salvation of the flesh, and treat with contempt its regeneration' (*haer.* 5.2.2). They do not understand, he claims, that as the breath of life animated the creature at the beginning so also at the end of the economy the Spirit vivifies that ancient substance of Adam's formation, rendering the human being 'living and perfect', so that, 'for this reason in the last times, not by the will of the flesh, nor by the will of man, but by the good pleasure of the Father, his Hands formed a living human being, in order that Adam might come to be according to the image and likeness of God'.[39] The whole economy, including our dissolution into the earth (which Irenaeus treats in eucharistic terms through a lengthy comparison with the way in which grain and grapes become the Body and Blood of Christ), has been arranged so that we might 'learn from experience' that we do not have life from ourselves and so be ever open to receiving it from God: 'for this purpose God bore [$\dot{\eta}\nu\acute{\epsilon}\sigma\chi\epsilon\tau o$] our dissolution into the dust, that we, being instructed in every way may in the future be precise in all things, being ignorant neither of God nor of ourselves' (*haer.* 5.2.3).

After this opening section, Irenaeus takes Christ's words to Paul, 'my strength is made perfect in weakness' (2 Cor. 12:9), as his guiding motif to treat, from various aspects, the power of God deployed in the weakness of the flesh, vivifying the flesh, so that it shares in the constructive wisdom

---

[37] For a lengthy and detailed line-by-line commentary on book five, see Antonio Orbe, *Teología de San Ireneo: Comentario al Libro V del 'Adversus haereses'*, 3 vols, BAC maior 25, 29, 33 (Madrid: BAC, 1985, 1987, 1988).

[38] Rousseau entitles this part 'The resurrection of the flesh proved by the epistles of Paul', correlating the resurrection of the flesh to the Incarnation. For another analysis, see Winfried Overbeck, *Menschwerdung: Eine Untersuchung zur literarischen und theologischen Einheit des fünften Buches 'Adversus Haereses' des Irenäus von Lyon*, Basler und Berner Studien zur historischen und systematischen Theologie, 61 (Bern: Peter Lang, 1995), who would designate this part as 'A theology of the flesh'.

[39] *haer.* 5.1.3; cf. John 1:13, Gen. 1:27.

and power of God (*haer.* 5.3–5). That 'God shall be glorified in his handiwork' is the reverse aspect of this creative work, and so Irenaeus devotes the following two chapters to considering how the body is the temple of the Spirit and members of Christ, and how perfection is reached not by a casting-away of the flesh but in the flesh, vivified by the Spirit, which is given even now as a pledge (*haer.* 5.6–8). The fourth and longest section of part one is an exegetical tour de force of 1 Corinthians 15 (5:9–14). Irenaeus argues that, although 'flesh and blood shall not inherit the kingdom' (1 Cor. 15:50), the power of God is such that flesh and blood will nevertheless '*be* inherited' by an engrafting into Christ by the Spirit. The flesh that we 'put off' is not the substance of our bodies, but rather the 'works of the flesh' (cf. Gal. 5:19), so that 'in the Spirit' we can put on incorruptibility, reconciled to God by the body of his flesh (cf. Col. 1:22) and glorify God in our body (1 Cor. 6:20). Irenaeus concludes this part by reminding his readers that, having been redeemed by the flesh of Christ and acquired by his blood, they should hold fast to the head of the body that is the Church, in whom it holds together and from whom it increases (*haer.* 5.14.4).

Irenaeus introduces the second part of book five with scriptural texts from Isaiah and Ezekiel referring to 'the second birth' consequent upon 'dissolution into the earth', promised by the one who created at the beginning.[40] The Lord who speaks in these scriptural texts—depicted as vivifying our dead bodies, promising resurrection, and conferring immortality—is shown to be the only God, the good Father, conferring life on those who do not have it in themselves. This continuous creative activity, encompassed within the one economy, is then exemplified through three aspects of Christ's work, each correlated to Genesis, demonstrating in this way Christ's role in creation. First, 'the Lord most clearly manifested himself and the Father to his disciples' by the way in which he healed the blind man, taking dust from the earth, mixing his own power with it, and completing that which was lacking from birth 'so that the work of God might be manifest', for 'the work of God is the fashioning of the human being' (*haer.* 5.15.2, John 9:3). Likewise, as God called out to Adam

---

[40] *haer.* 5.15.1, citing Isa. 26:19, 66:13–14; Ezek. 37:1–10, 12–14. Rousseau identifies part two of book five similarly. Overbeck, on the other hand, would divide the remainder of book five into three parts: part two, 'The Self-Revelation of God as the one Creator and Redeemer in the Recapitulation of all Things through the Son' (*haer.* 5.15.1–20.2); part three, 'The Battle with the Enemy as the Central Element in the Recapitulation Work of Christ' (*haer.* 5.21–30); and part four, 'The (Thousand Year) Reign of the Son and the Ultimate Consummation in the Kingdom of the Father'.

in the evening, so too Christ, the Word of God, came to call human beings at the end, being himself the very same voice, searching out his posterity and visiting them (*haer.* 5.15.4). In such ways, then, what was only *spoken* about at the beginning, and thereby easily lost, is now *seen*, Christ, at the end, showing the true image by himself becoming that image and thus re-establishing the likeness (*haer.* 5.16.2).

Christ's identity manifest in this way is also revealed through his Passion, to which Irenaeus devotes the next five chapters, correlating aspects of the Passion with the narrative of creation and with words from the prophets (*haer.* 16.3). For instance, as the Word came to ask after Adam when he sinned, so also he now comes to the human race with the same purpose, but reversing our situation and giving us a new starting point or head: 'he, the same against whom we had sinned in the beginning, grants forgiveness of sins in the end' (*haer.* 5.17.1). Likewise with the tree: by the tree we were made debtors to God but by the tree we have received remission of our debt (*haer.* 5.17.3). And from the prophets, Elisha's act of throwing wood into the water so that the axe rose to the surface is taken by Irenaeus, through the words of the Baptist (Matt. 3:10) and those of Jeremiah (Jer. 23:29), as making clear that, having lost the Word of God by means of a tree, it is by 'the economy of the tree' that we receive it again (*haer.* 5.17.4). As all creation is borne by the Father, so in turn it now bears the Word when he is hung upon the tree, recapitulating all in himself (*haer.* 5.18). And similarly the Church is the garden (*paradisus*) of God planted in this world, into which the Lord has introduced all those who respond to his call and in which we may eat from every Scripture of the Lord (*haer.* 5.20.2).

Recapitulating all things in himself, Christ, in his temptation, also recapitulates the temptation of Adam, and it is to this that Irenaeus devotes the next section of part two, paralleling the serpent's temptations in Genesis with those by which the devil tempted Christ in the desert, so demonstrating how Christ reversed the victory over and enmity against the human being by using, as human, the Father's commandments: acknowledging the one God, living by the food which comes from God, and not exalting himself (*haer.* 5.21–24). Being subject to the same temptations, but rebutting them by obedience to the Father, Christ sets free the human being and overcomes the strong man who had taken him captive. Recapitulating in himself the very days of creation, suffering in the day preceding the Sabbath, the sixth day on which the human being was created, Christ 'grants him a second creation by means of his Passion, which is that [creation] out of death' (*haer.* 5.23.2).

The third and final part of the last book of *Against the Heresies* is devoted to the final end (*haer.* 5.25–36.2): the coming of the Antichrist, his recapitulation of all error, evil, and apostasy, in an attempt to be worshipped as God in the Temple in Jerusalem. Dealing with the judgement of God, Irenaeus is at pains to emphasize that, in his advent, the Son comes alike to all, with the purpose of judging, granting life and communion with himself to all who orient themselves to God; but to those who, by their own choice, depart from God 'he inflicts that separation from himself which they have chosen of their own accord' (*haer.* 5.27.1–2). The number of the beast, 666, is taken as indicating the recapitulation 'of the whole apostasy which has taken place during six thousand years, for in as many days as this world was made, in so many thousand years shall it be concluded', for the narrative of Genesis 'is an account of things formerly created as it is also a prophecy of what is to come' (*haer.* 5.28.2–3). After dealing with the possible renderings in Greek and Latin of the name of the beast, Irenaeus turns, in the second section of part three (*haer.* 5.31.1–36.2), to a chiliastic interpretation of the resurrection, drawing upon the tradition of the elders who saw John as reported by Papias, describing a renovated creation of incredible bounty in which the righteous will be raised to reign with Christ. 'The fashion of this word will pass away' (1 Cor. 7:31), that is, not the substance or the essence of creation, but rather its temporal character, in which the human being has grown old (*haer.* 5.36.1). When this 'fashion' passes away, the human being shall be renewed, with a new heaven and a new earth, holding ever-new converse with God. Following the completion of the creation in six days, that is, six thousand years, this will be the rest of the seventh day, a seventh thousand-year period in which Christ shall reign in his kingdom, a renewed creation together with the sons of God in their glorious liberty.[41] This is the completion of the promise of the inheritance of land to the fathers, given by one who is thus shown to be the God and Father who fashioned human beings (*haer.* 5.32, 36.3). At the end of this period of the kingdom, the judged are raised and cast into 'the lake of fire, the second death', Gehenna or the eternal fire (*haer.* 5.35.2; Rev. 20.14). With death, the last enemy, thus destroyed, all is brought into subjection to Christ, who then in turn subjects himself to the One who put all things under him, so that God is all in all (1 Cor. 15:24–28), bestowing 'in a paternal

---

[41] A key passage from *haer.* 5.36.3 (after l. 55 in the SC edn) is omitted in the Latin version, and thus is not in the ANF translation; it is found only in the Armenian version (TU 35.2, 244.23–5.2).

manner things that no eye has seen nor ear heard nor the heart of man conceived' (*haer.* 5.36.3; 1 Cor. 2:9). Only one has seen the Father and made him known (cf. Matt. 11:27; Luke 10:22), and so Irenaeus concludes his work with a single sentence, quoted above, recapitulating the work of Christ is, to accomplish his Father's will, and to make the human being into the image and likeness of God.

We can thus outline the structure of book five as follows:

Book Five: 'The rest of the teachings of the Lord and the epistles of Paul'
Preface
   I. The power of God (*haer.* 5.1–14)
      The work of God, forming human beings through their death (*haer.* 5.1–2)
      The strength of God manifest in the weakness of the flesh (*haer.* 5.3–5)
      The glorification of God in his handiwork (*haer.* 5.6–8)
      'Flesh and blood shall not inherit the kingdom' (*haer.* 5.9–14)
   II. The work of Christ (*haer.* 5.15–24)
      Christ as Creator (*haer.* 5.15.1–16.2)
      The Passion (*haer.* 5.16.3–20)
      The temptation of Christ (*haer.* 5.21–24)
   III. The Final End (*haer.* 5.25–36.1)
      The Antichrist (*haer.* 5.25–30)
      The resurrection of the righteous (*haer.* 5.31–36.2)
Conclusion (*haer.* 5.36.3)

Although a voluminous work, each book of *Against the Heresies* is in fact thus tightly structured. Apart from book one, which is structured to expose his opponents, each book follows the same threefold pattern: One God, One Christ and the one economy, and the human being, as the creature fashioned by God but only becoming so in the last times, in the Church (in *haer.* 3), responding to the call/judgement of God (in *haer.* 4), and reigning with him (in *haer.* 5).

REFUTATION AND OVERTHROWAL (*haer.* 1–2)

Excellent work has been done over recent decades sympathetically reconstructing the theology of Valentinus and others. Compared with this, it might seem that Irenaeus has polemically distorted the teaching of his opponents. But we must nevertheless remember, however obvious the point is, that none of this scholarly work was available to him, nor, for that matter, did he have access to the full range of material rediscovered over the past century. From what we have seen, it is pretty certain that the only written texts he had to hand were those whose contents he reports in *haer.* 1.1–9, and probably also a text from which he recounts the teaching of Marcus, together with at least two earlier and distinct accounts of, first, the Valentinians and, second, the heretics. He mentions other writings, such as *The Gospel of Truth* and *The Gospel of Judas*, but does not appear to have had access to them. He says, and we have no reason not to take him at his word, that he has diligently perused the writings he had, and conversed with certain followers of Ptolemaeus. Even with all the material we now have to hand, especially from Nag Hammadi, and decades of scholarly work on them, it is still hard not to feel perplexed when reading these writings, and differences of interpretation of each text still abound. One can only imagine what verbal reports were given to Irenaeus by the Ptolemaeans he encountered and how they explained the texts they had and oral teachings they had heard. Irenaeus was certainly perplexed by what he read and heard, and, as we have seen, he regarded their 'exposure' as being their own 'refutation'. He was also pushed to exasperation, and occasionally let this show, with humour. At one point, for instance, he proposes his own version of such teaching:

> There is a certain royal First-Beginning, First-unthinkable, First-non-substantial Power, First-ever-forward-rolling. However, with this one there coexists a power, which I call Gourd; with this Gourd there coexists a Power, to which I give the name Utter-Emptiness. Now this Gourd and Utter-Emptiness, since they are one, brought forth a fruit, without bringing it forth—a fruit everywhere visible, edible, and delicious, which in our language we call Cucumber. With this Cucumber there coexists a consubstantial Power, to which I give the name Pumpkin. These Powers—Gourd, Utter-Emptiness, Cucumber, and Pumpkin—begot the rest of the multitude of delirious Pumpkins of Valentinus. (*haer.* 1.11.4)

Besides making fun of his opponents and dropping polemical jabs, Irenaeus does have serious points to make. In book two, as we have seen, he tackles his opponents on their own terms, to show into what inconsistencies and contradictions their teachings lead. In book one, on the other hand, after recounting 'their' teaching (*haer.* 1.1–8), and before narrating the genealogy of the Valentinians (*haer.* 1.10–21) and the heretics (*haer.* 1.22–31), Irenaeus devotes a chapter (*haer.* 1.9) to what, from his own perspective, he regards as being their fundamental error, and it is on this that we will now focus.

After having recounted the teaching he found in the documents given to him from the Ptolemaeans in *haer.* 1.1-7, Irenaeus continues with a striking visual image:

> Such is their hypothesis [ὑπόθεσις] which neither the prophets preached, nor the Lord taught, nor the apostles handed down [παρέδωκαν]. They boast rather loudly of knowing more about it than others do, citing it from non-scriptural [works] [ἐξ ἀγράφων];[42] and as people would say, they attempt to braid ropes of sand. They try to adapt to their own sayings in a manner worthy of credence, either the dominical parables [παραβολὰς κυριακὰς] or the prophets' sayings, or the apostles' words, so that their fabrication [πλάσμα] might not appear to be without witness. They disregard the order [τάξις] and the connection [εἱρμός] of the Scriptures and, as much as in them lies, they disjoint the members of the truth. They transfer passages and rearrange them, and, making one thing out of another, they deceive many by the badly composed fantasy of the dominical oracles [λογίων κυριακῶν] that they adapt. By way of illustration, suppose someone would take the beautiful image of a king, carefully made out of precious stones by a skilful artist, and would destroy the features of the man on it and change it around and rearrange the jewels, and make the form of a dog or of a fox out of them, and that rather a bad piece of work. Suppose he would then say with determination that this is the beautiful image of the king that the skilful artist had made, and at the same time pointing to the jewels which had been beautifully fitted together by the first artist into the image of the king, but which had been badly changed by the second into the form of a dog. And suppose he would through this fanciful arrangement of the jewels deceive the inexperienced who had no idea of what the king's picture looked like, and would persuade them that this base picture of a fox is that beautiful image of the king. In the same way these people patch together old women's fables, and then pluck words and sayings and parables from here and there and wish to adapt these oracles of God to their myths [μύθοις]. (*haer.* 1.8.1)

The terms that Irenaeus uses here—'hypothesis', 'fabrication', and 'myth'—are all technical terms in Hellenistic literary theory. 'Fabrication' (πλάσμα) and 'myth' (μῦθος) refer to stories that are, in the first case, not true but seem to be so, and in the latter case, manifestly untrue.[43] According to Irenaeus, his opponents have based their exegesis upon their own 'hypothesis' (ὑπόθεσις), rather than upon that foretold by the prophets, taught by Christ and delivered ('traditioned') by the apostles. In a literary context, the term 'hypothesis' referred to the plot or outline of

---

[42] This could also refer to unwritten, oral, traditions.
[43] Cf. Sextus Empiricus, *Math.* 1.252–68. For an excellent study, see R. Meijering, *Literary and Rhetorical Theories in Greek Scholia* (Groningen: Egbert Forsten, 1987), 72–90.

a drama or epic (what Aristotle, in the *Poetics*, had termed the μῦθος).[44] It is posited or presupposed by the poet as the basic outline for his subsequent creative work. It is not derived from reasoning, but rather provides the raw outline upon which the poet can exercise his talents. Irenaeus' point is clear: from his perspective, rather than taking the words of 'the dominical oracles' and seeing them as portraying Christ—as the prophets preached, the Lord himself taught, and the apostles handed down—they have instead adapted them to another hypothesis, that of events within the Fullness, fleshing out, as it were, their own hypothesis with scriptural words and so constructing their own fabrication. They have disregarded 'the order and the connection of the Scriptures', so distorting the picture and creating another. They have not accepted the coherence of the Scriptures, as speaking about Christ, but have preferred their own fabrication, created by adapting passages from Scripture to a different hypothesis, attempting to endow it with persuasive plausibility.

Irenaeus continues by describing how they do the same for what happened outside the Fullness, for instance, their claim that the 12-year-old daughter of the ruler of the synagogue (Luke 8:41–2) 'was a type of Achamoth, to whom their Christ, by extending himself, imparted shape and whom he led anew to the perception of that light which had forsaken her' (*haer.* 1.8.2), and similarly with the passages they interpret as pointing to three kinds of human beings, the material, the psychic, and the spiritual (*haer.* 1.8.3), and the wandering of Achamoth outside the Fullness, eventually receiving form from Christ and sought after by the Saviour (*haer.* 1.8.4). He then reproduces an extended passage interpreting the Prologue of John as an account of the origination of the various Aeons within the Fullness, which, though lengthy, deserves to be quoted in full:

John, the disciple of the Lord, wishing to narrate the origin of all things, according to which the Father emitted all things, proposes a certain Beginning, the first offspring by the Father, whom he called Son [John 1:34, 49; 3:18] and Only-begotten God [John 1:18], in whom the Father emitted all things seminally. By this one [the Beginning], he says, the Word was emitted and in him the whole substance of the Aeons, which the Word formed later. Since, then, he speaks of the first origin, he does well to start his teaching from the Beginning, that is, from the Son and the Word. He speaks thus: 'In the Beginning was the Word and the Word was with God and the Word was God. He was in the Beginning with God' [John 1:1–2]. First, he distinguishes these three: God, Beginning, and Word; then he unites them in order to show the emission of each one, namely of Son and of

---

[44] Cf. Sextus Empiricus, *Math.* 3.3–4; see also Meijering, *Literary and Rhetorical Theories*, 99–133, and Norris, 'Theology and Language'.

Word, and the union with one another and with the Father. For the Beginning is in the Father and from the Father; but Word is in the Beginning and from the Beginning. Therefore he said well: 'In the Beginning was the Word', for he was in the Son. 'And the Word was with God', for he was also the Beginning. And consequently: 'The Word was God', for whatever is born of God is God. 'He was in the Beginning with God' shows the order of the emission. 'All things were made through him, and without him was made not a thing' [John 1:3], for the Word was the cause of the formation and origin of all the Aeons that came after him. 'But what was made in him was Life' [John 1:3–4]. Here he indicated also the conjunction. 'For all things', he said, 'were made through him', but the Life, in him. She [Life], then, who was made in him is more closely related [to him] than the things that were made through him; for she is associated with him, and through him bears fruit. For when he continues: 'And the Life was the Light of Men' [John 1:4], though he now speaks of Men, he indicated also the Church by the like name, so that by the one name he might manifest the union of the conjunction. For Man and Church come to be from the Word and the Life. Besides, he called the Life 'Light of Men', because they were enlightened by her, that is, were formed and made manifest. Paul says the same thing: 'For anything that becomes visible is Light' [Eph. 5:13]. Since, therefore, the Life is manifested and gave birth to the Man and the Church, she is called their Light. By these words, then, John clearly manifested among other things the second Tetrad: Word and Life, Man and Church. But he also indicated the first Tetrad; for in discussing the Saviour and saying that all things outside the Fullness were formed by him, he said that he [the Saviour] is the fruit of the entire Fullness. For he said that he [Saviour] is the Light which shone in the darkness and was not comprehended by it [John 1:5], since in harmonizing [ἁρμόσας] all the products of the Passion, he remained ignorant of them. He also called him Son and Truth and Life and Word-become-flesh. He asserted: 'We have beheld his glory, glory as of the Only-begotten, full of Grace and Truth' [John 1:14], which was given to him by the Father. (But he says: 'And the Word became flesh and dwelt among us, and we beheld his glory, the glory of the Only-begotten of the Father, full of grace and truth').[45] Therefore he also accurately points out the first Tetrad, saying Father and Grace, Only-begotten and Truth. Thus John speaks of the first Ogdoad, which is the Mother of all the Aeons; for he mentions Father and Grace, Only-begotten and Truth, Word and Life, Man and Church. (*haer.* 1.8.5)

The Prologue of John is thus read as an account of the Aeons in the Fullness, with each noun personified and correlated by the various prepositions used. Quite why his opponents interpreted such texts in this manner, and what they thought they were doing in this, is unclear and has been the subject of many and various explanations. Some, such as Hans Jonas, have seen it as an expression of existential alienation in

---

[45] The words in parentheses are clearly Irenaeus' own indignant insertion.

creation, perceived as a vast prison in a dualistic system, from which only the spiritual part of the human being is saved through the work of various mediators.[46] Others have seen such mythological systems as an attempt to account for the transcendence of the divine, the origin of the world, and the reality of salvation, engaged in a dialogue about such matters that can be seen already in Plato's *Timaeus*, Philo, and Middle Platonism.[47] Others, following Irenaeus' comment that the Valentinians have projected their own inner states onto the heavens (*haer.* 2.13.3), have considered their mythology as a 'psychodrama'.[48] While yet others have taken such systems as an attempt to elaborate carefully the reality of the salvation enacted in history reflected in terms of protological myth.[49]

None of these brief comments does justice to the sophistication with which such explanations are elaborated. But whatever it was that his opponents thought that they were doing, Irenaeus makes a fundamentally simple point against them. The passage quoted above exemplifies, according to Irenaeus, 'the method' by which 'they abuse the Scripture by endeavouring to support their own fabrication [πλάσμα] out of them' (*haer.* 1.9.1). Regarding this, Irenaeus makes two concrete observations:

> In the first place, if John had intended to set forth that Ogdoad above, he would surely have preserved the order of its production, and would doubtless have placed the primary Tetrad first as being, according to them, most venerable and would then have annexed the second, that, by the order of the names, the order of the Ogdoad might be exhibited, and not after so long an interval, as if forgetful for the moment and then again calling the matter to mind, he, last of all, made mention of the primary Tetrad.
>
> In the next place, if he had meant to indicate their conjunctions, he certainly would not have omitted the [name of] Church; but, with respect to the other conjunctions, he either would have been satisfied with the mention of the male [Aeons], since they [the female] would be understood, so that the unity among all might be preserved, or if he enumerated the companions of the rest, he would also have announced the companion of Man and not have left us to divine her name. (*haer.* 1.9.1)

Whatever else one may think about their manner of reading the Prologue, Irenaeus' point is that it simply does not fit with the text, for it respects

---

[46] Hans Jonas, *The Gnostic Religion: The Message of the Alien God and the Beginnings of Christianity*, 2nd rev. edn (London: Routledge, 1992 [1958]); cf. Michael Waldstein, 'Hans Jonas' Construct "Gnosticism": Analysis and Critique', *JECS* 8/3 (2000), 340–72.

[47] Cf. Brakke, *The Gnostics*, 52–89.

[48] David Dawson, *Allegorical Readers and Cultural Revision in Ancient Alexandria* (Berkeley and Los Angeles: University of California Press, 1992), 127–82, at 171.

[49] See esp. Thomassen, *Spiritual Seed*.

neither the order of the words nor the actual words used. The Prologue, in other words, can be read as an account of the origination of the Aeons in the Fullness only by distorting the coherence of the text.

In contrast to this interpretation, Irenaeus offers his own reading of the Prologue:

Manifest, then, is the false fabrication [παραποίησις] of their exegesis. For while John, proclaiming one God, the Almighty, and one Jesus Christ, the Only-begotten, 'by whom all things were made' [John 1:3], declares that this is 'the Word of God' [John 1:1], this 'the Only-begotten' [John 1:18], this the Maker of all things, this 'the true Light who enlightens every man' [John 1:9], this 'the Maker of the world' [John 1:10], this the one who 'came to his own' [John 1:11], this the one who 'became flesh and dwelt among us' [John 1:14], they, speciously distorting the exegesis [παρατρέποντες κατὰ τὸ πιθανὸν τὴν ἐξήγησιν], hold that the Only-begotten, by emission, is another, whom they call the Beginning, and they hold that another became the Saviour, and another the Logos, the son of the Only-begotten, and another the Christ, emitted for the re-establishment of the Fullness. Wresting each of the things said from the truth, misusing the names, they transfer them to their own hypothesis, so that, according to them, in all these passages John makes no mention of the Lord Jesus Christ. For if he has named the Father, and Grace, and Only-Begotten, and Truth, and Logos, and Life, and Man, and Church, according to their hypothesis, he has, by thus speaking, referred to the primary Ogdoad, in which there was as yet no Jesus, and no Christ, John's teacher. But that the apostle did not speak concerning their conjunctions, but concerning our Lord Jesus Christ, whom he knew to be the Word of God, he himself has made evident. For, summing up concerning the Word in the beginning mentioned by him above [Ἀνακεφαλαιούμενος γὰρ περὶ τοῦ εἰρημένου αὐτῷ ἄνω ἐν ἀρχῇ λόγου], he adds, 'And the Word was made flesh, and dwelt among us' [John 1:14]. Yet, according to their hypothesis, it was not the Word who became flesh, since he never went outside the Fullness, but the Saviour, who was made out of all [the Aeons] and was generated later than the Word. (*haer.* 1.9.2)

The correct hypothesis of the Prologue is none other than the one Lord Jesus Christ, and it is to him that all the various terms and phrases refer, Word, Only-begotten, Maker, and Light, the one who came to his own and was made flesh, dwelling among us. His opponents, as Irenaeus points out, by personifying each term separately as distinct Aeons, have actually done away with the one Lord Jesus Christ.

As we will consider further in the next chapter, a similar manner of reading is in fact used by Irenaeus himself, and widely within early Christianity, for exegeting the Scriptures, that is, what we now call the 'Old Testament'. The paradigm for this is given by the apostle Paul, who 'delivered ['traditioned'] as of first importance what I also received, that

Christ died for our sins in accordance with the Scriptures, that he was buried, that he was raised on the third day in accordance with the Scriptures, and that he appeared to Cephas and to the twelve' (1 Cor 15:3–5), and depicted by Luke, with the resurrected Christ on the road to Emmaus opening the Scriptures to show how 'it was necessary that the Christ should suffer these things and enter into his glory; and beginning with Moses and all the prophets he interpreted to them in all the Scriptures the things concerning himself' (Luke 24:25–7). This Christocentric reading of the Scripture, focused upon the of the Christ, enables seeing the Scriptures (again, the 'Old Testament') as a mosaic depicting Christ composed out of different tiles. It also implies a differentiation, which we shall explore further in the next chapter, between the 'Old Testament' and the 'New Testament', not seeing the latter simply as a continuation of the former, treating them simply as yet more books of Scripture, but rather seeing the writings of the apostles and evangelists as already composed out of the material of Scripture, used in the interpretation of Christ and so seeing in the books of Moses and all the prophets a mosaic of the king. Irenaeus' opponents deploy the same exegetical methods but do so, however, upon the writings of the apostles and evangelists themselves, thereby treating them, certainly, as Scripture, but nevertheless in doing so substituting a different hypothesis from that of, in this case, John. This, Irenaeus repeatedly insists, is not as the prophets foretold, the Lord taught, and the apostles handed down. Although, as we have seen, Irenaeus repeatedly emphasizes that he has received this teaching and this method from Polycarp who had himself known John, he does not claim this pedigree to substantiate his claim here. Rather he allows it to stand on the two points he makes, both of which are immediately apparent, that his opponents' reading simply does not 'fit' the text.

Irenaeus continues his case by pointing out the difference between his opponents, who take the words of the Prologue as speaking about different Aeons, and John who wrote all this 'concerning our Lord Jesus Christ' (*haer.* 1.9.3). As he sees this, 'according to them, the Word did not originally become flesh, for they maintain that the Saviour assumed a psychic body, formed in accordance with the economy by an unspeakable providence, so as to become visible and palpable'. 'But flesh', Irenaeus points out, 'is the ancient handiwork [πλάσις] formed out of the dust by God for Adam, which John declares that the Word of God truly became' (*haer.* 1.9.3). We will take up this idea of the 'flesh' being the 'handiwork' again shortly. Irenaeus concludes the chapter by using a further literary example, that of how some people take diverse lines from the work of

Homer and then rearrange them to produce homeric-sounding verses that tell a tale not to be found in Homer (*haer.* 1.9.4). While these fabrications, called centos, can mislead those who have only a passing knowledge of Homer, they will not deceive those who are well versed in his poetry, for they will be able to identify the lines and restore them to their proper context. So, he concludes,

> anyone who keeps unswervingly in himself the canon of truth [τὸν κανόνα τῆς ἀληθείας] received through baptism will recognize the names and sayings and parables from the Scriptures, but this blasphemous hypothesis of theirs he will not recognize. For if he recognizes the jewels, he will not accept the fox for the image of the king. He will restore each one of the passages to its proper order and, having fit it into the body of the truth, he will lay bare their fabrication and show that it is without support (*haer.* 1.9.4).

This is followed by the fullest description given by Irenaeus of the faith received by the apostles, 'in one God the Father Almighty, Creator of heaven and earth... and in one Jesus Christ, the Son of God, who was enfleshed for our salvation; and in the Holy Spirit, who through the prophets preached the economies'[50]—that is, his coming (τὴν ἔλευσιν), the birth from the Virgin, the Passion, resurrection and bodily ascension into heaven, and his coming (παρουσία) from heaven, to recapitulate all things, bringing judgement to eternal separation or life (*haer.* 1.10.1).[51] It is striking that all the items pertaining to the work of Christ, which in the creeds from the fourth century onwards appear under the second article, are here given in the third article, as that which was foretold by the Spirit through the prophets. This is so precisely for the reason, noted above, that it is the words of the prophets that provide the material, the tiles of the mosaic, for the apostolic preaching. This 'canon of truth' is 'received through baptism', probably indicating its structuring upon the three central articles of belief found in the interrogatory baptismal creeds from the earliest times and going back to the baptismal command of Christ himself (Matt. 28:19). Elsewhere, in the context of discussing the rule of truth, Irenaeus also affirms that 'the baptism of our regeneration takes place through these three articles' (*Dem.* 7). Yet, despite this connection with

---

[50] 'Economy' (οἰκονομία) is another literary term, referring to the arrangement of a poem, or the purpose of a particular episode within it. Cf. Meijering, *Literary and Rhetorical Theories*, 171–81.

[51] For the suggestion that the canon had a narrative structure, see Paul M. Blowers, 'The *Regula Fidei* and the Narrative Character of Early Christian Faith', *Pro Ecclesia*, 6 (1997), 199–228, and, in response, Nathan MacDonald, 'Israel and the Old Testament Story in Irenaeus's Presentation of the Rule of Truth', *JTI* 3/2 (2009), 281–98.

baptism, the rule of truth is not given in a declarative form, as would be the creeds used in baptism from the fourth century onwards.[52] For Irenaeus, the canon of truth remained flexible in its wording, unlike the later declaratory creeds, and was used differently, as a guide for theology rather than as a confession of faith.

This appeal to a 'canon' brings out another dimension of the word 'hypothesis'. Besides its use in a literary context, considered earlier, the term is also used with a theoretical sense. According to Aristotle, 'hypotheses' are the starting points or first principles (ἀρχαί) of demonstrations.[53] For instance, the goal of health is presupposed as a 'hypothesis' by a doctor, who then deliberates on how it is to be attained, just as mathematicians hypothesize certain axioms and then proceed with their demonstrations.[54] In both cases, these hypotheses are tentative; if the goal proves to be unattainable or if the conclusions derived from the supposition turn out to be manifestly false, then the hypothesis in question must be rejected. Since the time of Plato, however, philosophy has aimed at discovering the ultimate first principles.[55] But, as Aristotle concedes, it is impossible to expect demonstrations of the first principles themselves: first principles cannot themselves be proved, otherwise they would be dependent upon something prior to them, and so the enquirer would be led into an infinite regress.[56] As Clement of Alexandria points out, this means that the search for the first principles of demonstration ends up with indemonstrable faith.[57] While not themselves being demonstrable, the first principles, grasped by faith, are the basis for subsequent demonstrations, and are also used to evaluate other claims to truth, and in this way act as a 'canon'. Originally this term simply meant a straight line, a rule by which

---

[52] For a recent discussion see W. Kinzig and M. Vinzent, 'Recent Research on the Origin of the Creed', *JTS* NS 50/2 (1999), 535–59.
[53] Aristotle, *Metaph.* 5.1.2 (1013^{a}17).
[54] Cf. Aristotle, *EE* 1227^{b}28–33; Meijering, *Literary and Rhetorical Theories*, 106.
[55] Cf. Plato, *Rep.* 6.20–1 (510–11).
[56] Aristotle, *Metaph.* 4.4.2 (1006^{a}6–12).
[57] Clement, *Strom.* 8.3.6.7–7.2; Cf. *Strom.* 7.16.95.4–6: 'He, then, who of himself believes the dominical Scripture and voice [τῇ κυριακῇ γραφῇ τε καὶ φωνῇ], which by the Lord acts for the benefit of men, is rightly faithful. Certainly we use it as a criterion in the discovery of things. What is subjected to criticism is not believed till it is so subjected, so that what needs criticism cannot be a first principle. Therefore, as is reasonable, grasping by faith the indemonstrable first principle, and receiving in abundance, from the first principle itself, demonstrations in reference to the first principle, we are by the voice of the Lord trained up to the knowledge of the truth'. Cf. Andrei Giulea Dragos, 'Apprehending "Demonstrations" from the First Principle: Clement of Alexandria's Phenomenology of Faith', *JR* 89/2 (2009), 187–213.

other lines could be judged. As Aristotle points out, only 'by that which is straight do we discern both the straight and the crooked; the carpenter's rule [ὁ κανών] is the test of both, but the crooked tests neither itself nor the straight'.[58] Epicurus' work entitled *The Canon* seems to have been the first work devoted to the need to establish 'the criteria of truth',[59] a need that, in the face of the Sceptical onslaught, made it almost obligatory in the Hellenistic period to begin any systematic presentation of philosophy with an account of 'the criterion'.[60] Without such a canon or criterion, it was recognized, it is simply not possible to gain any knowledge, for all enquiry would be drawn helplessly into an endless regression. It was generally held in Hellenistic philosophy that it is 'preconceptions' (προλήψεις, generic notions synthesized out of repeated sense perceptions, later held to be innate) that facilitate knowledge and act as criteria. The 'self-evidence' (ἐνάργεια) of the sense perceptions for the Epicureans, and the clarity of the cognitive impressions for the Stoics, provide the infallible criterion for examining what truly exists. But again, Clement points out, even Epicurus accepted that this 'preconception of the mind' is 'faith', and that without it, neither enquiry nor judgement is possible.[61]

With this background in mind, we can see that Irenaeus (and likewise Clement of Alexandria and Tertullian), countering the apparently constantly mutating teaching of their opponents, appealed to a 'canon' or 'criterion of truth' in much the same way as the Hellenistic philosophers argued against the infinite regression of the Sceptics.[62] It is by reference to such a canon, Irenaeus claims, that the believer is able to restore each passage of Scripture to its proper place in the body of truth, each tile of the mosaic to its proper place depicting the image of the king. The 'canon of truth' is not simply a set of inherited doctrines existing apart from Scripture, as it would later be for Lessing, but is, rather, an articulation of the hypothesis in a particular situation, outlining the presupposition needed for seeing in Scripture the image of the king, the Christ revealed in and through the Gospel, the apostolic preaching 'according to Scripture'.

[58] Aristotle, *de An.* 1.5 (411^{a}5–7).
[59] Diogenes Laertius, *Vitae* 10.31.
[60] Cf. G. Striker, 'Κριτήριον τῆς ἀληθείας', *Nachrichten der Akademie der Wissenschaften in Göttingen*, Phil.-hist. Kl., 2 (1974), 47–110; M. Schofield, M. Burnyeat, and J. Barnes (eds), *Doubt and Dogmatism: Studies in Hellenistic Epistemology* (Oxford: Oxford University Press, 1980); P. Huby and G. Neal (eds), *The Criterion of Truth* (Liverpool: Liverpool University Press, 1989).
[61] Clement, *Strom.* 2.5.16.3. Cf. S. R. C. Lilla, *Clement of Alexandria: A Study in Christian Platonism and Gnosticism* (Oxford: Oxford University Press, 1971), 120–31.
[62] Cf. Osborn, 'Reason and the Rule of Faith'.

Irenaeus himself gives no definition of what he means by the term 'canon', but Clement of Alexandria does, in precisely these terms: 'The ecclesiastical canon is the concord and symphony of the Law and the Prophets in the covenant delivered at the coming of the Lord.'[63]

The 'canon' of faith or truth is thus not an arbitrary principle, or set of inherited doctrines, which must be maintained, but an attempt to articulate the hypothesis of the Christian faith, which is itself found in the coherence of the image of Christ portrayed in the Scriptures or the symphony produced by these same Scriptures in the coming of Christ. Appeal is made to the 'canon' not to stymie further reflection or thought, but to make it possible. And so Irenaeus follows his account of the canon with numerous questions (*haer.* 1.10.3), reflection upon which opens up enquirers to the depths of the wisdom of God as revealed in Christ, rather than leading them to another construction based on another hypothesis.

Irenaeus admittedly does not provide a philosophically sophisticated account of terms such as 'canon' and 'hypothesis', as does Clement of Alexandria, but it is to his credit that they come to be deployed in this manner for the first time. The term 'canon' had only been used a couple of times prior to Irenaeus, in a manner that brings out further background and dimensions to his argument.[64] The first time is by Clement of Rome:

> Let us put aside empty and vain cares, and let us come to the glorious and venerable canon of our tradition [τὸν τῆς παραδόσεως κανόνα], and let us see what is good and pleasing and acceptable in the sight of our Maker. Let us fix our gaze on the Blood of Christ, and let us know that it is precious to his Father, because it was poured out for our salvation, and brought the grace of repentance to all the world.[65]

Turning to the canon seems to be set in apposition to fixing our attention on the Blood of Christ, which, in turn, apparently refers both to the

---

[63] Clement, *Strom.* 6.15.125.3: κανὼν δὲ ἐκκλησιαστικὸν ἡ συνῳδία καὶ ἡ συμφωνία νόμου τε καὶ προφητῶν τῇ κατὰ τὴν τοῦ κυρίου παρουσίαν παραδιδομένῃ διαθήκῃ.

[64] 'Canon' was used by Paul in Gal. 6:16: Καὶ ὅσοι τῷ κανόνι τούτῳ στοιχήσουσιν εἰρήνη ἐπ' αὐτοὺς καὶ ἔλεος καὶ ἐπὶ τὸν Ἰσραὴλ τοῦ θεοῦ. For an exploration of the role of this verse in the development of the appeal to the 'canon of truth' in the second and third centuries, and the suggestion that this verse, taken disjunctively ('And as many as shall walk by this rule, peace be upon them, and mercy also upon the Israel of God') was used by Marcion as the basis for the separation of the Law and the Gospel (cf. Tertullian, *Adv. Marc.* 1.20.1): 'They allege that in separating the Law and the Gospel, Marcion did not so much invent a new rule as refurbish a rule previously debased'), prompting the widespread appeal to the 'canon of truth' thereafter, see William R. Farmer, 'Galatians and the Second-Century Development of the *Regula Fidei*', *The Second Century*, 4/3 (1984), 143–70.

[65] Clement of Rome, *1 Clem.* 7.2–5.

sacrifice of Christ himself as well as to the celebration of the Eucharist, as that which is immediately and directly 'in view'. In a similar context, when Polycarp wrote to Victor about the Quartodeciman practice, he stated that all his predecessors kept the celebration of Pascha on the fourteenth day of the Passover, 'never swerving but following according to the rule of the faith' (*h.e.* 5.24.6).[66] This eucharistic context was also important for Irenaeus, especially in regard to the salvation of the flesh, for it confirms that 'our teaching is harmonious with the Eucharist and the Eucharist establishes our teaching' (*haer.* 4.18.5).

Clement's phrase, 'the canon of our tradition', is unusual, and its association with the Passion of Christ and the celebration of the Eucharist points to the background for the final term deployed by Irenaeus against his opponents, and that is 'tradition'. There are only two occasions when the apostle Paul uses the significant technical formula of 'handing down', or 'traditioning', what he has 'received'. One has already been noted, where he speaks of his handing-down 'as of first importance' that Christ died and rose 'in accordance with the Scriptures' (1 Cor. 15:3–5). On the other occasion, also in his first letter to the Corinthians, he asserts that 'I received from the Lord what I also delivered to you', that Christ took bread, gave thanks, broke it, and declared it to be his body, and likewise with the cup, enjoining his disciples to do likewise, 'in remembrance of me', 'for as often as you eat this bread and drink the cup, you proclaim the Lord's death until he comes' (1 Cor. 11:23–7). These two dimensions of what has been 'handed down' are depicted by Luke in his account of Christ on the road to Emmaus, who is recognized when, after 'opening the Scriptures', he breaks bread with his disciples, only to disappear from their sight (Luke 24:25–31). The 'tradition' appealed to by Irenaeus is not just some customary teaching or practice, but that which the apostles 'handed down' as the matrix and the means for encountering the Christ they proclaimed, a particular approach and practice, pivoted upon the Passion of Christ, understood through the Scriptures, and enacted in the Eucharist.

In this way, then, Irenaeus developed his argument against his opponents by deploying terms drawn from contemporary literary, rhetorical, and epistemological theory, and grounded it in the sacramental life of the

---

[66] A third time the term is used is in the Moscow postscript to the *Martyrdom of Polycarp*, where it states that in his writings Irenaeus 'mentions Polycarp, saying that he had been his pupil, and he ably refuted every heresy, and he also handed on the ecclesiastical and canonical rule, as he had received it from the saint' (*M. Polyc.* 22.2–4).

Church, the crux for both of which is the Passion of Christ. This structure enables us to keep to the revelation of God in Christ as the ground of all reality: 'we must keep the canon of faith unswervingly and perform the commandments of God' in faith, for such faith 'is established upon things truly real' and enables us to have 'a true comprehension of what is' (*Dem.* 3). Likewise, for Irenaeus, as we will see more fully in the next chapter, the economy of God is a divine pedagogy that has allowed us to learn of our weakness through the experience of death, in a process that is intertwined with and parallels the Eucharist itself—as the seeds sown in the ground receive growth from the Spirit and receiving the Word of God become the Body and Blood of Christ, so too do our bodies, nourished by this, when sown in the ground, rise again to receive immortality and incorruptibility from God—'so that we, being instructed in every way may be scrupulous in everything, being ignorant neither of God nor of ourselves' (*haer.* 5.2.3). As Hans Urs von Balthasar put it: 'The primary aim is not to think, to impose Platonic intellectual or even mythical categories on things, but simply to *see* what *is*.'[67]

In some ways, Irenaeus' method is phenomenological. Rather than speculating about beings, forces, or actions behind the appearances, Irenaeus keeps to the appearances, seeking out the wisdom of God in the revelation or manifestation of God in Christ, as this has shown itself, demonstrated through the interpretation of Scripture ('Old Testament' again) as preached by the apostles and enacted in the Eucharist, both handed down by the apostle as the means of encountering Christ, and as experienced by human beings in and through their own weakness and mortality, that which belongs without exception to all flesh, which, simply and profoundly, is what we are.[68] In book two, besides countering his opponents on their own terms to show the absurdities and contradictions into which they are led, Irenaeus devotes a section (*haer.* 2.25–28) to the ethos, as it were, of such enquiry, complementing his technical argument regarding 'hypothesis' and 'canon' in book one.[69]

He begins by affirming that the position of names, the election of the apostles, the deeds of the Lord, as they are found in Scripture, and also the

---

[67] Balthasar, *The Glory of the Lord*, 45.

[68] For a phenomenological reading of our existence as flesh, drawing extensively from Irenaeus, see Michel Henry, *Incarnation: Une philosophie de la chair* (Paris: Seuil, 2000).

[69] For the background of Irenaeus' stance here in the 'Empirical' school of physicians and the sceptical tradition in Greek philosophy, see W. R. Schoedel, 'Theological Method in Irenaeus (*Adversus Haereses* 2.25–28)', *JTS* NS 35 (1984), 31–49, and Norris, 'Theology and Language', 294–5.

whole arrangement of created things, are in no way meaningless or accidental. All things have been created by God with great wisdom and care, and so in all these cases we should 'harmonize them with what actually exists or with right reason' (*haer.* 2.25.1). The various numbers, syllables, and letters found in Scripture are not the starting point for understanding the revelation of God in Christ. Starting with them provides no solid hypothesis, and so leads inevitably to the many and diverse constructions of his opponents; they should instead 'adapt the numbers themselves and those things which have been formed to the underlying hypothesis of truth'.[70] When viewed individually, created things are 'mutually opposite and inharmonious'—they are each what they are and other than anything else—yet, when seen together, Irenaeus points out, they do indeed form one harmonious creation, as many distinct notes fit together in 'one unbroken melody' (*haer.* 2.25.2). Only seeing each individually, each creature or each note in the melody would seem to be from a different author, but starting with the hypothesis of one Creator, they are all known as belonging together. Only in this way will the judgement, goodness, skill, and wisdom be seen in the whole work. If we cannot, as yet, see this harmony, this is because we too are creatures within creation, 'infinitely inferior to God' and not seeing the whole from his perspective; we have 'received grace only in part', are 'not yet equal or similar to his Maker', and so 'cannot experience or form a conception of all things as God does' (*haer.* 2.25.3). So, Irenaeus urges, 'preserve therefore the proper order of your knowledge and do not, as being ignorant of things really good, seek to rise above God himself, for he cannot be surpassed' (*haer.* 2.25.4). Following the apostle's maxim that 'knowledge puffs up, but love edifies' (1 Cor. 8.1), Irenaeus holds that it is better 'to belong to the simple and unlettered, and by means of love attain nearness to God, rather than, by imagining ourselves as learned and skilful, be found among those who blaspheme their own God' (*haer.* 2.26.1). Just as Christ's statement that all the hairs on our head are numbered (Matt. 10:30) does not prompt us to count the hairs on each person's head and then devise explanations for why some have more and some less (*haer.* 2.26.2), so also, while accepting that all things are created by God in wisdom and with due order and measure, we would nevertheless think that anyone who attempts to count up all the grains of sand and pebbles on the earth, and then endeavours to think out the causes for these numbers, to be mad and insane (*haer.* 2.26.3).

From simple observations such as these, Irenaeus then concludes:

---

[70] *haer.* 2.25.1, following Rousseau's retroversion (SC 293.294–9).

A sound mind, and one which does not expose its possessor to danger, and is devoted to piety and the love of truth, will eagerly meditate upon those things that God has placed within the power of human beings, and has subjected to our knowledge, and will make advancement in them, rendering the knowledge of them easy to them by means of daily study. (*haer.* 2.27.1)

These are things such as 'fall under our observation' and as are 'clearly and unambiguously in express terms set forth in the sacred Scriptures' (*haer.* 2.27.1). The parables of Christ, then, should not 'be adapted to ambiguous expressions', but rather be explained by that which is clear, so that 'the parables will receive a similar interpretation from all, and the body of truth remain complete, structured harmoniously, and unshaken' (*haer.* 2.27.1). If this is not done, but rather if that which is unclear is interpreted as anyone chooses, 'no one will possess the rule of truth', each will work from his or her own hypothesis, setting out incompatible teachings, and ultimately 'one will always be enquiring but never finding, for they have rejected the very method of discovery' (*haer.* 2.27.1–2).

On the other hand, 'having the truth itself as our canon and the testimony concerning God set clearly before us' (*haer.* 2.28.1), we have a solid hypothesis for enquiring further into that which we can know, rather than pursuing that which we cannot and which ultimately has no solidity or real existence. As Irenaeus puts it, 'it is much more suitable that we, directing our enquiries after this fashion, should exercise ourselves in this investigation of the mystery and economy of the living God, and should increase in the love of him who has done, and still does, so great things for us' (*haer.* 2.28.1). And, if, in this enquiry, we find that 'we cannot discover explanations of all those things in Scripture which are made the subject of investigation', we should not turn to seek another God beside the Creator, for even those things at our own feet, such as the rising of the Nile or the circulating seasons, lie beyond our knowledge (*haer.* 2.28.2). Our limitation as creatures is not only with respect to knowledge of creation, but also that concerning God, so that, 'not only in the present world, but also in that which is to come, God should for ever teach and human beings should for ever learn the things taught them by God' (*haer.* 2.28.3). We should leave aside those things that are beyond our capacity for knowledge, and seek after that which is given. We cannot possibly, for instance, give a sensible answer to a question regarding what God was doing before he created the world; this lies with God alone (*haer.* 2.28.3). Likewise those who try to give an account of 'the birth and production both of God himself, of his Thought, of his Word, and Life, and Christ, form the idea of these from nothing other than a mere human experience' (*haer.* 2.28.4). If asked 'How then was the Son produced by the Father?', we can reply only 'that no one understands that production or generation or calling or revelation or whatever name one may use to describe his generation, which is in fact altogether indescribable' (*haer.* 2.28.6).[71] God is not subject to our scrutiny, as if we had some kind of vantage point to look down upon him as we might upon an object within creation; his revelation in Christ, however, is given to us, and leads us into the depths of the profundity of the mystery of his wisdom. Thus, when the proper method is followed, 'through the many diverse expressions [in Scripture] there shall be heard an harmonious melody in us, praising in hymns the God who created all things' (*haer.* 2.28.3).

In all these ways, then, Irenaeus argues that his opponents, with their faulty exegesis and their mythmaking, have substituted another hypothesis and so created their own fabrication ($\pi\lambda\acute{\alpha}\sigma\mu\alpha$). In doing so, he asserts, they have dissolved the one Lord Jesus Christ into a multitude of Aeons and so denied salvation to the flesh, for 'flesh is the ancient handiwork [$\pi\lambda\acute{\alpha}\sigma\iota\varsigma$] formed out of the dust by God for Adam, which John declares that the Word of God truly became' (*haer.* 1.9.3). When Irenaeus turns in the following books to examining 'the scriptural demonstration of the apostles who also composed the Gospel' (*haer.* 3.5.1), the term $\pi\lambda\acute{\alpha}\sigma\mu\alpha$ is used primarily to describe the 'fabrication of God', the flesh fashioned by the Hands of God, to which the Word is finally united, manifesting the image and likeness of God. The background for this usage is not the literary one that we examined above, but rather the fashioning of mud into flesh by God (Gen. 2:7), and the image of the potter and the vessel used by Isaiah and Paul: 'But who are you, a human being, to answer back to God? Will what is moulded [$\tau\grave{o}\ \pi\lambda\acute{\alpha}\sigma\mu\alpha$] say to its moulder, "Why have you made me thus?"' (Rom. 9.20; Isa. 29:16). Ultimately, however, the two uses turn upon the same point: who is the Creator or the poet (the $\pi o\iota\eta\tau\acute{\eta}\varsigma$)? Do we create our own fabrication or are we the ones being created in the Hands of God? For Irenaeus the human being is precisely the one created by God, flesh fashioned from mud by his Hands, animated

---

[71] Cf. Gregory of Nazianus, *Or.* 31.8: 'What, then, is "proceeding"? You explain unbegottenness of the Father and I will give you a biological account of the Son's begetting and the Spirit's proceeding—and let us go mad the pair of us for prying into God's secrets.'

by a breath of life to be vivified by the Spirit through their death in conformity with Christ, thus becoming at the end 'in the image and likeness of God'. It is to Irenaeus' own exposition of this economy of the one God worked through the one Christ upon the one handiwork that we now turn in the final chapter.

3

The Glory of God (haer. 3–5)

While exposing and refuting his opponents in the first two books of his *magnum opus, Against the Heresies*, Irenaeus also intimated, as we have seen, the lineaments of his own position: that, when viewed from the hypothesis preached by the prophets, taught by the Lord, and delivered by the apostles, the Scriptures are a mosaic portraying, in the arrangement of its tesserae, the image of the king. This hypothesis can be expressed as a canon, the rule of truth, affirming that there is but one God, the Father and Creator, who has revealed himself in and through his one Son, Jesus Christ, made known by the one Holy Spirit through the prophets. Read in this way, as we will see in this chapter, Scripture describes and the Hands of God, that is, Christ and the Holy Spirit, effect the one all-embracing economy, or arrangement, of God, which begins with his stated intention to create a human being in his own image and likeness and is completed at the end in Christ himself, who by the Spirit enables all men and women to become living human beings in the image and likeness of God.

At stake, then, are matters theological and anthropological, and the coincidence of both together in the person of Christ. These three themes, as we have seen, structure Irenaeus' own exposition in the remaining books of *Against the Heresies*: one God (*haer.* 3.6–15; 4.1–19; 5.1–14), one Christ (*haer.* 3.16–21; 4.20–35; 5.15–24), the human being (*haer.* 3.21–23; 4.36–41; 5.25–36). Irenaeus presents his case carefully, examining, for instance, how the word 'God' is used by Moses and the prophets and by the evangelists and Paul, in his 'hastily written' letters (*haer.* 3.6–7), thus demonstrating the faithfulness of his own exposition to the text of Scripture. Yet Irenaeus knows that his opponents cannot be refuted simply by laying claim to the canon of truth, tradition, or authority, or by paying close attention to the text of Scripture, without also providing an account of our existence and experience more persuasive and coherent than that which they have to offer, as fascinating as it was to some in his own time and in ours. And so, beyond his textual examination, he offers a profound analysis, running throughout his writings, of the work of God in and through the economy, touching, in the most direct way possible, issues concerning what it is to be human, the meaning of human existence and experience, life and death. In doing so, Irenaeus does not theologize in the manner of his opponents, offering a theogony describing the derivation of heavenly beings and then retelling the creation account of Genesis as a rather botched affair, but instead theologizes within the economy to offer an anthropogony, an account of how from the beginning and throughout the economy God himself fashions the mud taken from the earth, our own flesh and blood, into his own image and likeness, perfecting it in the end as a living human being, 'the glory of God' (*haer.* 4.20.7).[1]

At the heart of Irenaeus' exposition stands the person of Christ, the beginning and end of the economy, and the starting point for his theology. The figure of Christ is, of course, pivotally important for all Christian theologians, for his opponents as much as for Irenaeus. However, the difference between how Irenaeus and his opponents understood Christ, and approached the task of expounding his person, his work, and its significance, could not have been greater. Both focused on the opening chapters of Genesis, following Paul's correlation and contrast between Adam and Christ. But his opponents latched on to the apostle's statement that 'flesh and blood cannot inherit the kingdom' (1 Cor. 15:50) to find in Christ a figure providing the supposedly liberating knowledge that their earthy and material bodies were created not by God himself but by a demiurge, in which their true being, a spiritual seed from the Pleroma, had been deposited as a seed, unknown to the demiurge, and from which it could be liberated by growth in true knowledge. Irenaeus, in contrast, ever the careful reader, keeping closer to both Genesis and Paul, emphasizes the continuity between the first and second Adam, underscores the importance of the sequence between the two—the 'animated' being first, culminating in the 'spiritual' (1 Cor. 15:45–6)—and pivots his account, following Paul, on the Passion of Christ, as that which enables the 'animated body', sown into the earth, to be raised as a 'spiritual body' (1 Cor. 15:44). What Paul posits as a typological correlation between Adam and Christ, Irenaeus expands into an all-embracing account of the economy of God, understanding the end in terms of the beginning, with the end in turn shedding light on the beginning: the divine intention

---

[1] Cf. Thomas Holsinger-Friesen, *Irenaeus and Genesis: A Study of Competition in Early Christian Hermeneutics*, Journal of Theological Interpretation, Supplement 1 (Winona Lake, IN: Eisenbraus, 2009), 112: 'By declaring God to be the Creator (i.e. a *terminus a quo*), Irenaeus' rule of truth effectively stipulated that any accounting of God's activity—or Christ's—must begin with anthropogony rather than with theogony.'

expressed in Genesis 1:26 begins in Genesis 2:7 and concludes in Christ, who is thus the truly living human being; what is sketched out in Adam, clay animated by a breath of life, is brought to perfection by Christ vivified by Holy Spirit, the Hands of God through whom God himself has been at work throughout the whole economy. Within this economy, the sequence that Paul lays out in 1 Corinthians 15 does not result, on Irenaeus' reading, in a salvation *from* flesh and blood, but rather shows salvation—creation and re-creation—being worked out *in and through* flesh and blood, beginning with that of Christ himself. Flesh and blood do not, indeed, inherit the kingdom, but nevertheless it *is inherited* when humans allow themselves to be worked upon by the Hands of God.

The difference between Irenaeus and his opponents is a fundamentally hermeneutic one. For Irenaeus, Christ is not only the one who is 'preformed' in the earthy reality of Adam and the Hand who 'pre-forms' and perfects this earthy reality in himself, but also the lens who brings this scriptural account into focus.[2] To be precise, Irenaeus understands the work of Christ by beginning with the divine intention stated in Genesis, and in so doing continues in the footsteps of Paul, who began his exposition of Christ's work by 'handing down' ('traditioning') that Christ died and rose 'in accordance with Scripture' (1 Cor. 15:3–4). His opponents, on the other hand, began with a figure of Christ, by which they then reread the Genesis account as part of a larger mythological narrative, accounting for a radically different way of assessing the world and ourselves as human beings within it. For Irenaeus and his opponents, Scripture must be read in the light of Christ; but the Christ whom Irenaeus expounds is himself also understood within the mosaic or matrix of Scripture, as read and preached by the apostles. And so, as was noted in the previous chapter, Irenaeus has little time or patience for speculations about things not spoken of in Scripture, such as about what happened prior to creation, before God's act of taking clay in his Hands to fashion the human being.

Beyond the exegetical level, the hermeneutic contrast also pertains to our understanding of ourselves. Staying steadfastly within what can be known by creatures, in particular the fact of their being-created and all that this entails, Irenaeus finds within this experience the deployment of the wisdom and the power of God, divine strength made known in human weakness. This world is itself, then, the stage in which the economy of God is unfolded, and as such Irenaeus finds utterly incomprehensible his

---

[2] Cf. Holsinger-Friesen, *Irenaeus and Genesis*, 179.

opponents' description of it as the realm of a cruel god or the product of an inferior demiurge resulting from a disturbance within and exclusion from the divine realm. Beginning with the Passion of Christ, the climax of the work of God and the crux of his account, Irenaeus does not at all minimize or overlook the reality of evil and death within creation, but rather sees it as embraced and transformed by that work of Christ. If Christ's work had not touched everything, there would be an aspect of creation that does not lie within God's Hands. Death may well not have been created by God, but it would be a failure of the first order not to see it as transformed by the work of God, and indeed as the very instrument of that transformation, for the starting point for understanding the whole economy is nothing other than the Passion of Christ—that is, his victory over death *by his death*. Not only would an account of the economy that does not embrace and transform everything have failed to understand how God, as the Creator, is the Lord of all, but it would also have failed to understand the divine life, as Christ has shown it to be, that of the sacrifice of love, and so failed to provide an answer to our deepest human concern regarding our mortality.

THE CONCISE WORD

Irenaeus opens his own exposition, beginning in book three of *Against the Heresies*, with an emphatic statement regarding the basis of his hermeneutics:

For the Lord of all gave to his apostles the power of the Gospel, through whom also we have known the truth, that is, the doctrine of the Son of God; to whom also did the Lord declare: 'he who hears you, hears me; and he that despises you, despises me, and him that sent me' [Luke 10:16]. We have learned from none others the economy of our salvation, than from those through whom the Gospel has come down to us, which they did at one time proclaim in public, and, at a later period, by the will of God, handed down to us in the Scriptures, to be the pillar and foundation of our faith.[3]

The focus of Irenaeus' exposition is the 'economy of salvation'. The term 'economy' (οἰκονομία, *dispositio*, *dispensatio*) originally referred to the ordering or regulating of a household, but it had come to mean an administration or arrangement more generally, and, in rhetorical and literary

---

[3] *haer.* 3.Pr.-1.1, following Rousseau in taking the last sentence of the preface together with 3.1.

theory, it was used to refer to the arrangement of a poem or the purpose of a particular episode within it.[4] As such, the term could be used to denote both the action of arranging matters generally or a specific act for a particular purpose, as well as the arrangement or design itself, relating either to a particular act or to the comprehensive plan overall. Many theologians had used the term 'economy' to refer to particular acts of God, such as the Incarnation or the Passion, and Irenaeus himself could readily speak of such things in the plural, such as the 'economies of God' spoken of in his canon of truth (*haer.* 1.10.1). His opponents seem to have used the term also in the singular, to speak more comprehensively, referring to a plan of salvation undertaken to free the spiritual element lodged within some of the material bodies created by the Demiurge but unknown to him.[5] Irenaeus, in contrast, used the term with a truly universal sense, to bring together all the various aspects of God's work, creation as well as salvation, into one all-embracing and singular divine plan. This economy can be viewed both synchronically, seen synoptically in the scriptural mosaic of the king (*haer.* 1.8.10), and diachronically, in the symphony of salvation effected throughout history as the creature made from mud is gradually fashioned by the Hands of God to the point that created human eyes can rest upon the uncreated God.

As Irenaeus makes clear in the statement quoted above, however, the economy of salvation is not known simply from reading the Scriptures, but only from the preaching of the apostles—that is, as we shall see, the Gospel proclaimed 'in accordance with the Scriptures', so providing a 'concise word'. Their proclamation was made both through their preaching and through their writings, now to be counted as Scripture, and it is this that Irenaeus identifies, using words with which Paul had spoken of the Church (1 Tim. 3:15), as the basis and support of the faith. This opening statement is followed by a short account (*haer.* 3.1) describing the composition of the four Gospels, relating Mark to Peter and Luke to Paul, and an excursus (*haer.* 3.2–4) arguing that this preaching has been preserved publically by the successions of presbyter-bishops in the various churches, pre-eminently in Rome. Irenaeus' point is that the content of this apostolic tradition is identical to that handed down by the apostles in

---

[4] For the various terms used in the Latin and Armenian translation of Irenaeus, and the semantic range of the word in Irenaeus, his predecessors, and his opponents, see Jacques Fantino, *La Théologie d'Irénée: Lecture des Écritures en réponse à l'exégèse gnostique: Une approche trinitaire* (Paris: Cerf, 1994), 85–126. For the literary and rhetorical background of the term, see Meijering, *Literary and Rhetorical Theories*, 177–81.

[5] Cf. Fantino, *Théologie*, 98–101.

writing, so that, on the one hand, his opponents, who claim possession of a secret oral tradition by which they then interpret the Scriptures differently in fact follow neither Scripture nor tradition, and, on the other hand, those 'barbarians' who are not able to read nevertheless preserve the ancient tradition written in their hearts, believing in one God who created all things by his Son, Christ Jesus. After stating this to be the case, Irenaeus then begins his principal task of exposition that will occupy him for three further books:

> Since, therefore, the tradition from the apostles does thus exist in the Church, and is permanent among us, let us revert to the demonstration from the Scriptures provided by those apostles who wrote the Gospel [*reuertamur ad eam quae est ex scripturis ostensionem eorum qui euangelium conscripserunt apostolorum*], in which they recorded the doctrine regarding God, pointing out that our Lord Jesus Christ is the truth, and that no lie is in him. (*haer.* 3.5.1)

What counts for Irenaeus is not simply an appeal to the Church or tradition, but the apostolic demonstration from the Scriptures, and this he identifies with the Gospel. The Gospel, in other words, is not simply a liberating message independently proclaimed on its own terms; rather, the very shape and terms in which it is proclaimed by the apostles, to whom 'the power of the Gospel' has been given, are drawn from the Scriptures. Irenaeus speaks here of the 'Gospel' in the singular: he is not referring to the Gospels of Matthew, Mark, Luke, and John, in which we can see recourse to numerous texts from the Scriptures, fleshing out, as it were, the Gospel. Rather, the Gospel itself, in the singular, is understood to be already cast within the terms of Scripture, as expounded by the apostles.

Complementing his image of Scripture as a mosaic depicting the king (*haer.* 1.8.1), Irenaeus applies Christ's words about the treasure hidden in a field to elucidate further the hermeneutics at work in this apostolic demonstration, and much more, in a remarkable passage that, although lengthy, deserves to be quoted in full:

> If anyone, therefore, reads the Scriptures this way, he will find in them the Word concerning Christ, and a foreshadowing of the new calling. For Christ[6] is the 'treasure which was hidden in the field' [Matt. 13:44], that is, in this world—for 'the field is the world' [Matt. 13:38]—[a treasure] hidden in the Scriptures, for he was indicated by means of types and parables, which could not be understood by human beings prior to the consummation of those things which had been

---

[6] Following the Greek preserved in the *Catena in Matt.* (cf. SC 100, p. 712); the Latin simply has 'Hic', and similarly the Armenian.

predicted, that is, the advent of the Lord. And therefore it was said to Daniel the prophet, 'Shut up the words, and seal the book, until the time of the consummation, until many learn and knowledge abounds. For, when the dispersion shall be accomplished, they shall know all these things' [Dan. 12:4, 7]. And Jeremiah also says, 'In the last days they shall understand these things' [Jer. 23:20]. For every prophecy, before its fulfilment, is nothing but an enigma and ambiguity to human beings; but when the time has arrived, and the prediction has come to pass, then it has an exact exposition [ἐξήγησις]. And for this reason, when at this present time the Law is read by the Jews, it is like a myth, for they do not possess the explanation [ἐξήγησις] of all things which pertain to the human advent of the Son of God; but when it is read by Christians, it is a treasure, hid in a field, but brought to light by the Cross of Christ, and explained, both enriching the understanding of human beings, and showing forth the wisdom of God, and making known his economies with regard to the human being, and prefiguring the kingdom of Christ, and preaching in anticipation the good news of the inheritance of the holy Jerusalem, and proclaiming beforehand that the human being who loves God shall advance so far as even to see God, and hear his Word, and be glorified, from hearing his speech, to such an extent, that others will not be able to behold his glorious countenance [cf. 2 Cor. 3:7], as was said by Daniel, 'Those who understand shall shine as the brightness of the firmament, and many of the righteous as the stars for ever and ever' [Dan. 12:3]. In this manner, then, I have shown it to be, if anyone read the Scriptures. (*haer.* 4.26.1)

It is Christ himself who is hidden in the Scriptures and brought to light by the Cross. Or, as he puts it elsewhere, commenting on Christ's words that Moses 'wrote of me' (John 5:46), Christ is 'sown' throughout the Scriptures.[7] He is hidden, as the previous chapters of *Against the Heresies* make clear, in the prophecies and types, the words and deeds, of the patriarchs and the prophets, which prefigure what was to happen to Christ in his advent as preached by the apostles. The patriarchs and prophets 'disseminated the word concerning Christ' preparing the field for the harvest reaped by the Church (*haer.* 4.25.3). They 'prefigured our faith and disseminated throughout the earth the advent of the Son of God, who and what he should be', so that the posterity 'might easily accept the advent of Christ, having been instructed by Scripture' (*haer.* 4.23.1). Those, therefore, who

---

[7] *haer.* 4.10.1: Christ said this, 'no doubt, because the Son of God is implanted everywhere throughout his writings [*inseminatus est ubique in Scripturis eius Filius Dei*]: at one time, indeed, speaking with Abraham; at another time with Noah, giving him the dimensions [of the Ark]; at another enquiring after Adam; at another time, bringing down judgement upon the Sodomites; and again, when he becomes visible, and directs Jacob on his journey, and speaks with Moses from the bush. The occasions are innumerable in which the Son of God is shown forth by Moses.'

are familiar with Scripture (Irenaeus gives the example of Joseph and the Ethiopian eunuch) are ready to be instructed in the advent of the Son of God, needing only to be told of whom Scripture speaks, whereas those who do not know these Scriptures present a harder task, and for this reason, Irenaeus claims, Paul can justly say, 'I laboured more than the rest' (*haer.* 4.24.1; 1 Cor. 15:10).

However, such things are only prophecies and prefigurations; what they foreshadow is not yet known. They could not be known, Irenaeus claims, as in fact they were not, prior to their consummation, that is, 'the advent of the Lord', or as he puts it, when they are 'brought to light by the Cross of Christ'. So, for those who read Scripture without this vantage point, the Scriptures are nothing but ambiguities and enigmas, myths and fables; the book remains shut, as the prophet Daniel had said, waiting till the last times to be opened. Yet now that the book has been unsealed, those who read the same Scripture with an understanding of its proper exegesis are themselves transfigured to become like Moses in his descent from the mountain after his encounter with God, themselves shining with the glory of God.

Scripture and Gospel

There are a number of points here which must be carefully and clearly noted, so as not to miss the force of what Irenaeus is saying. First, and most striking, is that it implies a way of reading Scripture, and indeed what constitutes a text as sacred Scripture, very different from our modern assumptions. After the last couple of centuries of scriptural scholarship, we have become accustomed to reading Scripture primarily in historical terms, debating what we believe to be 'historically true', what was the historical context in which it was written and redacted, and its reception by the initial readers, and, if we still think of it as 'sacred', its inspiration will probably be understood as an interaction between God and the author in their own historical context. The task of exegesis thus becomes to expound the 'meaning' of the text, either within its historical context, or, as more recent scriptural scholarship has argued, within its canonical or rhetorical context. Irenaeus, however, is not concerned with any of this. Instead, as the image of the mosaic already indicates, he sees Scripture as being, as it were, a compendium or 'thesaurus', that is, a 'treasury', of images, words, and reports, which gives flesh to the Christ proclaimed by the apostles, who in turn reveals the work of God deployed throughout the whole economy described in Scripture.

As odd as it may seem to us, the approach of Irenaeus in fact exemplifies what James Kugel identifies as 'four assumptions about Scripture that characterize all ancient biblical interpretation'.[8] The first is that Scripture is 'a fundamentally cryptic text'. If it were not cryptic, if it did not need explanation, it would not be Scripture. This point is abundantly clear in the passage from Irenaeus cited above. The second assumption is that Scripture is 'a fundamentally *relevant* text'. Scripture is not written simply to inform us about events that happened in the past, but rather written for us, now: as the apostle put it, 'now these things [what happened in the desert] happened to them as a type [$\tau υ π ι κ ῶ ς$], but they were written down for our instruction upon whom the end of the ages has come' (1 Cor. 10:11). The translation by the RSV of the word $\tau υ π ι κ ῶ ς$ by 'as a warning' obscures the grounding of Irenaeus' 'typological' reading in the apostle himself. Not only is the account given in Scripture to be understood 'typologically', but this is done for our benefit, for those, that is, who stand 'at the end of the ages', or 'the last times' in Jeremiah's words quoted by Irenaeus, as the point at which the types and prophecies are fulfilled and the books opened. The third assumption is that 'Scripture is perfect and perfectly harmonious'. If it is cryptic, but opened in the last times, then it will be found to speak of the one who opens the books. Or, as Irenaeus put it, it is Christ himself who is disseminated throughout Scripture. It is the act of opening the Scriptures by Christ that enables them to be read synchronically, as a mosaic depicting himself, and diachronically, as the economy of God unfolded throughout time, culminating in Christ. This third presupposition, together with the first one, is dramatically depicted in the account of the appearance of the risen Christ to his disciples on the road to Emmaus, when he opens the Scriptures, which to this point had been cryptic, and 'beginning with Moses and all the prophets interpreted to them in all the Scriptures the things concerning himself' (Luke 24:27). Kugel's fourth assumption is that Scripture 'is somehow divinely sanctioned, of divine provenance, or divinely inspired'. Kugel makes the further important point that it 'would be a mistake, in my view, to assume that this fourth assumption stands behind the other three', if for no other reason than that the divine inspiration of the whole of Scripture appears to have developed later than the other three assumptions. More directly to our point would be that Irenaeus' account of how Scripture is to be read assumes that the divinely inspired content of

---

[8] James Kugel, *Traditions of the Bible: A Guide to the Bible as it was at the Start of the Common Era* (Cambridge, MA: Harvard University Press, 1998), 15, and 15–19 for what follows.

Scripture is not known until the books are opened by the Cross of Christ, and so their 'inspiration' cannot be separated from the act of opening nor, for that matter, from the inspired reading: the 'inspired' writing of Scripture cannot be separated from the 'inspired' reading, and both, together, turn upon the act of opening the Scriptures by the one of whom they speak, or, in reverse, the one who speaks in them.[9]

As Kugel makes clear, these assumptions were operative for all readers of Scripture in antiquity. 'Reading' the present in terms drawn from the past, from the Scripture, is, moreover, something that we can see at work even within the Scriptures themselves. The writers of Israel had long since been using the events and figures of earlier Scripture to understand, explicate, and describe the events and figures at hand. For example, Isaiah (or 'Second-Isaiah') draws upon the image of Abraham to encourage Israel in exile. However small the remnant has become, there will nevertheless be a national renewal if only they imitate Abraham's action and return to their ancestral land: 'Recall Abraham your forefather and Sarah who bore you: for he was one when I called him, but I blessed him and made him numerous' (Isa. 51:2). Abraham thus becomes a type for a new exodus, and this in turn is based upon an earlier typology already inscribed in the earliest level of the Abrahamic traditions, describing his migration to and exodus from Egypt in terms drawn directly from the description of the exodus under Moses (cf. Gen. 12): in this way, as Michael Fishbane puts it, 'in all these various forms Abraham came to serve as the prototype of Israel for later generations'.[10]

Paul's own conversion exemplifies many of these points regarding the reading of Scripture in ways important for understanding much of what we will see in Irenaeus. Before his encounter with Christ, he considered himself to be 'blameless with respect to righteousness under the law' (Phil. 3:6), not needing salvation, and in fact persecuting Christians on the grounds of their obvious impiety. However, after his encounter, whatever

---

[9] Commenting on Christ's claim that 'Moses wrote of me' (John 5:46), Irenaeus says this means that 'the writings of Moses are his [i.e. Christ's] words', and extends this to include 'the words of the other prophets' (*haer.* 4.2.3). For the problems that arise when the synchronic character of Scripture, as the product of one author or as speaking of a single subject throughout, is replaced by a diachronic study of the text, attempting to reconstruct the 'original meaning' of its various parts, see Jon D. Levenson, 'The Eighth Principle of Judaism and the Literary Simultaneity of Scripture', *JR* 68 (1988), 205–25, repr. in Levenson, *The Hebrew Bible, The Old Testament, and Historical Criticism: Jews and Christians in Biblical Studies* (Louisville, KY: Westminster/John Knox, 1993).

[10] Cf. Michael Fishbane, *Biblical Interpretation in Ancient Israel* (Oxford: Clarendon Press, 1985), 376.

that may in fact have been, he concluded, with reference to the same Scripture, that all human beings since Adam have been held under the power of sin and death. The text of Scripture had not changed, but rather his starting point, his first principle or 'hypothesis'—the person and work of Christ—was new. Correlating and contrasting Adam and Christ, he understood the end in terms of the beginning and the beginning in terms of the end: Adam, who, prior to Paul's insight, appears very rarely in Scripture, is now understood as 'a type of the one to come' (Rom. 5:14). Paul also reflects on this hermeneutical turn, comparing it to the removal by the Lord, for all who turn to him, of the veil that lay over the face of Moses as he descended from the mountain and which still remains over the minds of those who now read Moses (now a text) without having turned to the Lord. That the veil is removed by Christ means that it is only in Christ that the glory of God is revealed, and revealed in the right reading of the Scriptures. Behind the veil, then, is nothing other than 'the light of the Gospel of the glory of Christ, who is the likeness of God', though this remains 'veiled' to those whose 'minds are blinded by the god of this world'. In this way, he identifies the God who said 'let light shine out of darkness' as the one who 'has shone in our hearts to give the light of the knowledge of the glory of God in the face of Christ' (2 Cor. 3:12–4:6). As Richard Hays points out, in this hermeneutical reading of the veiling and unveiling of Moses, the man and the text, and the Gospel, as Christ himself and the Gospel preached by the apostles, 'Scripture becomes—in Paul's reading—a metaphor, a vast trope that signifies and illuminates the Gospel of Jesus Christ'.[11]

This does not mean, however, that the Gospel is simply or straightforwardly a new interpretation or reading of an ancient Scripture, but rather that it is so on the basis of a new event, the death and resurrection of Christ, which provides the catalyst for the veil to be removed and the books to be opened, and itself now becomes the subject of interpretation. As God has acted in Christ in a definitive, an unexpected manner, making all things new (cf. Rev. 21:5), Scripture itself must be read anew. The 'word of the Cross', the preaching of 'Christ crucified', may well be a scandal for the Jews and folly for the Gentiles, but it alone, according to Paul, is 'the power of God' making known 'the wisdom of God' (1 Cor. 1:18–25). The goal now is not to understand the 'original meaning' of an ancient text, as in so much modern scriptural scholarship, but to

---

[11] Richard Hays, *Echoes of Scripture in the Letters of Paul* (New Haven and London: Yale University Press, 1989), 149.

understand Christ, who, by being explained 'according to the Scriptures', becomes the sole subject of Scripture throughout.[12]

The apostle's proclamation of Christ 'in accordance with the Scriptures' is clearly evident in the four Gospels accepted by Irenaeus, or rather in the four forms of the one Gospel (τὸ εὐαγγέλιον τετράμορφον, haer. 3.11.8), the forms of which he expounds by reference to passages from Scripture. In these Gospels, the accounts of Christ and his activity, culminating in the Passion and always told from that perspective and leading inexorably towards it, are described with constant allusion to scriptural imagery, from the very 'beginning of the Gospel of Jesus Christ', illustrated by a passage from Isaiah (Mark 1:1–3; Isa. 40:3), to the opening of the books by the risen Christ, mentioned earlier, and, most emphatically, in the statement of Christ himself in John: 'If you believed Moses, you would believe me, for he wrote of me' (John 5:46). The reasons Irenaeus gives for there only being four Gospels—that there are only four corners of the earth and four winds—are clearly secondary reflections on what is already a given fact, that, by this time, the number of Gospels had become an established part of the broad consensus and tradition, rather than a serious attempt to argue the case.[13] As such, since the 'Gospel of Truth' was but 'recently composed', it cannot lay claim to the same authority, and, in any case, as Irenaeus argues, it is totally 'unlike those which have been handed down by the apostles, as is shown from the Scriptures themselves' (haer. 3.11.9).

The exposition of the Gospel in terms drawn almost exclusively from the Scriptures can be seen in other subsequent writings, most poetically in *On Pascha*, by Melito of Sardis, another orator of the second sophistic period from Asia Minor alongside Irenaeus.[14] It is the very subject to which Irenaeus devotes a specific short work, *The Demonstration of the Apostolic Preaching*. Here he gives a clear, coherent, and concise exposition of the apostolic preaching without, however, making any extensive use of the apostolic writings, but rather by deriving the whole content of their preaching from the Scriptures themselves. He begins by briefly outlining

---

[12] James Barr makes a similar point, noting that 'large elements in the text [of the Genesis story of Adam] cannot be made to support Paul's use of the story without distortion of their meaning'. This is, he continues, because 'Paul was not interpreting the story in and for itself; he was really *interpreting Christ* through the use of images from this story' (*The Garden of Eden and the Hope of Immortality* (Minneapolis: Fortress Press, 1993), 89).

[13] The collection of four authoritative Gospels seems to go back to the turn of the second century, very likely in Asia Minor and perhaps associated with the shadowy figure of John the Elder. Cf. Hill, *Who Chose the Gospels?*

[14] See Hainsworth, 'The Force of the Mystery'.

the faith handed down by the elders who had known the apostles, summarized in the three articles of the 'canon of faith' through which the baptismal regeneration is effected (*Dem.* 3–7). After laying out his first principles, he then turns to the two interrelated tasks at hand in this demonstration: first, to recount, in the manner of the great apostolic speeches in Acts, the narrative of God's work of salvation that culminates in Christ (*Dem.* 8–42a), and, second, to demonstrate that what the apostles proclaimed to be fulfilled in Christ was indeed foretold in Scripture (*Dem.* 42b–97). Importantly, before beginning the second part, Irenaeus notes that, while, for God, the Son is indeed in the beginning, from all eternity, yet, as he has only now been revealed to us, 'before this he was not for us who did not know him' (*Dem.* 43). So, although, in the first part, Irenaeus recounted the scriptural narrative that, on his hypothesis, culminates in Christ, as preached by the apostles, a preaching that, as we have seen, is articulated in the texture of the same Scriptures, it is only in the second part that he is able to describe, retrospectively, how Jesus Christ was present throughout the economy, already being seen, in anticipation by the patriarchs (cf. esp. *Dem.* 44–5) and being spoken of, in anticipation, by the prophets.

The second point to note, from *haer.* 4.26.2 quoted above, is the apocalyptic and eschatological finality and completeness of the Gospel. The consummation of the things spoken of in Scripture, through types and parables, occurs with the Cross of Christ. The work of God is concluded and brought to completion: it is finished or perfected ($\tau\epsilon\tau\epsilon\lambda\epsilon\sigma\tau\alpha\iota$), as Christ himself says on the Cross (John 19:30). There are no further acts for God to perform or revelations to be given, but rather everything thereafter is determined and understood by this definitive revelation: the sealed books are opened, and the faith is 'delivered, once for all' (Jude 3), requiring now the exposition of the Scriptures in the preaching of the Gospel. Thus, for Irenaeus, the Gospel is unique precisely as apocalyptic and eschatological: it is only through this act of God in Christ, as preached by the apostles, that the types and prophecies of Scripture are unveiled to speak of the one and only Word of God, rather than mere myths and fables. Irenaeus appeals directly to this apocalyptic imagery in *haer.* 4.20.2, where he points out that, as Christ has been given all things by his Father (Matt. 11:27), he alone, as the judge of the living and the dead, has the key of David, and so he alone opens and shuts (Rev. 3:7). Using the imagery of Revelation 5, Irenaeus continues:

'No one, either in heaven or on earth, or under the earth, was able to open the book' of the Father, 'nor to look into it', with the exception of 'the Lamb who was slain and who redeemed us with his own blood', receiving from the same God, who made all things by the Word and adorned them by [his] Wisdom, power over all things when 'the Word became flesh'. (*haer.* 4.20.2; Rev. 5:3, 6, 9; John 1:14) The slain Lamb alone has received all power, wealth, wisdom, and might (Rev. 5:12), and so he alone is able to open the book, and this, Irenaeus specifies, is the book of the Father. Irenaeus very strikingly associates revelation of the content, the Word, of the paternal book by the slain Lamb with the Word becoming flesh, for it is the enfleshed, revealed, Word who alone makes known or exegetes (ἐξηγήσατο) the Father, as the Prologue of John concludes (John 1:18).[15] Just as the Gospel alone unlocks the treasures of Scripture, so also it is only in the Son, as preached in the Gospel, that the invisible and immeasurable God becomes visible and comprehensible (cf. *haer.* 4.4.2, 6.6).

The third point to note is that, for Irenaeus, the Cross is *the* definitive event in the revelation of God, occurring within our history yet with a significance that is eternal; the only perspective from which one can speak of the Word of God is that of the Cross.[16] The evangelical rereading of Scripture in the proclamation of the crucified Lord is the unique locus for the revelation of God, and so this 'eschatological *apokalypsis* of the Cross', in Richard Hays's words, provides the hermeneutical lens through which Scripture is now refracted with 'a profound new symbolic coherence'.[17] Irenaeus continues the passage from 4.26.1, cited above, by noting how this manner of reading the Scriptures was revealed only after the Passion, when the risen Christ demonstrated to his disciples from the Scriptures that 'the Christ must suffer and enter into his glory' (*haer.* 4.26.1; Luke 24:26, 47). As such, the Passion of Christ is revealed to be the subject of the Law and the Prophets.

In this manner, therefore, they did also see the Son of God as a human conversing with human beings; they prophesied what was to happen, saying that he who was

---

[15] As Rolf Noorman (*Irenäus als Paulusinterpret: Zur Rezeption und Wirkung der paulinischen und deuteropaulinischen Briefe im Werke des Irenäus von Lyon*, Wissenschaftliche Untersuchungen zum Neuen Testament, 2.66 (Tübingen: Mohr, 1994), 451) notes, Irenaeus does not differentiate too sharply between the 'Incarnation' and the 'Passion', neither as 'events' nor in terms of their effects; both are embraced in the 'coming' of Christ in the last times. Cf. *haer.* 3.16.6; 4.10.2; 5.17.3. All the 'works' of God throughout the economy are told only from the perspective of the opening of the books in 'the last times' and so are embraced together in this apocalyptic revelation.
[16] For the role of the Cross in Irenaeus more generally, see Daniel Wanke, *Das Kreuz Christi bei Irenäus von Lyon*, Beihefte zur ZNTW 99 (Berlin: Walter de Gruyter, 2000).
[17] Hays, *Echoes*, 169.

not come as yet is present [*eum qui nondum aderat adesse*] and proclaiming the impassible as passible, and declaring that the One in the heavens had descended into the 'dust of death'. (*haer.* 4.20.8; Ps 21:16 LXX)

Christ is not yet present, but his saving Passion, proclaimed in the Gospel, is already the subject of the prophets' words and visions. Having the Gospel pre-preached to him by the Scripture, that in him all nations will be blessed (cf. Gal. 3:8), 'the prophet Abraham saw in the Spirit the day of the Lord's coming and the dispensation of his suffering', so that those who follow his example, trusting in God and taking up the Cross as Isaac did the wood, might be saved (*haer.* 4.5.4–5). The same subject is also revealed in the actions of the prophets. Discussing Elisha's actions in 2 Kings 6:1–7, and interpreting the axe by means of the words of John the Baptist (Matt. 3:10), Irenaeus comments:

By this action the prophet pointed out that the sure Word of God, which we, having negligently lost by means of a tree, did not discover, we should receive anew by the dispensation of a tree ... This Word, then, which was hidden from us, did the dispensation of the tree make manifest, as we have said. For as we lost it by means of a tree, by means of a tree again was it made manifest to all, showing the height, the length, and the breadth, in itself; and, as one of our predecessors observed, 'Through the extension of the hands, gathering together the two peoples to one God'. (*haer.* 5.17.4)[18]

This emphasis, that it is through the Cross that the Word is revealed, means that the Word of God is always related to the Cross, is always, as it were, cruciform. Just as Scripture is permeated, in this way, by the figure of the Cross, Irenaeus also points out, following Justin, that the Word of God who adorned and arranged the heavens and earth does so in a likewise cruciform manner.[19]

---

[18] The explanation given here for the significance of the Cross, the inclusion of the Gentiles, supports Hays's conclusion that Paul's interpretative strategies are more ecclesiocentric than Christocentric, so that 'his typological reading strategy extends a typological trajectory begun already in the texts themselves', referring to the typological reading of Yahweh's dealings with Israel in Deut. 32 and Isaiah. Hays, *Echoes*, 164, cf. 84–7.

[19] Cf. *Dem.* 34, and Justin, *1 Apol.* 60. A. Rousseau, 'Le Verbe "imprimé en forme de croix dans l'univers": A propos de deux passages de saint Irénée', in *Armeniaca: Mélanges d'études arméniennes* (Venice: S. Lazarus, 1969), 67–82. This tradition is echoed, a couple of centuries later, by Gregory of Nyssa (*de Tridiu spatio*, GNO 9.303; trans S. G. Hall, 48). Similarly, in the seventh century, Isaac of Syria (*The Second Part*, chapter 11.3) comments: 'We do not speak of a power in the Cross that is any different from that (power) through which the worlds came into being, (a power) which is eternal and without beginning, and which guides creation all the time, without any break, in a divine way and beyond the understanding of all, in accordance with the will of his divinity.'

136   *Irenaeus of Lyons*

The fourth point to note is how Irenaeus understands the relationship between the Scriptures and the Gospel. His arresting association in *haer.* 4.20.2, considered above, of the Word becoming flesh with opening of the books by the slain Lamb is paralleled by *haer.* 1.9.2, in which he quotes this verse from John's Prologue for the first time and connects it to the final literary or rhetorical term that is important for the structure and method of Irenaeus' theology—'recapitulation'. For Irenaeus the subject of Scripture is clearly always the crucified and risen Christ, as preached by the apostles 'in accordance with Scripture', and so it is to him that all the various divine titles are attributed, as in the book of Revelation, where it is to the one 'clad in a robe dipped in blood' that the title 'Word of God' is ascribed (Rev. 19:13). This stands in stark contrast, as we saw in the previous chapter, to his opponents' personification of these various titles as diverse heavenly beings. After emphasizing that John spoke only of one Jesus Christ—declaring of Christ that 'this "the Word of God" [John 1:1], this "the Only-begotten" [John 1:18], this the Maker of all things, this "the true Light who enlightens every man" [John 1:9], this "the Maker of the world" [John 1:10], this the one who "came to his own" [John 1:11], this the one who "became flesh and dwelt among us"' [John 1:14]—rather than the various conjunctions of Aeons in his opponents' systems, he concludes: 'For, summing up concerning the Word in the beginning mentioned by him above [Ἀνακεφαλαιούμενος γὰρ περὶ τοῦ εἰρημένου αὐτῷ ἄνω ἐν ἀρχῇ λόγου], he adds, "And the Word was made flesh, and dwelt among us"' (*haer.* 1.9.2). John's statement that 'the Word became flesh' is interpreted by Irenaeus in terms of the recapitulation of everything that has previously been said by him.[20] It is, as we have seen, only in the apostolic preaching 'in accordance with Scripture' that we 'see' the revelation of God in Christ, and so it is, in a very real sense, here, in the Gospel, that the Word becomes flesh.[21]

The term 'recapitulation', as other important terms for Irenaeus such as 'hypothesis' and 'economy', has a well-defined meaning in Hellenistic literary and rhetorical theory.[22] The Roman rhetorician Quintilian,

---

[20] Robert M. Grant notes that 'his context is strictly literary when he asserts that the evangelist John "sums up" the account in his Prologue (John 1:1–13) by saying that the Word became flesh (1:14)' (*Irenaeus of Lyons* (New York: Routledge, 1997), 50).

[21] Ignatius had already drawn this comparison, exhorting his readers to 'take refuge in the Gospel as in the flesh of Christ' (*Phil.* 5.1).

[22] A weakness of many accounts of Irenaeus' use of 'recapitulation' is that they have not paid attention to this literary dimension, but instead see it as a controlling 'idea' or 'concept' for his theology, analysing it into its various components. Eric Osborn (*Irenaeus*, 97–8), for

writing a century before Irenaeus, provides a succinct and useful statement of the meaning of this term:

> The repetition and grouping of the facts, which the Greeks call ἀνακεφαλαίωσις [recapitulation] and some of our own writers call enumeration, serves both to refresh the memory of the judge and to place the whole case before his eyes, and, even although the facts may have made little impression on him in detail, their cumulative effect is considerable.[23]

That is, the rhetorical device of 'recapitulation' serves to provide a summary of the whole case or a restatement of the argument in an epitome or résumé, bringing together the whole into one conspectus, so that, while the particular details will have made little impact because of their number or apparent insignificance, the picture summarily stated as a whole will be more forceful, giving new significance to each particular detail and bringing them all together into one. In this way, recapitulation provides a résumé which, as a succinct synopsis, is clearer and therefore more effective.

The apostle Paul uses 'recapitulation' as a literary summary when he comments that the various commandments of Scripture have been 'summed up in this word [ἐν τῷ λόγῳ τούτῳ ἀνακεφαλαιοῦται], "You shall love your neighbour as yourself"' (Rom. 13:9). And it is precisely in this way, and in reference to this passage, that Irenaeus explains how God has provided us with an epitome or résumé of the Law in the Gospel:

> And that, not by the prolixity of the Law, but according to the brevity of faith and love, men were going to be saved, Isaiah, in this fashion, says, 'he will complete and cut short [his] Word in righteousness; for God will make a concise Word in all the world'.[24] And therefore the Apostle Paul says, 'Love is the fulfilment of the Law' [Rom. 13:10], for he who loves God has fulfilled the Law. Moreover, the Lord

---

instance, devoting two chapters to 'recapitulation', begins with this disclaimer: 'The complexity of the concept is formidable. At least eleven different ideas—unification, repetition, redemption, perfection, inauguration and consummation, totality, the triumph of Christus Victor, ontology, epistemology, and ethics (or being, truth, and goodness)—are combined in different permutations.' All these themes are certainly at play in Irenaeus, but we should not forget the grounding of all this in the relationship between the Scriptures and the Gospel which is that of a literary 'recapitulation'. For a summary of the century of scholarship on this term following in the wake of Harnack, see Holsinger-Friesen, *Irenaeus and Genesis*, 1–26, who rightly reminds us that, when we read Irenaeus himself, we 'shall discover "recapitulation" to involve Irenaeus' performance of biblical *texts* rather than of concepts' (p. 22), though he himself does not look to the background of the term in rhetorical and literary theory or expound it in terms of the relationship between Scripture and Gospel.

[23] Quintilian, *Inst.* 6.1.1.
[24] Isa. 10:22–3; Rom. 9:28. This point is lost in the RSV translation: 'for the Lord will execute his sentence upon the earth with rigour and dispatch.'

also, when he was asked, which is the first commandment, said, 'You shall love the Lord your God with [your] whole heart and [your] whole strength; and the second is like it, you shall love your neighbour as yourself. On these two commandments', he says, 'depend all the Law and the Prophets' [Matt. 22:37–40]. So he has increased, by means of our faith in him, our love towards God and towards the neighbour, rendering us godly, righteous and good. And therefore he made 'a concise word < ... > in the world'. (*Dem.* 87)[25]

Although the Scriptures speak of the Word of God, their prolixity effectively renders the Word obscure, hidden under a veil, and so invisible and incomprehensible—types and parables that are enigmas and ambiguities. The work of God in Christ, therefore, as preached by the apostles 'in accordance with Scripture', has 'cut short' the Law and produced a 'concise word', which as an epitome or résumé is clearer and therefore more effective, increasing our faith in God and our love for him and our neighbour, and so providing salvation. Yet, while being 'cut short', it is nevertheless identical in content: the Gospel, as the recapitulation of Scripture in a 'concise word', is its fulfilment. The apostolic proclamation of the crucified Christ is composed from the texture of Scripture, no longer proclaimed in the obscurity of types and prophecies, but clearly and concisely, in a résumé: what was prolix becomes condensed, what was incomprehensible becomes comprehensible, the unseen becomes seen, the invisible visible—the Word becomes flesh.[26]

---

[25] In quotations from the *Demonstration* words in angled brackets < > indicate a correction of the text printed in PO 12.5, and words in square brackets [ ] are supplementary additions to the text.
[26] Thomas F. Torrance (*Divine Meaning: Studies in Patristic Hermeneutics* (Edinburgh: T&T Clark, 1995), 121), puts the matter well, illustrating the synchronic and diachronic aspect of the economy: 'In the whole course of Christ's life from birth to Passion and resurrection, there is presented an epitome of God's saving acts, so that it is to the pattern enshrined in the humanity of Jesus Christ that Irenaeus turns for his precise understanding of the universal economy of God. The principle term he uses to express this is ἀνακεφαλαίωσις or *recapitulatio*, which he applies both to what happened in the life of Jesus himself and to what God accomplished through him and will accomplish in the final actualization of his saving will within creation. "Recapitulation" means that redemptive activity of God in Jesus Christ was not just a transcendent act that touched our existence in space and time at one point, but an activity that passed into our existence and is at work within it, penetrating back to the beginning in the original creation retracing and reaffirming in it the divine Will, and reaching forward to the consummation in the new creation in which all things are gathered up, thus *connecting the end with the beginning.*' It is necessary to specify, however, that this epitome of God's saving acts throughout the economy in the life of Christ is seen in the Gospel as preached by the apostles 'in accordance with the Scriptures', so recognizing the scriptural or literary dimension of this recapitulation.

It is necessary to have a firm grasp of Irenaeus' understanding of the relationship between the Scriptures and the Gospel if we are not to misunderstand his exposition of the economy of God described therein. Irenaeus does not understand this in terms of a history recorded in the 'Old Testament' continuing on to a new phase in the 'New Testament', as two bodies of literature between which, if we so wish, we might be able to discern correspondences, or 'types', and continuities. There is, rather, a strict identity between the Scriptures and the Gospel, both speaking of the 'once for all' work of God in Christ: at length and diachronically, on the one hand, through various figures in the Scriptures; in brief, on the other hand, recapitulated together, synchronically, in the Gospel, drawing from the Scriptures. On the basis of this identity, Irenaeus can counter his opponents, both those who would broaden this scriptural revelation and those who would curtail it. Against the Valentinians, Irenaeus can point to the eschatological completeness of what is revealed through the Cross of Christ expounded through the Scriptures: although there are abundantly more treasures to bring forth from the Scriptures in proclaiming Christ, there is no new hypothesis. And, on the other hand, he can maintain, against Marcion, that there is in fact nothing new in the Gospel: what Christ is preached as having done, in the Gospel, is what he has done in directing the economy from the beginning, in all the symbolic actions and words recorded in Scripture. So, he exhorts Marcion: 'read with earnest care that Gospel which has been given to us by the apostles, and read with earnest care the prophets, and you will find that the whole conduct, and all the doctrine and all the sufferings of our Lord, were predicted through them' (haer. 4.34.1).

To those who would then ask 'what new thing then did the Lord bring by his advent?' Irenaeus simply answers: 'Christ himself!' Irenaeus compares this to the announcement of the arrival of a king and his actual arrival: the king's arrival is heralded beforehand, so that those who will entertain the king can prepare; the king's arrival brings nothing new apart from himself, though the joyful fulfilment of what had previously only been announced is itself a novelty—'Know that he brought all novelty by bringing himself who had been announced' (haer. 4.34.1).

Finally, this recapitulation of Scripture in the Gospel provides Irenaeus with the key to understanding and explaining the person and work of Jesus Christ himself and his relationship to God, his Father. The recapitulation of Scripture in the Gospel is, according to Irenaeus, complete: there is no part of Scripture that speaks of God independently from Christ, and so what is revealed in Christ in this way is nothing other than a revelation of

God himself, the God who *is* the Father and Creator. Moreover, to suppose, as some did, that the Son who has been revealed is distinct, as 'another God', from the Father, who in turn, by virtue of the supreme transcendence of his divinity, is unable to come into contact with created reality and manifest himself, would undermine the very revelation given in Christ: Christ would no longer reveal the Father, in looking at him we would not be granted a vision of the one true God, and so would not be brought into communion with him.[27] For Irenaeus, the Father is indeed invisible and infinitely beyond human comprehension, and so, he argues, if human beings are to see him and to enter into communion with him, to share in his life, rather than just hear reports about him, then, just as the Gospel provides a visible synopsis of the Scriptures, the Christ that it proclaims provides a 'measure' of the 'immeasurable Father' (*haer.* 4.4.2), *in* whose human nature, rather than behind it, we can see the invisible Father.[28] Thus, as Irenaeus puts it, 'the Father is the invisible of the Son, but the Son the visible of the Father' (*haer.* 4.6.6). Yet, at the same time, the Son preserves the invisibility of the Father, in order that we might never think we comprehend all there is to know, and so come to think little of the Father and then turn away from him, the only source of life, but rather that there might always be something to which we might advance, in order that the glory of God might continue to be demonstrated, for this glory is, as Irenaeus puts it, the 'living human being', whose life is 'the vision of God' (*haer.* 4.20.7).

The coming Christ

Pivoted, as this recapitulation is, on the person of Christ and his Cross, the Gospel affirms, as we have seen, the *one* Jesus Christ, the subject about whom Scripture speaks and to whom all the divine titles apply. Thus when Irenaeus sets out to expound 'the entire mind of the apostles regarding our Lord Jesus Christ' (*haer.* 3.16.1), he begins by pointing out that John 'knew one and the same [R. εἷς καὶ ὁ αὐτός] Word of God, the

---

[27] It is noteworthy that Irenaeus criticizes those who 'allege that, the Father of all being invisible, the one seen by the prophets was another [God]' for being 'altogether ignorant of prophecy' (*haer.* 4.20.5). The unity of the one God is connected with the singular opening of the Scriptures by Christ determining thereby the prophetic nature and character of what had been written.

[28] Cf. D. Minns, *Irenaeus* (London: Geoffrey Chapman, 1994), 38–43; Real Tremblay, *La Manifestation et la vision de Dieu selon saint Irénée de Lyon*, Münsterische Beiträge zur Theologie, 41 (Münster: Aschendorff, 1978).

Only-begotten, incarnate for our salvation, Jesus Christ our Lord' (*haer.* 3.16.2). Likewise Matthew also 'recognized one and the same Jesus Christ', when he recounted 'his human birth from the Virgin': Matthew did not write that the 'birth of Jesus took place in this way', but that 'the birth of Christ took place in this way', who was called Emmanuel, so demonstrating that 'the Son of God was born from a Virgin', in order that 'we should not imagine that Jesus was one, and Christ another, but should know them to be one and the same' (*haer.* 3.16.2). Paul also knew only one God and one Son, Jesus Christ (*haer.* 3.16.3), bringing together his statements concerning the appointing of Christ as the Son of God at the resurrection (Rom. 1:1–4), his descent according to the flesh (Rom. 9:5), and his birth at the fullness of time (Gal. 4:4–5). After demonstrating a similar position in Mark and Luke, Irenaeus concludes, apropos of Luke:

> The Gospel, therefore, knew of no other Son of Man but him who was of Mary, who also suffered, and no Christ who flew away from Jesus before the Passion; but it recognizes as the Son of God this Jesus Christ who was born, this same one who suffered and rose again, as John the disciple of the Lord confirms, saying, 'These things are written so that you might believe that Jesus is the Christ, the Son of God, and believing you might have eternal life in his name' [John 20:31], foreseeing these blasphemous canons [*regulas*] that divide the Lord, as far as lies in their power, saying that he was formed of two different substances [*ex altera et altera substantia dicentes eum factum*]. (*haer.* 3.16.5)

In context, this statement that Jesus Christ was not 'formed of two different substances' refers to his opponents' teaching that an Aeon called 'Christ' or 'Saviour' descended upon the man Jesus and departed from him prior to the Passion (*haer.* 3.16.1; 11.3). For Irenaeus, in contrast, there is one Jesus Christ, the one Son of God: he it was who was born, suffered, and rose again. Yet it also suggests that we should not conceptualize the relation between divinity and humanity in the one Christ in terms of two distinct 'parts', one passible and visible, the other impassible and invisible. For Irenaeus, the distinction between God and created reality is not thought of in terms of distinct substances existing in parallel, and therefore commensurate with each other, but rather in terms of the relationship between God as Creator and the created reality he brings about: 'In this God differs from the human being, that God makes and the human being is made' (*haer.* 4.11.2). For Irenaeus there is no question but that Jesus Christ is everything that it is to be God and everything that it is to be human, but this is not revealed separately or in division, as if one 'face', as it were, revealed one aspect and another 'face' revealed the other, but together, without confusion or change: on the one hand, Christ is the one who *creates*, fashioning human beings into the image and likeness of God; on the other hand, he does this by himself fulfilling the economy, *being made* the living human being. The one Jesus Christ, as God, creates and fashions us, by himself being made human and undergoing the Passion.

There are not two 'parts', then, to the one Jesus Christ, one invisible the other visible, but it is he himself who, as we have seen, is both invisible and visible, being hidden in the type and prophecies of Scripture, yet revealed in the Gospel recapitulating Scripture. Understanding Christ in this hermeneutic manner has further implications not appreciated, Irenaeus claims, by his opponents:

[They] stray from the truth, because their teaching forsakes him who is truly God, not knowing that his only-begotten Word, who is always present with the human race, was united and closely grafted to his own handiwork, according to the Father's good pleasure, and who 'became flesh' [John 1:14], is himself Jesus Christ our Lord, who did also suffer for us, and rose for our sakes, and who is again coming in the glory of his Father, to raise up all flesh, and for the manifestation of salvation, and to reveal the rule of just judgement to all who were made subject to him. There is, therefore, as we have shown, one God the Father and one Christ Jesus, who is coming throughout the whole economy,[29] 'recapitulating all things in himself' [Eph. 1:10]. But in this 'all things' is the human being, the handiwork of God, and thus he recapitulated the human being in himself—the invisible becoming visible; the incomprehensible becoming comprehensible; the impassible becoming passible; and the Word, human—'recapitulating all things in himself', so that just as in the super-celestial, spiritual and invisible things, the Word of God is the Sovereign Ruler, so also in the things visible and corporeal he might possess sovereign rule, and thus, by taking to himself the primacy and constituting himself the head of the Church, he might draw all things to himself at the proper time. (*haer*. 3.16.6; cf. Col. 1:15–18; Eph. 1:22)

The identity between the Scriptures and the Gospel, preached by the apostles 'in accordance with' and recapitulating Scripture, means that the Christ it proclaims has always been present with the human race,

---

[29] Steenberg translates the clause *veniens per universam dispositionem* as 'who comes through every economy', wanting to emphasize that 'the Word was present in every one of the "lesser economies", not simply that he was present in the whole of the final economy; much less that he is in the universal economy, as Sagnard (SC 34, p. 293) has it' (ACW 64, 164). However, given what we have seen, and will consider further below, of the connection between the beginning and the end of the one economy, I have preferred to remain with the SC translation, preserved in the later edition by Rousseau, in which he suggests for a retroversion: ὁ ἐλθὼν καθ' ὅλην τὴν οἰκονομίαν (SC 211, 313).

'grafted to his handiwork': Jesus Christ, 'coming throughout the whole economy', always is, and remains, even in the Gospels, the Coming One (ὁ ἐρχόμενος, cf. e.g. Matt. 11:3). It is again, as we saw earlier, by recapitulating all things in himself, including the human being, that the invisible, incomprehensible, impassible Word becomes visible, comprehensible, and passible—becomes human. The mention of the 'proper time' as the point at which Christ draws all things to himself, that is, by ascending the Cross,[30] as the crux by which Scripture is focused into an epitome, is picked up in the following paragraph where Irenaeus interprets the exchange between Christ and his mother at Cana (John 2:3–4) as his mother urging Christ to perform the miracle because she 'desired before the appointed time to partake of the cup of concision [*compendii poculo*]' (*haer.* 3.16.7): the cup that results from Christ's Passion is the epitome in which salvation is granted.

These themes are picked up again in *haer.* 3.18, where the continual presence of the Word, 'united to his own handiwork' (*haer.* 3.16.6), is reaffirmed:

the Word, who existed in the beginning with God, by whom all things were made, who was also always present with the human race, was in the last times, according to the time appointed by the Father, united to his own workmanship, inasmuch as he became a human being liable to suffering. (*haer.* 3.18.1)

After voicing the objection that, if Christ was born then, he could not have previously existed, Irenaeus continues:

For we have shown that the Son of God did not begin to exist then, being eternally with the Father; but when he became incarnate, and was made human, he recapitulated in himself the long unfolding [*expositionem*] of human beings, furnishing us with salvation by way of a compendium [*in compendio*], so that what we lost in Adam—to be according to the image and likeness of God—that we might recover in Christ Jesus. (*haer.* 3.18.1)

The Word becoming flesh is an eschatological event, in the 'last times'. As one coming throughout the whole economy, it is only at the end that Christ, recapitulating the long narrative given in Scripture, provides salvation in the concise word, the Gospel, which makes what had been

---

[30] Cf. *haer.* 5.17.4, cited above, and *haer.* 4.2.7: 'For the Law never hindered them from believing in the Son of God; but it even exhorted them to do so, saying that human beings can be saved in no other way from the old wound of the serpent than by believing in him who, in the likeness of sinful flesh, is lifted up from the earth upon the tree of martyrdom and draws all things to himself and vivifies the dead.'

invisible and incomprehensible to be visible and comprehensible. And this is done, as Irenaeus specifies and we will examine in what follows, in order that what we lost in Adam we might regain in Christ, recapitulating us in himself and rendering us in the image and likeness of God.

THE ARC OF THE ECONOMY

As was noted in the previous chapter, adherence to the canon of truth was not understood by Irenaeus to curtail further reflection or analysis, but rather to provide a firm basis upon which this can be done, for all reflection, if it is not to dissolve into endless speculation, requires a criterion. Thus, after giving his fullest statement of the canon in *haer.* 1.10.1, Irenaeus continues in *haer.* 1.10.3 by indicating possible lines of enquiry for those who want to understand the faith more fully. This cannot be done, Irenaeus asserts, by changing the 'hypothesis' itself, by postulating, for instance, another God other than the Creator, maker, and nourisher of this universe, or another Christ or Only-begotten, for, quite simply, this would be a different project altogether. Rather one should bring out more clearly the meaning of those things spoken of in parables in accord with 'the hypothesis of the truth'. In particular, one should seek:

to expound the dealings and economy of God, which occurred for the sake of humanity; to make clear that God was long-suffering with regard to the apostasy of the angels who transgressed and the disobedience of humans; to set forth why God made some things temporal, others eternal, some heavenly, others eternal; to understand why God, being invisible, yet appeared to the prophets, not in one form but differently to different ones; to indicate why several covenants were made with humanity, and to teach the character of each covenant; to search out why 'God consigned all to disobedience, that he may have mercy on all' [Rom. 11:32], and to acknowledge thankfully [εὐχαριστεῖν] why the Word of God 'became flesh' [John 1:14] and suffered, and to relate why the coming [παρουσία] of the Son of God was in the last times [ἐπ' ἐσχάτων τῶν καιρῶν], that is, [why] the Beginning appeared at the end; to unfold as much as lies in Scripture concerning the end and the things to come; and not pass over in silence why God made the Gentiles, who were despaired of, co-heirs, co-incorporated, and co-partakers with the saints; and to expound how this mortal, fleshly [body] shall put on immortality and the corruptible incorruptibility [cf. 1 Cor. 15:53–4]; and to proclaim how he says '[Those who were] not a people, are a people, and she who was not beloved is beloved' [cf. Hos. 2:25; Rom. 9:25], and how 'The children of her who was desolate are more than her who is married' [cf. Isa. 54:1; Gal. 4:27]. For regarding these, and other such points, the apostle exclaims: 'O the depths of riches and wisdom and knowledge of God; how unsearchable are his judgements and inscrutable his ways!' [Rom. 11:33].[31]

All these points are not theological items deriving from the rule of truth, nor do they, together, form a 'system' of theological doctrine; they are rather, as the concluding quotation from Paul indicates, openings into the mysteries of the wisdom and riches of God deployed in his dealings with the human race, the economy. They are, moreover, ones that are not given to be reflected upon for one's own intellectual satisfaction, but rather, as the various verbs indicate—to preach, expound, demonstrate—to be made public rather than kept in silence. Despite the apostle's awe at the inscrutability of God's ways, Irenaeus expounds each of these topics during the course of *Against the Heresies*, by following the apostle's lead in correlating Adam and Christ, expanding this parallel into an all-embracing understanding of the economy of God or the symphony of salvation.

Adam and Christ

Perhaps the most striking, and certainly the most characteristically Irenaean, point set before the theologian is that the beginning appeared at the end. As we have seen, Irenaeus is clear that the only perspective from which one can contemplate the economy of God, from its beginning to its conclusion, is from the end point, the apocalyptic opening of the Scriptures at the end of the ages in the light of the Cross of Christ. Irenaeus is prepared to accept, moreover, that this structure of revelation qualifies how we speak of Christ himself. The genealogy given in the Gospel of Luke (*haer.* 3:23–38), tracing the lineage of Christ back to Adam, demonstrates, according to Irenaeus, how Christ has recapitulated all generations in himself, connecting the end to the beginning. It is for this reason, he says, that Paul could describe Adam as 'the type of the one to come' (Rom. 5:14),

> because the Word, the Fashioner of all things, prefigured in him the future economy relating to the Son of God on behalf of the human race, God having predetermined the first, the animated human that is, so that he should be saved by the spiritual [one]; for, since the Saviour pre-exists, it was necessary that the one to

---

[31] *haer.* 1.10.3, following, largely, the textual emendations proposed by Rousseau (SC 263, pp. 226–9) and Unger (ACW 55, 188–90). On this text, see Alfred Bengsch, *Heilsgeschichte und Heilswissen: Eine Untersuchung zur Struktur und Entfaltung des theologischen Denkens im Werk 'Adversus Haereses' des hl. Irenäus von Lyon* (Leipzig: St Benno, 1957), 51–6, and W. C. van Unnik, 'An Interesting Document of Second Century Theological Discussion (Irenaeus, Adv. Haer. 1.10.3)', *VC* 31 (1977), 196–228.

be saved should also exist, so that the Saviour should not be without purpose. (*haer.* 3.22.3)[32]

In Adam, the Word sketched out in advance what would be revealed and established in the Son of God, Christ himself. The description of Adam as a 'type' implies the prior existence of the one of whom he is a type.[33] As such, the one who was to come exists before Adam; it was by him and for him that Adam came into existence, and, furthermore, as he exists as the Saviour, Adam came into existence to be saved by him. Thus, though only appearing at the end, this one is, nevertheless, the true beginning.

This is a remarkable statement and for our modern theological sensibilities perhaps rather jarring. Yet it is entirely consequential and coherent, and a position held right through to the end of the Byzantine era.[34] It highlights the fact, as we have been emphasizing, that Irenaeus theologizes strictly from within the economy, from what can in fact be known and spoken about, with the right hermeneutic, of God's activity and revelation in Christ. He resists any attempt to seek a higher perspective to speak about God prior to and independent from creation, a standpoint that would have to be supra-human and, indeed, above God himself; to attempt to speak from such a perspective would, for Irenaeus, be not only presumptuous but also groundless. Yet, since the starting point for Christian theology is the work of God in Christ, understood through the opening of the Scriptures, the Christ who is now known to be the one to whom God said 'Let us make the human being' is already known to be the Saviour, to

---

[32] This is a difficult text; for full discussion see Rousseau (SC 210, pp. 371–2) and Steenberg (ACW 64, 195–8) with reference to prior literature. I have adopted Rousseau's suggestion of *in eo* instead of *in semetipsum*, which Steenberg retains and renders 'with a view to himself', rather than 'in him', though he accepts that 'if *in semetipsum* is retained, Adam must in any case be implied in the clause'. I have adopted Steenberg's reading of *generis humani* 'as if it were a dative of advantage'.

[33] The word 'type', τύπος, comes from τύπτω, 'to strike', 'to blow', and so primarily means 'impression'—for instance, the 'stamp' left in wax when it is struck by a seal; the seal must exist prior to the impression.

[34] See, for instance, the statement of Nicholas Cabasilas: 'It was for the new human being that human nature was created at the beginning, and for him mind and desire were prepared... It was not the old Adam who was the model for the new, but the new Adam for the old... For those who have known him first, the old Adam is the archetype because of our fallen nature. But for him who sees all things before they exist, the first Adam is the imitation of the second. To sum it up: the Saviour first and alone showed to us the true human being, who is perfect on account of both character and life and in all other respects' (*The Life in Christ*, 6.91–4. ed. and French trans. M.-H. Congourdeau, SC 361 (Paris: Cerf, 1990); Eng. trans. C. J. deCatanzaro (Crestwood, NY: St Vladimir's Seminary Press, 1974), where it is numbered as 6.12).

'pre-exist' as Saviour, and so Adam's relation to his maker is always already that of being saved by the Saviour. We are here far removed from the debate between Thomas Aquinas and Duns Scotus about whether the Word would have become incarnate had Adam not fallen, a debate that has all too frequently set the parameters for interpreting Irenaeus.[35] We are also far removed from any attempt to think of creation and salvation as being respectively, in rather crude terms, 'Plan A', followed by the 'Fall', which is then rectified by 'Plan B'. Starting with Christ, Irenaeus would rather see creation *and* salvation, with carefully defined nuances considered below, as being not two moments within one economy, but rather as coextensive, as the *one* economy: God's continuously creative work throughout the economy, resulting in the end in the one who is in the image and likeness of God, is salvation. And, as such, Irenaeus can even say that it was necessary for Adam to come into existence, not implying any lack or need in God himself, but simply as a consequence of the fact that the starting point for all theology is Jesus Christ, the Saviour.

This point is fundamental and follows on from Irenaeus' understanding of the relation between Scripture and Gospel, in which the Gospel is not simply the next stage or a new step in God's dealings with the human race, but rather the recapitulation of Scripture through the Cross in a concise word. The significance of this can again be illustrated by the example of Paul, whose hermeneutic turn we considered in the previous section: it is only after his encounter with Christ that Paul understood the human predicament, which he then expounded in terms of the contrast between Adam and Christ. To paraphrase E. P. Sanders, the solution comes first, and then the problem is understood, or, in more Irenaean terms, starting from the perfected and completed work of God in Christ, we now understand the preliminary nature of what came before.[36] Seen in this way, from the very beginning Adam is always and already 'the type of the

---

[35] As Gustav Wingren comments, these debates in Irenaean scholarship 'might lead one to ask if the main question is really whether Irenaeus followed Thomas or Duns Scotus!' (*Man and the Incarnation*, 92–3, n. 37).

[36] Cf. E. P. Sanders, *Paul and Palestinian Judaism* (Philadelphia: Fortress Press, 1977), 475: 'Paul's logic seems to run like this: in Christ God has acted to save the world; therefore the world is in need of salvation; but God also gave the law; if Christ is given for salvation, it must follow that the law could not have been; is the law then against the purpose of God which has been revealed in Christ? No, it has the function of consigning everyone to sin *so that* everyone could be saved by God's grace in Christ.' For further reflection on the implications of starting with Christ, see John Behr, *The Mystery of Christ: Life in Deaths* (Crestwood, NY: SVS Press, 2006), ch. 3.

one to come' and so cannot simply be considered in himself, as a finished product. Thus the death he subsequently brought into the world through his disobedience, and that disobedience itself, must be placed within the scope of the larger arc that moves from the original formation of Adam to its completion in Christ. In other words, the person and work of Christ cannot be understood simply as a response to the death that Adam brought upon himself. To take it as such would be to treat Adam as already sufficient unto himself and Christ's work as merely restoring that condition. Rather, starting instead with the person of Christ, the one whom the type prefigures, Adam is seen to be an initial sketch or a preliminary imprint of the figure of Christ. And the difference between the two, for Irenaeus, is that Christ alone first shows us the life of God in human form, so that the life of Adam, before as well as after subjecting himself to death, is but a foreshadowing of this. The difference between them then is not simply, though it certainly includes, the contrast between the disobedience shown by the human creature, Adam, and the obedience of the Son of God, Christ. Nor does it turn only upon Adam's subjecting himself to death through disobedience, as if it were mortality alone that needs to be overcome, for this would only return Adam to his former life, which is already set in an arc leading to something greater. As it is in the life-giving death of Christ, in obedience to the Father and voluntarily assumed for the sake of others, that the uncreated life of God is revealed and communicated to his creature, the contrasting position of Adam from the very beginning is that he did not live this life, but rather, as created and a preliminary sketch of what is to come, this life of Christ is something that he needs to grow into by learning through experience. The unfolding of the economy cannot, therefore, be told by beginning with Adam, considered in himself, proceeding to the 'Fall', then the 'history of salvation', and finally to Christ, but must be told in such a manner that the end and the beginning mutually inform each other in one arc, both synchronously, in that the arrangement of the whole is revealed together in its recapitulation, and diachronically, as it is unfolded throughout time.[37]

---

[37] The attempt to do this here marks the major departure from my earlier work, *Asceticism and Anthropology in Irenaeus and Clement*, OECS (Oxford: Oxford University Press, 2000), a slight revision of my doctoral dissertation ('Godly Lives: Asceticism and Anthropology, with Special Reference to Sexuality, in the Writings of St Irenaeus of Lyons and St Clement of Alexandria', D.Phil. Oxford University, 1995), in which I did indeed recount the economy of God by beginning with Adam and concluding with the beginning that appears at the end (*Asceticism and Anthropology*, 35–85), noting that the end is in fact the starting point, but not

To ask whether this means that God planned 'the Fall', or in Irenaeus' terms our apostasy and our death in that apostasy, would be, for Irenaeus, a mistaken question, or rather one that arises from a mistaken standpoint, imagining ourselves in the position of God before creation. As we have seen, for Irenaeus the task of theology is, as Balthasar put it, 'to *see* what *is*', rather than imagining a different starting point or another first principle. Rather, beginning from what has been revealed in Christ, we can see that his work encompasses the whole of creation and its history, *including* our apostasy and *transforming* it into one movement of salvation. This is in fact a theme that runs throughout Scripture, from Joseph being sold into slavery in Egypt, yet telling his brothers that 'God sent me before you to preserve life . . . So it was not you who sent me here but God' (Gen. 45:5, 8), to Christ himself, who, though he 'was crucified and killed by the hand of lawless men', yet he was, nevertheless, 'delivered up according to the definite plan and foreknowledge of God' (Acts 2:23). If human apostasy, and the death that is its consequence, cannot be turned inside out, as it were, to be utilized by the God who in Christ destroyed death by his death, so granting not only a restored (yet still mortal) breath of life but the life granted by the Spirit, which can no longer be touched by death since it is entered into through death, God would not, in fact, be almighty and all things would not be in his Hands. As difficult as Irenaeus' claims might seem to us, they testify to his sense that God's overwhelming omnipotence works through the paradox of strength in weakness and articulates this transforming power consistently and forcefully.

The Breath and the Spirit

It is not only the relation between Adam and Christ that is presented in the passage (3.22.3) cited above, but also the contrast between the two ends of the arc, which Irenaeus describes in terms of the different 'lives' by which they live: the type, Adam, is an animated human being, who is saved by the 'spiritual' one. Irenaeus is again drawing from Paul, this time from the contrast he makes between the first Adam, who by the 'breath of life' became a 'living soul' ($\psi\upsilon\chi\grave{\eta}\nu$ $\zeta\hat{\omega}\sigma\alpha\nu$), and 'the last Adam' who 'became a life-creating spirit'.[38] As the context in 1 Corinthians 15 makes clear, the

---

yet presenting the economy that way nor being explicit about the hermeneutic stance upon which it is based.

[38] 1 Cor. 15:45; Gen. 2:7. Cf. Jacques Fantino, 'Le Passage du Premier Adam au Second Adam comme expression du salut chez Irénée de Lyon', *VC* 52/4 (1998), 418–29.

transformation from one to the other is effected by the resurrection from the dead, in which what is sown in dishonour and weakness will be raised in glory and power, and what is sown as an 'animated body [σῶμα ψυχικόν]' will be raised as a 'spiritual body [σῶμα πνευματικόν]' (1 Cor. 15:44, 46). Unlike the RSV, which renders the first as 'physical body' in contrast to the 'spiritual body', with the implication that, when raised, the body is no longer 'physical', Irenaeus reads Paul as contrasting two different modes of life: the first is the 'animation' effected by the 'breath of life', and the second, the 'vivification' effected by the Holy Spirit, bestowed in Christ, rendering the same body as 'spiritual', with the transition between the two turning upon death, that of Christ himself and then those who die in him to be raised to life in him: 'what you sow does not come to life unless it dies' (1 Cor. 15:36). It is worth noting that when Irenaeus cites John 1:3–4 he does so in the form, also witnessed by many other early writers and manuscripts: 'All things came to be by him and without him nothing came to be. What came to be in him was life [ὃ γέγονεν ἐν αὐτῷ ζωὴ ἦν], and the life was the light of human beings.'[39] 'Life', strictly speaking, is what comes through Christ, and, in turn, those who do not live by this life are, simply, 'dead'.[40]

This contrast and the transformation from the first to the last is also treated by Irenaeus in *haer.* 5.1.3, which sets out the contrast between the 'animated' and the 'living' with the same intentionality and within the full scope of the economy. Irenaeus here tackles the 'Ebionites' who regard Jesus as a human son of Joseph and Mary, rather than accepting 'the union of God and human', and so remain in 'the old leaven of birth [*generationis*]'. They do not want to understand, Irenaeus says, that the Holy Spirit came upon Mary and the Power of the Most High overshadowed her, so that 'what is born [*quod generatum est*] is holy and the Son of the Most High God, the Father, who effected his [the Son's] Incarnation and demonstrated a new generation [*novam generationem*], so that as by the former generation we inherited death, so by this generation we might

---

[39] *haer.* 3.11.1, cf. 1.8.5. Cf. Origen, *Jo.* 2.132: 'Some copies, however, have, and perhaps not without credibility, "what came to be in him was life". Now if life is equivalent to "the light of human beings", no one who is in darkness is alive, and no one who is alive is in darkness, but everyone who is alive is also in light, and everyone who is in light is alive.' The Codex Sinaiticus and the Western text have this reading of John 1:3–4.

[40] Cf. *haer.* 5.9.1: 'Those, then, not having that which saves and forms into life, shall be, and shall be called, "flesh and blood" [1 Cor. 15:50], not having the Spirit of God in themselves. Wherefore they were spoken of by the Lord as "dead", for, he says, "Let the dead bury their dead" [Luke 9:60], because they do not have the Spirit which vivifies the human being.'

inherit life'. Rejecting the 'heavenly wine', wanting only the 'water of this world', they do not 'receive God so as to have communion with him, but remain in Adam who had been conquered and was expelled from paradise'. The mention of Adam is the occasion for Irenaeus to set out the arc of the economy in the terms that we have been considering. His opponents, he says, do not understand that

just as, at the beginning [*ab initio*] of our formation [*plasmationis*] in Adam, the breath of life from God, having been united [*unita*] to the handiwork [*plasmati*], animated [*animavit*] the human being and showed him to be a rational being, **so also**, at the end [*in fine*], the Word of the Father and the Spirit of God, having become united [*adunitus*] with the ancient substance of the formation [*plasmationis*] of Adam, rendered [*effecit*] the human being living [*viventem*] and perfect, bearing the perfect Father, **in order that just as** in the animated we all die, **so also** in the spiritual we may all be vivified [*vivificemur*]. For never at any time did Adam escape the Hands of God, to whom the Father speaking, said, 'Let us make the human being in our image, after our likeness' [Gen. 1:26]. And for this reason at the end [*fine*], 'not by the will of the flesh, nor by the will of man' [John 1:13], but by the good pleasure of the Father, his Hands perfected a living human being [*vivum perfecerunt hominem*], in order that Adam might become in the image and likeness of God. (*haer.* 5.1.3, emphasis added)

The two 'just as—so also' parallels are linked by a statement of intent: the beginning of our formation, in Adam, is animation by a breath of life, whereas its end, in Christ, is vivification of the ancient substance by the Holy Spirit, rendering the handiwork a living and perfect human being, and this has been established with the intention that as we all die in the animated life of Adam we may be vivified in the spiritual life of Christ. That the beginning and the end are united in one intentional economy is further emphasized by the statement that Adam 'never escaped the Hands of God', being continuously fashioned and prepared to live the life of God. The perfected living human being does not result, for Irenaeus, from the 'old generation', or, borrowing words from John's Prologue, 'from the will of the flesh or the will of man', but rather by the good pleasure of the Father in the 'new generation', and so the living human being is none other than Christ himself, who enables Adam also to become 'in the image and likeness of God'.[41]

---

[41] Holsinger-Friesen, *Irenaeus and Genesis*, 155, notes that 'Irenaeus' reading of John 1.13 follows the Western tradition where the verb "born" is singular in tense (ἐγεννήθη) rather than plural (ἐγεννήθησαν) as is the case in all Greek manuscripts'. Cf. *haer.* 3.19.2: 'He who "was not born of the will of the flesh nor by the will of man" is the Son of Man, he is the Christ, the Son of the living God.'

What more then can be said of the difference between animation by the breath of life and vivification by the Spirit, the relation between them, and between them and the soul?[42] In the passage just cited (*haer.* 5.1.3), Irenaeus describes the breath of life as animating the human being and showing him to be a rational animal. Throughout his writings, Irenaeus shows a remarkable lack of interest in the soul, as the bearer of the identity of the person or as the domain of interiority. In one of his very few comments on the soul itself, he describes it as being the intellect of the human being, containing 'mind, thought, mental intuition, and such like' (*haer.* 2.29.3), but he is led to make this remark only because here he is discussing his opponents' claim that each 'part' of the human being has a separate destiny. His gaze is focused much more on the body, or more specifically on the flesh, the handiwork (πλάσμα) of God; it is, by and large, only with respect to its contribution to the body that Irenaeus is interested in the soul. The soul uses the body as an artist does an instrument and even adopts its shape.[43] On one occasion, in the context of considering what Paul meant by the 'mortal body' that will be raised by the Spirit (Rom. 8:11), Irenaeus does call the soul 'the breath of life', to emphasize that it is flesh, again his primary interest, that will be raised.[44] But, while animating the body, and as such a breath of life, the soul emphatically does not have life in itself. This point is made explicitly in *haer.* 2.34.2–4, an important passage that seems to be dependent upon Justin's *Dialogue with Trypho*.[45] Here, commenting on Psalm 20:5 (LXX),

---

[42] The relationship between the soul, the breath of life, and the Holy Spirit is examined in detail in Behr, *Asceticism and Anthropology*, 91–109.

[43] Cf. *haer.* 2.33.4. Irenaeus never says that the soul is itself a 'body' (as did some Stoics, e.g. SVF 2.790, 219.24–8), but that it retains the form of the body. Cf. *haer.* 2.19.6, and 2.34.1, commenting on the account of Lazarus and the rich man in Luke 16:19–31.

[44] *haer.* 5.7.1: 'But souls are incorporeal when compared to mortal bodies; for God "breathed into the face" of the human "a breath of life, and the human became a living soul" [Gen. 2:7], and the breath of life is incorporeal. But one cannot call it mortal, since it is the breath of life.' What the 'it' in the previous sentence refers to is unclear: the Latin has *ipsum*, referring back to the breath of life, but Rousseau (SC 152, pp. 236–7) suspects this to be a mistranslation and would correct it to *ipsam*, referring back to the soul, the Greek in either case being αὐτήν. A few lines later, commenting on the death of the body, Irenaeus states that this does not happen to the soul 'for it is a breath of life'. For the distinction between 'immortality' and the possession of life, see Henri Lassiat, *Promotion de l'homme en Jésus-Christ d'après Irénée de Lyon* (Tours: Mame, 1974), esp. 165–6, responded to by Adelin Rousseau, 'L'Éternité des peines de l'enfer et l'immortalité naturelle de l'âme selon saint Irénée', NRT 99 (1977), 834–64, to which Lassiat replied with 'L'Anthropologie d'Irénée', NRT 100 (1978), 399–417. For comment on this debate, see Behr, *Asceticism and Anthropology*, 94–6.

[45] Cf. *Dial.* 6.1–3. The similarity with Justin is denied by Rousseau (SC 293, p. 348) but upheld by J. C. M. van Winden, *An Early Christian Philosopher: Justin Martyr's Dialogue with*

'He asked life of you and you gave him length of days for ages and ages', Irenaeus asserts that 'life does not arise from us, nor from our own nature; but is bestowed according to the grace of God' (*haer.* 2.34.3). As a gift, it must be received, and so 'those who, in this brief temporal life, have shown themselves ungrateful to him who bestowed it' will not receive 'length of days for ages of ages'. Irenaeus then turns to Genesis 2:7:

> But as the animated body is certainly not itself the soul, yet participates in the soul as long as God pleases, so also the soul herself assuredly is not life, but partakes in that life bestowed from God himself. Wherefore also the prophetic word declares of the first-formed, 'he became a living soul', teaching us that by participation of life the soul was made 'living' so that the soul is thought of separately, and separately also the life which is in her. With God therefore bestowing life and perpetual continuance, it comes to pass that even souls which did not at first exist should henceforth continue, since God will have both willed them to be and to continue. (*haer.* 2.34.4)

The soul becomes a 'living soul' by receiving life from God, through the breath of life, and thus is able to animate the body. The life lived by the human creature in this way is, however, a 'brief temporal life'. Showing themselves thankful in this life, ready to accept life rather than reject it, the human being will also be able to receive 'length of days for ever and ever'.

The description of the life of the human animated by the breath of life as being 'brief' and 'temporal', is developed in *haer.* 5.3.3, where Irenaeus explains further how this life relates to eternal life given in Christ by the Spirit in the resurrection. Those who claim that it is not possible for the flesh to receive life in the resurrection, he points out, contradict the self-evident fact that their bodies already now participate in life.

> If, then, the present temporal life, which is much weaker than that eternal life, is nevertheless able to vivify our mortal members, why should not eternal life, being much more powerful than this, vivify the flesh, already exercised and accustomed to sustain life? For that the flesh is capable of receiving life is shown from the fact of its being alive; for it lives as long as God wants it to live. It is manifest, too, that God has the power to confer life upon it, for when he grants life, we live. (*haer.* 5.3.3)

All life is a gift from God, lived by the human being. And the life we now live in the body shows that the same body is indeed capable of receiving the eternal life of God himself. The only distinction that Irenaeus makes

---

Trypho, *Chapters One to Nine: Introduction, Text and Commentary* (Leiden: Brill, 1971), 105–8, and Ysabel de Andia, *Homo vivens: Incorruptibilité et divinisation de l'homme selon Irénée de Lyon* (Paris: Études Augustiniennes, 1986), 271–3, who helpfully prints both texts in parallel.

between the two is one of relative degrees: weaker or stronger, temporal or eternal.[46]

The Pauline distinction between the breath of life and the life-creating spirit, used by Irenaeus to describe the arc of the economy of God, is treated most fully during the course of his rebuttal of his opponents' literal reading of Paul's assertion that 'flesh and blood cannot inherit the kingdom' (1 Cor. 15:50). Irenaeus argues that flesh and blood can indeed *be inherited by* the Spirit when vivified by the Spirit (*haer.* 5.9–10)—that is, when we no longer bear the image of the earthly one by working the deeds of the flesh, but rather bear the image of the heavenly one, having been washed in Christ and 'made alive by working the works of the Spirit' (*haer.* 5.11; 1 Cor. 15:48–9). Irenaeus then further explains the relationship between the breath of life and the life-creating Spirit by turning to the previous verses from the apostle's epistle. Although the flesh is capable of receiving both the breath of life and the life given by the Spirit, and while the difference between these can be put in relative terms (temporal/eternal, weaker/stronger), they cannot, however, coexist together in the same body. Just as death cannot coexist in the same body with life, so Irenaeus asserts, apropos of a quotation from Isaiah (25:8), that 'the former life is expelled, because it was not given by the Spirit but by the breath, for the breath of life, which made the human an animated being, is one thing, and the vivifying Spirit, which rendered him spiritual, another' (*haer.* 5.12.1–2). Citing two further verses from Isaiah (42:5; 57:16), Irenaeus concludes from the first that the 'breath' is given in common to all people upon earth, but the Spirit only to those who tread down earthly desires, and following the language of the second, 'For the Spirit shall go forth from me, and I have made every breath', that the Spirit is placed 'particularly on the side of God [$\vec{\iota}\delta\iota\omega\varsigma\ \vec{\epsilon}\pi\grave{\iota}\ \tau o\hat{\upsilon}\ \Theta\epsilon o\hat{\upsilon}$]', bestowed upon the human race in the last times through the adoption of sons, while the 'breath' is common to all creation and is 'created [$\pi o\iota\eta\mu a$]' (*haer.* 5.12.2). As 'the created is other than him who creates', the breath is temporal while the Spirit is eternal; the breath increases in strength, flourishes for a period of time, and then departs, leaving its abode destitute of breath, while the Spirit 'embraces the human being inside and out' and remains with him permanently (*haer.* 5.12.2). And then returning to 1 Corinthians 15:45–6, Irenaeus reminds us that the animated is first, followed by the spiritual: 'it was necessary that, first, the human being should be

---

[46] Cf. Noormann, *Irenäus*, 277, 486–7. In *haer.* 4.9.2 Irenaeus points out that the terms 'more' and 'less' can be applied only to things of the same nature.

fashioned, then that what was fashioned should receive the soul; and that afterwards it should thus receive the communion of the Spirit.' That he uses the term 'soul' here, rather than 'breath', is due to the fact that he is commenting on 1 Corinthians 15:45–6, and the use it makes of Genesis 2:7, rather than the Genesis text itself. Irenaeus then concludes his discussion stating: 'Therefore, just as the one who became a living soul, turning to evil, lost life, so again, that same one, turning to what is better and receiving the life-creating Spirit, shall find life' (*haer.* 5.12.2). Turning to evil, the animated human being lost the life of the breath, but what he or she will receive in Christ is more than this, it will be the life-creating Spirit himself.

The relationship between the breath of life and the Spirit is thus described, throughout this passage, in terms of the Spirit's activity as life-creating, and therefore the breath as being created. Yet, as created, the breath is nevertheless placed in direct relationship to, and dependent upon, the Spirit. There is no life, as we have seen, apart from that given by God. However, the life received at the beginning is received, as it were, on the creature's own terms and capacity—that is, as created: it is a created breath, that abides and flourishes for a period, but is not strong enough to remain permanently. Those, however, who receive the adoption of sons in Christ receive life as the life-creating Spirit himself, vivifying them permanently 'inside and out'. But reception of this requires that the breath be 'expelled'; it requires that the creature die, with Christ, to receive the life given in Christ. In one passage, Irenaeus suggests that human beings, animated by a breath of life, could have remained as they were—'that is, immortal'—had they kept the commandment and acknowledged God as the Lord of all—that is, the source of all life—but that if they failed to recognize this they would become mortal and be dissolved into the earth from which they were taken (*Dem.* 15). Or, as he had just put it, while 'the breath of life remains in its order and strength', Adam and Eve had no comprehension of what is evil, and so '"were not ashamed" [Gen. 2:25], kissing and embracing each other in holiness as children'.[47] But even this apparent 'immortality' is not the same thing as the life given by the possession of the Spirit to adopted sons in Christ: the 'breath' remaining with its 'proper strength', while the human being acknowledges that God is Lord of all, the source of all life, by obedience to his law, is still but a breath, a created effect of the life-creating Spirit, rather than the possession

---

[47] *Dem.* 14, mistranslated by Smith, who renders 'breath' as 'spirit', on the grounds that 'it is hardly possible to use "breath" in what follows' (ACW 16, pp. 151–2, nn. 82–3).

of the Spirit enjoyed by those adopted in Christ, and so those living by the 'breath' can be called merely 'flesh and blood', or even simply 'dead'.[48] Irenaeus does not hold that in their initial formation human beings 'possessed' the Spirit, which they then 'lost' and then regained in Christ. Rather, for Irenaeus, the Spirit is present throughout the whole economy ('For never at any time did Adam escape the Hands of God', *haer.* 5.1.3), from the first stage, imparting what the human being receives as a 'breath', and thereafter preparing human beings to learn to live not by or from themselves, but from God, who alone provides life through his life-creating Spirit, in different modalities, to all living upon earth.

Two further passages mention this distinction of modalities. The first is a long discussion in *haer.* 4.20, in which Irenaeus speaks of life in terms of the vision of God. He is emphatic that it is not possible to live without life, and that life is to be found in communion with God, which is to see God and enjoy his blessings.[49] After discussing the proleptic nature of the vision of God enjoyed by the prophets of old, Irenaeus continues:

For the glory of God is a living human being; and the life of the human consists in beholding God. For if the manifestation of God which is made by means of the creation, affords life to all living in the earth, much more does that revelation of the Father which comes through the Word, give life to those who see God.

There is, again, only one source of life—that is, God, which is received through the vision of him, in two distinct modes, first, through creation, as God, for his fatherhood is not yet known, and then, secondly, in a stronger fashion, through the vision of the Father through the Word. The second passage, *haer.* 5.18.2, presents a similar distinction, in terms of the bestowal of the Spirit:

For the Father simultaneously bears the creation and his own Word, and the Word borne by the Father bestows the Spirit on all as the Father wills: to some, who are in a created state, which is made, he gives the Spirit pertaining to creation; to others, who are according to adoption, an engendering, he gives the Spirit of the Father.[50]

---

[48] Cf. *haer.* 5.9.1, cited in Ch. 3, n. 40.

[49] *haer.* 4.20.5: Ἐπεὶ ζῆσαι ἄνευ ζωῆς [ἀδύνατον], ἡ δὲ ὕπαρξις τῆς ζωῆς ἐκ τῆς τοῦ Θεοῦ περιγίνεται μετοχῆς, μετοχὴ δὲ Θεοῦ ἐστι τὸ [ὁρᾶν] Θεὸν καὶ ἀπολαύειν τῆς χρηστότητος αὐτοῦ. The words in square brackets are Rousseau's emendations to the Greek text, found in the *Sacra Parallela*, on the basis of the Latin and the Armenian.

[50] The Latin text of this passage is particularly problematic but clarified somewhat by the Armenian version. For a full analysis of the textual difficulties, see Behr, *Asceticism and Anthropology*, 102–5.

Those who remain as they are created, receive the Spirit in a manner befitting their state, as what we have seen him elsewhere speak of as 'the breath of life'. On the other hand, those who are born as adopted sons of God receive the Spirit of the Father.

The role of the Spirit in the human being whom the Spirit 'embraces inside and out' in a permanent fashion to such an extent that the Spirit can be called 'their Spirit' is described most fully in the following passage, which analyses what Paul means by the perfect or complete human being:

> Now the soul and the Spirit can be a part of the human being, but by no means a human being; the complete [*perfectus*] human being is the commingling and the union of the soul receiving the Spirit of the Father and joined to the flesh that was moulded after the image of God. For this reason the Apostle says 'We speak wisdom among them that are perfect [*perfectos*]' [1 Cor. 2:6], calling those 'perfect' who have received the Spirit of God . . . these the Apostle also calls 'spiritual', being spiritual by a participation in the Spirit and not by a deprivation and removal of the flesh {and merely that itself alone}. For if anyone take away the substance {of the flesh, that is} of the handiwork, and merely considers only the Spirit itself, such is no longer what is a spiritual human, but the Spirit of the human being or the Spirit of God.[51] But when this Spirit, commingled with the soul, is united to the handiwork, because of the outpouring of the Spirit the human being is rendered spiritual and complete [*perfectus*], and this is the one who was made in the image and likeness of God. But if the Spirit is lacking from the soul, such a one, remaining indeed animated and fleshly, will be incomplete [*imperfectus*], having the image, certainly, in the handiwork, but not receiving the likeness through the Spirit. Likewise this one is incomplete, in the same manner again, if someone takes away the image and rejects the handiwork; one can no longer contemplate a human being, but either some part of the human, as we have said, or something other than the human being. For neither is the handiwork of the flesh itself, by itself, a complete human being, but the body of a human and a part of a human being; nor is the soul itself, by itself, a human, but the soul of a human and a part of a human

---

[51] The words in curly brackets {} are only in the Latin version and are perhaps an attempt to soften Irenaeus' words. Rousseau's translation of 'Spiritus' in these sentences with a capital for 'l'Esprit de Dieu', but lower case for 'l'esprit de l'homme', and his note that the latter refers to the 'soul' (SC 152, pp. 231–2), are unwarranted. Irenaeus never refers to the soul as *spiritus*, and the whole emphasis here is that the Spirit of God is present in the perfect human being to such an extent that it can be considered 'their Spirit', yet without it being a 'part' of the human being, as Rousseau accepts in his comments on the quotation of 1 Thess. 5:23 (ὑμῶν τὸ πνεῦμα) in the same passage (SC 152, pp. 233–4). Rousseau also interprets the phrase 'their Spirit[s]' in *haer.* 2.33.5 in this way (SC 293, pp. 339–42); only in *haer.* 2.31.2 might Irenaeus use the term 'spirit' to refer to the 'soul', though the choice of words here probably reflects Luke 8:55, cited earlier, which would thus be consistent with the interpretation of *haer.* 5.6.1 given here, and with *haer.* 2.33.5 and 5.18.2.

being; nor is the Spirit a human being, for it is called Spirit and not human. But the commingling and union of all of these constitutes the complete human being. And for this reason the Apostle, explaining himself, clarifies [what makes] the complete and spiritual saved human being [*perfectum et spiritalem salutis hominem*], saying, in the First Epistle to the Thessalonians, 'May the God of peace sanctify you completely [*perfectos*], and may your Spirit and soul and body be preserved in the coming of the Lord Jesus Christ' [1 Thess. 5.23]. (*haer.* 5.6.1)

The complete or the perfect human being is saved in body, soul, and Spirit, preserved as such in the coming of Christ. Neither element can individually be called the human being. But the body and soul can be called 'parts' of the human being, in the way that the Spirit cannot, for the Spirit is not human, but of God; if we were to remove the Spirit, what we would have left is an animated and fleshly being.[52] Nevertheless, the Spirit is given to the perfect and complete spiritual human being, or perhaps rather inherits and embraces that human being, in such a manner that it becomes integral to the human being: if we were to remove 'the substance of the handiwork'—that is, the flesh animated by the soul—we would be left with 'only the Spirit itself', which can be spoken of as 'the Spirit of the human being'.

Death and life

The arc of the economy thus moves from Adam to Christ and from the breath to the Spirit, with Christ and the Spirit being the Hands that fashion and animate the human creature, leading the handiwork from animation to vivification. As we have seen, as yet only in passing, it was by his disobedience that Adam turned to evil and 'lost life', becoming not just capable of death but subject to death. Yet, as told from the end, death and disobedience are integral to the movement from one end of the arc to the other: it is by death that the animation by the breath is 'expelled', giving way to the vivification of the flesh by the Spirit; and it is also by the effect of disobedience that the human being learns obedience—that is, learns to receive life, which God alone can give, and so receive it securely. The ultimately pedagogical, and salvific, role of disobedience and death within the economy is brought out in a further passage where Irenaeus again depicts the span of the economy and makes clear that the salvific work of Christ is both the beginning and culmination.

---

[52] Cf. *haer.* 5.8.2: 'but our substance, that is, the union of soul and flesh, receiving the Spirit of God, constitutes the spiritual human being.'

The Glory of God (haer. 3–5)   159

God, therefore, was long-suffering when the human being defaulted, foreseeing that victory which should be granted to him through the Word. For when strength was made perfect in weakness [cf. 2 Cor. 12:9], [the Word] showed the kindness and transcendent power of God. For **just as** he did bear[53] Jonah to be swallowed up by the whale, not that he should be swallowed up and perish altogether, but **so that**, having been cast out again, he might be more subject to God and might glorify him the more who had conferred upon him such an unhoped-for salvation and brought a firm repentance to the Ninevites, that they might convert to the Lord who delivered them from death when they were struck with awe by that sign that had been wrought on Jonah . . . **so also**, from the beginning, God did bear the human being to be swallowed up by the great whale, who was the author of the transgression, not that he should perish altogether when so engulfed, but arranging in advance the finding of salvation, which was accomplished by the Word, through the 'sign of Jonah' [Matt. 12:39–40], for those who held the same opinion as Jonah regarding the Lord, and who confessed, and said, 'I am a servant of the Lord, and I worship the Lord God of heaven, who made the sea and the dry land' (Jonah 1.9), **so that** the human being, receiving an unhoped-for salvation from God, might rise from the dead, and glorify God, and repeat, 'I cried to the Lord my God in my affliction, and he heard me from the belly of hell' [Jonah 2:2], and that he might always continue glorifying God, and giving thanks without ceasing for that salvation which he had obtained from him, 'that no flesh should glory in the Lord's presence' [1 Cor. 1:29], nor should the human being ever adopt an opposite opinion with regard to God, supposing that the incorruptibility which surrounds him is his own by nature, nor, by not holding the truth, should boast with empty superciliousness, as if he were by nature like to God. (haer. 3.20.1)

From the beginning God has borne human beings while they were swallowed up by the great whale—that is, death. God, emphatically, did not create human beings *in* this condition. It was the 'animated' human

---

[53] The Latin here is *patienter sustinuit*, and variations thereof in the following sentences, for which Rousseau suggests that the Greek would have been ἠνέσχετο, and translates by 'a permis'. However, as Roger Berthouzoz notes, such a translation reflects a later theological perspective, and so he proposes instead 'a supporté' (*Liberté et grâce suivant la théologie d'Irénée de Lyon* (Fribourg en Suisse: Éditions Universitaires; Paris: Cerf, 1980), 216, n .79). The term is used elsewhere in *Against the Heresies*: in haer. 5.2.3, in a similar context, where the Greek is preserved; and haer. 4.37.8, where the Armenian version seems to be an attempt to explain the middle voice, 'he took to himself' (TU 35.2, 137.23; for 5.2.3, see 157.5). Both passages will be considered below. In the New Testament (the background for much of Irenaeus' vocabulary), the verb ἀνέχω always appears in the middle voice, generally with the sense of 'to bear, to endure' (e.g. Matt. 17:17). I have preferred 'to bear' to emphasize God's support of the human being in and through this, rather than simply permitting or enduring it from a distance. Indeed, if the parallel with Jonah is to hold, God is in fact actively involved, appointing a whale to swallow him up. The background for Irenaeus' use of this term and the idea of the forbearance of God in Polycarp and the *Letter to Diognetus*, was noted in Ch. 2.

being who 'turned to evil and lost life' (*haer.* 5.12.2). And, as he puts it in the above passage, there was 'an author of the transgression'. The lesson learnt by Jonah through his misadventure, according to Irenaeus, was that he 'is a servant of the Lord', which is nothing other, as we have seen, than the law given to Adam and Eve at the beginning (cf. *Dem.*15). As such, the 'author of the transgression' tempts the human being to think that he or she has life of his or her own nature, 'as if he were like to God', or, as Irenaeus puts it elsewhere, he beguiled Adam and Eve with 'the pretext of immortality', that which is God's alone to give.[54] However, God's forbearance has a purpose, which is that, as in the case of Jonah, the human being might learn to subject herself or himself to God, to glorify him the more, and so be glorified in return. Moreover, God is forbearing in allowing the human race to be swallowed up from the beginning because, although unknown to the human race, he had also 'arranged in advance the finding of salvation'—a salvation that therefore was, from the human perspective, 'unhoped-for'.

In this way, then, the 'finding of salvation' was effected through 'the sign of Jonah', who in turn becomes a type both of the perishing human race and of the salvation worked by Christ. That Jonah can represent both is because it is in and through his death that Christ brings about salvation, as it is through their death that the human beings come to know their own inherent weakness and, simultaneously, the strength of God, just as it is also through death that the human being passes from animation to vivification. So, Irenaeus concludes:

Such then was the patience of God, that the human being, passing through all things and acquiring knowledge of death,[55] then attaining to the resurrection from the dead, and learning by experience from whence he has been delivered, may thus always gives thanks to the Lord, having received from him the gift of incorruptibility, and may love him the more, for 'he to whom more is forgiven, loves more' [cf. Luke 7:42–3], and may himself know how mortal and weak he is, but also understand that God is so immortal and powerful as to bestow immortality on the mortal and eternity on the temporal, and that he may also know the other powers of God made manifest in himself, and, being taught by them, may think of God in accordance with the greatness of God. For the glory of the human being is God,

---

[54] *haer.* 3.23.5; 4.Pref.4. For the Devil's role in the human apostasy, see also *haer.* 3.23.1–3; 4.40.3; *Dem.* 16.

[55] Following the emendation of 'morum' to 'mortum' proposed by Grabe and adopted by Rousseau (SC 210, 349–50), who notes *haer.* 3.23.1 (referring back to the previous passage) and *haer.* 4.39.1 as parallels.

while the vessel of the workings of God, and of all his wisdom and power is the human being. (*haer.* 3.20.2)

Subjection to death, brought upon human beings by their own disobedience at the instigation of the Devil, is thus turned inside out within the full arc of the economy, which, as we have seen repeatedly, can be understood only from the end point, Christ and his Passion. In this way, then, Irenaeus has explicated one of the key points that he set before the theologian in 1.10.3—that is, to proclaim the reason why God 'was long-suffering' with regard to the apostasy of angels and the disobedience of human beings and 'consigned all to disobedience that he may have mercy on all' (Rom. 11:32).

'The glory of the human being is God' (*haer.* 3.20.2), and in turn 'the glory of God is the living human being' (*haer.* 4.20.7); and it is precisely in terms of this glory that Irenaeus explains why God initiated the whole economy. In the context of explaining that God accepted the friendship of Abraham, not because he was in need of it, but so that he might bestow eternal life upon Abraham, for 'friendship with God imparts immortality to those who embrace it' (*haer.* 4.13.3), Irenaeus extrapolates the point on the basis of Christ's high priestly prayer:

> Neither in the beginning was it because God had need of the human being that he formed Adam, but that he might have someone on whom he might confer his benefits. For not only before Adam, but also before all creation, did the Word glorify his Father, remaining in him, and was himself glorified by the Father, as he did himself declare, 'Father, glorify me with the glory which I had with you before the world was'. (*haer.* 4.14.1; John 17:5)

Since to follow the light is to be enlightened, he continues, so also to follow the Saviour is to partake in salvation, and likewise to serve and follow God gives nothing to God, but rather God bestows upon those who follow him 'life, incorruptibility, and eternal glory' (*haer.* 4.14.1). Only by orienting himself towards God, by following him, is the human being able to receive life and share in the incorruptibility and glory of God. As created, the human being ever stands in dependency upon the Creator: 'For as much as God is in want of nothing, by so much does the human being stand in need of communion with God; for this is the glory of the human being, to continue and remain permanently in the service of God' (*haer.* 4.14.1). Picking up on the theme of glory evoked by the prayer of Christ, 'I will that where I am there they may also be, that they may behold my glory' (John 17:24), Irenaeus adds that Christ did not want to boast of his glory, but rather that his disciples, by beholding his glory, should also participate in it. Irenaeus returns to the inspiration for creation in terms of this participation by human beings in the glory of God. Connecting a passage from Isaiah, regarding the gathering of the posterity from the four corners, of 'everyone who is called by my name, whom I created for glory, whom I formed and made' (Isa. 43:6–7) to the enigmatic words of Christ, he concludes:

> Inasmuch, then, as 'wheresoever the carcase is, there shall also the eagles be gathered together' [Matt. 24:28], participating in the glory of the Lord, who has both formed us and prepared us for this, that when we are with him, we may partake of his glory. (*haer.* 4.14.1)

The economy of God, which is 'for the sake of the human race' (*haer.* 1.10.3), thus begins with the glory that the Word has with the Father in eternity and culminates in the glorification of Christ by the Father, a glory in which the disciples, by beholding it, participate. 'The glory of God is the living human being, and the life of the human being is to see God' (*haer.* 4.20.7).

THE WORK OF GOD

Fashioning human beings

The arc of economy thus moves, as we have seen, from Adam to Christ, from the human being animated by a breath of life to the spiritual human being vivified by the Holy Spirit, with the beginning and the end being understood in terms of each other. The economy is 'for the sake of the human race' and leads from the preliminary sketch to the perfect and complete living human being. That this is indeed the work of God is shown, for Irenaeus, by the manner in which Christ healed the man blind from birth (John 9). It was not merely by a word that he was healed, but 'by an outward action, doing this not without purpose or by chance, but that he might show forth the Hand of God that had at the beginning moulded the human being' (*haer.* 5.15.2). So, just as 'the Lord took mud from the earth and formed the human being' (Gen. 2:7), Christ spat on the ground and made mud, smeared it upon his eyes, 'pointing out the original fashioning, how it was effected, and manifesting the Hand of God to those who can understand by what [Hand] the human being was formed out of the dust' (*haer.* 5.15.2). As, in Christ's words, the man was born blind not because of his own sin or that of his parents, 'but that the works of God should be manifest in him' (John 9:3), so Irenaeus sets this particular work within the intentionality of the economy as a whole:

For that which the artificer, the Word, had omitted to form in the womb, he then supplied in public, that the works of God might be manifested in him, in order that we might not seek out another hand by which the human being is fashioned, nor another Father, knowing that this Hand of God which formed us in the beginning, and which does form us in the womb, has in the last times sought us out who were lost, winning back his own, and taking up the lost sheep upon his shoulders, and with joy restoring it to the fold of life. (*haer.* 5.15.2; cf. Luke 19:10, 15:4–6)

If all of this was done so that 'the works of God should be manifest in him', Irenaeus concludes that 'the work of God is fashioning the human being' (*haer.* 5.15.2, *opera autem Dei plasmatio est hominis*). By putting the healing of the blind man together with the formation of the human being as described in Genesis, Irenaeus can focus Christ's words about 'the works of God' specifically upon the formation of human beings, which is, in fact, the only creative work that the first chapter of Genesis describes as being God's own project: 'Let us make a human being in our image and likeness' (Gen. 1:26).

The paradigmatic description of the fashioning of the human being in the opening chapters of Genesis, now seen as the beginning of an arc culminating in Christ, is used by Irenaeus to understand Christ's own birth from the Virgin.

And **just as** the first-fashioned Adam had his substance from untilled and yet virgin soil, 'for God had not yet sent rain, and there was no human being to till the ground' [Gen. 2:5], and was fashioned by the Hand of God, that is, by the Word of God, for 'all things were made through him' [John 1:3], and the Lord took mud from the ground and fashioned the human being [Gen. 2:7], **so also**, when the Word himself, recapitulated Adam in himself, he rightly received from Mary, who was as yet a virgin, that generation which was the recapitulation of Adam. If then the first Adam had a man for his father, and was born from male seed, they would be right to say that the second Adam was begotten of Joseph. But if the former was taken from the mud, and fashioned by the Word of God, so the Word himself, when bringing about the recapitulation of Adam within himself, ought to have the likeness of generation itself. Why then did God not once again take mud, rather than work this fashioning from Mary? So that there should not be another fashioning, nor that it should be another fashioning which would be saved, but that the same thing should be recapitulated, preserving the similitude. (*haer.* 3.21.10)[56]

Preserving the pattern of Adam's formation, yet not being a new beginning of a new formation, Christ's virgin birth, rather than undermining

---

[56] Cf. *haer.* 1.9.3; 3.18.7, 21.9, 22.1; 5.1.2, 12.4, 14.1–3.

the genuineness of Christ's humanity, in fact guarantees it. By recapitulating the ancient formation of Adam, Christ preserves both our own substance, the mud from which we are made, and the manner in which Adam came to be.

In the *Demonstration*, Irenaeus expounds further on the action of God taking mud from the earth to fashion his handiwork. After the opening chapters, in which he presents the rule of truth and various matters pertaining to angels, Irenaeus begins his discussion of God's work this way:

> But he fashioned the human being with his own Hands, taking the purest, the finest <and the most delicate> [elements] of the earth, mixing with the earth, in due measure, his own power; and because he <sketched upon> the handiwork his own form, in order that what would be seen should be godlike, for the human being was placed upon the earth fashioned <in> the image of God; and that he might be alive, 'he breathed into his face a breath of life' [Gen. 2:7]: so that both according to the inspiration and according to the formation, the human being was like God. Accordingly, he was free and master of himself, having been made by God in this way, [in order] that he should rule over everything upon earth. And this great created world, prepared by God before the fashioning of the human being, was given to the human being as [his] domain, having everything in it. (*Dem.* 11)

Irenaeus strikingly combines both creation accounts together: there is no distinction between the 'making' (ποίησις) of Genesis 1:26 and the 'fashioning' (πλάσις) of Genesis 2:7, as there would be for other writers.[57] It is the mud taken from the earth that is itself fashioned into the image of God. Irenaeus adds to the text of Genesis a supplementary action of God, that of 'mixing his own power' into the earth. This should probably be understood in terms of the creative activity of God, whose strength is made perfect in weakness (2 Cor. 12:9).[58] In *haer.* 5.3.1–3, commenting on

---

[57] For instance, Philo, *Opif.* 46.134, who distinguished between Gen. 1:26, the creation of the ideal human, neither male nor female, created in the image, the true human being or νοῦς, and Gen. 2:7, the mud fashioned into the sensible and corruptible body. Origen (*Jo.* 20.182) seems to make a distinction between a descending gradation of 'create' (κτίζειν), 'make' (ποιεῖν), and 'mould' (πλάσσειν): 'Because, therefore, the first man fell away from the superior things and desired a life different from the superior life, he deserved to be a beginning neither of something created nor made, but "of something moulded by the Lord to be mocked by the angels" [Job 40:19, LXX]. Now, our true substance [ἡ προηγουμένη ὑπόστασις] too is our being according to the image of the Creator, but the substance resulting from a cause [ἡ ἐξ αἰτίας] is in the thing moulded [πλάσματι], which was received from the dust of the earth.'

[58] On the basis of what Irenaeus says elsewhere regarding baptism, that the dry earth cannot be made into a body or bear fruit unless it receives 'the willing Rain from above' (*haer.* 3.17.2), some have suggested that the 'power' spoken of in *Dem.* 11 is the 'Spirit of God' mentioned in Gen. 1:2, understood as an *anima mundi* rather than a 'Personal Spirit'. Cf.

these words of Christ to Paul, he notes that the flesh, which was skilfully formed by God in the beginning, will be raised from the dead by the same power. Irenaeus describes with awe how the bones, the nerves, the veins, and the rest of 'the arrangement [οἰκονομία] of the human being' have come together by the power of God: this is for something more miraculous than bringing them back together in the resurrection. So he concludes:

> One cannot enumerate all the harmonious structure of the human being [τῆς κατὰ τὸν ἄνθρωπον μελοποιΐας],[59] which was not made without the great wisdom of God. Whatever participates in the art and wisdom of God also participates in his power. The flesh, therefore, is not without part in the art, the wisdom and the power of God, but his power, which produces life, is made perfect in weakness, that is, in the flesh. (haer. 5.3.2-3)

Whatever is worked upon by God is the recipient of his power, and this is especially so in the case of the human being, who is, as we saw earlier, 'the vessel of the workings of God and of all his wisdom and power' (haer. 3.20.2). God took dust from the earth and fashioned (ἔπλασε) it, so that it, receiving his creative power and wisdom, becomes flesh, the 'handiwork' (πλάσμα) of God. In previous chapters, we have seen how Irenaeus uses this term *plasma* to refer to the 'fabrication' created by his opponents from the Scriptures read according to their own hypothesis. Here, now, the same term refers directly to the human being, as the 'handiwork' of God. The term emphasizes both the essentially, and profoundly, earthy character of the human being—skilfully fashioned mud—and, at the same time, the literally hands-on immediacy of God's creative work, who as an artist or potter fashions the mud in his hands.[60]

Antonio Orbe, *Antropología de San Ireneo*, BAC (Madrid: BAC, 1969), 59–61; Andia, *Homo vivens*, 76–8.

[59] The term μελοποιΐα is rare; LSJ attests it only in the sense of 'making a melody', but, as Rousseau (SC 152, p. 218) notes, the context strongly suggests μέλος in the sense of 'members' or 'limbs'. Nevertheless, given Irenaeus' frequent deployment of musical imagery, for instance, that God has 'harmonized the human race to the symphony of salvation' (haer. 4.14.2), the allusion to melody-making here is probably not accidental.

[60] The background here is clearly Isa. 45:9 and Rom. 9:20. For Irenaeus' use of the term *plasma*, see Godehard Joppich, *Salus Carnis: Eine Untersuchung in der Theologie des hl. Irenäus von Lyon*, Münsterschwarzacher Studien, 1 (Münsterschwarzach: Vier-Türme, 1965), 49–55. See also Orbe, *Antropología*, 527–8, who would characterize Irenaeus' anthropology as 'sarcology', compared with the 'pneumatology' of the Gnostics and the 'psychology' of Origen. See also Henry, *Incarnation*.

In the passage from *Dem.* 11 cited above, before turning to the second part of Genesis 2:7, the animation of the handiwork by the breath of life, Irenaeus turns to Genesis 1:27 to specify in what form it is that God has fashioned this mud—that is, in his own form, for the human being was set upon the earth 'in the image of God'. We have already seen a passage, cited above, in which Irenaeus states explicitly that it is 'the flesh that was moulded after the image of God' (*haer.* 5.6.1). Irenaeus is emphatic that an image must have a form, and can therefore exist only in matter, not in an immaterial part or aspect of the human being.[61] An image must reveal that of which it is an image, and so the human being, who is in the image of God in his very flesh, points forward to Christ, as we have seen when examining Paul's description of Adam as a 'type of the one to come' (Rom. 5:14). As Irenaeus puts it: '"For <I made> man <in> the image of God" [Gen. 9.6 LXX] and the image of God is the Son, according to whose image was man made; and for this reason, he appeared in the last times, to render the image like himself' (*Dem.* 22).[62] The distinction that Irenaeus makes between the human being made *in* the image of God and Christ who *is* the image of God (cf. Col. 1:15) is clearly related to his understanding of Adam as the 'type' of Christ, stamped, as it were, to be an impression of the seal. Being inscribed in the very flesh of human beings, their being 'in the image' of God is indelible.[63] Alongside being in the image, the human 'godlike' existence is shown by his being 'free and master of himself', which Irenaeus elsewhere describes as indicating his 'similitude' with God.[64] This freedom includes the freedom of faith (cf.

---

[61] Cf. *haer.* 2.7, 19.6; J. Fantino, *L'Homme, image de Dieu chez saint Irénée de Lyon* (Paris: Cerf, 1984), 87–9.

[62] Cf. Fantino, *L'Homme*, 145–54. Tertullian also makes the same point: 'Whatever [form] the clay expressed, in mind was Christ who was to become human (which the clay was) and the Word flesh (which the earth then was). For the Father had already said to his Son, "Let us make the human being unto our image and likeness; and God made the human being", that is the same as "fashioned" [cf. Gen. 2:7], "unto the image of God made he him" [Gen. 1:26-7]— it means of Christ. And the Word is also God, who "being in the form of God, thought it not robbery to be equal to God" [Phil. 2:6]. Thus that clay, already putting on the image of Christ, who was to be in the flesh, was not only the work, but also the pledge of God.' *Res.* 6 (modifying the translation of Evans).

[63] Passages such as *haer.* 3.18.1, which speak of what we lost in Adam, that is, being in the image and likeness of God, we regain in Christ, are often taken to mean that human beings lost the status of being 'in the image' (e.g. Grant, *Irenaeus*, 52); yet it is the possession of both that is said to be lost; Irenaeus never asserts that the human being stopped being 'in the image'.

[64] e.g. *haer.* 4.37.4: 'Because man is possessed of free will from the beginning, and God is possessed of free will, in whose similitude man was created, advice is always given to him to keep fast the good, which is done by means of obedience to God.' Fantino (*L'Homme*, 110–18)

haer. 4.27.5), and, as the basis for our response towards God, it too has always been preserved intact by God (cf. *haer.* 4.15.2). The final aspect of the passage from *Dem.* 11 cited above is the second divine action in Genesis 2:7, animation with the breath of life, so that 'both according to the inspiration and according to the formation, the human being was like God'. The typological relation in which Adam stands to Christ pertains both to his bodily character as 'image', and also to their respective modes of life, as we have considered fully in the previous section: the animation of the handiwork prefigures the vivification of the same handiwork by the Holy Spirit in the last times.

There are three further actions of God described in the opening chapters of Genesis that figure in Irenaeus' account of the work of God in Christ that fashions living human beings. The first is that, having fashioned his handiwork, God prepared a place, better than this present world, to provide suitable 'nourishment' for the human being who, as newly created, was but an 'infant' needing to grow to reach full development (*Dem.* 12).[65] So beautiful and good was this garden, that 'the Word of God was always walking in it; he would walk and talk with the human being, prefiguring the future, which would come to pass, that he would dwell with him and speak with him and would be with humankind teaching them righteousness' (*Dem.* 12). The future that is prefigured here is clearly the Church, so that Irenaeus can in turn say that 'the Church has been planted as a garden [*paradisus*] in this world', and interpret the instruction to eat of every tree in the garden as a direction to 'eat from every Scripture of the Lord' (*haer.* 5.20.2; Gen. 2:16). Before examining further Christ's establishment of the Church, and its own prefigurative aspect, the second action of God, which, as we will see, is related to the Church, is the

---

convincingly argues that the Latin translation of *Against the Heresies* uses the word *similitudo* to render both ὁμοιότης, where it speaks of human free will making the human being like or similar to God, and the ὁμοίωσις of Gen. 1:26. The latter term, not repeated in Gen. 1:27 to describe what God 'made', has, for Irenaeus, an eschatological character, and will be further considered below.

[65] It is for this reason that the human being, although intended to be the lord of the earth with the angels appointed as his servants, was only 'secretly' established as their Lord (*Dem.* 12). It is important to note that Irenaeus never characterizes or assimilates the human being or life to the angelic: it is the becoming fully human of both God and the handiwork that is the goal of the economy, according to Irenaeus. On infancy of Adam and Eve, probably deriving from Theophilus of Antioch (*Autol.* 2.25), see M. C. Steenberg, 'Children in Paradise: Adam and Eve as "Infants" in Irenaeus of Lyons', *JECS* 12/1 (2004), 1–22, and *Irenaeus on Creation: The Cosmic Christ and the Saga of Redemption*, Supplements to Vigiliae Christianae 91 (Leiden: Brill, 2008), 142–5.

formation of a partner for the human being. In *Dem.* 13, Irenaeus paraphrases and extends Genesis 2:18–23:

> And he decided also to make a helper for the man, for in this manner, 'God said "It is not good for man to be alone, let us make him a helper fit for him,"' since among all the other living things no helper was found equal and like to Adam; and God himself 'cast a deep sleep upon Adam and put him to sleep', and, that a work might be accomplished out of a work, sleep not being in Paradise, it came upon Adam by the will of God; and God 'took one of Adam's ribs and filled up flesh in its place, and he built up the rib which he took into a woman and, in this way, brought [her] before Adam'. And he, seeing [her], said, 'This at last is bone of my bones, and flesh of my flesh; she shall be called "woman", for she was taken from her man.' (*Dem.* 13)

Irenaeus follows the scriptural text, but adds an intriguing explanatory comment regarding God's act of putting Adam to sleep so as to form the woman, noting that, as sleep did not yet exist in paradise, God suspended, as it were, Adam's existence so as to 'accomplish a work from a work'. Irenaeus clearly wants to emphasize the point that, as taken from his side, Eve belongs to the same formation as Adam, the unity of the work from the work.[66] Irenaeus does not explicitly relate this 'sleep' of Adam, resulting in the emergence of Eve, to the Passion of Christ and the Church, as others in this period would do.[67] The final action of God is to give the newly created infants, Adam and Eve, the commandment not to eat of the tree of the knowledge of good and evil, for, on the day that you do so, you will die (cf. Gen. 2:16–7). Irenaeus interprets this commandment, as we have already seen, in terms of needing to recognize that they have 'as their lord the Lord of all' (*Dem.* 15), the lesson learnt by Jonah and by all human beings through their own death.

Christ's work of recapitulating the whole economy to bring about the perfect or complete 'living human being' does not encompass, however, only the initial actions of God, but also actions of the human beings themselves,

---

[66] Cf. Theophilus, *Autol.* 28: 'so that no one might suppose that one god made man and another made woman, he made the two together. Moreover, he formed only man from earth so that thus the mystery of the divine unity might be demonstrated. At the same time, God made woman by taking her from his side so that the man's love for her might be greater.'

[67] e.g. Tertullian, *An.* 43.10: 'As Adam was a figure of Christ, Adam's sleep shadowed out the death of Christ, who was to sleep a mortal slumber, that from the wound inflicted on his side might be figured the true Mother of the living, the Church.' The Church, which came from the side of the crucified Christ (referring to the blood and the water, cf. John 19:34), is foreshadowed by the formation of Eve from the side of Adam when he was asleep, the sleep which foreshadowed Christ's own sleep in death. Thus while Eve was certainly called the mother of the living (Gen. 3:20), it is really the Church that is this.

and in so doing reverses their effects. As Adam and Eve were newly created, they were but infants, inexperienced and untrained in divine ways, and so immediately gave way to the seduction of the Devil, losing the 'strength' of the breath and becoming subject to death. The Word of God became human, therefore, 'in order to undergo temptation' (*haer.* 3.19.3). While Adam was defeated through disobedience, Christ, in recapitulating these temptations, was obedient and emerged victorious. The parallels between the temptations of Adam in the garden and Christ in the desert are worked out in great detail in *haer.* 5.21–2. Drawing upon Scripture in his replies to the Devil, 'casting down the apostasy by means of these sayings', Christ 'overcomes the strong man by his Father's voice', confounding the adversary by nothing else than the commandments of his own Father (*haer.* 5.22.1; Matt. 12:29).[68] Likewise, while Adam was disobedient with respect to the tree, Christ demonstrated his obedience by means of the tree (*haer.* 5.16.3; Phil. 3:8): 'So, by means of the obedience by which he obeyed unto death, hanging upon the tree, he undid the old disobedience occasioned by the tree' (*Dem.* 34; Gal. 3:13). And again, waging war against the enemy in his work of recapitulation, Christ also recapitulated the enmity between the woman and the serpent, and between their offspring (Gen. 3:15):

> and therefore does the Lord profess himself to be the Son of Man, recapitulating in himself that original man out of whom woman was fashioned, in order that, as our race went down to death through a vanquished man, so we may ascend to life again through a victorious one, and as through a man death received the palm [of victory] against us, so again, by a man we may receive the palm against death. (*haer.* 5.21.1)[69]

Christ's work of recapitulating Adam's defeat is thus twofold: 'For he fought and conquered; for, on the one hand, he was human contending for the fathers, and through obedience doing away with disobedience completely; and on the other hand, he bound the strong man, and set free the weak, and endowed his own handiwork with salvation, by destroying sin' (*haer.* 3.18.6; Rom. 5:19; Matt. 12:29). The liberation of human beings from the tyranny of the Devil is thus effected by Christ, who, as human, fought the enemy and untied the knot of disobedience through his obedience, and, as God, destroyed sin, set free the weak, giving salvation to his handiwork. So, Irenaeus continues:

---

[68] For the image of Christ binding the 'strong man', see *haer.* 3.18.2, 6, 23.1; 4.33.4; 5.21.3, 22.1; *Dem.* 31.
[69] Cf. *haer.* 4.40.3.

Therefore, as I have already said, he attached and united the human being to God. For unless the human being had overcome the enemy, the enemy would not have been legitimately vanquished. And, again, unless it had been God who had freely given salvation, we could never have possessed it securely. And unless the human being had been joined to God, he could never have become a partaker of incorruptibility. For it was incumbent upon the Mediator between God and humans [1 Tim. 2:15], by his kinship to both, to bring both to friendship and concord, and to bring it about that God would take the human to himself and that the human would give itself to God. For in what way could we be partakers of the adoption of sons, unless we had received through the Son participation in himself, unless his Word had not entered into communion with us by becoming flesh? Therefore he also passed through every stage of life, restoring all to communion with God... It behoved him who was to put sin to death and redeem the human being under the power of death that he should himself be made that very thing which he was, that is, human, who had been drawn into slavery by sin and held bound by death, so that sin should be destroyed by a human being, and that the human being should go forth from death. For just as through the disobedience of the one human being, who was fashioned first from untilled soil, many were made sinners and lost life, so it was necessary that by the obedience of one human being, who was the first born of the Virgin [*qui primus ex Virgine natus est*], that many should be made just and receive salvation [cf. Rom. 5:19]. Thus, then, was the Word of God made human, as Moses also says, 'God, true are his works' [Deut. 32.4]. But if he seemed to be flesh, not having been made flesh, his work was not true; but what he seemed to be, that he also was: God, recapitulating in himself the ancient formation of the human being, that he might kill sin, deprive death of its power, and vivify the human being; and therefore his works are true. (*haer.* 3.18.7)

Recapitulating the ancient formation of the human being, and therefore also passing through every stage of human life,[70] by his obedience unto death Christ undoes the slavery of sin and the bondage in death, into which Adam, fashioned from the untilled soil, had drawn the human race, and in doing so Christ vivifies the human being. By recapitulating in himself the whole economy prefigured, and conquered, in Adam, Christ

---

[70] Cf. *haer.* 2.22.4: 'He therefore passed through every age, becoming an infant for infants, thus sanctifying infants, a child for children, a youth for youths, and an old man for old men, offering to each an example appropriate to their age.' That Christ became an 'old man' is shown, for Irenaeus, by the Jews' question, 'You are not yet fifty years old, and you have seen Abraham?' (John 8:57), which, he argues, is applicable only to one who has passed the age of 40, and is not yet 50; so, he concludes, ten years must have passed between Christ's baptism and death (*haer.* 2.22.6). Similarly, as he was born about the forty-first year of the reign of Augustus (*haer.* 3.21.3, starting from 44 BCE), but crucified under Pontius Pilate, 'the procurator of Claudius Caesar' (*Dem.* 74), he would have been in his forties when Claudius began his reign (41–57 CE). As Grant puts it (*Irenaeus*, 50), Irenaeus is 'convert[ing] grammar into theology'.

accomplishes the economy, becoming himself the human being, 'the first born of the Virgin'. In recapitulating in himself the economy of the human formation, Christ establishes himself as the new head of the human race. This is a further dimension of the term 'recapitulation', brought out well by Thomas Holsinger-Friesen:

> To press the language a bit, one might say that humanity, originally 'capitulated' by virtue of its relationship to its 'head', has found itself 'de-capitulated' (or decapitated). What is needed is a re-capitulation wherein the original connection between creation and Creator is restored, thus replacing death with life.[71]

In the head of the human race, Adam, the human being, turned from God and so lost contact with the source of life, becoming 'dead in Adam'. Through Christ's salvific work, the human being is brought back to God, given a new head, and so finds life in him.

Christ himself, as we have seen repeatedly, is the first human being, strictly speaking, of whom Adam was but a foreshadowing. He is the firstborn of the Virgin, and is himself the image of God. As such, it was not simply because he was inexperienced, as a newly created infant, that Adam was disobedient, nor because the breath of life is 'weaker' than the Spirit, but because, even though he had been created 'in the image', the one who is the image had not yet appeared. As Irenaeus puts it:

> For in times long past it was said the human being was made in the image of God, but it was not shown [to be so]; for the Word was as yet invisible, after whose image the human was created; and because of this he easily lost the likeness. When, however, the Word of God became flesh, he confirmed both of these: for he both showed forth the image truly, himself becoming that which was his image, and he re-established the likeness in a sure manner, by co-assimilating [συνεξομοιώσας] the human being to the invisible Father through the Word become visible. (*haer.* 5.16.2)

The Word was as yet invisible, or, as we have seen, the crucified Christ was hidden under the veil of Scripture, in types and prophecies not yet understood. And so, as Irenaeus puts it in the *Demonstration*, 'Christ, by being embodied in the same manner as Adam, became the human being, who was written in the beginning, "according to the image and likeness of God".'[72] The 'likeness' that the human race lost in Adam is not the Spirit,

---

[71] Holsinger-Friesen, *Irenaeus and Genesis*, 128; cf. pp. 87–8, commenting on 5.14.2: 'Its particular rendering of original "capitulation" and "decapitulation" (the introduction of death into human flesh) points to an interpretation of Christ's salvific work as "re-capitulation".'

[72] *Dem.* 32, for which Rousseau (in a retroversion that he kindly supplied to me) suggests: καὶ γένηται ὁ γεγραμμένος ἐν ἀρχῇ ἄνθρωπος.

for the Spirit was then present, bestowing the breath of life, and continuously thereafter, together with Christ, preparing the human race to be perfected in Christ and by the life-giving Spirit. Nor is it that the human race lost life, waiting for life to be restored in Christ, for, as we have seen, the arc of the economy moves from animation to vivification, two distinct modalities of life. Nor, finally, is it simply that human beings became mortal; for they always were mortal, that is, capable of death, even had they retained the 'strength' of the breath and had not died. What happened to the human race in Adam is, specifically, that it became *subject* to mortality, caught in sin and death, unable to escape from the strong man who had beguiled them under 'the pretext of immortality'. They lost, as the passage cited above suggests, the ability to live like God, for the Word as yet had not shown himself and his life in this world. Yet, when Christ does so, it is in fact by using death to conquer death. 'Likeness' to God is thus manifest in the *way* that human creatures live the life given to them, if, that is, they do so in the manner revealed by Christ, by laying down their life, rather than trying to preserve their own life (of the breath) in perpetuity. Since this had not yet been clearly shown, though with hindsight, as we have seen, the Law and the Prophets speak of this throughout, Adam, though a model of the one to come, had as yet no one on whom to model himself, and so lost this 'likeness'.[73]

The Church and the Virgin, Baptism and Eucharist

It is, however, in this very way, by death, that human beings in Adam now enter into the fullness of humanity manifested in Christ: 'Do you not know that all of us who have been baptized into Christ Jesus were baptized into his death?' (Rom. 6:3). Although Irenaeus knows of baptism as given 'for the remission of sins',[74] for him the primary function of baptism is the 'regeneration' of the human being as an adopted son of

---

[73] James Barr (*Garden of Eden*, 21) makes a similar point in his reading of the Genesis account of Adam and Eve: 'Adam and Eve were not immortal beings who by sin fell into a position where they must die; they were mortal beings who had a remote and momentary chance of eternal life but gained this chance only through an act of their own fault, and who because of that same act were deprived of that same chance.' Irenaeus would add, however, that, starting with the work of Christ in his Passion, this disobedience and death are incorporated within the arc of the economy, to become the means by which the creature learns to receive and live the divine life.

[74] The connection is made explicit only in *Dem.* 3 and *haer.* 3.12.7, where he comments on Acts 10:43. In *haer.* 5.14.3, Irenaeus writes of the 'remission of sins' of those who have been reconciled to the Father by being incorporated into the righteous flesh of Adam, but no

God.⁷⁵ Thus Irenaeus defines baptism as 'the seal of eternal life and rebirth unto God, that we may no longer be sons of mortal men, but of the eternal and everlasting God' (*Dem.* 3). This 'new generation' is intimately connected with the Christ's own formation as 'the first born of the Virgin' (*haer.* 3.18.7, cited above). As Irenaeus asks of the Ebionites:

> how can they be saved unless it was God who wrought their salvation upon earth? Or how shall the human being pass into God [χωρήσει], unless God has passed into the human? And how shall he escape from the generation of death [*mortis generationem*], if not by a new generation [*in novam generationem*], given in a wonderful and unexpected manner by God as a sign of salvation, that which is from the Virgin, they being regenerated through faith [*quae est ex Virgine, per fidem regenerentur*]? Or how shall they receive adoption from God, remaining in that generation which is according to the human being in this world?... And for this reason in the last days he exhibited the 'likeness', the Son of God being made human, assuming the ancient handiwork into himself, as I have shown in the preceding book. (*haer.* 4.33.4)⁷⁶

The new generation from the Virgin is manifested by Christ's own arrival in this world, but it is no less a new birth for all believers regenerated through faith. Similarly, a few paragraphs later, Irenaeus says:

> There are those who say that 'He is a man, and who shall know him?' [Jer. 17:9]; and, 'I came unto the prophetess, and she bore a son, and his name is called Wonderful Counsellor, the Mighty God' [Isa. 8:3, 9:6]; and those who proclaimed the Immanuel, born of the Virgin [Isa. 7:14]: declaring the union of the Word of God with his own handiwork, that the Word would become flesh, and the Son of God the Son of Man, the pure one opening purely that pure womb which regenerates human beings unto God and which he himself made pure, having become that which we are, he is 'God Almighty' and has a generation which cannot be declared. (*haer.* 4.33.1)

Becoming human, Christ opens the pure womb, the womb by which human beings are also regenerated unto God. The background for this idea is a scriptural verse that Irenaeus set before the theologian in *haer.* 1.10.3: that 'the children of her who was desolate are more than her who is married' [cf. Isa. 54:1; Gal. 4:27]. The 'barren woman', who as a result of Christ's Passion (the suffering servant described by Isaiah in the previous

---

explicit mention in made of baptism. Cf. A. Houssiau, 'Le Baptême selon Irénée de Lyon', *ETL* 60 (1984), 45–59.
⁷⁵ Cf. *haer.* 1.21.1; 3.17.1; *Dem.* 7.
⁷⁶ See also *haer.* 3.19.1; 5.1.3, cited above.

chapter, Isa. 52:13–53:12) now has many children, is the Church who now gives birth to those adopted in Christ by themselves being regenerated in the same pure womb.[77]

Irenaeus thus understands Mary, as the pure Virgin, in terms of a larger scriptural thematics, extending the dynamism of typological parallelism that we have seen between Adam and Christ to include the Virgin. The most important passage for this is *haer.* 3.22.4, which follows on directly from Irenaeus' comment on Adam as 'the type of the one to come', the one who therefore pre-exists as Saviour.

> Consistently, then, also the Virgin Mary was found to be obedient when she said, 'Behold I am the handmaid of the Lord, let it be done to me according to your word' [Luke 1:38]; but Eve was disobedient, for she did not obey when she was yet a virgin. **Just as** she, having a husband yet still being virgin ('for they were both naked', in Paradise, 'and were not ashamed' [Gen 2:25], because they had recently been made and had no knowledge about generating children; for they had first to grow up and then multiply [cf. Gen 1:28]), was disobedient, and became the cause of death for herself and the entire human race, **so also** did Mary, though having a man destined for her beforehand, and still a virgin, by being obedient became the cause of salvation for herself and the entire human race. And on this account, does the law call her who is espoused to a man, though she is still a virgin, the wife of him who espoused her, pointing out thereby the recircling [*recirculationem*][78] from Mary to Eve, because in no other way is that which is tied together loosed, except that the cords of the tying are untied in the reverse order, so that the first cords are loosed by [loosening] the second; in other words, the second cords release the first. And so it happens that the first cord is untied by the second cord, and the second cord serves as the first's untying. With this in view, the Lord said, the first will be last, and the last first [cf. Matt. 19:30; 20:16]. The prophet, too, pointed out the same thing: 'in place of your fathers, sons were born to you', he said [Ps. 44 (45):17]. For the Lord, who was born 'the firstborn of the dead' [Col. 1:18], receiving the ancient fathers into his bosom regenerated them to the life of God, having become the beginning of those who live, as Adam had become the beginning of those who die. (*haer.* 3.22.4)

It is as 'the first born of the dead' that Christ was born from the Virgin, so himself becoming the beginning of life for all those who are regenerated in his own new generation. Christ's birth from the Virgin cannot be

---

[77] We will see this again in the last section of this chapter, on the martyrs, especially in *The Letter of the Churches of Vienne and Lyons*, which is almost certainly by Irenaeus himself. For further reflection on this, see Behr, *Mystery of Christ*, ch. 4, 'The Virgin Mother'.

[78] As SC. The alternative reading in the MSS, *recircumlatio*, is followed by Steenberg, who translates it as 'return-circuit'. Rousseau suggests ἀνακύκλησις as the underlying Greek. More generally, see Matthew C. Steenberg, 'The Role of Mary as Co-Recapitulator in St Irenaeus of Lyons', *VC* 58 (2004), 117–37.

separated from the Passion, indeed it is already understood in terms of it; his recapitulation of the human being is specifically of those who have sacramentally died in baptism; and the life he gives those who are incorporated in him is a pledge of the resurrection to come.

Born again in the Church, believers receive the gift of the Holy Spirit, which is set again in a typological relationship with the breath of life:

> It is to the Church itself that this gift of God has been entrusted, as was the breath to the handiwork, for this purpose, that all the members receiving it may be vivified; and in it [the Church] is deposited the communion with Christ, that is, the Holy Spirit, the pledge of incorruptibility, the means of confirming our faith, and the ladder of ascent to God. (*haer.* 3.24.1)

As the Church is the locus of the Spirit, Irenaeus continues: 'Where the Church is, there is the Spirit of God, and where the Spirit of God is, there is the Church, and every kind of grace, and the Spirit is truth.' The Church is, as we have seen, 'planted as a Paradise in this world', in which we can 'eat from every Scripture of the Lord', but not with an uplifted mind or touching any heretical discord, lest we be cast out of the 'Paradise of life',

> into which the Lord has introduced those who obey his proclamation, 'recapitulating in himself all things which are in heaven, and which are on earth' [Eph. 1:10]; but the things in heaven are spiritual, while those on earth are the arrangements concerning man. These things, therefore, he recapitulated in himself, uniting the human being to the Spirit and making the Spirit to dwell in the human, becoming himself the head of the Spirit, and giving the Spirit to be the head of the human being: through him we see and hear and speak. (*haer.* 5.20.2)

In the paradise that is the Church, newly regenerated human beings can be trained to follow the Word and bear the Spirit.

According to Irenaeus, at his baptism Jesus was anointed by the Father with the Spirit, to be the Christ, so that human beings might also share in the abundance of his Unction (*haer.* 3.9.3). The Spirit thus initially became accustomed to dwell in the human race in Christ, 'working the will of the Father in them and renewing them from oldness to the newness of Christ' (*haer.* 3.17.1; cf. *Dem.* 6). But after his Passion and resurrection, the same Spirit was bestowed at Pentecost upon all the disciples, uniting them together, opening the New Covenant, and bringing them all to life, so that with one accord they could praise God in many languages, thus reversing the divisions introduced at Babel.[79] This same Spirit now

---

[79] *haer.* 3.17.2, and for what follows. For water imagery applied to the Spirit, see also *haer.* 4.14.2, 33.14, 36.4, 39.2; 5.18.2, and Andia, *Homo vivens*, 205–23.

works through the waters of baptism, so that, 'as a lump of dough or loaf of bread cannot be made from dry flour without water, so neither could we, being many, be made one in Christ Jesus without the Water from heaven'. Likewise: 'Just as dry earth, unless it receives water, does not fructify, so also we, who formerly were dry wood, would never have borne, as fruit, life without the willing Rain from above [cf. Ps. 67:10 LXX]'. In this way, the baptized also receive the 'living Water' promised by Christ to the Samaritan woman (cf. John 4:14), which the Lord received as a gift from the Father but which now 'wells up to eternal life' in the believer.

However, just as Jesus received this Unction at the time of his baptism, yet it was, nevertheless, not until his Passion, his death and resurrection, that 'the paternal light' fell 'upon our Lord's flesh' so that his flesh rendered fully incorruptible radiates his glory to us (cf. *haer.* 4.20.2), so also what believers have received of the Spirit through baptism is but a 'pledge' of what is to come.

> For now we receive a certain portion of the Spirit towards perfection and preparation for incorruptibility, being slowly accustomed to contain and to bear God, which the Apostle called 'a pledge', that is, a part of the honour which God has promised us, saying, in the Epistle to the Ephesians, 'In him you also, having heard the word of truth, the Gospel of your salvation and believing in him, have been sealed with the Holy Spirit of the promise, which is the pledge of our inheritance' [Eph. 1:13–14]. This pledge, therefore, thus dwelling in us, renders us spiritual even now, and the mortal is swallowed up by immortality, for he declares, 'you are not in the flesh, but in the Spirit, if the Spirit of God dwells in you' [Rom. 8:9], and this is not by a casting away of the flesh, but by the communion of the Spirit, for those to whom he was writing were not without flesh, but those who had received the Spirit of God, 'in whom we cry Abba, Father' [Rom. 8:15]. If then now, having the pledge, we cry 'Abba, Father', what shall it be when rising again we behold him face to face, when all the members shall burst forth in an exuberant hymn of exultation, glorifying him who raised them from the dead and gave them eternal life? For if the pledge, gathering the human being together into himself, makes him now say 'Abba, Father', what shall the full grace of the Spirit, which shall be given to human beings by God, effect? It will render us like unto him, and perfect the will of the Father: for it shall make the human being in the image and likeness of God. (*haer.* 5.8.1)

It is but a 'certain portion [*partem aliquam*]' of the Spirit that believers now receive through baptism, working towards their perfection and preparing them for incorruptibility, when they will be able to contain and bear God. Believers are made spiritual even now, able to call upon God as 'Abba

Father', not by the rejection of the flesh, but by the flesh beginning to be vivified by the Spirit. Its fullness remains for the time when, 'rising again', that is, after death, the flesh is fully vivified, inherited by the Spirit, so that the human being may behold the Father 'face to face' and, by the full grace of the Spirit, be made 'in the image and likeness of God'.

Regenerated in baptism, receiving the pledge of the Spirit, believers are adopted as sons of God. According to Irenaeus, the term 'son of God' can be taken in various senses. One of his predecessors observed that the term 'son' has two different meanings: according to nature or according to teaching (*haer.* 4.41.2–3).[80] In the first sense, it applies to both an 'offspring' or a product of a creator, the first being begotten, the latter being created. As created, all human beings can therefore be called sons of God. However, in the second sense, that of teaching, only those who remain in obedience to God and adhere to true belief can be called sons of God; if they turn away from this filial relationship, joining instead the apostasy of the Devil, by doing his works they become sons of the Devil. Elsewhere, Irenaeus distinguishes three different relations between God and his handiwork: while he is the God of all, to the Gentiles God is the Maker and Creator (sons as created by their Maker), to the Jews he is the Lord and Lawgiver (sons by virtue of the Law), but 'to the faithful he is as Father, since "in the last times" he opened the testament of the adoption of sons' (*Dem.* 8). This relationship of the believer to God is thus more than that of being created, or that of obeying the Law, but that of a son to the Father. Incorporated into Christ by baptism, regenerated in the Virgin, believers share in the sonship of the Son of God, 'for it was for this that the Word of God was made human, and the Son of God, the Son of Man, that the human being, having been taken [*commixtus*] into the Word, and receiving adoption, might become a son of God' (3.19.1). Becoming 'sons of God' in this manner, believers can themselves be called 'gods': '"God stood in the congregation of gods, he judges in the midst of the gods" [Ps. 81.1 LXX] [this text] speaks of the Father and the Son and those who have received the adoption, for they are the Church' (*haer.* 3.6.1).[81]

This new status of believers as 'sons of God' and themselves 'gods' is manifest, paradoxically, in an increased subjection to God. As sons, they

---

[80] Irenaeus does not name his source, though one might reasonably conjecture Polycarp. I have followed Rousseau (SC 100, pp. 283–5) in giving preference to the Armenian version of *haer.* 4.41.2. A similar point is made by Origen in his *Hom. on Jer.* 9.4.

[81] This passage is referred to in *haer.* 4.Pr.4: 'I have shown that there is none other called "God" by the Scriptures, except the Father of all, and the Son, and those who possess the adoption.'

are no longer subject to the law of slavery, the pedagogue that led us to Christ (cf. Gal. 3.24), for this has been cancelled by Christ in 'the new covenant of liberty' (*haer.* 4.16.5).[82] In annulling the laws of slavery imposed upon Israel when they turned to the golden calf in the desert, Christ has not abrogated the natural precepts of love for God and justice towards one's neighbour planted in the heart, the free and willing keeping of which justified those before the Law, but has 'extended and fulfilled them' (*haer.* 4.13.1)[83]: the Law prohibited adultery, Christ forbade lust (Matt. 5:27–8). It is not the internalization of the commandments that is of interest to Irenaeus, for, as we have seen, he says very little about 'interiority' altogether, but rather the greater subjection to God that this demonstrates: the glorious liberty of the sons of God is thus manifest, for Irenaeus, in the higher degree of their subjection to God. If the primary relationship between God and his handiwork is that 'God makes and the human being is made' (*haer.* 4.11.2), then the more that the handiwork subjects herself or himself to the creative activity of God, the more God can in turn fashion him or her.[84]

Having passed through the waters of baptism and receiving the pledge of the Spirit, believers are now nourished by eating from the Scriptures, as Adam was to eat from every tree, and, as Israel was fed by manna, so now believers are fed by the Eucharist. As the Body and Blood of Christ are themselves a union of flesh and spirit, they provide us with a taste of incorruptibility and the hope of resurrection:

> For we offer to him his own, fittingly proclaiming the communion and union of the flesh and the Spirit. For just as the bread from the earth, when it has received the invocation of God, is no longer ordinary bread, but Eucharist, consisting of two things, earthly and heavenly, so also our bodies, receiving the Eucharist, are no longer corruptible, having the hope of the resurrection. (*haer.* 4.18.5).

The flesh of believers is nourished, even now, by that for which they are being prepared—that is, the reception of incorruption. As the Eucharist itself is no longer common bread, by partaking of the Eucharist, the bodies of believers are no longer corruptible flesh, but, just as the Eucharist is both earthly and heavenly, so do their bodies have the 'hope of the

---

[82] The whole section *haer.* 4.9–16 is a reflection on the Law and the Gospel, and the growth from one to the other. Cf. M. F. Berrouard, 'Servitude de la Loi et liberté de l'Evangile selon saint Irénée', *LV* 61 (1963), 41–60.

[83] Cf. *haer.* 4.13.2–4, 16.4–5; *Dem.* 96.

[84] Cf. Julie Canlis, 'Being Made Human: The Significance of Creation for Irenaeus' Doctrine of Participation', *SJT* 58/4 (2005), 343–54.

resurrection', so that believers proclaim 'the communion and union of the flesh and the Spirit'.

Nourishing believers in this way, the Eucharist is the paradigm of what will happen to them in and through their own death, when the pledge of the Spirit blossoms into its fullness, just as the Unction by which Christ was baptized transfigured his body through his Passion such that it became resplendent with the paternal light (cf. *haer.* 4.20.2). This connection between the Eucharist and the death and resurrection of the believer is treated in *haer.* 5.2.3. He begins by emphasizing that, just as the flesh of believers 'has grown and strengthened' by the 'mixed cup and manufactured bread', which, having received the Word of God, is the Body and Blood of Christ, so also their flesh is capable of receiving eternal life from God. Moreover, if the Apostle speaks of believers as 'members of his body and of his flesh and of his bones' (cf. Eph. 5:30), he is speaking not of fleshless spiritual beings, 'for a spirit has neither flesh nor bones' (cf. Luke 24:39), but of a genuine human being, made of flesh and blood, and nourished by Christ's Body and Blood. He then continues:

> **Just as** the wood of the vine, planted in the earth, bore fruit in its own time, and the grain of wheat, falling into the earth and being decomposed, was raised up manifold by the Spirit of God who sustains all, then, by wisdom, they come to the use of human beings and, receiving the Word of God, become Eucharist, which is the Body and Blood of Christ, **so also**, our bodies, nourished by it, having been placed in the earth and decomposing in it, shall rise in their time, when the Word of God bestows on them the resurrection to the glory of God the Father, who secures immortality for the mortal and bountifully bestows incorruptibility on the corruptible [cf. 1 Cor. 15:53], because the power of God is made perfect in weakness [cf. 2 Cor. 12:9], **in order that** we may never become puffed up, as if we had life from ourselves, nor exalted against God, entertaining ungrateful thoughts, but learning by experience that it is from his excellence, and not from our own nature, that we have eternal continuance, that we should neither undervalue the true glory of God nor be ignorant of our own nature, but should know what God can do and what benefits the human, and that we should never mistake the true understanding of things as they are, that is, of God and the human being. (*haer.* 5.2.3)

The parallelism between the processes that lead to the Eucharist and to the resurrection of the believer is intertwined in a dynamic manner. By receiving the Eucharist, as the wheat and the vine receive growth from the Spirit, believers are prepared, as they make the fruits of the earth into bread and wine, for their own resurrection effected by the Word, through which, as the bread and wine receive the Word to become the Body and Blood of Christ, the Eucharist, so also the bodies of believers will receive immortality and incorruptibility from the Father. The distinctively human activity of preparing the fruits of this earth,[85] which then receive the invocation (ἐπίκλησις, *haer.* 4.18.5) and the Word to become the Body and Blood of Christ, corresponds to their preparation, through receiving the Eucharist, for the bestowal of immortality in the resurrection effected by Christ. In a very real sense, then, the whole of the divine economy, ordered towards and culminating in the death and resurrection of Christ and believers in him, can be seen as the Eucharist of the God and Father. Moreover, in a very characteristically Irenaean fashion, all of this has been arranged with a purpose, an intentionality structured by Christ's words to Paul that his strength is made perfect in weakness. As with the 'Sign of Jonah' considered earlier, by undergoing the experience of weakness to its ultimate point, becoming dust in the earth, the human being simultaneously learns the strength of God and so comes to the true knowledge of things as they are—that is, of God and the human being, and so is able to remain continuously thankful thereafter to God who in this way fashions the living human being, who we can now add is a 'eucharistic' being.

The completion of creation

Although members of the Church are dispersed throughout the world (*haer.* 1.10.1; 4.36.2), the Church is located in the Spirit (3.24.1), just as believers, having passed through the waters of baptism, have received a 'pledge' of the Spirit and now are fed by Scripture and the Eucharist, but have not yet been inherited by the Spirit nor entered the Promised Land. Their regeneration in baptism is but a prelude of what is to come—that is, the 'second generation [*secundam generationem*] after their dissolution into the earth' promised in the prophecies of Isaiah and Ezekiel by the one 'who at the beginning created the human being'.[86] As the patriarchs learnt to follow the Word, but did not enter the Promised Land before their death, so too their descendants, the followers of Christ, do not receive the fullness of the promise until their resurrection; and, as it was specifically

---

[85] Nicholas Cabasilas (*A Commentary on the Divine Liturgy*, trans. J. M. Hussey and P. A. McNulty (London: SPCK, 1960), iii. 4), points out that human beings alone are cooking animals: 'We call human that which belongs to the human being alone. Now, the baking of bread to eat and the making of wine to drink is peculiar to the human being. That is why we offer bread and wine.'

[86] *haer.* 5.15.1, citing Isa. 26:19, 66:13–14; Ezek. 37:1–14. The connection between the παλιγγενεσία (not translated in the RSV) and the kingdom is made in Matt. 19:28. Cf. Orbe, *Teología*, ii. 7–8.

land that was promised to the patriarchs, so it will be in a transfigured, but fully material, world that the righteous are raised. The object of the economy of God is, as we have seen, the flesh moulded, animated, and ultimately vivified by the Hands of God, and the economy has been arranged in such a way as to acquaint the handiwork with its weakness, that it is flesh, so that the human being can simultaneously come to know, in this way, the strength of God deployed in the flesh. As such, the economy culminates not in a mystical union of the soul with God, but with the perfecting of the mud in the image and likeness of God. Conditioned as this may have been by Irenaeus' reaction to the teaching of his opponents, it is nevertheless integral to his understanding of the single and complete economy of God, as revealed in Christ, and is therefore articulated by him in an uncompromising and unparalleled manner.[87] Irenaeus' teaching on the last times is not, therefore, an aberrant appendage to his work, but shows him to be, as Christopher Smith puts it, 'a consistent creationist'.[88]

As Irenaeus turned to the opening chapters of Genesis to understand Christ's work, so too he looked to the opening verses to understand the last times: for 'this is an account of what happened, as it happened, as also it is a prophecy of what is to come' (*haer.* 5.28.3). As a day of the Lord is as a thousand years (cf. 2 Pet. 3:8), if God finished his work on the sixth day and rested on the seventh (cf. Gen. 2:2), creation is completed in six thousand years, when there is inaugurated the seventh thousand-year period, which will be that of the kingdom of the Son, in which the just will reign with him in a renewed earthly Jerusalem. The period before the resurrection and the coming of the kingdom is a time of tribulation and martyrdom, in which the wheat will be separated from the chaff. This era culminates, before the return of Christ, with the coming of the Antichrist, who will devastate all things in this world, recapitulate all error, evil, and apostasy, and, for three years and six months, attempt to be worshipped as God in the Temple in Jerusalem.[89] Recapitulating in himself all apostasy, error, and iniquity, the whole apostasy, summed up together in him, can

---

[87] As Hans Urs von Balthasar (*Glory of the Lord*, ii. 93) puts it: 'In his eschatology Irenaeus produces an important counterweight to the flight from the world and the failure to take seriously the resurrection of the flesh which marks the Platonizing Christian eschatologies of a later period and indeed the average Christian consciousness.'

[88] Christopher R. Smith, 'Chiliasm and Recapitulation in the Theology of Ireneus', *VC* 48 (1994), 313–31, at 320.

[89] Cf. *haer.* 5.25–6, 28–30. The three years and six months (5.30.4) probably refer to the 'half week' of Dan. 9:27.

be consigned to the eternal furnace.[90] Christ will cast the Antichrist into the lake of fire (Rev. 19:20), when he comes in the glory of the Father to bring the just into the seventh-day rest of the kingdom (*haer.* 5.30.4). In dealing with the judgement that Christ brings, Irenaeus emphasizes that the Son comes to all alike, with the express purpose of judging, granting life, and communion with himself to all who are willing to receive it. The meaning of the term 'judgement' is separation, and, as everyone has been created with free will and understanding, the choice whether to join the just or the judged rests with them, not with God who 'makes his sun to rise on the evil and on the good' (*haer.* 5.27.1; Matt. 5:45). It is, therefore, not the light that has blinded the judged, but rather that they have preferred the darkness, and so God's 'judgement' is an acknowledgement of their own freely chosen separation: 'he inflicts that separation from himself which they have chosen of their own accord' (*haer.* 5.27.2).

When he comes, Christ will raise the just to reign with him in his kingdom. In one passage, a large part of which is preserved only in Armenian, Irenaeus describes this period of the kingdom as being the seventh thousand-year period:

John, therefore, foresaw precisely the first resurrection of the just [cf. Luke 14:14, Rev. 20:5–6] and the inheritance of the earth in the kingdom, and the prophets have also prophesied concerning it in the same terms. For this is what the Lord also taught, promising to drink the new mingled cup with his disciples in the kingdom [cf. Matt. 26:29], {and again when he said, 'the days are coming when the dead in their tombs will hear the voice of the Son of Man and those who have done good will rise to the resurrection of life, but those who have done evil will rise to the resurrection of judgement' [cf. John 5:28–9], saying that those doing good will be raised first, going to the rest, and then those who are to be judged will be raised, just as the Book of Genesis has the completion of this world on the sixth day, that is, the sixth thousand-years, and then the seventh day of rest, of which David says, 'this is my rest, the just shall enter into it' [cf. Pss 131:14, 117:20 LXX], that is, the seventh thousand-years of the kingdom of the just, in which the just shall grow accustomed to incorruptibility, when the whole of creation will be renewed for those who have been preserved for this.} The apostle, also, has confessed that the creation shall be set free from the bondage of corruption for the glorious liberty of the children of God [Rom. 8:21]. (*haer.* 3.36.3)[91]

---

[90] Cf. *haer.* 5.25.1, 5; 28.2; 29.2; 30.1. The number of the Antichrist, 666, also recapitulates the apostasy that had taken place at the beginning, the middle, and the end of the six thousand-year periods (*haer.* 5.30.1).

[91] The words in curly brackets {} are found only in Armenian (TU 35.2, 244.23–5.2).

The just are now raised to enjoy the land promised to the patriarchs and drink the fruit of the vine with Christ as he promised to his disciples (*haer.* 5.33.1; Matt. 26:29). In expounding this eschatological banquet, Irenaeus draws upon the tradition of the elders who saw John as reported by Papias, who taught that:

> The days will come, in which vines shall grow, each having ten thousand branches, and in each branch ten thousand twigs, and in each true twig ten thousand shoots, and in each one of the shoots ten thousand clusters, and on every one of the clusters ten thousand grapes, and every grape when pressed will give twenty-five metretes of wine. And when any one of the saints shall lay hold of a cluster, another shall cry out, 'I am a better cluster, take me; bless the Lord through me'. In like manner [the Lord declared] that a grain of wheat would produce ten thousand ears, and that every ear should have ten thousand grains, and every grain would yield ten pounds of clear, pure, fine flour; and that all other fruit-bearing trees, and seeds and grass, would produce in similar proportions; and that all animals feeding [only] on the productions of the earth, should [in those days] become peaceful and harmonious among each other, and be in perfect subjection to man. (*haer.* 5.33.3)

Isaac's blessing on Jacob (Gen. 27:27–9), is extended to the field of the world (cf. Matt. 13:38), and so the blessing foreshadows the kingdom, when 'creation, also, having been renovated and set free, shall fructify with an abundance of all kinds of food, from the Dew of heaven and from the fertility of the earth' (*haer.* 5.33.3). This time of the kingdom, life in a liberated and fruitful creation, also provides a further occasion for the human being to be trained in divine ways and become accustomed to bear God, to partake of his incorruptibility, and to receive the glory of the Father (*haer.* 5.32.1, 35.1–2).

After Christ's kingdom comes the general resurrection and judgement, when 'the book of life' is opened and the dead judged according to their works and 'cast into the lake of fire, the second death', Gehenna or the eternal fire (*haer.* 5.35.2, Rev. 20:12–15). John's words immediately following this, 'Then I saw a new heaven and a new earth', together with Isaiah's prophecy that 'there shall be a new heaven and a new earth', are understood by Irenaeus in terms of Paul's words that 'the fashion of this world shall pass away'.[92] The passing-away of the fashion of this world happens when 'the new Jerusalem shall descend, as a bride adorned for her husband, and this is the tabernacle of God in which God will dwell with human beings' (*haer.* 5.35.2; Rev. 21:2–3). The earthly Jerusalem is an

---

[92] *haer.* 5.35.2, citing Rev. 21:1, Isa. 65:17, and 1 Cor. 7:31.

image of the new Jerusalem, and of this tabernacle Moses received a pattern on the mountain. Regarding the new creation, Irenaeus emphasizes that 'nothing is able to be allegorized, but all things are steadfast and true and substantial, having been made by God for the enjoyment of the righteous' (*haer.* 5.35.2). It is the 'fashion of this world' that passes away, that is 'that in which the transgression occurred, for the human being has grown old in them', while 'neither the nature nor substance is not destroyed, for true and firm is he who has established it' (*haer.* 5.36.1). When the human being shall be 'renewed and flourishing in an incorruptible state', then there shall be the new heaven and the new earth, 'in which the human being will remain always holding fresh converse with God' (*haer.* 5.36.1). When this 'fashion' has passed away, 'the human being is renewed and flourishes with incorruptibility, as no longer able to grow old; "there shall be a new heaven and a new earth" in which the new human being will remain holding converse with God in an always new manner' (*haer.* 5.36.1). The 'many mansions' of the Father's house provide a continual mode of ascent towards God (*haer.* 5.36.2; John 14:2). With death, the 'last enemy', thus destroyed, the Son will yield up his work to the Father, that he might be 'all in all' (*haer.* 5.36.2; 1 Cor. 15:24–8).

Irenaeus concludes his work with two sentences, the first emphasizing that the whole economy, as one economy, manifests one God, the Father, and the second recapitulating the work of Christ, bringing his handiwork to existence as the image and likeness of God:

And in all these things, and by them all, one and the same God the Father is shown, fashioning the human being and promising the inheritance of the earth to the fathers, giving it[93] in the resurrection of the just and fulfilling the promises in the kingdom of his Son, then bestowing paternally those things which neither the eye has seen, nor the ear has heard, nor has [the thought] arisen within the heart of the human being [1 Cor. 2:9].[94] And there is one Son, who accomplished the Father's will, and there is one human race, in which the mysteries of God are wrought, 'which the angels desire to see' [1 Pet. 1:12], not being able to search out

---

[93] Following the Armenian, with Rousseau, rather than the Latin *eduxit illam*.

[94] As to what is bestowed 'paternally' at this point, Irenaeus does not speculate. Undaunted, Orbe (*Teología*, iii. 628–33, 646–51) analyses this statement in terms of the vision of God with corporeal eyes. *haer.* 4.20.5, with its threefold modes of seeing God (*prophetice, adoptive, paternaliter*), might suggest that there is a vision of God directly, but it is also qualified by Irenaeus' assertion that God has manifested himself in (and only in) Christ, who preserves the visibility of the Father so that we might always have something towards which we can advance, and it is 'incorruption for eternal life that comes to us from seeing God'. Likewise, in *haer.* 5.36, he does not speak so much of seeing God directly, but rather of flourishing in incorruptibility and holding ever-new converse with God.

the wisdom of God, through which his handiwork, conformed and incorporated with the Son, is perfected—that his Offspring, the First-begotten Word, should descend to the creature, that is, to the handiwork, and be borne by it, and, again, [that] the creature should bear the Word and ascend to him, passing beyond the angels and becoming in the image and likeness of God. (*haer.* 5.36.3)

The divine intention expressed in Genesis, to create a human being 'in the image and likeness' of God, is now complete: the handiwork, mud taken up from the earth and animated by a breath of life, fashioned by the Hands of God throughout the economy, culminates in its being raised up, again from the earth, to be vivified by the Holy Spirit in a second generation, which is already anticipated in the believers' regeneration through baptism into Christ and their reception of the pledge of the Spirit. The beginning and the end have been expounded by Irenaeus in terms of each other, within the arc of one economy, the defining shape of which is given by the work of God in Christ: Scripture, in particular the opening chapters of Genesis, typifies what happens in him, as he realizes what will be wrought in those who follow him. For Irenaeus, protology and eschatology are thoroughly, from beginning to end, Christocentric.

THE SYMPHONY OF SALVATION

In the previous section we have seen how Irenaeus understands the work of God in and through the economy, following Paul's lead of putting Adam and Christ in parallel and filling in the details from a broad range of Scripture but especially from the opening chapters of Genesis: Adam is a preliminary and animated sketch of Christ, the complete and living spiritual human being, whose stature believers in the present anticipate, again in a preliminary manner, through the regeneration of baptism and reception of the pledge of the Spirit. This is, to use the terms we have employed previously, a synchronic picture, seeing in the mosaic of Scripture, in its types and accounts, the image of the King proclaimed in the recapitulation of Scripture in the Gospel. Christ is the culmination of the arc of the economy, but he also comes first, before Adam, being the reality impressed on the handiwork and the Word sown throughout Scripture.

This synchronic view of the economy, however, goes together with the diachronic unfolding of the economy and the growth of human beings in time. In the points laid before theologians, Irenaeus invites them 'to set forth why God made some things temporal, others eternal' (*haer.* 1.10.3).

Or, as he puts it in a short statement of the rule of truth in *haer.* 1.22.1: 'It is the Father who made all things through him [the Word], whether visible or invisible, whether sensible or intelligible, whether temporal, for the sake of a certain economy, or eternal.' God has created all things in the same manner, that is, through his Word. Some things, however, were created invisible and with an intellectual nature, the spiritual beings who are eternal, and therefore neither subject nor able to change, at least within the course of human temporality, while others are created visible and sensible, and they also are temporal, and thus subject to change.

It is, therefore, God himself who is responsible for the temporal nature of the sensible universe, and hence its mutability. This temporality and mutability is inscribed into the very nature of the relationship between God and his handiwork, based as this is on the logic of creation—that is, that it is God who skilfully fashions the human being while the human being is made by God. Being made, the human being must have a beginning, the starting point for their growth:

> For he formed him for growth and increase, as the Scripture says, 'increase and grow' [Gen 1:28]. And indeed in this respect God differs from the human, that God indeed makes, but the human is made. And he who makes is always the same, while he who is made must receive a beginning, a middle, addition and increase.[95] And God indeed makes well, while the human is well made. (*haer.* 4.11.1-2)

Irenaeus continues by saying that, while God is 'perfect in all things, equal to himself and similar to himself', the human being receives advance and growth towards God; 'as God is always the same, so also the human being, when found in God, shall always go on towards God' (*haer.* 4.11.2). Likewise, God never ceases from bestowing gifts upon the human being, nor does the human being ever cease from receiving these benefits and being enriched. It is for each human being to determine how he or she will respond, whether thankfully or ungratefully, and everything depends upon this response:

> For the vessel of his goodness and the instruments of his glorification is the human being who is thankful towards him that made him; and again, the vessel of his just

---

[95] Rousseau (SC 100, p. 228) argues that *adjectionem et augmentum*, while the Armenian text repeats the same word (*augmentum*), reflects an underlying single Greek word, ἀκμή, as, following the beginning and middle, one would 'a prior' expect 'le point culminant ou maturité'. However, the first line of the quotation given above (the last line of *haer.* 4.11.1), in both the Latin and Armenian, would support the Latin *adjectionem et augmentum*. Irenaeus sees human perfection lying in an unceasing movement towards God, as indeed he points out in the following sentence. Cf. Bacq, *De l'ancienne à la nouvelle alliance selon S. Irénée*, 96, n. 2.

judgement is the ungrateful human, who despises his Maker and is not subject to his Word. (*haer.* 4.11.2)

Following on from the basic dynamic of the relationship between the Creator and the created, is the need for created beings to respond to the creative activity of God by *allowing* themselves to be created, an attitude that Irenaeus characterizes as thankfulness. If the intention of God is to create human beings 'in his image and likeness', the handiwork must give its assent to become human in the stature of Christ. In an intriguing manner, Irenaeus seems to be picking up on a distinction within the opening chapter of Genesis, where every other aspect of creation is simply brought into existence by a divine 'fiat', while the work that God identifies as his own project, to make the human being in his image and likeness, is not completed until Christ's own work as human, and now in those who respond in faith and thankfulness in Christ.

Irenaeus provides a further analysis of the rationale of the temporality of the fashioning of the handiwork by God in the economy in *haer.* 4.4.1–5.1. His opponents argued that, if Jerusalem had indeed been 'the city of the great King' (Matt. 5:35), then it should never have been deserted. But, Irenaeus points out, this would be like claiming that, if straw or vine twigs were created by God, then they should never be separated from the wheat or grapes. Rather, the truth of the matter is that they were not originally made for their own sake, but for the fruit that they produce, and they are abandoned once the harvest is gathered. So, likewise, with Jerusalem, which had in herself borne the yoke of bondage, to which the human race had been reduced, but by so being subdued became a fit subject for liberty; 'when the fruit of liberty had come and reached maturity and been reaped' and carried away from Jerusalem, scattered throughout the world, then Jerusalem was forsaken. So, he concludes, 'all things which have a beginning in time must of course have an end in time also' (*haer.* 4.4.1). Likewise with the Law that originated with Moses and terminated with John, so that 'Jerusalem beginning with David, and completing its own time, must have an end of legislation when the new covenant was revealed' (*haer.* 4.4.2; Luke 16:16). And, on a universal scale, 'the fashion of the whole world must also pass away when the time of its disappearance has come, in order that the fruit may be gathered into the granary, but the chaff, left behind, may be consumed by fire' (*haer.* 4.4.3). In *haer.* 5.36.1, referring to a 'preceding book' in which he has 'shown, as far as possible, the cause of the creation of this world of temporal things', Irenaeus specifies, as we have seen, following Paul (1 Cor. 7:31), that it is the 'fashion' of the world that passes, but not its 'nature of substance', for this remains as its Creator is true and faithful. The beginning and end of all these things, says Irenaeus, lies with God himself, 'who does all things by measure and in order', so that, as a predecessor put it, 'the unmeasurable Father was measured in the Son, for the Son is the measure of the Father since he also comprehends him' (haer. 4.4.2).

However, in the midst of all these changeable and transitory things is the human being, who, as created, is also changeable, but who has nevertheless been created for immortality. Unlike the wheat and the chaff, where the one who created them is also the one who separates them, the human being, created with reason, free will, and power over himself, 'is himself the cause to himself' whether he becomes wheat or chaff.[96] Thus the human being is part of the world of temporal and changeable things, but differs from the rest of creation in that its transience provides the context in which she or he can grow into immortality (haer. 4.4.3).[97] So, Irenaeus concludes:

> God, therefore, is one and the same, who rolls up the heaven like a book and renews the face of the earth; who made the temporal things for the human being, so that, maturing in them, he may bear as fruit immortality, and who, through his kindness, also confers eternal things, 'that in the ages to come he may show the exceeding riches of his grace'. (haer. 4.5.1, Eph. 2:7)

The temporality and mutability of creation, and the human being within creation, are therefore, for Irenaeus, provided by God as the context in which the human being can learn to grow into the immortality of God. As it is the present fashion ($\sigma\chi\hat{\eta}\mu a$) of this world that passes away, so, in turn, when the human being comes to participate in the immortality of God, God will 'transfigure' ($\mu\epsilon\tau a\sigma\chi\eta\mu a\tau\iota\sigma\epsilon\iota$) the initial 'fashion' of the 'body of humiliation' to conform it to 'the body of his glory'.[98]

Irenaeus adds a further dimension to this growth and change, in haer. 4.38.3, when he explains how God demonstrates his power, wisdom, and goodness

---

[96] For Irenaeus' understanding of 'free will', see Orbe, Antropología, 165–95, and Berthouzoz, Liberté et grâce, 195–8.

[97] Cf. haer. 5.29.1, again referring back to a previous discussion: 'In the previous books I have set forth the causes for which God permitted these things to be made, and have pointed out that all such have been created for the benefit of that human nature which is saved, ripening for immortality that which is [possessed] of its own free will and its own power, and preparing and rendering it more adapted for eternal subjection to God. And therefore the creation is suited to [the needs of] the human being; for the human being was not made for its sake, but creation for the sake of the human being.'

[98] haer. 5.13.3, citing 1 Cor. 15:53–5 and Phil. 3:20–1.

simultaneously together: his power and goodness, in that he brings things into being that previously were not; his wisdom, in that, in proportion, measure, and harmony, he brought things into being, those who,

> through his super-eminent goodness, receiving growth and abiding for a long period of existence, will obtain the glory of the Uncreated [ἀγενήτου δόξαν ἀποίσεται], of the God who bestows what is good ungrudgingly. By virtue of being created, they are not uncreated; but by virtue of continuing in being throughout a long course of ages, they shall receive the power of the Uncreated [δύναμιν ἀγένητου προσλήψεται], of the God who freely bestows upon them eternal existence. (haer. 4.38.3)

This is, as we have seen, the fruit of the economy that is for the sake of the human being, and the completion of creation. But it has now become clearer that freedom and temporality are preconditions for its fulfilment. Only things subject to time are capable of growth, and this opens the possibility that, while remaining what they are by nature, the mode or the 'fashion' of their existence can change: human beings can come to share in the power and the glory of the Uncreated. Yet this is but a possibility, which requires the free response of human beings, to allow themselves to be fashioned in this manner.

The temporal unfolding of the economy is enacted in two registers, that narrated within Scripture and that lived out by each human being, though the depiction of Adam as an infant and Christ as the perfect living human being suggests an underlying correspondence or similar pattern of growth for the human race and the individual human being. The unfolding of the economy in the first register is described at length in the first half of the *Demonstration of the Apostolic Preaching*. It is also summarized succinctly in *haer.* 4.14.2, where it follows his analysis (in *haer.* 4.14.1, considered earlier) of the intentionality of the act of creation as bringing human beings to share in the glory that Christ had with the Father before the creation of the world:

> Thus God, from the beginning, fashioned the human being for his munificence; and chose the patriarchs for the sake of their salvation; and formed in advance a people, teaching the uneducated to follow God; and prepared the prophets, accustoming the human being on the earth to bear his Spirit and to have communion with God; he himself, indeed, having need of nothing, but granting communion with himself to those who stood in need of it. To those that pleased him, he sketched out like an architect, the construction of salvation;[99] and to those who did not see, in Egypt, he himself gave guidance; and to those who were

---

[99] Bacq (*De l'ancienne à la nouvelle alliance selon S. Irénée*, 117) suggests the allusion is to God describing the plan of the ark to Noah in Gen. 6: 13–16.

unruly, in the desert, he promulgated a very suitable Law; while to those who entered into the good land he bestowed the appropriate inheritance; finally, for those converted to the Father, he killed the fatted calf and presented them with the finest robe.[100] Thus, in many ways, he harmonized the human race to the symphony of salvation.[101]

The first two sentences of this passage recount, twice, the history unfolded in Scripture. Following his initial bountiful creation, God chose the patriarchs 'for their salvation'; that is, he chose those who were to be the fathers of a race, individuals whose lives and actions were to have a universal significance. To these, he sketched out 'the construction of salvation'—that is, in the various theophanies and actions of God in Genesis, where the future economy of Christ is already foreshadowed and foreseen in the Spirit, finding a response in the faith of the patriarchs (cf. haer. 4.5.2–5). Having chosen the heads of the race, God then forms a people for himself through the guidance given in Egypt and the Law given through Moses, and through the tabernacle and temple, the sacrifices and oblations, as 'types' by which 'they learned to fear God and continue in his service' (haer. 4.14.3). Again this preparatory formation of the people points forward to Christ's work of salvation and the establishment of the Church. Having journeyed through the desert, God bestows upon the people who entered the good land an appropriate inheritance. The next stage is that of the prophets, who, like the patriarchs, have a twofold significance: on the one hand, they are, individually, moved by the Spirit, and, on the other hand, this is a further stage in the accustoming of the human being in bearing the Spirit and holding communion with God. It also, again, points forward, as

---

[100] Following Rousseau's translation of *primam stolam*. Others have taken the adjective *prima* in the sense of 'original', and linked the *stola* to 'the robe of holiness from the Spirit' (haer. 3.23.5) with which Adam was clothed in Paradise, identifying this as the Spirit and the 'likeness' which he lost. Cf. Orbe, *Antropología*, 214–18; H. J. Jaschke, *Der Heilige Geist im Bekenntnis der Kirche: Ein Studie zur Pneumatologie des Irenäus von Lyon im Ausgang vom altchristlichen Glaubensbekenntnis*, Münsterische Beiträge zur Theologie, 40 (Münster: Aschendorff, 1976), 254–6, and Andia, *Homo vivens*, 95–9. However, the context here is an interpretation of the parable of the Prodigal Son (Luke 15:11–32), where the father simply bestows on his son the finest that he has, with no indication of what clothing he wore before setting out on his misadventures. As Bacq (*De l'ancienne à la nouvelle alliance selon S. Irénée*, 118, n. 1) notes, the verb used is *donans* not *restaurans* or *restituens*.

[101] Following, in the last words, the Armenian version, which suggests a musical context. Bacq (*De l'ancienne à la nouvelle alliance selon S. Irénée*, 118, n. 2) points out that this 'symphony' is a further reference to the parable of the Prodigal Son, who, when approaching his father's house, heard music (συμφωνία, Luke 15:25). For Irenaeus' image of God and the human being becoming 'accustomed' to one another, see Paul Évieux, 'La Théologie de l'accoutumance chez saint Irénée', *RSR* 55 (1967), 5–54.

the people now learn to recognize those sent from God, and to see in their suffering the suffering of the one to come, the one who will impart the fullness of the Spirit and establish full communion between God and the human being. Finally, for those who convert to the Father, that is, the Gentiles,[102] God sacrifices his Son, the 'fatted calf', and bestow on them the 'finest robe', so making those who were not a people into his people, another point that Irenaeus set before the theologian (*haer.* 1.10.3; Hos. 2:23; Rom. 9:25).

Such, then, is the 'symphony of salvation' to which the human race has been 'harmonized', played out through the economy narrated in Scripture: God choosing his friends, forming a people out of them, and finally grafting in the Gentiles through the sacrifice of his Son, to which all the prior episodes narrated in Scripture also pointed. Although 'simple' (cf. *haer.* 2.13.3, 28.5), God has worked out human salvation through this economy in a manifold fashion. So Irenaeus continues the passage by adding to the 'many ways of the symphony of salvation' the words of John, that 'his voice [φωνή] is as the sound of many waters' (*haer.* 4.14.2, Rev. 1.15), commenting that 'the Spirit is truly many waters as the Father is both rich and multiple'. As only the Son has declared the Father (John 1:18), the Word who is the interpreter of the Father is likewise 'rich and multiple', for it was 'not in one figure, nor in one character, that he appeared to those seeing him, but according to purpose and effect of the economies' (*haer.* 4.20.11). All the diverse types and parables by which Christ is present throughout Scripture are brought together, again in the image of a symphony or melody, in *haer.* 4.20.7, so that the 'richness' of God is unfolded in a harmonious manner, each with their appropriate moment, all for the benefit of the human being:

> Thus, from the beginning, the Son is the Revealer [*Enarrator*] of the Father, since he is with the Father from the beginning: the prophetic visions, the diversity of graces, his ministries, the glorification of the Father, all these, in the manner of a melody, compositely and harmoniously, he has unfolded to the human race at the appropriate time for their advantage. For where there is a melody, there is a composition; where there is a composition, there is appropriate time; and where there is appropriate time, there is advantage. (*haer.* 4.20.7)

In this way, Irenaeus continues, the Word became 'the dispenser [οἰκονόμος] of the paternal grace', the one who arranges and effects the

---

[102] Cf. Bacq, *De l'ancienne à la nouvelle alliance selon S. Irénée*, 117, and *haer.* 4.36.7, the only other place where Irenaeus refers to the parable, to show that both those called first, Israel, and those called later, the Gentiles, have one and the same Father.

economy, for the advantage of human beings, 'revealing God to human beings and presenting the human being to God'. In doing so, Irenaeus points out, the Word always preserves the invisibility of the Father, lest human beings come to despise God, and that they may always have something towards which to advance; yet, on the other hand, he reveals God to human beings through many economies, that they should not cease to be (*haer.* 4.20.7). Human beings cannot of themselves see God, but God shows himself as and when he wills; previously he had been seen 'prophetically' in the Spirit; now he is seen 'adoptively' in the son; while in the kingdom he will be seen 'paternally', having been prepared by the Spirit for the Son who leads the human being to the Father who bestows incorruptibility and eternal life (*haer.* 4.20.5). This symphony of salvation, then, has led the human being through the different stages of life, to become the living human being that sees God and is the glory of God (*haer.* 4.20.7).

The same process of growth and maturation is evident within the temporal span of a human lifetime. Irenaeus addresses this in a most intriguing fashion in *haer.* 4.37–9, where he provides an exposition from Scripture of 'the ancient law of human liberty', the fact that 'God created man free, having, from the beginning, power over himself' (*haer.* 4.37.1).[103] As we have seen, only creatures created with freedom are capable of initiative and response, and only in this way are they capable of changing the mode or fashion of their existence, growing into the immortality of God. After citing many passages from Scripture to demonstrate human freedom, a freedom that extends to faith (*haer.* 4.37.5), and the corresponding responsibility and accountability that follow on from this, Irenaeus turns to those who would deny this, representing, Irenaeus claims, the Lord as destitute of power, unable to accomplish what he willed, or as ignorant that some human beings are merely 'material', not able to receive immortality. He draws out the presuppositions of his opponents, as a question:

'But', they say, 'he should not have created angels such that they were able to transgress, nor human beings such that they immediately [*statim*] became ungrateful towards him, because they were created rational and capable of examining and judging, and not like irrational or inanimate creatures which are not able to do anything of their own will but are drawn by necessity and force towards the good, with one inclination and one bearing, unable to deviate and without

---

[103] On the place of 4.37–9, the so-called 'Treatise on Free Will', in *Against the Heresies*, see Bacq, *De l'ancienne à la nouvelle alliance selon S. Irénée*, 363–88. For a more comprehensive analysis of this section, see Berthouzoz, *Liberté et grâce*, 189–243.

the power of judging, and unable to be anything other than what they were created.' (*haer.* 4.37.6)

Had this been the case, Irenaeus replies, it would have benefited neither God nor human beings: communion with God would not be precious, desired, or sought after; it would be by nature, and not as a result of their own proper endeavour, care, or study. As such, it would be misunderstood and no pleasure would be found in it.

Irenaeus continues by citing Christ's words that 'the violent take it by force' (Matt. 11:12) and Paul's exhortation to run the race (1 Cor. 9:24–7) to emphasize the need for struggle, on the grounds that endeavour heightens the appreciation of the gift: 'as it lies with us to love God the more, the Lord has taught and the apostle has handed down that this will happen with struggle, for otherwise this, our good, would be unknown, not being the result of striving' (*haer.* 4.37.7). Irenaeus gives an example by way of explanation: as the faculty of seeing is desired more by those who know what it is like to be without sight, so also is health prized more by those who know disease, light by contrast with darkness, and life by death (*haer.* 4.37.7). As we have seen, especially with the example of Jonah, the whole economy, from beginning to end, has been arranged in such a manner that human beings come to know their own weakness, for it is here that they simultaneously know the strength of God (cf. 2 Cor. 12:9), and having known the experience of death they might thereafter hold ever more firmly to the source of life.

A little later, Irenaeus develops this analysis by contrasting two different types of knowledge: that gained, on the one hand, through experience, and that, on the other hand, learned through hearsay (*haer.* 4.39.1). It is, he points out, only through experience that the tongue comes to learn of both bitterness and sweetness, and likewise, it is only through experience of both good and evil, the latter being disobedience and death, that the mind receives the knowledge (*disciplina*) of the good—that is, obedience to God, which is life for human beings. By experiencing both, and casting off disobedience through repentance, the human being (as in the case of Jonah) becomes ever more tenacious in obedience to God, growing into the fullness of life. The alternative, Irenaeus says dramatically, is that, 'if anyone shuns the knowledge of both of these, and the twofold perception of knowledge, forgetting himself he destroys the human being'.[104]

---

[104] *haer.* 4.39.1: *Si autem utrorumque eorum cognitionem et duplices sensus cogitationis quis defugiat, latenter semetipsum occidit hominem.* Cf. Berthouzoz, *Liberté et grâce*, 236:

Returning to *haer.* 4.37.7, Irenaeus continues that therefore the heavenly kingdom will be more precious to those who have known the earthly kingdom, and, if they prize it more, they will also love it more, and, loving it more, they will be glorified more by God. He then concludes this section:

> God therefore has borne[105] all these things for our sake, in order that, having been instructed through all things, henceforth we may be scrupulous in all things and, having been taught how to love God in accordance with reason, remain in his love, God exhibiting patience [*magnanimitatem*] in regard to the apostasy of the human being, and the human being taught by it, as the prophet says: 'Your own apostasy shall heal you.' (*haer.* 4.37.7; Jer. 2:19)

Irenaeus immediately continues by placing this particular action of God within the economy as a whole:

> God, thus, determining all things beforehand for the perfection of the human being, and towards the realization and manifestation of his economies, that goodness may be displayed and righteousness accomplished, and that the Church may be 'conformed to the image of his Son' [Rom. 8:29], and that, finally, the human being may be brought to such maturity as to see and comprehend God. (*haer.* 4.37.7)

Human disobedience, apostasy, and death are, as we have already seen, inscribed into the very unfolding of the economy; death results from human action, but it is nevertheless a result that is subsumed and transformed within the larger arc of the economy, as it brings the creature made from mud to share in the very life, glory, and power of the Uncreated, so demonstrating the goodness and righteousness of God. Worked out in and through the life of each individual human being, if they should respond with faith and thankfulness, the conclusion is also corporate, for in this way the Church is conformed to Christ as each human being is brought to see God.

In *haer.* 4.38, Irenaeus analyses the question with which he began these chapters, but from a different angle. Here he suggests that God could indeed have created the human being perfect or as a 'god' from the beginning, for all things are possible to him. However, he points out, created things, simply by virtue of being created, are necessarily inferior to the one who created them; they fall short, to begin with, of the perfect; as

---

'En conséquence, l'humanisation de l'homme demande un engagement de sa part, ce qui est évident à l'expérience, et comporte l'acceptation corrélative d'un risque, en particulier celui de se tromper. Par là se trouvent exclues l'éthique de l'abstention préventive, toute valorisation de l'innocence originelle et indifférenciée et, surtout, l'hétéronomie comme instance de conduite moral, adulte.'

[105] On this term, see above, Ch. 3, n. 53.

created, they are initially 'infantile', and so 'unaccustomed to and unexercised in perfect conduct' (haer. 4.38.1). Using another example, he points out that, as it would be possible for a mother to give solid food to her infant, but the infant would not benefit from this, 'so also, it was possible for God himself to have made the human being perfect from the first, but the human being could not receive this, being as yet an infant' (haer. 4.38.1).

This need not be taken to suggest that the infantile state is itself 'imperfect', but simply that it has not yet reached the stature to which growth will bring it; an infant may well be born with 'perfect' limbs, but will nevertheless be unable to walk.[106] Nor need it suggest that the omnipotence of God is restricted by the nature of that upon which he is working.[107] By definition the created cannot be uncreated, but more importantly the omnipotence of God *is* in fact demonstrated, for Irenaeus, by the way that the created is brought in time to share in the uncreated life of God, a change in the 'fashion' of its existence or the mode of its life, which requires preparation and training, for this is what the whole economy, including disobedience and death, effects. There is, moreover, no end to this process; never becoming uncreated, the perfection of human beings lies, instead, in their continual submission to the creative activity of God, through which he is brought to share in the glory and power of the Uncreated (haer. 4.38.3).[108] As he puts it, again with musical resonance:

By this order and such rhythms and such a movement the created and fashioned human becomes in the image and likeness of the uncreated God: the Father planning everything well and commanding, the Son executing and performing, and the Spirit nourishing and increasing, and the human being making progress day by day and ascending towards perfection, that is, approaching the Uncreated One. For the Uncreated is perfect, and this is God.

Now, it was first necessary for the human being to be created;
and having been created, to increase;
and having increased, to become an adult;
and having become an adult, to multiply;

---

[106] Cf. Wingren, *Man and the Incarnation*, 20, and, more generally, 26–45.

[107] As Minns, *Irenaeus*, 73–4, argues. As Robert F. Brown points out: 'Irenaeus does not accept the Platonic view that the recalcitrance of a pre-existent matter constitutes a limit to what God can make of it' ('On the Necessary Imperfection of Creation: Irenaeus' *Adversus Haereses* IV, 38', *SJT* 28/1 (1975), 17–25, at 23.

[108] Cf. *haer.* 4.11.2, discussed above. The whole tenor of Irenaeus' thought on this point is strikingly similar to that of Gregory of Nyssa, e.g. *Perf. GNO* 8.1, 214; cf. J. Daniélou, *L'Être et le temps chez Grégoire de Nysse* (Leiden: Brill, 1970), 114.

and having multiplied, to become strong;
and having been strengthened, to be glorified;
and being glorified, to see his Master;
for God is he who is yet to be seen, and the vision of God produces incorruptibility, and 'incorruptibility renders one close to God' [Wis. 6:19]. (*haer.* 4.38.3)

Such are the rhythm and movement of human life, which recapitulates the movement of the economy. We can no more escape its pattern or anticipate its conclusion than we can expect a newborn infant to live in an adult manner. 'Irrational, therefore, in every way are those who await not the time of increase and ascribe to God the infirmity of their nature,' Irenaeus continues, 'knowing neither God nor themselves, being insatiable and ungrateful, they are unwilling to be at the outset as they have been created, human beings subject to passions [*homines passionum capaces*]' (*haer.* 4.38.4). Wanting 'to be gods from the beginning', rather than 'at first human, and only then gods' (*se primo quidem hominess, tunc demum dii*), they blame God and show their ingratitude for what he has given them, 'even though God has adopted this course out of his pure benevolence'.[109] Irenaeus cites the two contrasting verses of Psalm 81.6–7 (LXX) to demonstrate this point: '"I said you are gods, sons of the Most High", but since we could not sustain the power of divinity, he adds, "but you shall die like human beings".' This, he says, 'sets forth both truths: by his kindness, he graciously gave good and made the human being self-governing like himself, but by his foreknowledge he knew the weakness of human beings and what would come of it, yet by love and power he conquered the substance of our created nature' (*haer.* 4.38.4).[110] Finally, Irenaeus concludes by sketching out his analysis of the economy of the growth of the human being, in a few brief strokes:

---

[109] Cf. Jeff Vogel, 'The Haste of Sin, the Slowness of Salvation: An Interpretation of Irenaeus on the Fall and Redemption', *ATR* 89/3 (2007), 443–59, at 443: 'This graspingness is the fundamental problem in the way that human beings comport themselves in relation to God. Though they have an original capacity to be incorporated into the divine life, they lose it through their impatience, what I call the "haste of sin".'

[110] Bacq (*De l'ancienne à la nouvelle alliance selon S. Irénée*, 384) points out that this implies that God did indeed bestow the power of his divinity on the human race, but the human being, unable to bear it, lost it, though it can now be regained through Christ's work of recapitulation. It must be borne in mind, however, that for Irenaeus what God bountifully bestows is set within the whole economy of the arc, which includes the loss by human beings of what is given to them in the beginning, that is, the breath of life, but yet through this loss, dying and rising, comes to acquire something more, the fullness of the Holy Spirit, which the breath anticipated.

It was necessary, first, for nature to be manifest; after which, for what was mortal to be conquered and swallowed up by immortality, and the corruptible by incorruptibility, and for the human being to be made in the image and likeness of God, having received the knowledge of good and evil. (*haer.* 4.38.4)[111]

Irenaeus takes the words of God in Genesis 3:22, 'Behold, the human being has become like one of us, knowing good and evil', as spoken without any sense of irony, but as a statement reflecting just how it is that the creature made from dust, coming to know both good and evil, and rejecting the latter through repentance, becomes a human being in the image and likeness of God.

To become human in this stature, to become a god, cannot be done by setting our own agenda, 'wishing to be even now like God'. Such an attempt demonstrates an ignorance of all that we have seen: on the one hand, the fact that God has revealed himself in Christ as the perfect living human being, dying for others, and, on the other hand, the comprehensiveness of the arc of the economy through which the Creator brings his handiwork to this stature, by themselves undergoing the long pedagogy of the economy, culminating in their death and resurrection. To become a living human being, a god upon this earth, then, the creature must allow God to fashion him by being open and responsive to his creative activity. Irenaeus concludes these chapters with a beautiful passage, picking up on various themes that we have already seen: the artistic work of the Word of God, the presence of the Spirit, as Water, enabling this formation, and the response of the human being by trusting in God, letting him be the Creator:

> How then will you be a god, when you are not yet made human? How perfect, when only recently begun? How immortal, when in mortal nature you did not obey the Creator? It is necessary for you first to hold the rank of human, and then to participate in the glory of God. For you do not create God, but God creates you. If, then, you are the work of God, await the Hand of God, who does everything at the appropriate time, the appropriate time for you, who are being made. Offer to him your heart, soft and pliable, and retain the shape with which the Fashioner shaped you, having in yourself his Water, lest you turn dry and lose the imprint of his fingers. By guarding this conformation, you will ascend to perfection; the mud in you will be concealed by the art of God. His Hand created your substance; it will gild you, inside and out, with pure gold and silver, and so adorn you that the King himself will desire your beauty. But if, becoming hardened, you reject his art and being ungrateful towards him, because he made you a human being, ungrateful,

---

[111] Cf. 2 Cor. 5:4; 1 Cor. 15:53; Gen. 1:26; 3:5, 22.

that is, towards God, you have lost at once both his art and life. For to create is the characteristic of the goodness of God; to be created is characteristic of the nature of the human. If, therefore, you offer to him what is yours, that is, faith in him and subjection, you will receive his art and become a perfect work of God. But if you do not believe in him, and flee from his Hands, the cause of imperfection will be in you who did not obey, and not in him who called you. For he sent messengers to call people to the feast; but those who did not obey deprived themselves of his royal banquet. (*haer.* 4.39.2–3; cf. Matt. 22:3)

For the handiwork to be fashioned to the stature of Christ, the truly living human being, rather than hardening himself, trying to be what he wants to be, he must remain pliable, open, and responsive to the creative work of God. As Denis Minns puts it: 'What the earth creature needs to learn above all is to relax in the Hands of God, to let God be the creator.'[112]

LIVING HUMAN BEINGS, THE MARTYRS

If it is the crucified and exalted Christ who is the starting point for expounding the economy of God, through the parallelism between Adam and Christ, and who brings the preliminary sketch to its fulfilment in himself as the living human being, no longer animated by a breath but vivified by the Spirit, then it is the martyrs, who have followed Christ on this path, who witness and manifest the power of God and are therefore the culmination of his creative work. For Irenaeus they exemplify the words of Christ that the Spirit is ready, while the flesh is weak, and so demonstrate what happens to the 'pledge' of the Spirit given in baptism when it fully bears life in the witness of one dying in Christ:

For it is testified by the Lord that as 'the flesh is weak', so 'the Spirit is ready' [Matt. 26:41], that is, is able to accomplish what it wills. If, therefore, anyone mixes the readiness of the Spirit as a stimulus to the weakness of the flesh, it necessarily follows that what is strong will prevail over what is weak, so that the weakness of the flesh will be absorbed by the strength of the Spirit, and such a one will no longer be carnal but spiritual because of the communion of the Spirit. In this way, therefore, the martyrs bear witness and despise death: not after the weakness of the flesh, but by the readiness of the Spirit. For when the weakness of the flesh is absorbed, it manifests the Spirit as powerful; and again, when the Spirit absorbs the weakness, it inherits the flesh for itself, and from both of these is made a living

---

[112] Minns, *Irenaeus*, 64.

human being: living, indeed, because of the participation of the Spirit; and human, because of the substance of the flesh. (*haer.* 5.9.2)[113]

It is not that they think death to be of no account, or simply embrace it nihilistically, but rather do so as a martyr following Christ. It is, moreover, not only in the resurrection that God's creative work comes to fulfilment, but it is actually in the very death of the martyrs, imaging Christ, who is himself the image of God, that his handiwork is perfected as a truly living human being bearing witness to the paradoxical words of Christ that his strength is made perfect in weakness (2 Cor. 12:9). The Spirit inherits the flesh, possesses it in such a manner that the flesh itself adopts the quality of the life-giving Spirit, and so is rendered like the Word of God (cf. *haer.* 5.9.3). The paradigm of the living human being—flesh vivified by the Spirit—is the martyr.[114]

With regard to martyrdom, Irenaeus is emphatic that the Cross of Christ, his suffering and death, is the same as that which his disciples must endure and undergo. The Cross is 'the tree of martyrdom', by which Christ draws all to himself and vivifies all (*haer.* 4.2.7). Apropos of Christ's words 'If any man would come after me, let him deny himself and take up his Cross and follow me. For whoever would save his life, will lose it; and whoever loses his life for my sake shall find it' (Matt. 16:24–5), and 'You will stand before governors and kings for my sake, and they shall scourge some of you, and shall slay you and persecute you from city to city' (cf. Matt. 10:18; Mark 13:9; Luke 21:16), Irenaeus comments:

> He knew, therefore, those who would suffer persecution, and he knew those who would be scourged and slain because of him; and he did not speak of any other Cross, but of the Passion which he should himself undergo first, and then his disciples afterwards. (*haer.* 3.18.5)

Thus those who would be disciples of Christ must take up his Cross, deny themselves, and lose their lives for his sake, and this, Irenaeus stipulates, refers to nothing other than the Passion of Christ, which he and his disciples following him must suffer (cf. Luke 24:26, it was 'necessary'). As such, his disciples are those 'who are slain on account of the confession

---

[113] Cf. PO 12.5, 738–9 (frag. 6); TU 36.3, 14–19 (frag. 10).

[114] As H. J. Jaschke puts it: 'Das Martyrium is die Grundform christlicher Existenz' ('Pneuma und Moral: Der Grund christlicher Sittlichkeit aus der Sicht des Irenäus von Lyon', SM 14 (1976), 239–81; at 265); cf. also Ysabel de Andia, 'La Résurrection de la chair selon les Valentiniens et Irénée de Lyon', *Les Quatre Fleuves*, 15–16 (1982), 69; Real Tremblay, 'Le Martyre selon saint Irénée de Lyon', SM 16 (1978), 167–89.

of the Lord, and who endure all things predicted by the Lord, and who in this way strive to follow the footprints of the Lord's Passion, becoming martyrs of the suffering One' (*haer.* 3.18.5). As he himself was the 'faithful martyr' (Rev. 1:5), the disciples of Christ must likewise be martyrs in their witness to him, losing their lives, their animation by the breath of life, in order to enter into the life that Christ has brought into this world.

There are two particular figures that feature in Irenaeus, writings who exemplify all that we have seen. The first is Ignatius of Antioch, whom Irenaeus regards as 'one of our own' and from whose letters Irenaeus cites a striking image:

And therefore throughout all time, the human being, formed at the beginning by the Hands of God, that is, by the Son and the Spirit, becomes after the image and likeness of God: the chaff, that is, the apostasy, being cast away, while the wheat, that is, those who bear as fruit faith in God, being gathered into the granary. And therefore tribulation is necessary for those who are being saved, that, in a certain way, having been threshed and kneaded together, through endurance, with the Word of God, and baked in the fire, they may be suitable for the banquet of the King, as one of ours said, when condemned to the wild beasts because of his testimony [μαρτυρία] to God: 'I am the wheat of Christ, and I am ground by the teeth of the wild beasts, that I may be found [to be] pure bread of God.'[115]

The parallel Irenaeus draws between the Eucharist and human death (*haer.* 5.2.3), considered earlier, is here applied by Ignatius directly to himself, and interpreted by Irenaeus within the scheme of the whole economy: threshed by tribulation, the chaff or apostasy being cast away, the human being is kneaded together with Christ, and through fire made into bread for the Father's banquet. This is, moreover, the culmination of the fashioning of the creature throughout all time by the Hands of God into the image and likeness of God.

Elsewhere in his *Letter to the Romans*, Ignatius intimates many of the other themes that we have seen Irenaeus develop. Asking the Christians in Rome not to interfere with his coming martyrdom, he comments: 'If you keep silent about me, I will be a word of God; but if you desire my flesh, I will once again be a mere noise.'[116] Even more strikingly:

---

[115] *haer.* 5.28.4, referring to Ignatius of Antioch, *Rom.* 4.1. The eucharistic framework for understanding martyrdom is also evident in *The Martyrdom of Polycarp*, where the structure of the narrative closely parallels that of the Last Supper.

[116] *Rom.* 2; this is paralleled by Ignatius' description of Jesus Christ as 'the Word proceeding from silence' (*Magn.* 8), the silence, that is, of the Father, for he is also 'the mouth that does not lie, by whom the Father spoke the truth' (*Rom.* 8): the Father neither speaks nor says anything apart from Christ, the Word of God. The background for this connection between

It is better for me to die in Christ Jesus than to rule the ends of the earth. This is the one I seek, who died on our behalf; this is the one I desire, who arose for us. The pains of birth are upon me. Grant this to me, brothers; do not keep me from living; do not wish me to die; do not hand over to the world the one who wants to belong to God or deceive him by what is material. Allow me to receive the pure light; arriving there, I shall be a human being [ἄνθρωπος ἔσομαι]. Allow me to be an imitator of the suffering of my God.[117]

Only through his martyrdom, his birth, does Ignatius consider that he will become a human being, in the stature of Jesus Christ, the 'perfect man'.[118] At the end of his letter to the Ephesians, Ignatius mentions that, if Christ will, he will send a second small book that he is about to write, discussing 'the economy that leads to the new human being, Jesus Christ, involving his faithfulness and love, his suffering and resurrection'.[119] With this set before us, he can urge his readers that, 'if we do not choose to die voluntarily in his sufferings, his life is not in us', for 'our life arose through him and his death'.[120] And finally, by sharing in the sufferings of Christ in this way, by being born in him into life, we become members of his body. This is the very birth of Christ himself: 'Through the Cross, by his Passion, he calls you who are parts of his body. Thus the head cannot be born without the other parts, because God promises unity, which he himself is.'[121]

The other example held up by Irenaeus, accepting that *The Letter of the Churches of Vienne and Lyons* is his, is the slave girl Blandina. As we saw in the first chapter, the letter describes in graphic detail the sufferings of Christians in Gaul during the persecutions there around the year 177 CE. During the first round in the arena, some of the Christians 'appeared to be unprepared and untrained, as yet weak and unable to endure such a great conflict'. About ten of these, the letter says, proved to be 'stillborn' or 'miscarried', causing great sorrow to the others and weakening the resolve of those yet to undergo their torture (*h.e.* 5.1.11). However, these stillborn Christians were encouraged through the zeal of the others, foremost among whom was Blandina, very much the heroine of the whole account: she is named, while her mistress is not, and as a young slave girl she is the epitome of weakness in the ancient world, and therefore also the vessel in which the power of God can be fully manifest. The *Letter* describes how

---

Ignatius 'becoming a word of God' by suffering martyrdom Christ as the Word from silence seems to be the silence of the Father when Christ calls out from the Cross.

[117] Ignatius, *Rom.* 6.   [118] Ignatius, *Smyrn.* 4.   [119] Ignatius, *Eph.* 20.
[120] Ignatius, *Magn.* 5, 9.   [121] Ignatius, *Trall.* 11.

Blandina, hung on a stake [ἐπὶ ξύλου], was offered as food for the wild beasts that were let in. She, by being seen hanging in the form of a cross, by her vigorous prayer, caused great zeal in the contestants, as, in their struggle, they beheld with their outward eyes, through the sister, him who was crucified for them, that he might persuade those who believe in him that everyone who suffers for the glory of Christ has for ever communion with the living God... the small and weak and despised woman had put on the great and invincible athlete, Christ, routing the adversary in many bouts, and, through the struggle, being crowned with the crown of incorruptibility. (*h.e.* 5.1.41–2)

In her suffering, Blandina became an image, a living icon, of Christ, for those, specifically, who suffer alongside her. In her weakness, the strength of God is victorious, and through her martyrdom incorruptibility is bestowed upon her. This account so clearly draws upon what we have seen in Irenaeus that we must suspect that he is its author: the strength of God is manifest in the weakness of human beings, bestowing incorruptibility on those who follow him, through martyrdom, and so who become, in this way, living images of Christ, in the image and likeness of God.

After describing her suffering, and that of another Christian called Attalus, the letter continues:

Through their continued life the dead were made alive, and the witnesses [the martyrs] showed favour to those who had failed to witness. And there was great joy for the Virgin Mother in receiving back alive those whom she had miscarried as dead. For through them the majority of those who had denied were again brought to birth and again conceived and again brought to life and learned to confess; and now living and strengthened, they went to the judgement seat. (*h.e.* 5.1.45–06)

As with Ignatius, life and death are completely reversed: those who had turned away from making their confession (that is, who stayed 'alive' in this world) are simply dead. Their lack of preparation has resulted in their condition of being stillborn children of the Virgin Mother. The Virgin Mother here is simply the Church, as we have also seen above, in considering Irenaeus' expounding of the typological parallelism between Eve and Mary. However, strengthened by the witness of others, especially Blandina, they were able to go to their martyrdom, so that the Virgin Mother, with great joy, can receive them back as alive, finally giving birth to living children of God. It is for this reason, the letter says later on, that the death of the martyrs is their 'second generation'.[122]

---

[122] *h.e.* 5.1.63: παλιγγενεσία. See Ch. 3, n. 86, for Irenaeus' use of this term to describe the death and resurrection of the human being.

Such figures are, for Irenaeus, the very glory of God, truly living and truly human. The whole arc of the economy, the long pedagogy that leads from our first breath in Adam to the power of the life-creating Spirit given by Christ, vivifying the very same flesh as was animated by the breath, begins and ends with Christ. The glory that he had with the Father 'before the world was', is the glory with which he asks to be glorified as he approaches the Cross (John 17:5), asking that his disciples should be there with him to behold that glory (John 17:24). Following the words in Isaiah, which speak of the gathering of the posterity of everyone, that is, 'who is called by my name, whom I created for glory, whom I formed and made' (Isa. 43:6–7), the disciples of Christ are gathered around his body, as the eagles gathered around the carcass (Matt. 24:28), 'participating in the glory of the Lord who has both formed us and prepared us for this, that when we are with him, we may partake of his glory' (haer. 4.14.1).

Conclusion

It would be hard to overstate the importance of Irenaeus of Lyons, both with respect to what came before him and for the history of Christian theological reflection and identity thereafter. With Irenaeus we have, for the first time, a fully articulate account of 'orthodoxy' and 'heresy', which recognizes the self-chosen separation of those who did not want to share in the broader fellowship of the Christian communities in Rome, or looked down on others as inferior, and which was prepared to see in the diversity of those who remained together the unity of faith. With Irenaeus we have, for the first time, an account of the 'canon' or 'rule' of truth, not as a list of abstract doctrines supposedly given as an apostolic deposit, but as the coherence of the Scriptures (that is, the 'Old Testament') seen as a mosaic of Christ as preached by the apostles. This, for the first time, enables Irenaeus to use explicitly almost the full range of writings by the apostles and evangelists thereafter recognized as 'canonical', seeing in them a 'recapitulation' of the Scriptures, making the Word visible and accessible. In doing this, Irenaeus speaks, for the first time, of the 'economy' of God in the singular sense of an all-embracing coherence of everything spoken by Scripture, from Adam to Christ, with both understood in terms of each other and within a dynamic movement from the first to the second. And, set within the comprehensive scope of the economy, we have with Irenaeus, again for the first time, a full account of the human being, the clay moulded by God throughout the whole economy from Adam to Christ, to bring about the stated intention of God in Genesis, spoken of as his own particular work, to make a human being in his image and likeness, the 'glory of God [that] is a living human being' (*haer.* 4.20.7).

In and through all of this, Irenaeus establishes a foundation and identifies Christianity in a manner that becomes a given for most Christian history thereafter. In fact, what he establishes is so much taken for granted that it is perhaps not surprising that, paradoxically, his works were not read extensively thereafter, apart from the heresiologists, that is, who mined his work for details about the early heretics. It is thus again perhaps not surprising that it is not only his opponents' works that were lost for many centuries but also his own, at least in the original Greek, *Against the Heresies* surviving only in a Latin translation, with the last books of that work and the *Demonstration* newly discovered in an Armenian translation at the beginning of the twentieth century. If recent discoveries of his opponents' works have allowed us to catch a glimpse of 'lost Christianities', to use the title of Bart Ehrman's book, our investigation of Irenaeus' own works has also enabled us to see afresh something that was equally 'lost', for, after having been adapted to centuries of new contexts—imperial Christianity, Scholasticism, Reformation, Enlightenment, and so on—the foundations and identity of Christianity as elaborated by Irenaeus, despite all its apparent familiarity, when investigated closely can appear strangely unfamiliar territory.

For these reasons, as noted in the Preface and Introduction, the context for the study of Irenaeus undertaken here has not only been the second century, but also our own times, allowing the presuppositions of modern scholarship regarding such matters as orthodoxy and heresy, identity and diversity, Scripture and its exegesis, creation and salvation, as these have come to be shaped at least since the Reformation, to be called into question and challenged by Irenaeus. I would draw particular attention to three key features of what we have seen in this study: the elaboration of 'orthodoxy' and correspondingly of 'heresy'; the comprehensiveness of his understanding of the single economy of God; and his attention to the flesh as the focus of the economy of God. Undergirding these three themes, finally, there is perhaps the most important aspect of his work, which is his understanding of the nature and task of theology.

Irenaeus is, of course, the most important theologian in the articulation of Christian orthodoxy to his time, and, arguably, thereafter. From what we have seen, the standard accepted picture assumed by much contemporary scholarship, that Irenaeus is a leading figure in the emergence of an intolerant, patriarchal, hierarchy, excluding the 'heretics' on the basis of an increasing rigidity regarding what he claimed to be an apostolic deposit, where this is understood as items of theological doctrine in creedal form, simply does not stand up, and in fact is the reverse of what happened. Marcion broke from the common fellowship of the Christian communities when his efforts at 'reforming' those communities along the lines of what he considered to be the original Gospel failed. The 'Valentinians' likewise were already aware of the distance that separated themselves, as truly 'spiritual', from the lower 'psychic' Christians of the other communities before Irenaeus intervened. Irenaeus is moreover very careful with his use of the term 'heretic', initially reserving it for those who had *already* separated themselves from the common fellowship, and gradually extending it to those who had *already* distanced themselves. And, as we have also seen, it is as the upholder of diversity among and between the communities that he eventually intervenes in affairs in Rome, restoring peace to the strife that such diversity could cause, recalling certain communities to the tradition of toleration exemplified by their predecessors. Christianity in his day was catholic not by being a universally monolithic institution, but rather by embracing diverse communities in a common fellowship, as the one Body.

Now, clearly, this was not a fellowship that tolerated anything and everything. But, at least in Irenaeus' era, it was not by exercising already demarcated parameters that 'heretics' were excluded. Rather, it was their self-chosen departure that provided occasions for identifying the points at issue and thereby establishing parameters and a framework for understanding what such parameters might be and how they might function. As we have seen, Irenaeus did not understand this in terms of the preservation of a static deposit of teaching, but rather in terms of the functioning of a community of interpretation: seeing in the Scriptures (the 'Old Testament') a mosaic of the Christ preached by the apostle 'in accordance with the Scriptures', effecting the salvation of the flesh. This interpretative endeavour had been 'delivered' or 'traditioned' by the apostle (cf. 1 Cor. 15:3–5), but it was only in the context of Marcion's proposed retrieval of what he considered to be the original Gospel that it became necessary to specify that it is only ever in relation to Scripture that the Gospel is proclaimed; and only in the context of the various soteriologies proposed by Valentinus and others was it necessary to emphasize that God's handiwork is nothing other than the flesh itself. The 'others' thus not only provided an occasion for greater reflection, but also influenced the direction that this reflection would take. Yet the 'hypothesis' of that reflection, and the 'canon' or 'criterion' that it provides, is not thereby changed to something else: it remains that 'delivered' in the beginning, to be explored in a multitude of ways as the symphony of theology, as discussed in the Introduction, is played out throughout time, with different voices lending different notes and tones, harmonizing the human race to the symphony of salvation.

This symphony of salvation, the divine economy, is at the heart of Irenaeus' work: the way and ways in which the Hands of God fashion the clay taken from the earth throughout time into the image and likeness of God, 'for never at any time did Adam escape the Hands of God, to whom the Father said: "Let us make a human being in our image and likeness"'(*haer.* 5.1.3). Irenaeus' manner of holding this divine economy together as a single economy is strikingly, and significantly, different from the way in which we have become accustomed to think of creation–fall–redemption almost as 'plan A' followed, after humans disrupt a 'good' creation by introducing sin and death, by 'plan B'. Christ, for Irenaeus, is emphatically not 'plan B'! Such an approach would begin by imagining a good and perfect creation sufficient unto itself, and then see Christ's work as excising a cancerous growth, as it were, the deformity of sin and death introduced by Adam and Eve. Approached in this way, there would remain something, our own sin and death, that is ultimately outside of God's contro, and that would also be, in the final analysis, meaningless. Irenaeus, instead, holds the wisdom and omnipotence of God as revealed in Christ and deployed throughout the whole economy, from beginning to end as seen from the end, to be such that it embraces and transforms, turns inside out, as it were, human apostasy, to make it subservient to God's project: death was certainly introduced into the world through sin, but the starting point or first principle for that very recognition is Christ's own work of conquering death by his own death, such that we can, in his light, now see that, although death is indeed 'the last enemy', it is also, nevertheless, the means by which it is conquered. Thus, by beginning with what Christ has shown us to be the life and existence of God, that of laying down one's life for others in freedom and love, we can see that the whole economy, embracing our apostasy, has been oriented in such a manner that it provides a pedagogy for the creature made from clay to enter into the life of God and finally in this way become human. God's power, known from the end, in the end turns all things to himself. As Joseph embraced his brothers consoling them that, although they thought that they had sold him into slavery (which, in fact, they had sinfully done), nevertheless it was in truth God who sent him into Egypt to preserve life (Gen. 45:5, 8), so also, in the light of Christ, it turns out that even our apostasy and its result in death lie in God's Hands. As Irenaeus quotes Jeremiah, 'Your own apostasy shall teach you' (Jer. 2:19; *haer.* 4.37.7), and death turns out to be the means of life, for 'what you sow does not come to life unless it dies' (1 Cor. 15:36). That this is known only from the end, moreover, means that we can never put ourselves in the position of God 'before' creation (and how indeed could we speak from such a perspective?) to ask whether it could have been otherwise. The language of foreknowledge is deployed only retrospectively from the perspective of having been called; to deploy it ourselves prospectively inevitably introduces irresolvable problems regarding free will and reduces God to an arbitrary despot.

Yet, for all his importance as an architect of 'orthodoxy' and an expositor or exegete of the divine economy, Irenaeus is *par excellence* the theologian of the flesh. His theological vision is 'incarnational' through and through, focused on the becoming flesh of God and his handiwork. While much modern theology wants to emphasize the 'incarnational' dimension of Christianity, to underscore the fact that the body and material reality are good, its focus on human beings as 'persons' betrays something of an uneasiness about the body, as something the 'person' has rather than is. For Irenaeus, on the other hand, the human being *is* essentially and profoundly skilfully fashioned mud: the flesh is the handiwork of God, fashioned in a hands-on manner by Christ and the Spirit, the Hands of God, leading it from animation by a breath of life to vivification by the Spirit directly, transfiguring the flesh 'inside and out' (*haer.* 4.39.2), to be a living human being, 'the glory of God' (*haer.* 4.20.7).

What is meant by 'incarnational' here is very different from how that term has come to be used in modern times. For us, the term 'Incarnation' refers to a movement from God to us, with the second person of the Trinity taking a body by being born of the Virgin. But it is a stubborn fact that the affirmation that 'the Word became flesh' (John 1:14) can be made only once we no longer know the Word according to the flesh (cf. 2 Cor. 5:16). The assumption of the flesh by the Word is less a reduction of the Word to the level of the flesh than it is the raising of the flesh to the level of the Word. It is as the one whose Passion is spoken of by 'Moses and all the prophets' that we come to know Jesus Christ as the Word of God, encountering him in the breaking of the bread, only for him to disappear from our sight (Luke 24:25–35). The revelation of God in a body thus transforms that body so that it is no longer an object of physical sight, and consequently the revelation of God, his revelation, his truth, and his light, is not subsumed or caught within the horizon of this world.[1] As such, theological reflection can only ever be interpretative or exegetical, and its point of reference is the transformation effected by Christ in and through his Passion. In turn, the 'glory of God [that] is the living human being' is

---

[1] For reflections on such matters, as they are treated by contemporary phenomenology, see Michel Henry, *I am the Truth: Towards a Philosophy of Christianity*, trans. Susan Emanuel (Stanford, CA: Stanford University Press, 2003), and Jean-Luc Marion, *God without Being*, trans. Thomas A. Carlson (Chicago: University of Chicago Press, 1991), *In Excess: Studies of Saturated Phenomena* (New York: Fordham University Press, 2002), and *The Visible and the Revealed*, trans. Christina M. Gschwandtner (New York: Fordham University Press, 2008).

not, as we might be tempted to think, what we already are, but rather it is the martyr, the one who takes up the Cross to follow Christ, being born into life as the body of Christ in the womb of the Virgin Mother.

Each of these three points was important in his own time, and just as much in ours, addressing as they do the question of Christian identity and its truth claims in a pluralistic culture, the meaning of suffering and death, and what it is to be human. Yet it is not simply these particular points themselves, but the manner in which Irenaeus addresses them, that is perhaps most important. For a variety of reasons, over recent centuries the discipline of theology has fragmented into a variety of more or less independent disciplines, some historically oriented (such as the study of Scripture and the Fathers), others more constructive (such as systematic or foundational theology), each increasingly unable to comprehend and engage each other.[2] As such, it has become increasingly unclear just what is the nature and mode of the particular and peculiar discourse that is theology *as theology*. It does indeed have its own coherence. But, as Rowan Williams noted: 'Theology ... is perennially tempted to be seduced by the prospect of bypassing the question of how it *learns* its own language.'[3] With Irenaeus, however, standing as he does at the beginning of a self-conscious articulation of the discourse of theology, we have the opportunity to learn again its coherence.

---

[2] Cf. Edward Farley, *Theologia: The Fragmentation and Unity of Theological Education* (Philadelphia: Augsburg Fortress, 1983); John Behr, *The Nicene Faith*, The Formation of Christian Theology, vol. 2 (Crestwood, NY: SVS Press, 2004), pt 1, pp. 1–17; *Mystery of Christ*, 15–20, 173–81.

[3] Rowan Williams, *On Christian Theology* (Oxford: Blackwell, 2000), 131.

Bibliography

PRIMARY WORKS

Texts

Against the Heresies

Erasmus, D., *Opus eruditissimum divi Irenaei episcopi Lugdunensis in quinque libros digestum* ... (Basle, 1526).

Harvey, W. W., *Sancti Irenaei episcopi Lugdunensis libros quinque adversus haereses*, 2 vols (Cambridge, 1857).

Massuet, E., *Sancti Irenaei episcopi Lugdunensis et martyris detectionis et eversionis falso cognominatae agnitionis libri quinque* (Paris, 1710); repr. PG 7 (Paris, 1857).

Rousseau, A., and Doutreleau, L., *Irénée de Lyon: Contre les Hérésies, Livre I*, SC 263–4 (Paris: Cerf, 1979).

Rousseau, A., and Doutreleau, L., *Irénée de Lyon: Contre les Hérésies, Livre II*, SC 293–4 (Paris: Cerf, 1982).

Rousseau, A., and Doutreleau, L., *Irénée de Lyon: Contre les Hérésies, Livre III*, SC 210–11 (Paris: Cerf, 1974).

Rousseau, A., Hemmerdinger, B., Doutreleau, L., and Mercier, C., *Irénée de Lyon: Contre les Hérésies, Livre IV*, SC 100, 2 vols (Paris: Cerf, 1965).

Rousseau, A., Doutreleau, L., and Mercier, C., *Contre les Hérésies, Livre V*, SC 152–3 (Paris: Cerf, 1969).

Ter-Mekerttschian, K., and Ter-Minassiantz, E., *Irenäus, Gegen die Häretiker.* [Ἔλεγχος καὶ ἀνατροπὴ τῆς ψευδωνύμου γνώσεως], *Buch IV u. V in armenischer Version*, TU 35.2 (Leipzig: Hinrichs, 1910).

Demonstration of the Apostolic Preaching

Ter-Mekerttschian, K., and Ter-Minassiantz, E. (eds and trans.), *Des heiligen Irenäus Schrift zum Erweise der apostolischen Verkündigung... in armenischer Version entdeckt und in Deutsche übersetzt... mit einem nachwort und Anmerkungen von A. Harnack*, TU 31.1 (Leipzig: Hinrich, 1907).

Ter-Mekerttschian, K., and Wilson, S. G., with Prince Maxe of Saxony (eds) and Eng. trans., French trans. J. Barthoulot, Εἰς ἐπίδειξιν τοῦ ἀποστολικοῦ κηρύγματος; *The Proof of the Apostolic Preaching, with Seven Fragments*, PO 12.5 (Paris, 1917; repr. Turnhout: Brepols, 1989).

Fragments

Holl, K., *Fragmente vornicänischer Kirchenväter aus den Sacra Parallela*, TU 20.2 (Leipzig: Hinrich, 1899).

Jordan, H., *Armenische Irenaeusfragmente*, TU 36.3 (Leipzig: Hinrich, 1913).
Renoux, C., *Nouveaux fragments armeniens de l' 'Adversus Haereses' et de l' 'Epideixis'*, PO 39.1 (Turnhout: Brepols, 1978).

Translations

Against the Heresies

Grant, R. M., *Irenaeus of Lyons* (New York: Routledge, 1997) [Extracts].
Keble, J., *Five Books of S. Irenaeus, Against Heresies* (London: James Parker, 1872).
Roberts, A., and Donaldson, J. (eds), ANF 1 (Edinburgh, 1887; repr. Grand Rapids: Eerdmans, 1987).
Unger, D. J., rev. J. J. Dillon, *St Irenaeus of Lyons Against the Heresies, Book 1*, ACW 55 (New York: Paulist Press, 1992).
Unger, D. J., rev. J. J. Dillon, *St Irenaeus of Lyons Against the Heresies, Book 2*, ACW 65 (New York: Paulist Press, 2012).
Unger, D. J., rev. M. C. Steenberg, *St Irenaeus of Lyons: Against the Heresies, Book 3*, ACW 64 (New York: Newman Press, 2012).

Demonstration of the Apostolic Preaching

Armitage Robinson, J., *St. Irenaeus: The Demonstration of the Apostolic Preaching* (London: SPCK, 1920), repr. in I. M. Mackenzie, *Irenaeus' Demonstration of the Apostolic Preaching: A Theological Commentary and Translation* (Farnham: Ashgate, 2002).
Behr, J. (trans.), *St Irenaeus of Lyons: On the Apostolic Preaching* (Crestwood, NY: SVS, 1997).
Froidevaux. L. M., *Irénée de Lyon: Démonstration de la Prédication Apostolique*, SC 62 (Paris: Cerf, 1959).
Rousseau, A. (ed. and trans.), *Démonstration de la prédication apostolique*, SC 406 (Paris: Cerf, 1995).
Smith, J. P., *St Irenaeus: Proof of the Apostolic Preaching*, ACW 16 (New York: Newman 1952).
Weber, S., *Des Heiligen Irenäus Schrift zum Erweis der apostolischen Verkündigen*, BKV (Kempton and München: Kösel, 1912), 1–68 (583–650).

Reference works

Reynders, B. (ed.), *Lexique comparé du texte grec et des versions latine, arménienne et syriaque de l' 'Adversus Haereses' de saint Irénée*, CSCO 141–2, subsidia 5–6 (Louvain: Peeters, 1954).
Reynders, B. *Vocabulaire de la 'Démonstration' et des fragments de S. Irénée* (Louvain: Éditions de Chevetogne, 1958).
Sanday W., and Turner, C. H. (eds), *Novum Testamentum Sancti Irenaei* (Oxford: Clarendon, 1923).

Bibliography

Other Texts

Agapius (Mahboud) of Mendibj, *Kitab al-'Unvan*, PO 7.4.

Aristotle, *On the Soul*, ed. and trans. W. S. Hett, LCL Aristotle, 8 (Cambridge, MA: Harvard University Press, 1936).

Aristotle, *Eudemian Ethics*, ed. and trans. H. Rackham, LCL Aristotle, 20 (Cambridge, MA: Harvard University Press, 1935).

Aristotle, *Metaphysics*, ed. and trans. H. Tredennick, LCL Aristotle, 17–18 (Cambridge, MA: Harvard University Press, 1933).

Aristotle, *Nicomachean Ethics*, ed. and trans. H. Rackham, LCL Aristotle, 19 (Cambridge, MA: Harvard University Press, 1990).

Aristotle, *Posterior Analytics*, ed. and trans. H. Tredennick, LCL Aristotle, 15 (Cambridge, MA: Harvard University Press, 1976).

Aristotle, *Rhetoric*, ed. and trans. J. H. Freese, LCL Aristotle, 22 (Cambridge, MA: Harvard University Press, 1926).

Barnabas, *The Epistle of Barnabas*, ed. and trans. K. Lake, LCL Apostolic Fathers, 1 (Cambridge, MA: Harvard University Press, 1985).

Cabasilas, Nicholas, *A Commentary on the Divine Liturgy*, trans. J. M. Hussey and P. A. McNulty (London: SPCK, 1960).

Cabasilas, Nicholas, *The Life in Christ*, ed. and French trans. M.-H. Congourdeau, SC 361 (Paris: Cerf, 1990); Eng. trans. C. J. deCatanzaro (Crestwood, NY: St Vladimir's Seminary Press, 1974).

Clement of Alexandria, *Stromata I–VI*, ed. O. Stählin, 3rd edn., rev. L. Früchtel, GCS 52 (Berlin: Akademie Verlag, 1972); trans. in ANF 2 (1887: repr. Grand Rapids: Eerdmans, 1989), 299–520.

Clement of Alexandria, *Stromata VII, VIII, Excerpta ex Theodoto, Eclogae Propheticae, Quis Dives Salvetur, Fragmente*, ed. O. Stählin, 2nd edn. rev. L. Früchtel and U. Treu, GCS 17 (Berlin: Akademie Verlag, 1970); trans. in ANF 2 (1887: repr. Grand Rapids: Eerdmans, 1989), 523–567 (*Strom.* 7–8); 591–604 (*Who is the Rich Man that shall be Saved?*).

Clement of Rome, *First Letter*, ed. J. B. Lightfoot, in *The Apostolic Fathers* (Macmillan, 1889; repr. Peabody, MA: Hendrickson, 1989), pt 1, vols 1–2; ed. and trans. B. Ehrman, LCL Apostolic Fathers, 1 (Cambridge, MA: Harvard University Press, 2003).

The Epistle to Diognetus, ed. and trans. K. Lake, LCL Apostolic Fathers, 1 (Cambridge, MA: Harvard University Press, 1985).

Epiphanius, *Panarion*, ed. K. Holl: Epiphanius I (heresies 1–33), GCS 25 (Leipzig: Hinrichs Verlag, 1915); Epiphanius II (heresies 34–64), rev. J. Dummer, GCS 31 (Berlin: Akademie Verlag, 1980); Epiphanius III (heresies 65–80), rev. J. Dummer, GCS 37 (Berlin: Akademie Verlag, 1985). Selective English trans. P. R. Amidon, *The Panarion of Epiphanius of Salamis: Selected Passages* (Oxford: Oxford University Press, 1990).

Eusebius of Caesarea, *Ecclesiastical History*, ed. and trans. K. Lake, LCL (Cambridge, MA: Harvard University Press, 1980).

The Gospel of Truth, ed. and trans. Harold W. Attridge, *The Nag Hammadi Codex I (The Jung Codex)*, The NHS 22 (Leidon: Brill, 1985); also trans. in Bentley Layton, *The Gnostic Scriptures: Ancient Wisdom for the New Age*, Anchor Bible Reference Library (New York: Doubleday, 1987), 253–64.

Gregory of Nazianzus, *Orations 27–32*. Ed. A. J. Mason, *The Five Theological Orations of Gregory of Nazianzus* (Cambridge: University Press, 1899). Ed. and French trans. P. Gallay, with M. Jourjon, *Grégoire de Nazianze: Discours 27–31 (Discours Théologiques)*, SC 250 (Paris: Cerf, 1978). Trans. in NPNF 7, and in L. Wickham and F. Williams (trans.), *St Gregory of Nazianzus: On God and Christ: The Five Theological Orations and Two Letters to Cledonius* (Crestwood, NY: St Vladimir's Seminary Press, 2002).

Gregory of Nyssa, *On the Three Day Period*, ed. E. Gebhardt, GNO 9 (Leiden: Brill, 1967), 273–306; trans. S. G. Hall, in A. Spira and C. Klock (eds), *The Easter Sermons of Gregory of Nyssa*, Patristic Monograph Series, 9 (Philadelphia: Philadelphia Patristic Foundation, 1981), 31–50.

Gregory of Nyssa, *On Perfection*, ed. W. Jaeger, GNO 8.1 (Leiden: Brill, 1986 [1952]), 173–214; trans. in V. Woods Callahan, *Saint Gregory of Nyssa: Ascetical Works*, FC 58 (Washington: Catholic University of America Press, 1967), 95–122.

Hermas, *The Shepherd*, ed. and trans. K. Lake, LCL Apostolic Fathers, 2 (Cambridge, MA: Harvard University Press, 1976).

Hippolytus, *Refutation of all Heresies*, ed. P. Wendland, GCS 26 (Leipzig: Hinrichs Verlag, 1916); ed. M. Marcovich, PTS 25 (Berlin: De Gruyter, 1986); trans. in ANF 5 (1887; repr. Grand Rapids: Eerdmans, 1986), 9–153.

Ignatius of Antioch, *Letters*, ed. and trans. B. Ehrman, LCL Apostolic Fathers, 1 (Cambridge, MA: Harvard University Press, 2003).

Isaac of Syria, *Isaac of Nineveh (Isaac the Syrian): 'The Second Part', Chapters IV–XLI*, ed. S. Brock, CSCO 555, scriptores syri 225 (Louvain: Peeters, 1995).

Justin Martyr, *Apologies*, ed. M. Marcovich, PTS 38 (Berlin, New York: De Gruyter, 1994); trans. L. W. Barnard, *St Justin Martyr: The First and Second Apologies*, ACW 56 (New York: Paulist, 1997).

Justin Martyr, *Dialogue with Trypho*, ed. M. Marcovich, PTS 47 (Berlin and New York: De Gruyter, 1997); trans. in ANF 1 (Edinburgh, 1887; repr. Grand Rapids: Eerdmans, 1987), 194–270.

The Martyrdom of Justin and Companions, ed. and trans. in Herbert Musurillo, *The Acts of the Christian Martyrs* (Oxford: Clarendon Press, 1972), 42–61.

Maximus the Confessor, *Centuries on Theology and the Economy*, trans. in *The Philokalia*, vol. 2, trans. G. E. H. Palmer, Philip Sherrard, and Kallistos Ware (London: Faber and Faber, 1981), 114–63.

Origen, *Commentary on John*, ed. and French trans. C. Blanc, SC 120, 157, 222, 290, 385 (Paris: Cerf, 1966, 1970, 1975, 1982, 1992); English trans. R. E. Heine, *Origen:*

Commentary on the Gospel according to Saint John, FC 80, 89 (Washington: Catholic University of America, 1989, 1993).

Origen, *Contra Celsum*, ed. and French trans. M. Borret, SC 132, 136, 147, 150, 227 (Paris: Cerf, 1967, 1968, 1969 [2], 1976); English trans. H. Chadwick (Cambridge: Cambridge University Press, 1953).

Origen, *Homilies on Jeremiah*, ed. P. Nautin, French trans. P. Husson and P. Nautin, SC 232, 238 (Paris: Cerf, 1976, 1977); English trans. J. C. Smith, *Origen: Homilies on Jeremiah; Homily on 1 Kings 28*, FC 97 (Washington: Catholic University of America, 1998).

Philo, *On the Account of the World's Creation given by Moses*, ed. and trans. F. H. Colson and G. H. Whitaker, LCL Philo, 1 (Cambridge, MA: Harvard University Press, 1991).

Philostratus, *Lives of the Sophists*, ed. and trans. W. C. Wright, LCL, *Philostratus and Eunapius* (London: Heinemann, 1922).

Photius, *Bibliotheca*, ed. and French trans. R. Henry, 8 vols (Paris: Belles Lettres, 1959–77); English trans. (to ch. 145) J. H. Freese (London: SPCK, 1920).

Plato, *Laws*, ed. and trans. R. G. Bury, LCL Plato, 10–11 (Cambridge, MA: Harvard University Press, 1961).

Plato, *Republic*, ed. and trans. P. Shorey, LCL Plato, 5–6 (Cambridge, MA: Harvard University Press, 1963).

Plato, *Timaeus*, ed. and trans. R. G. Bury, LCL Plato, 9 (Cambridge, MA: Harvard University Press, 1981).

The Martyrdom of Polycarp, ed. and trans. B. Ehrman, LCL Apostolic Fathers, 1 (Cambridge, MA: Harvard University Press, 2003).

Ptolemaeus, *Letter to Flora*. Text from Epiphanius, *Panarion* 33.3–7. *Ptolémée: Lettre à Flora*, ed. and trans. G. Quispel, SC 24 bis (Paris: Cerf, 1966); English trans. in P. R. Amidon, *The Panarion of Epiphanius of Salamis: Selected Passages* (Oxford: Oxford University Press, 1990), 119–23; R. Grant, *Second-Century Christianity: A Collection of Fragments* (London: SPCK, 1946), 30–7; and also trans. in Bentley Layton, *The Gnostic Scriptures: Ancient Wisdom for the New Age*, Anchor Bible Reference Library (New York: Doubleday, 1987), 308–15.

Quintilian, *Institutio Oratoria*, ed. and trans. Donald A. Russell, LCL Quintilian: *The Orators Education* (Cambridge, MA: Harvard University Press, 2002).

Sextus Empiricus, *Against the Grammarians*, ed. and trans. R. G. Bury, LCL Sextus Empiricus, 4 (Cambridge, MA: Harvard University Press, 1937).

Tertullian, *Against Marcion*, ed. and trans. E. Evans, OECT (Oxford: Clarendon Press, 1972).

Tertullian, *On the Resurrection of the Flesh*, ed. and trans. E. Evans (London: SPCK, 1960).

Tertullian, *On the Soul*, ed. J. H. Waszink, (Amsterdam: North-Holland Publishing Company, 1947); trans. in ANF 3 (Edinburgh, 1887; repr. Grand Rapids: Eerdmans, 1989), 181–235.

Tertullian, *Prescription against the Heretics*, ed. R. F. Refoulé and French trans. by P. de Labriolle, SC 46 (Paris: Cerf, 1957); trans. in ANF 3 (Edinburgh, 1887; repr. Grand Rapids: Eerdmans, 1989), 243–65.

Tertullian, *Against the Valentinians. Contre les Valentiniens*, ed. and French trans. J. C. Fredouille, SC 280-1 (Paris: Cerf, 1980, 1981); trans. in ANF 3 (Edinburgh, 1887; repr. Grand Rapids: Eerdmans, 1989), 503–20.

Ps-Tertullian, *Adversus omnes Haereses*, ed. E. Kroymann, CCSL 2 (1954), 1399–1410.

Theophilus of Antioch, *To Autolycus*, ed. and trans. R. M. Grant, OECT (Oxford: Clarendon, 1970).

SECONDARY WORKS

Aland, B., 'Fides und subiectio: Zur Anthropologie des Irenäus', in A. M. Ritter (ed.), *Kerygma und Logos: Beiträge zu den geistesgeschichtlichen Beziehungen zwischen Antike und Christentum. Festschrift für Carl Andresen zum 70. Geburtstag* (Göttingen: Vandenhoeck and Ruprecht, 1979), 9–28.

Aldama, J. A. de, 'Adam, typus futuri', *Sacris Erudiri*, 13 (1962), 266–80.

D'Alès, A., 'La Doctrine de la récapitulation en S. Irénée', *RSR* 6 (1916), 185–211.

D'Alès, A., 'La Doctrine de l'Esprit en saint Irénée', *RSR* 14 (1924), 497–538.

Altermath, F., 'The Purpose of the Incarnation according to Irenaeus', *StPatr* 13, TU, 116 (Berlin: Akademie, 1975), 63–8.

Altermath, F., *Du corps psychique au corps spirituel: Interprétation de 1 Cor. 15.35–49 par les auteurs chrétiens de quatre premiers siècles*, Beiträge zur Geschichte der biblische Exegese, 18 (Tübingen: Mohr, 1977).

Anderson, G., 'Celibacy or Consummation in the Garden? Reflections on Early Jewish and Christian Interpretations of the Garden of Eden', *HTR* 82/2 (1989), 121–48.

Andia, Y. de, 'La Résurrection de la chair selon les Valentiniens et Irénée de Lyon', *Les Quatre Fleuves*, 15–16 (1982), 59–70.

Andia, Y. de, *Homo vivens: Incorruptibilité et divinisation de l'homme selon Irénée de Lyon* (Paris: Études Augustiniennes, 1986).

Andia, Y. de, 'Modèles de l'unité des testaments selon Irénée de Lyon', *StPatr* 21 (Leuven: Peeters, 1989), 49–59.

Ashbrook Harvey, Susan, and Hunters, David G. (eds), *The Oxford Handbook of Early Christian Studies* (Oxford: Oxford University Press, 2008).

Bacq, P., *De l'ancienne à la nouvelle alliance selon S. Irénée: Unité du livre IV de l'Adversus Haereses* (Paris: Éditions Lethielleux, Presses Universitaires de Namur, 1978).

Balás, D. L., 'The Use and Interpretation of Paul in Ireneaus' Five Books Adversus Haereses', *Second Century*, 9/1 (1992), 27–39.

Balthasar, H. U. von, *Herrlichkeit: Eine theologische Aesthetik*, Bd II: *Fächer der Stile*, I: *Klerikale Stile* (Einsiedeln: Johannes Verlag, 1962); trans., *The Glory of the Lord: A Theological Aesthetics*, ii (Edinburgh: T&T Clark, 1984).

Bibliography

Barr, James, *The Garden of Eden and the Hope of Immortality* (Minneapolis: Fortress Press, 1993).

Bauckham, Richard, *Jesus and the Eyewitnesses: The Gospels as Eyewitness Testimony* (Grand Rapids: Eerdmans, 2006).

Bauer, Walter, *Rechtglaübigkeit und Ketzerei im ältesten Christentum* (Tübingen: Mohr, 1934); trans. of 2nd edn. (1964, ed. G. Strecker) by R. Kraft et al., *Orthodoxy and Heresy in Earliest Christianity* (Philadelphia: Fortress Press, 1971).

Behr, John, 'Shifting Sands: Foucault, Brown and the Framework of Christian Asceticism', *HJ* 34.1 (1993), 1–21.

Behr, John, 'Irenaeus *AH* 3.23.5 and the Ascetic Ideal', *SVTQ* 37.4 (1993), 305–13.

Behr, John, 'Godly Lives: Asceticism and Anthropology, with Special Reference to Sexuality, in the Writings of St Irenaeus of Lyons and St Clement of Alexandria' (D.Phil. Oxford University, 1995).

Behr, John, *Asceticism and Anthropology in Irenaeus and Clement*, OECS (Oxford: Oxford University Press, 2000).

Behr, John, *The Way to Nicaea*, Formation of Christian Theology, vol. 1 (Crestwood, NY: SVS Press, 2001).

Behr, John, *The Nicene Faith*, The Formation of Christian Theology, vol. 2 (Crestwood, NY: SVS Press, 2004).

Behr, John, *The Mystery of Christ: Life in Death* (Crestwood, NY: SVS Press, 2006).

Behr, John, 'Gaul', in Mitchell and Young (eds), *The Cambridge History of Christianity*, i, *Origins to Constantine*, 366–79.

Bengsch, A., *Heilsgeschichte und Heilswissen: Eine Untersuchung zur Struktur und Entfaltung des theologischen Denkens im Werk 'Adversus Haereses' des hl. Irenäus von Lyon* (Leipzig: St Benno, 1957).

Benoît, A., *Saint Irénée: Introduction à l'étude de sa théologie*, Études d'Histoire et de Philosophie Religieuses, 52 (Paris: Presses Universitaires de France, 1960).

Bentivegna, G., *Economia di salvezza e creazione nel pensiero di S. Ireneo* (Rome: Herder, 1973).

Berrouard, M. F., 'Servitude de la Loi et liberté de l'Evangile selon saint Irénée', *LV* 61 (1963), 41–60.

Berthouzoz, R., *Liberté et grâce suivant la théologie d'Irénée de Lyon* (Fribourg en Suisse: Éditions Universitaires; Paris: Cerf, 1980).

Beyschlag, Karlmann, *Simon Magus und die christliche Gnosis*, WUNT (Tübingen: Mohr Siebeck, 1974).

Blanchard, Y. M., *Aux sources du canon: Le Témoignage d'Irénée* (Paris: Cerf, 1993).

Blowers, Paul M., 'The *Regula Fidei* and the Narrative Character of Early Christian Faith', *Pro Ecclesia*, 6 (1997), 199–228.

Boersma, Hans, 'Irenaeus, Derrida and Hospitality: On the Eschatological Overcoming of Violence', *MT* 19/2 (2003), 163–80.

Bonner, G., 'Martyrdom: Its Place in the Church', *Sobornost*, 5/2 (1983), 6–21.

Bonwetsch, N., *Die Theologie des Irenäus*, Beiträge zur Förderung christlicher Theologie, 2/9 (Gütersloh: C. Bertelsmann, 1925).

Boulluec, Alain Le, *La Notion d'hérésie dans la literature greque IIe–IIIe siècles* (Paris: Études Augustiniennes, 1985).

Bousset, W., *Jüdisch-christlicher Schulbetrieb in Alexandria und Rom: Literarische Untersuchungen zu Philo und Clemens von Alexandria, Justin und Irenäus*, Forschung zur Religion und Literatur der Alten und Neuen Testaments, N.F. 6 (Göttingen: Vandenhoeck & Ruprecht, 1915).

Bousset, W., *Kyrios Christos: Geschichte des Christusglaubens von den Anfängen des Christentums bis Irenaeus*, 2nd edn. (Göttingen: Vandenhoeck and Ruprecht, 1921); trans. J. E. Steely, *Kyrios Christos: A History of Belief in Christ from the Beginnings of Christianity to Irenaeus* (New York, Nashville: Abingdon Press, 1970).

Brakke, David, *The Gnostics: Myth, Ritual, and Diversity in Early Christianity* (Cambridge, MA: Harvard University Press, 2010).

Brent, Allen, 'Diogenes Laertius and the Apostolic Succession', *JEH* 44/3 (1993), 367–89.

Brent, Allen, *Hippolytus and the Roman Church in the Third Century: Communities in Tension before the Emergence of a Monarch-Bishop* (Leiden: Brill, 1995).

Briggman, Anthony, 'The Holy Spirit as the Unction of Christ in Irenaeus', *JTS* NS 61/1 (2010), 171–93.

Briggman, Anthony, 'Re-Evaluating Angelomorphism in Irenaeus: The Case of *Proof of the Apostolic Preaching* 10', *JTS* NS 61/2 (2010), 583–96.

Briggman, Anthony, 'Revisiting Irenaeus' Philosophical Acumen', *VC* 65/2 (2011), 115–24.

Briggman, Anthony, 'Spirit-Christology in Irenaeus: A Closer Look', *VC* 66/1 (2012), 1–19.

Brown, R. F., 'On the Necessary Imperfection of Creation: Irenaeus *Adversus Haereses* IV.38', *SJT* 28/1 (1975), 17–25.

Burrus, V., 'Hierarchalization and Genderization of Leadership in the Writings of Irenaeus', *StPatr* 21 (Leuven: Peeters, 1989), 42–8.

Cabrol, F., and Leclercq, H. (eds), *Dictionnaire d'Archéologie Chrétienne et de Liturgie* (Paris: Letouzey et Ané, 1907–53).

Canlis, Julie, 'Being Made Human: The Significance of Creation for Irenaeus' Doctrine of Participation', *SJT* 58/4 (2005), 434–54.

Constantelos, D. J., 'Irenaeus of Lyons and his Central Views on Human Nature', *SVTQ* 33/4 (1989), 351–65.

Coolidge, J. S., *The Pauline Basis of the Concept of Scriptural Form in Irenaeus*, in W. Wuellner (ed.), *Protocol of the Eighth Colloquy: 4 November 1973*, The Center for Hermeneutical Studies in Hellenistic and Modern Culture (Berkeley and Los Angeles: University of California, 1974).

Culpepper, Alan R., *John, the Son of Zebedee: The Life of a Legend*, Studies on Personalities of the New Testament (Columbia: University of South Carolina Press, 1994).

Czesz, B., 'La continua presenza dello Spirito Santo nei tempi del Vecchio e del Nuovo Testamento secondo S. Ireneo (*Adv. haer.* IV,13,15)', *Augustinianum*, 20/3 (1980), 581–5.

Daley, B. E., *The Hope of the Early Church: A Handbook of Patristic Eschatology* (Cambridge: Cambridge University Press, 1991).

Daniélou, J., *L'Être et le temps chez Grégoire de Nysse* (Leiden: Brill, 1970).

Dawson, David, *Allegorical Readers and Cultural Revision in Ancient Alexandria* (Berkeley and Los Angeles: University of California Press, 1992).

Dehandschutter, B., 'The Martyrium Polycarpi: A Century of Research', *ANRW* 2.27.1 (1993), 485–522.

Dodwell, H., *Dissertationes in Irenaeum* (Oxford, 1689).

Donovan, M. A., 'Irenaeus in Recent Scholarship', *Second Century*, 4/4 (1984), 219–41.

Donovan, M. A., 'Alive to the Glory of God', *TS* 49/2 (1988), 283–97.

Donovan, M. A., 'Irenaeus: At the Heart of Life, Glory', in A. Callahan (ed.), *Spiritualities of the Heart* (New York: Paulist, 1989), 11–22.

Doutreleau, L., 'Irénée de Lyon (saint). I. Vie. II. Œuvres', in *Dictionnaire de spiritualité*, ed. M. Viller et al. (1937–), fasc. L–LX, pp. 1923–38.

Dragos, Andrei Giulea, 'Apprehending "Demonstrations" from the First Principle: Clement of Alexandria's Phenomenology of Faith', *JR* 89/2 (2009), 187–213.

Droge, A. J., *Homer or Moses? Early Christian Interpretation of the History of Culture* (Tübingen: Mohr, 1989).

Dunderberg, Ismo O., *Beyond Gnosticism: Myth, Lifestyle, and Society in the School of Valentinus* (New York: Columbia University Press, 2008).

Dunning, Benjamin H., *Aliens and Sojourners: Self as Other in Early Christianity* (Philadelphia: University of Pennsylvannia Press, 2009).

Dunning, Benjamin H., 'Virgin Earth, Virgin Birth: Creation, Sexual Difference and Recapitulation in Irenaeus of Lyons', *JR* 89/1 (2009), 57–88.

Dunning, Benjamin H., *Specters of Paul: Sexual Difference in Early Christian Thought* (Philadelphia: University of Pennsylvania Press, 2011).

Edwards, Mark J., 'Gnostics and Valentinians in the Church Fathers', *JTS* NS 40/1 (1989), 26–47.

Edwards, Mark J., 'Neglected Texts in the Study of Gnosticism', *JTS* NS 41 (1990), 26–50.

Edwards, Mark J., 'Justin's Logos and the Word of God', *JECS* 3/3 (1995), 261–80.

Ehrman, Bart D., *Lost Christianities: The Battles for Scripture and the Faiths We Never Knew* (Oxford: Oxford University Press, 2003).

Évieux, P., 'La Théologie de l'accoutumance chez saint Irénée', *RSR* 55 (1967), 5–54.

Fantino, J., *L'Homme, image de Dieu chez saint Irénée de Lyon* (Paris: Cerf, 1984).

Fantino, J., 'La Création *ex nihilo* chez saint Irénée: Étude historique et théologique', *RSPT* 76/3 (1992), 421–42.

Fantino, J., *La Théologie d'Irénée: Lecture des Écritures en réponse à l'exégèse gnostique: Une approche trinitaire* (Paris: Cerf, 1994).

Fantino, J., 'Le Passage du Premier Adam au Second Adam comme expression du salut chez Irénée de Lyon', *VC* 52/4 (1998), 418–29.

Farkasfalvy, D., 'Theology of Scripture in St Irenaeus', *RB* 78 (1968), 319–33.

Farley, Edward, *Theologia: The Fragmentation and Unity of Theological Education* (Philadelphia: Augsburg Fortress, 1983).

Farmer, William R., 'Galatians and the Second-Century Development of the *Regula Fidei*', *Second Century*, 4/3 (1984), 143–70.

Ferguson, Thomas C., 'The Rule of Truth and Irenaean Rhetoric in Book 1 of *Against Heresies*', *VC* 55.4 (2001), 356–75.

Fishbane, Michael, *Biblical Interpretation in Ancient Israel* (Oxford: Clarendon Press, 1985).

Fishwick, D., 'The Federal Cult of the Three Gauls', in *Les Martyrs de Lyon (177)*, 33–45.

Förster, Niclas, *Marcus Magus: Kult, Lehre und Gemeindeleben einer valentinianischen Gnostikergruppe. Sammlung der Quellen und Kommentar*, WUNT 114 (Tübingen: Mohr-Siebeck, 1999).

Gächter, P., 'Unsere Einheit mit Christus nach dem hl. Irenäus', *ZKT* 58 (1939), 503–32.

Gamble, Harry Y., 'Marcion and the "Canon"', in Mitchell and Young (eds), *The Cambridge History of Christianity*, i, *Origins to Constantine*, 195–213.

Gonzalez Faus, J. I., *Creación y progreso en la teología de San Ireneo* (San Cugat del Valles: Facultad de theología de Barcelona, 1968).

Gonzalez Faus, J. I., *Carne de Dios: Significado salvador de la Encarnación en la teología de San Ireneo* (Barcelona: Herder, 1969).

Grant, Robert M., 'Irenaeus and Hellenistic Culture', *HTR* 42 (1949), 41–51; repr. in R. M. Grant, *After the New Testament* (Philadelphia: Fortress Press, 1967), 158–69.

Grant, Robert M., 'Eusebius and the Martyrs of Gaul', in *Les Martyrs de Lyon (177)*, 129–36.

Grant, Robert M., *Irenaeus of Lyons* (New York: Routledge, 1997).

Griffe, Élie, *La Gaule Chrétienne à l'Époque Romaine*, i, *Des origines chrétiennes à la fin du IVe siècle* (Paris: Picard, 1947).

Hainsworth, John, 'The Force of the Mystery: Anamnesis and Exegesis in Melito's *Peri Pascha*', *SVTQ* 46/2 (2002), 107–46.

Harnack, Adolf von, *History of Dogma*, trans. of 3rd German edn (London, 1896).

Harnack, Adolf von, 'Der Presbyter-Prediger des Irenäus (IV, 27,1–32,1). "Bruchstücke und Nachklänger der ältesten exegetisch-polemischen Homilien', in *Philotesia: Paul Kleinert zum LXX Geburtstag* (Berlin: Trowitzsch, 1907), 1–37.

Harnack, Adolf von, *Marcion: Das Evangelium vom fremden Gott: Neue Studien zu Marcion*, 2nd edn (1924; repr. Darmstadt: Wissenschaftlich Buchgesellschaft, 1996); abridged translation, *Marcion: The Gospel of the Alien God*, trans. John E. Steely and Lyle D. Bierma (Durham, NC: Labyrinth Press, 1990).

Hays, Richard, *Echoes of Scripture in the Letters of Paul* (New Haven and London: Yale University Press, 1989).

Henry, Michel, *Incarnation: Une philosophie de la chair* (Paris: Seuil, 2000).

Henry, Michel, *I am the Truth: Towards a Philosophy of Christianity*, trans. Susan Emanuel (Stanford, CA: Stanford University Press, 2003).

Hemmerdinger, B., 'Les "Notices et extraits" des bibliothèques grecques de Bagdad par Photius', *REG* 69 (1956), 101–3.

Hemmerdinger, B., 'Observations critiques sur Irénée, IV (*Sources chrétiennes* 100), ou les mesaventures d'un philologue', *JTS* NS 18/2 (1966), 308–22.

Hill, Charles E., 'What Papias said about John (and Luke): A "New" Papian Fragment', *JTS* NS 49 (1998), 582–629.

Hill, Charles E., *Regnum Caelorum: Patterns of Millennial Thought in the Early Church*, 2nd edn (Grand Rapids: Eerdmans, 2001).

Hill, Charles E., *The Johannine Corpus in the Early Church* (Oxford: Oxford University Press, 2004).

Hill, Charles E., *From the Lost Teaching of Polycarp*, WUNT 186 (Tübingen: Mohr Siebeck, 2006).

Hill, Charles E., 'The "Orthodox Gospel": The Reception of John in the Great Church prior to Irenaeus', in Tuomas Rasimus (ed.), *The Legacy of John* (Leiden: Brill, 2009), 233–300.

Hill, Charles E., *Who Chose the Gospels? Probing the Great Gospel Conspiracy* (Oxford: Oxford University Press, 2010).

Hitchcock, F. R. M., *Irenaeus of Lugdunum: A Study of his Teaching* (Cambridge: Cambridge University Press, 1914).

Hitchcock, F. R. M., 'Loofs' Theory of Theophilus of Antioch as a Source of Irenaeus', *JTS* 38 (1937), 130–9, 255–66.

Hitchcock, F. R. M., 'Loofs Asiatic Source (IQA) and the Pseudo-Justin *De resurrectione*', *ZNTW* 36 (1937), 35–60.

Hodge, A. Trevor, *Ancient Greek France* (Philadelphia: University of Pennsylvania Press, 1999).

Hoffman, D. L., *The Status of Women and Gnosticism in Irenaeus and Tertullian* (Lewiston: Edwin Mellen, 1995).

Holsinger-Friesen, Thomas, *Irenaeus and Genesis: A Study of Competition in Early Christian Hermeneutics*, Journal of Theological Interpretation, Supplement 1 (Winona Lake, IN: Eisenbrauns, 2009).

Holzhausen, Jens, 'Irenäus und die valentinianische Schule: zur Praefatio von *Adv. Haer.* 1', *VC* 55/4 (2001), 341–55.

Holte, R., 'Logos Spermatikos: Christianity and Ancient Philosophy According to St Justin's *Apologies*', *ST* 12 (1958), 109–68.

Houssiau, A., *La Christologie de saint Irénée* (Louvain: Publicationes Universitaires, 1955).

Houssiau, A., 'Le Baptême selon Irénée de Lyon', *ETL* 60 (1984), 45–59.

Huby, P., and Neal, G. (eds), *The Criterion of Truth* (Liverpool: Liverpool University Press, 1989).

L'Huillier, Peter, *The Church of the Ancient Councils: The Disciplinary Work of the First Four Ecumenical Councils* (Crestwood, NY: SVS Press, 1996).

Jacobsen, Anders-Christian, 'The Importance of Genesis 1–3 in the Theology of Irenaeus', *ZAC* 8/2 (2004), 299–316.

Jaschke, H. J., *Der Heilige Geist im Bekenntnis der Kirche: Ein Studie zur Pneumatologie des Irenäus von Lyon im Ausgang vom altchristlichen Glaubensbekenntnis*, Münsterische Beiträge zur Theologie, 40 (Münster: Aschendorff, 1976).

Jaschke, H. J., 'Pneuma und Moral: Der Grund christlicher Sittlichkeit aus der Sicht des Irenäus von Lyon', *SM* 14 (1976), 239–81.

Jeffers, James S., *Conflict at Rome: Social Order and Hierarchy in Early Christianity* (Minneapolis: Fortress Press, 1991).

Jenkins, D. E., 'The Make-up of Man According to St Irenaeus', *StPatr* 6, TU 81 (Leipzig, 1962), 91–5.

Jonas, H., *The Gnostic Religion: The Message of the Alien God and the Beginnings of Christianity*, 2nd rev. edn (London: Routledge, 1992 [1958]).

Joppich, G., *Salus Carnis: Eine Untersuchung in der Theologie des hl. Irenäus von Lyon*, Münsterschwarzacher Studien, 1 (Münsterschwarzach: Vier-Türme, 1965).

Jouassard, G., 'La Théologie mariale de saint Irénée', in *L'Immaculée Conception*, 7e Congrès Marial National, Lyon 1954 (Lyon, 1954), 265–76.

Jouassard, G., 'Amorces chez saint Irénée pour la doctrine de la maternité spirituelle de la Sainte Vierge', *Nouvelle revue mariale*, 7 (1955), 217–32.

Jouassard, G., 'Le "Signe de Jonas" dans le Livre IIIe de l'*Adversus haereses* de saint Irénée', in *L'Homme devant Dieu: Mélanges offerts au Père Henri de Lubac*, v. 1, *Exégèse et patristique* (Paris: Aubier, 1963), 235–46.

Kalvesmaki, Joel, 'The Original Sequence of Irenaeus, *Against Heresies* 1: Another Suggestion', *JECS* 15/3 (2007), 407–17.

O'Keefe, John J. 'The New Irenaeus', *JTI* 5/1 (2011), 113–19.

Kereszty, R., 'The Unity of the Church in the Theology of Irenaeus', *Second Century*, 4/4 (1984), 202–18.

Klebba, E., *Die Anthropologie des hl. Irenaeus*, Kirchengeschichtliche Studien, 2.3 (Münster, 1894).

King, Karen, *What is Gnosticism?* (Cambridge MA: Belknap Press of Harvard University Press, 2003).

King, Karen, *The Secret Revelation of John* (Cambridge, MA: Harvard University Press, 2006).

King, Karen, 'Which Early Christianity?', in Ashbrook Harvey and Hunters (eds), *The Oxford Handbook of Early Christian Studies*, 66–84.

Kinzig, W., and Vinzent, M., 'Recent Research on the Origin of the Creed', *JTS* NS 50/2 (1999), 535–59.

Koch, H., 'Zur Lehre von Urstand und von der Erlösung bei Irenäus', *TSK* 96–7 (1925), 183–214.

Koschorke, K., *Die Polemik der Gnostiker gegen das kirchliche Christentum*, NHS 12 (Leiden: Brill, 1978).

Köstenberger, Andreas J., and Kruger, Michael J., *The Heresy of Orthodoxy: How Contemporary Culture's Fascination with Diversity has Reshaped our Understanding of Early Christianity* (Wheaton, IL: Crossway, 2010).

Kugel, James, *Traditions of the Bible: A Guide to the Bible as it was at the Start of the Common Era* (Cambridge, MA: Harvard University Press, 1998).

Kurz, Joel R., 'The Gifts of Creation and the Consummation of Humanity: Irenaeus of Lyons' Recapitulatory Theology of the Eucharist', *Worship*, 83/2 (2009), 112–32.

Kürzinger, J., *Papias von Hierapolis und die Evangelien des Neuen Testaments* (Regensburg: R. Pustet, 1983).

Lampe, Peter, *From Paul to Valentinus: Christians at Rome in the First Two Centuries*, trans. M. Steinhauser (Minneapolis: Fortress Press, 2003).

Lanne, D. E., 'La Vision de Dieu dans l'œuvre de saint Irénée', *Irénikon*, 33 (1966), 311–20.

Lassiat, H., *Pour une théologie de l'homme. Création ... Liberté ... Incorruptibilité: Insertion du thème anthropologique de la jeune tradition romaine dans l'oeuvre d'Irénée* (Lille: Service de reproduction des thèses, Univ. de Lille, 1972).

Lassiat, H., *Promotion de l'homme en Jésus-Christ d'après Irénée de Lyon* (Tours: Mame, 1974).

Lassiat, H., 'L'Anthropologie d'Irénée', NRT 100 (1978), 399–417.

Lawson, J., *The Biblical Theology of St Irenaeus* (London: Epworth Press, 1948).

Layton, Bentley, 'Prolegomena to the Study of Ancient Gnosticism', in L. Michael White and O. Larry Yarbrough (eds), *The Social World of the First Christians: Essays in Honor of Wayne A. Meeks* (Minneapolis: Fortress, 1995), 334–50.

Lebeau, P., 'KOINONIA: LaSignification du salut selon S. Irénée', in J. Fontaine and C. Kannengiesser (eds), *EPEKTASIS: Mélanges offerts au Cardinal J. Daniélou* (Paris: Beauchesne, 1972), 121–7.

Lessing, Gotthold, 'Necessary Answer to a Very Unnecessary Question of Herr Hauptpastor Goeze of Hamburg', in *Lessing: Philosophical and Theological Writings*, ed. H. B. Nisbet, Cambridge Texts in the History of Philosophy (Cambridge, Cambridge University Press, 2005), 172–7.

Levenson, Jon D., 'The Eighth Principle of Judaism and the Literary Simultaneity of Scripture', *JR* 68 (1988), 205–25.

Levenson, Jon D., *The Hebrew Bible, The Old Testament, and Historical Criticism: Jews and Christians in Biblical Studies* (Louisville, KY: Westminster/John Knox, 1993).

Lieu, Judith M., *Christian Identity in the Jewish and Graeco-Roman World* (Oxford: Oxford University Press, 2004).

Lightfoot, J. B., *The Apostolic Fathers* (Macmillan, 1889; repr. Peabody, MA: Hendrickson, 1989).

Lilla, S. R. C., *Clement of Alexandria: A Study in Christian Platonism and Gnosticism* (Oxford: Oxford University Press, 1971).

Lipsius R., 'Irenaeus', *DCB* iii (London, 1888), 253–79.

Long, A. A., and Sedley, D. N. (eds), *The Hellenistic Philosophers* (Cambridge: Cambridge University Press, 1987).

Logan, Alistair H. B., *The Gnostics: Identifying an Early Christian Cult* (London: T&T Clark, 2006).

Loofs, F., *Theophilus von Antiochien Adversus Marcionem und die anderen theologischen Quellen bei Irenäus*, TU 46.2 (Leipzig: Hinrichs, 1930).

Lündstrom, S., *Studien zur lateinischen Irenäusübersetzung* (Lund: Gleerup, 1943).

Lündstrom, S., *Neue Studien zur lateinischen Irenäusübersetzung*, Lunds Universitets Årsskrift, N.F. Aud. 1, Bd. 44, n. 8 (Lund: Gleerup, 1948).

Lündstrom, S., *Übersetzungstechnische Untersuchungen auf dem Gebiete der christlichen Latinität*, Lunds Universitets Årsskrift, N.F. Aud. 1, Bd. 55, n. 3 (Lund: Gleerup, 1955).

Lyman, Rebecca, 'Hellenism and Heresy', *JECS* 11/2 (2003), 209–22.

MacDonald, Nathan, 'Israel and the Old Testament Story in Irenaeus' Presentation of the Rule of Faith', *JTI* 3/2 (2009), 281–98.

Marion, Jean-Luc, *God without Being*, trans. Thomas A. Carlson (Chicago: University of Chicago Press, 1991).

Marion, Jean-Luc, *In Excess: Studies of Saturated Phenomena* (New York: Fordham University Press, 2002).

Marion, Jean-Luc, *The Visible and the Revealed*, trans. Christina M. Gschwandtner (New York: Fordham University Press, 2008).

Marjanen, Antti, 'Gnosticism', in Ashbrook Harvey and Hunters (eds.), *The Oxford Handbook of Early Christian Studies*, 203–20.

Markschies, Christoph, *Valentinus Gnosticus? Untersuchungen zur valentinianischen Gnosis mit einem Kommentar zu den Fragmenten Valentins*, WUNT 65 (Tübingen: Mohr Siebeck, 1992).

Markus, R. A., 'Pleroma and Fulfillment: The Significance of History in St Irenaeus' Opposition to Gnosticism', *VC* 8 (1954), 193–224.

Markus, R. A., 'The Problem of Self-Definition: From Sect to Church', in E. P. Sanders (ed.), *Jewish and Christian Self-Definition*, i, *The Shaping of Christianity in the Second and Third Centuries* (Philadelphia: Fortress, 1980), 1–15.

Les Martyrs de Lyon (177), Colloques Internationaux du Centre National de la Recherche Scientifique, no. 575 (Paris: CNRS, 1978).

May, G., *Creation Ex Nihilo: The Doctrine of 'Creation out of Nothing' in Early Christian Thought*, trans. A. S. Worrall (Edinburgh: T&T Clark, 1994).

May, Gerhard, and Greschat, Katharine (eds), *Marcion und seine kirchengeschichtlich Wirkung: Marcion and his Impact on Church History. Vorträge der Internationalen Fachkonferenz sur Marcion, gehalten vom 15–18 August 2001 in Mainz* (Berlin: de Gruyter, 2002).

May, Jordan Daniel, 'The Four Pillars: The Fourfold Gospel before the Time of Irenaeus', *Trinity Journal*, 30/1 (2009), 67–79.

Meer, F. van der, and Mohrmann, C., *Atlas of the Early Christian World*, trans. M. F. Hedlund and H. H. Rowley (London: Nelson, 1958).

Meijering, E. P., 'Irenaeus' Relation to Philosophy in the Light of his Concept of Free Will', in W. den Boer . . . [et al.] (eds), *Romanitas et christianitis: Studia Iano Henrico Waszink oblata* (Amsterdam and London: North Hollons, 1973), 221–32.

Meijering, R., *Literary and Rhetorical Theories in Greek Scholia* (Groningen: Egbert Forsten, 1987).

Meyer, John R., 'Assumptio carnis and the Ascent to God: Hilary's Revision of Irenaeus' Doctrine of salus carnis', *ZAC* 9/2 (2005), 303–19.

Minns, D., *Irenaeus* (London: Geoffrey Chapman, 1994).

Mitchell, Margaret M., *Paul, The Corinthians and the Birth of Christian Hermeneutics* (Cambridge: Cambridge University Press, 2010).

Mitchell, Margaret M., and Young, Frances M. (eds) *The Cambridge History of Christianity*, i, *Origins to Constantine* (Cambridge: Cambridge University Press, 2006).

Moll, Sebastian, *The Arch-Heretic Marcion*, WUNT 250 (Tübingen: Mohr Siebeck, 2010).

Moringiello, Scott D., 'Irenaeus Rhetor' (Ph.D., University of Notre Dame, 2008).

Mosshammer, Alden A., *The Easter Computus and the Origins of the Christian Era*, OECS (Oxford: Oxford University Press, 2008).

Mutschler, Bernhard, *Irenäus als johanneischer Theologe: Studien zur Schriftauslegung bei Irenäus von Lyon*, Studien und Texte zu Antike und Christentum, 21 (Tübingen: Mohr Siebeck, 2004).

Mutschler, Bernhard, *Das Corpus Johanneum bei Irenäus von Lyon: Studien und Kommentar zum dritten Buch von* Adversus Haereses, WUNT 189 (Tübingen: Mohr Siebeck, 2006).

Mutschler, Bernhard, 'John and his Gospel in the Mirror of Irenaeus of Lyons: Perspectives of Recent Research', in Tuomas Raismus (ed.), *The Legacy of John: Second-Century Reception of the Fourth Gospel*, Supplements to Novum Testamentum, 132 (Leiden: Brill, 2010), 319–43.

Nautin, P., *Lettres et écrivains chrétiens des IIe et IIIe siècles* (Paris: Cerf, 1961).

Nielsen, J. T., *Adam and Christ in the Theology of Irenaeus of Lyons: An Examination of the Function of the Adam–Christ Typology in the Adversus Haereses of Irenaeus, against the Background of the Gnosticism of his Time*, Van Gorcum's Theologische Bibliothek, 40 (Assen: Van Gorcum, 1968).

Noormann, R., *Irenäus als Paulusinterpret: Zur Rezeption und Wirkung der paulinischen und deuteropaulinischen Briefe im Werke des Irenäus von Lyon*, WUNT 2.66 (Tübingen: Mohr, 1994).

Norris, R. A., *God and the World in Early Christian Theology: A Study on Justin Martyr, Irenaeus, Tertullian and Origen* (London: Adam and Charles Black, 1966).

Norris, R. A., 'Irenaeus' Use of Paul in his Polemic against the Gnostics', in W. S. Babcock (ed.), *Paul and the Legacies of Paul* (Dallas: Southern Methodist University Press, 1990), 79–98.

Norris, R. A., 'Theology and Language in Irenaeus of Lyon', *ATR* 76/3 (1994), 285–95.

Ochagavía, J., *Visibile Patris Filius: A Study of Irenaeus' Teaching on Revelation and Tradition*, OCA 171 (Rome: Pont. Inst. Orientalium Studiorum, 1964).

Olson, M. J., *Irenaeus, the Valentinian Gnostics and the Kingdom of God (AH Book V): The Debate about 1 Corinthians 15.50* (New York: Mellin, 1992).

Orbe, A., *Estudios Valentinianos*, 1, *Hacia la primera theología de la procesión del Verbo* (Rome, 1958).

Orbe, A., 'El hombre ideal en la teología de s. Ireneo', *Greg.* 43 (1962), 449–91.

Orbe, A., 'El pecado de Eva, signo de division', *OCP* 29 (1963), 305–30.

Orbe, A., 'El pecado original y el matrimonio en la teología del s. II', *Greg.* 45 (1964), 449–500.

Orbe, A., 'Homo nuper factus: En torno a S. Ireneo, *adv. haer.* IV.38.1', *Greg.* 46 (1965), 481–544.

Orbe, A., 'El sueño y el paraíso: Iren., *Epid.* 13', *Greg.* 48 (1967), 346–9.

Orbe, A., 'La definición del hombre en la teología del siglo IIe', *Greg.* 48 (1967), 522–76.

Orbe, A., 'La atonia del espiritu en los Padres y teólogos del s.II', *La Ciudad de Dios*, 181 (1968), 484–528.

Orbe, A., *Antropología de San Ireneo*, BAC (Madrid: BAC, 1969).

Orbe, A., *Parábolas evangélicas en San Ireneo*, 2 vols (Madrid: BAC, 1972).

Orbe, A., 'Supergrediens angelos: AH V.36.1', *Greg.* 54 (1973), 5–69.

Orbe, A., 'Los Valentinianos y el matrimonio espiritual: Hacia los orígenes de la mística nupcial', *Greg.* 58/1 (1977), 5–53.

Orbe, A., 'San Ireneo y la creación de la materia', *Greg.* 59/1 (1978), 71–127.

Orbe, A., 'Adversarios anónimos de la *salus carnis* (Iren. *adv. haer.* V.2.2s)', *Greg.* 60/1 (1979), 9–53.

Orbe, A., 'San Ireneo y la doctrine de la reconciliación', *Greg.* 61/1 (1980), 5–50.

Orbe, A., 'Cinco exegesis ireneanas de Gn. 2.17b: *adv. haer.* V, 23,1–2', *Greg.* 62 (1981), 75–113.

Orbe, A., 'La virgen María abrogada de la virgen Eva: En torno a s. Ireneo, *adv. haer.* V.19.1', *Greg.* 63/3 (1982), 453–506.

Orbe, A., 'Visión del Padre e incorruptela según san Ireneo', *Greg.* 64/2 (1983), 199–241.

Orbe, A., '¿San Ireneo adopcionista? En torno a *adv. haer.* III.19.1', *Greg.* 65/1 (1984), 5–52.

Orbe, A., *Teología de San Ireneo: Comentario al libro V del 'Adversus Haereses'*, 3 vols (Madrid: BAC, 1985, 1987, 1988).

Orbe, A., 'Deus facit, homo fit: Un axioma de san Ireneo', *Greg.* 69/ (1988), 629–61.

Orbe, A., 'Gloria Dei vivens homo: Análisis de Ireneo, *adv. haer.* IV.20.1–7', *Greg.* 73/2 (1992), 205–68.

Orbe, A., 'Los hechos de Lot, mujer e hijas vistos por san Ireneo (*adv. haer.* IV, 32,1, 15/3, 71)', *Greg.* 75/1 (1994), 37–64.

Orbe, A., 'Sobre los "Alogos" de san Ireneo (adv. haer. III, 11, 9)', Greg. 76/1 (1995), 47–68.

Orbe, A., 'El Espíritu en el bautismo de Jesús (en torno a san Ireneo),' Greg. 76/4 (1995), 663–99.

Orbe, A., 'El signo de Jonás según Ireneo', Greg. 77/4 (1996), 637–57.

Osborn, E. F., 'Reason and the Rule of Faith in the Second Century', in Rowan Williams (ed.), The Making of Orthodoxy: Essays in Honour of Henry Chadwick (Cambridge: Cambridge University Press, 1989), 40–61.

Osborn, E. F., Irenaeus of Lyons (Cambridge: Cambridge University Press, 2001).

Osiek, Carolyn, and Koester, Helmut, Shepherd of Hermas, Hermeneia (Minneapolis: Augsburg Fortress, 1999).

Overbeck, Winfried, Menschwerdung: Eine Untersuchung zur literarischen und theologischen Einheit des fünften Buches 'Adversus Haereses' des Irenäus von Lyon, Basler und Berner Studien zur historischen und systematischen Theologie, 61 (Bern: Peter Lang, 1995).

Pagels, Elaine, The Gnostic Gospels (London: Penguin, 1980).

Pagels, Elaine, Adam, Eve and the Serpent (London: Weidenfeld and Nicolson, 1988).

Pagels, Elaine, 'Irenaeus, the "Canon of Truth", and the Gospel of John: "Making a Difference" through Hermeneutics and Ritual', VC 56/4 (2002), 339–71.

Pagels, Elaine, Beyond Belief: The Secret Gospel of Thomas (New York: Random House, 2003).

Paice, R. J. R., 'Irenaeus on the Authority of Scripture, the "Rule of Truth" and Episcopacy', in two parts, Churchman, 117/1 (2003), 57–71, and 117/2 (2003), 133–52.

Palashkovsky, V., 'La Théologie eucharistique de S. Irénée, évêque de Lyon', StPatr 2, TU 64 (Berlin: Akademie, 1957), 277–81.

Petersen, W. L., 'Eusebius and the Paschal Controversy', in Harold W. Attridge and Gohei Hata (eds), Eusebius, Christianity and Judaism (Leiden: Brill, 1992).

Pétrement, S., Le Dieu séparé: Les Origines du gnosticisme (Paris: Cerf, 1984); trans. C. Harrison, A Separate God: The Origins and Teachings of Gnosticism (San Francisco: Harper, 1990).

Piana, George La, 'The Roman Church at the End of the Second Century', HTR 18 (1925), 201–77.

Piana, George La, 'Foreign Groups in Rome during the First Centuries of the Empire', HTR 20 (1927), 183–403.

Prümm, K., 'Göttliche Planung und menschliche Entwicklung nach Irenäus Adversus Haereses', Scholastik, 13 (1938), 206–24, 342–66.

Prümm, K., 'Zur Terminologie und zum Wesen der christliche Neuheit bei Irenäus', in T. Klauser and A. Rucker (eds), Pisciculi: Studien zur Religion und Kultur des Altertums, Franz Joseph Dölger zum sechzigsten Geburtstag dageboten von Freunden, Verehrern und Schülern (Münster: Aschendorff, 1939), 192–219.

Purvis, James G. M., 'The Spirit and the Imago Dei: Reviewing the Anthropology of Irenaeus of Lyons', Evangelical Quarterly, 68 (1996), 99–120.

Quasten, J., *Patrology*, i (Utrecht: Spectrum, 1950).
Quentin, H., 'La Liste des martyrs de Lyon de l'an 177', *AB* 39 (1921), 113–38.
Ramos-Lissón, D., 'Le Rôle de la femme dans la théologie de saint Irénée', *StPatr* 21 (Leuven: Peeters, 1989), 163–74.
Reed, Annette Yoshiko, 'EUANGELION: Orality, Textuality, and the Christian Truth in Irenaeus' *Adversus haereses*', *VC* 56/1 (2002), 11–46.
Reimarus, Herman, 'The Intention of Jesus and his Disciples', in *Reimarus: Fragments*, ed. Charles H. Talbert, trans. Ralph S. Fraser (Eugene, OR: Wipf and Stock, 2009).
Reimherr, O., 'Irenaeus Lugdunensis', in V. Brown (ed.), *Catalogus translationum et commentariorum: Mediaeval and Renaissance Latin Translations and Commentaries, Annotated Lists and Guide*, 7 (Washington: Catholic University of America, 1992), 14–54.
Reumann, J., '$Oἰκονομία$ as "Ethical Accommodation" in the Fathers, and its Pagan Background', *StPatr* 3.1, TU 78 (Berlin: Akademie, 1961).
Robinson, J. A., 'Notes on the Armenian Version of *Adv. Haereses* IV, V', *JTS* 32 (1930–1), 153–166, 370–93.
Robinson, James M., and Koester, Helmut, *Trajectories through Early Christianity* (Philadelphia: Fortress Press, 1971).
Rousseau, A., 'Le Verbe "imprimé en forme de croix dans l'univers": A propos de deux passages de saint Irénée', in *Armeniaca: Mélanges d'études arméniennes* (Venice: S. Lazarus, 1969), 67–82.
Rousseau, A., 'La Doctrine de saint Irénée sur la préexistence du Fils de Dieu dans Dém. 43', *Muséon*, 89 (1971), 5–42.
Rousseau, A., 'L'Éternité des peines de l'enfer et l'immortalité naturelle de l'âme selon saint Irénée', *NRT* 99 (1977), 834–64.
Rousseau, Philip, *Pachomius: The Making of a Community in Fourth Century Egypt*, The Transformations of the Classical Heritage (Berkeley and Los Angeles: University of California Press, 1985).
Rudolph, K., *Gnosis: The Nature and History of an Ancient Religion*, trans. R. McL. Wilson (Edinburgh: T&T Clark, 1983).
Sagnard, F. M. M., *La Gnose valentinienne et le témoignage de saint Irénée* (Paris: Vrin, 1947).
Sanders, E. P., *Paul and Palestinian Judaism* (Philadelphia: Fortress Press, 1977).
Sanders, E. P. (ed.), *Jewish and Christian Self-Definition*, i, *The Shaping of Christianity in the Second and Third Centuries* (Philadelphia: Fortress, 1980).
Scharl, E., 'Der Rekapitulationsbegriff des heiligen Irenäus', *OCP* 6 (1940), 376–416.
Schoedel, W. R., 'Theological Method in Irenaeus (*Adversus Haereses* 2.25–28)', *JTS* NS 35 (1984), 31–49.
Schofield, M., Burnyeat, M., and Barnes, J. (eds), *Doubt and Dogmatism: Studies in Hellenistic Epistemology* (Oxford: Oxford University Press, 1980).
Schüngel, Paul, 'Das Valentinreferat des Irenäus von Lyon (*Haer.* I 11,1)', *VC* 55/4 (2001), 376–405.

Schutz, D. R., 'The Origin of Sin in Irenaeus and Jewish Pseudoepigraphical Literature', *VC* 32.3 (1978), 161–90.

Simonin, H. D., 'A propos d'un texte eucharistique de S. Irénée: AH. IV.xviii.5', *RSPT* 23 (1934), 281–92.

Simpson, R. L., 'Grace and Free Will: A Study in the Theology of St Irenaeus', in R. L. Simpson (ed.), *One Faith: It's Biblical, Historical, and Ecumenical Dimensions. A Series of Essays in Honour of Stephen J. England* (Enid, OK: Phillips University Press, 1966), 59–72.

'Sites and Museums in Roman Gaul I', *Athena Review: Journal of Archaeology, History, and Exploration*, 1/4 (1998) <http://www.athenapub.com> (accessed 10 September 2012).

Skarsaune, Oscar, *The Proof from Prophecy: A Study in Justin Martyr's Proof-Text Tradition: Text-Type, Provenance, Theological Profile* (Leiden: Brill, 1987).

Smith, Christopher R., 'Chiliasm and Recapitulation in the Theology of Irenaeus', *VC* 48/4 (1994), 313–31.

Smith, Daniel, 'Irenaeus and the Baptism of Jesus', *TS* 58/4 (1997), 618–42.

Smith, J. P., 'Hebrew Christian Midrash in Irenaeus Epid. 43', *Biblica*, 38 (1957), 24–34.

Smith, M., *Clement of Alexandria and a Secret Gospel of Mark* (Cambridge, MA: Harvard University Press, 1973).

Snyder, Harlow Gregory, '"Above the Bath of Myrtinus": Justin Martyr's "School" in the City of Rome', *HTR* 100/3 (2007), 335–62.

Stanton, Graham N., 'The Fourfold Gospel', *NTS* 43/3 (1997), 317–46.

Starr, Raymond, 'The Circulation of Literary Texts in the Roman World', *CQ* 37/1 (1987), 213–23.

Steenberg, M. C., 'Children in Paradise: Adam and Eve as "Infants" in Irenaeus of Lyons', *JECS* 12/1 (2004), 1–22.

Steenberg, M. C., 'The Role of Mary as Co-Recapitulator in St Irenaeus of Lyons', *VC* 58 (2004), 117–37.

Steenberg, M. C., *Irenaeus on Creation: The Cosmic Christ and the Saga of Redemption*, Supplements to Vigiliae Christianae 91 (Leiden: Brill, 2008).

Steenberg, M. C., 'Irenaeus on Scripture, Graphe, and the Status of Hermas', *SVTQ* 53/1 (2009), 29–66.

Stevenson, J., *A New Eusebius: Documents Illustrative of the History of the Church to A. D. 337* (London: SPCK, 1963).

Stewart-Sykes, A., *The Lamb's High Feast: Melito, Peri Pascha and the Quartodeciman Paschal Liturgy at Sardis* (Leiden: Brill, 1998).

Striker, G., 'Κριτήριον τῆς ἀληθείας', *Nachrichten der Akademie der Wissenschaften in Göttingen*, Phil.-hist. Kl., 2 (1974), 47–110.

Swete, H. B., foreword in F. R. M. Hitchcock, *Irenaeus of Lyons: A Study of his Teaching* (Cambridge: Cambridge University Press, 1914).

Thomassen, Einar, 'Orthodoxy and Heresy in Second Century Rome', *HTR* 97/3 (2004), 241–56.

Thomassen, Einar, *The Spiritual Seed: The Church of the 'Valentinians'* (Leiden: Brill, 2008).
Thornton, Claus-Jürgen, *Der Zeuge des Zeugen: Lukas als Historiker der Paulusreisen*, WUNT 56 (Tübingen: Mohr Siebeck, 1991).
Thornton, L. S., 'St Irenaeus and Contemporary Theology', *StPatr* 2, TU 64 (Berlin: Akademie, 1957), 317–27.
Tiessen, T. L., *Irenaeus on the Salvation of the Unevangelized* (Metuchen, NJ, and London: Scarecrow Press, 1993).
Timothy, H., *The Early Christian Apologists and Greek Philosophy Exemplified by Irenaeus, Tertullian and Clement of Alexandria* (Assen: Van Corcum, 1973).
Torrance, Thomas F., *Divine Meaning: Studies in Patristic Hermeneutics* (Edinburgh: T&T Clark, 1995.)
Tortorelli, K., 'Some Notes on the Interpretation of St Irenaeus in the Works of Hans Urs von Balthasar', *St Patr.* 23 (Leuven: Peeters, 1989), 284–8.
Tremblay, R., *La Manifestation et la vision de Dieu selon saint Irénée de Lyon*, Münsterische Beiträge zur Theologie, 41 (Münster: Aschendorff, 1978).
Tremblay, R., 'Le Martyre selon saint Irénée de Lyon', *SM* 16 (1978), 167–89.
Trevett, Christine, *Montanism: Gender, Authority, and the New Prophecy* (Cambridge: Cambridge University Press, 1996).
Tripp, David H., 'The Original Sequence of Irenaeus' "Adversus Haereses" I: A Suggestion', *Second Century*, 8 (1991), 157–62.
Unger, D. J., 'The Divine and Eternal Sonship of the Word According to St Irenaeus of Lyons', *Laurentianum*, 14 (1973), 357–408.
Unnik, W. C. van, 'An Interesting Document of Second Century Theological Discussion (Irenaeus, Adv. Haer. 1.10.3)', *VC* 31 (1977), 196–228.
Vallée, G., 'Theological and Non-Theological Motives in Irenaeus' Refutation of the Gnostics', in E. P. Sanders (ed.), *Jewish and Christian Self-Definition*, i, *The Shaping of Christianity in the Second and Third Centuries* (Philadelphia: Fortress, 1980). 174–85.
Vinzent, Markus, 'Rome', in Mitchell and Young (eds), *The Cambridge History of Christianity*, i, *Origins to Constantine*, 397–412.
Vogel, Jeff, 'The Haste of Sin, the Slowness of Salvation: An Interpretation of Irenaeus on the Fall and Redemption', *ATR* 89/3 (2007), 443–59.
Waldstein, Michael, 'Hans Jonas' Construct "Gnosticism": Analysis and Critique', *JECS* 8/3 (2000), 340–72.
Wanke, Daniel, 'Irenäus und die Häretiker in Rom: Thesen zur geschichtlichen Situation von *Adversus haereses*', *ZAC* 3/2 (1990), 202–40.
Wanke, Daniel, *Das Kreuz Christi bei Irenäus von Lyon*, Beihefte zur ZNTW 99 (Berlin: Walter de Gruyter, 2000).
Weidmann, Frederck W., *Polycarp and John: The Harris Fragments and their Challenge to the Literary Traditions* (Notre Dame, IN: University of Notre Dame Press, 1999).

Werner, J., *Der Paulinismus des Irenaeus: Eine Kirchen- und Dogmengeschichtliche Untersuchung über das Verhältnis des Irenaeus zu der Paulinischen Briefsammlung und Theologie* (Leipzig: Hinrichs, 1889).

Widmen, M., 'Irenäus und seine theologischen Väter', *ZKT* 54 (1957), 156–73.

Williams, Michael Allen, *Rethinking 'Gnosticism': An Argument for Dismantling a Dubious Category* (Princeton: Princeton University Press, 1996).

Williams, Rowan, *On Christian Theology* (Oxford: Blackwell, 2000).

Winden, J. C. M. van, *An Early Christian Philosopher: Justin Martyr's Dialogue with Trypho, Chapters One to Nine: Introduction, Text and Commentary* (Leiden: Brill, 1971).

Wingren, G., *Människan och Inkarnationen enligt Irenäus* (Lund: Cleerup, 1947); trans. R. Mackenzie, *Man and the Incarnation: A Study in the Biblical Theology of Irenaeus* (London: Oliver and Boyd, 1959).

Winling, R., 'Une façon de dire le salut: La Formule "être avec Dieu être avec Jésus Christ" dans les écrits de saint Irénée', *RSR* 58 (1984), 105–35.

Wood, A. S., 'The Eschatology of Irenaeus', *Evangelical Quarterly*, 41 (1969), 30–41.

Young, Frances, *Biblical Exegesis and the Formation of Christian Culture* (Cambridge: Cambridge University Press, 1997).

Index

Abercius Marcellus 71
Adam 92–3, 99, 100–1, 122–3, 131, 143–4, 145–9, 151, 155, 160, 161, 163, 166–72, 185, 190
Agapius (Mahboud) of Mendibj 53
Andia, Ysable de 153, 164–5, 175, 190, 199
Anicetus of Rome 25, 27, 44, 45, 48, 49–50, 55–6
Aristotle 11, 45, 67, 106, 112–13

Bacq, Philippe 15, 73, 94, 95, 186, 189, 190, 191, 192, 196
Balthasar, H. Urs von 14, 116, 149, 181
Baptism 33, 35, 71, 79, 90, 111–12, 133, 164, 170, 172–3, 175–8, 180, 181, 198
Barr, James 132, 172
Bauckham, Richard 59, 76
Bauer, Walter 5–6
Behr, John 19, 37, 68, 147, 148–9, 152, 156, 174, 210
Berthouzoz, Roger 159, 188, 192, 193–4
Blanchard, Yves-Marie 68
Blandina 19, 201–2
Blastus 14, 53–4
Bousset, W. 15
Brakke, David 6, 7, 8–9, 16, 40, 45, 84, 108
breath 93, 99, 149–58, 167, 169, 175, 196
Brent, Allen 49
Brown, Robert 195

Cabasilas, Nicholas 146, 180
canon 4, 11, 54, 67, 79, 83, 111–16, 118, 121
Carpocrates 44–5, 64, 83, 84, 87
Cerdo 24–5, 27, 46, 47, 64, 83, 84

Cerinthus 64, 65, 83, 84
chiliasm 68, 70, 102, 181–4
Church 2–3, 7, 9, 23–4, 27, 29, 38, 40, 45–6, 70, 79, 93, 101, 167–8, 172–5, 180, 194, 202
Clement of Alexandria 58, 78, 112–14
Clement of Rome 22, 23, 48, 49, 50, 114–15
creation 100–1, 122–3, 163, 180–5
Cross 91, 127–8, 133–5, 143, 199, 201
see also Passion
Culpepper, Alan R. 58

Dawson, David 108
death 91, 97, 99, 101, 102, 116, 124, 148–9, 150, 158–62, 168–72, 183–4, 193, 194, 198–9, 200, 201, 202, 208
Demonstration of the Apostolic Preaching 13, 68–9, 76, 88, 132–3, 138, 164, 171, 189
Dodwell, H. 14
Doutreleau, L. 19, 79–80
Dunderberg, O. 27, 31, 43, 79

economy 90, 92, 93, 96, 99, 103, 111, 116, 121–3, 124–5, 129, 138–9, 142, 144–62, 165, 181, 184–5, 189, 191–2, 194, 196–7, 200, 201, 203, 207–9
Ebionites 64, 83, 84, 92, 99, 150, 173
Ehrman, Bart D. 1, 3, 6, 61, 206
Eleutherus of Rome 16, 21, 47–50, 68, 69, 88
Epicurus 11, 113
Eucharist 11, 33, 35, 41, 41, 55–7, 99, 114–16, 178–80, 200

Eusebius of Caesarea 13, 14, 16, 20, 36, 49, 50, 52, 53, 54–7, 61, 68, 69, 76
Eve 93, 155, 160, 167, 168, 169, 172, 174, 202

fabrication *see* plasma
Fantino, Jacques 125, 149, 166–7
flesh 99–100, 110, 116, 119–20, 123, 152, 153, 157–8, 164–6, 176–7, 178–9, 181, 198–9, 209–10
see also human being, plasma
Flora 31–32, 34
Florinus 13–14, 31, 34, 50–3, 58, 60, 63, 64, 68, 69–70
forbearance 51, 52, 99, 159–60, 194

Gnosticism 4, 8–9, 15, 107–8
Gnostics 8–9, 16, 45, 80, 84, 85, 87, 97
Gospel 66, 88, 89, 95, 124–6, 131–2, 133–4, 136–40, 142–3, 147
Gospel of Truth 30, 32, 140
Grant, Robert M. 16, 67, 136, 166, 170
Gregory of Nazianzus 119
Gregory of Nyssa 135, 195

handiwork *see* plasma
harmony 9, 50, 52, 107, 115, 117, 119, 129, 165, 189, 190, 191, 207
see also symphony
Harnack, Adolf von 4, 5, 14, 25, 26, 27, 137
Harvey, W. W. 52, 76
Hays, Richard 131, 134, 135
Hegesippus 28, 49–50, 58
heresy 1–12, 27, 38–41, 46–7, 80, 83–4, 206–7
Hermas 22–4, 27, 29, 30, 40, 46, 93
Hill, Charles 15, 25–6, 44, 51, 52, 58–9, 61–6, 67, 68–70, 132
Holsinger-Friesen, Thomas 122, 123, 137, 151, 171

human being 92–3, 95–6, 97, 99, 100, 103, 119–20, 141, 151, 152, 154–5, 156, 157–8, 161, 162–72, 175–7, 178, 179–80, 184–5, 186–7, 188, 192–203
see also flesh, plasma
hypothesis 11, 78–9, 105–6, 109, 112–14, 116, 117, 118, 121, 144–5, 207

Ignatius of Antioch 22, 39, 47, 60, 65, 136, 200–1, 202
image of God 77, 99, 101, 119–20, 121, 122, 143–4, 151, 157, 163, 164, 166–7, 171, 176–7, 181, 184–5, 187, 195, 197, 200
Isaac of Syria 135

Jaschke, H. J. 190, 199
Jesus Christ 89–93, 95–7, 100–1, 109–10, 121–3, 126–7, 131–2, 136, 139–44, 145–8, 158, 166–7, 170, 175–6, 184–5, 198
John 50, 51, 54, 56, 58–9, 65, 66, 70, 71, 79, 88, 90, 106–10, 132, 136, 140, 150, 151, 182–3
Jonah 91, 159–60, 168, 193
Jonas, Hans 107–8
Justin Martyr 28, 29, 34–44, 47, 82, 135, 152

Kalvesmaki, Joel 78
King, Karen 4–5, 6, 7, 84
Kugel, James 129–30

Lampe, Peter 6, 21–2, 25, 26, 27, 28, 32, 33, 34, 35, 36, 42, 43, 45, 48
Lassiat, Henri 152
Le Boulluec, Alain 38, 39
Lessing, Gotthold 3, 4, 10, 11, 113
Letter of the Churches of Vienne and Lyons 14, 16–17, 18–19, 21, 48, 174, 201–2

Index

Letter to Diognetus 52, 59, 159
Lipsius, R. 67
likeness to God 101, 157, 166, 171–2, 173, 190
 see also image of God
Loofs, Friedrich 14–15
Lyman, Rebecca 7, 37–8, 39, 42

Marcion 2–3, 5, 9, 25–7, 29, 31 36, 39, 40, 41–2, 44, 46, 47, 51, 62, 63, 64, 65, 70, 83, 84, 97, 114, 206–7
Marcellina 45, 75, 83, 84
Marcus 20, 44, 61, 80–1, 82, 84, 104
Markschies, Christoph 29, 82
martyrs 18–20, 91, 97, 143, 198–203
Mary 93, 150, 163, 174
 see also Virgin
Maximus the Confessor 14, 66
Meijering, R. 105, 106, 111, 112, 125
Melito of Sardis 54, 66, 132
Menander 39, 40, 64, 83
Minns, D. 140, 195, 198
Moll, Sebastian 25, 27
More, Henry 8
Moringiello, Scott D. 74

Nautin, P. 14, 19, 20
Nicolaitans 64, 83
Noorman, Rolf 134, 154
Norris, Richard A. 31, 106, 116

Orbe, Antonio 99, 164–5, 180, 184, 188, 190
Origen 10, 36, 150, 164, 165, 177
orthodoxy 1–12, 41–2, 46–7, 58, 206–7
 see also canon
Osborn, Eric 11, 113, 136–7
Overbeck, Winfried 99, 100

Pagels, Elaine 53
Papias 58–9, 69–70, 76, 102, 183

Passion of Christ 10, 92, 101, 115–16, 124, 133–5, 143, 168, 172, 175–6, 179, 199, 209
 see also cross
Paul 7, 11, 22, 38–9, 46, 47, 65, 83, 89, 90, 91, 92, 109–10, 114, 115, 119, 122–3, 125, 128, 130–1, 132, 135, 137, 141, 145, 147, 150, 154, 157, 183, 185
Pectorius 71
Pétrement, Simone 83
plasma 105–6, 108–9, 110, 119, 142–3, 151, 152, 157–8, 164–5, 167, 178, 184–5, 187, 198, 207, 209
Polycarp 28, 44, 47, 50–2, 54, 55–6, 57–67, 70, 71, 81, 84, 97, 110, 115, 159, 177, 200
Polycrates 54, 56–7
Pothinus 19, 23
Ptolemaeus 20, 28, 31–2, 34, 43, 74, 78, 79, 81–3, 84, 87, 104

Quartodeciman controversy 54–7, 115
Quasten, Johannes 15
Quintilian 136–7

recapitulation 90, 92–3, 101, 136–40, 142–3, 163, 169, 170–1, 181–2, 184–5
Rousseau, A. 68, 76, 79, 89, 92, 92, 94, 99, 100, 117, 124, 135, 142, 145, 146, 152, 157, 159, 160, 165, 171, 174, 177, 184, 186, 190

Sanders, E. P. 147
Scripture 3–4, 10, 53, 37, 65–6, 76, 96–7, 101, 109–10, 113, 123, 124–40, 185, 191, 205
Simon Magus 10, 15, 39, 40, 64, 80, 83
Smith, Christopher 181
Spirit, the 93, 95, 99–100, 111, 149–58, 164–5, 167, 171–2, 175–7, 189–92, 196, 198–9
Steenberg, M. C. 142, 146, 167, 174

Swete, H. B. 13
symphony 9–11, 114, 125, 165, 190–2, 207
  see also harmony

Tertullian 25, 26, 28, 29, 36, 48, 114, 166, 168
Theophilus of Antioch 167, 168
Thomassen, Einar 23, 24, 27, 28–30, 31, 32, 42, 46, 53, 78, 80, 81–3, 108
Torrance, Thomas F. 138
tradition 32, 54, 79, 88, 105, 109, 114–15, 125–6, 207
Tripp, David H. 78

Valentinus 2, 9, 20, 27–34, 40–1, 42–3, 44, 47, 52, 69, 70, 73, 74, 79–80, 81–3, 84–5, 97, 103–4, 108, 206–7
Victor of Rome 13, 14, 28, 31, 34, 48, 52–3, 54–7, 63, 68, 69
Virgin, the 91, 92, 163, 170–1, 172–5, 177, 202, 209–10
  see also Eve, Mary
Vogel, Jeff 196

Weidmann, Frederick W. 58
Williams, Rowan 210
Wingren, Gustaf 15, 147, 195

Printed and bound by CPI Group (UK) Ltd, Croydon, CR0 4YY